INSTANT POT

COOKBOOK

TOP 500

Easy and Delicious Recipes for Your
Instant Pot Electric Pressure Cooker

Pamela Steven

Legal & Disclaimer

The information and contents herein are not designed to replace or take the place of any form of medical or professional advice and are not meant to replace the need for independent medical, financial, legal or other professional advice or services, as may be required. The content and information in this book have been provided for educational and entertainment purposes only.

The content and information in this book have been compiled from reliable sources and are accurate to the author's best knowledge, information, and belief. The author cannot guarantee this book's accuracy and validity and cannot be held liable for any errors and/or omissions. Further, changes will be periodically made to this book when needed. It is recommended that you consult with a health professional who is familiar with your personal medical history before using any of the suggested remedies, techniques, or information in this book.

Upon using the contents in this book, you agree to hold harmless the author from and against any damages, costs, and expenses, including any legal fees potentially resulting from the application of the information provided You agree to accept all risks associated with using the information presented inside this book.

Table of Content

Instant Pot Seafood Recipes   **123**

Instant Pot Soup Recipes   194

Instant Pot Rice & Pasta Recipes   220

Instant Pot Dessert Recipes   252

Introduction

Dear Reader,

Thank you for choosing the **Instant Pot Cookbook: Top 500 Easy and Delicious Recipes for Your Instant Pot Electrical Pressure Cooker**.

Instant Pot electric pressure cooker utilizes the pressure, steam, and high temperatures to speed up the cooking time. You can cook a wide variety of delicious meals with your multi-cooker and save your precious time and hard-earned money!

It can cook even the most complicated dishes quickly. No matter what you cook, whether it is meat, poultry, grains, or other dishes, the maximum time of cooking will be under 2 hours.

This cookbook includes 500 Instant Pot recipes that will inspire you to create new culinary masterpieces. You can find the best 500 **breakfast recipes, meat recipes, seafood recipes, vegetarian recipes, soup recipes and dessert recipes** in this book.

Whether you're in the mood for eggs, seafood. meat, grains, poultry or vegetables - you can find everything inside!

Just follow the easy directions provided in this cookbook to cook all of the delicious dishes you wish.

Start Cooking Healthy and Deliciously Now!

About the Instant Pot

We all have much better things to do with our valuable time than spending it slaving over a hot stove, thawing frozen ingredients, watching contents bake in the oven, and spending tons of time cleaning up after meals.

I am here to inform you that there is a way to reduce the time you spend in your kitchen and still make delicious, healthy meals. And the best part? You may already have this kitchen gadget in one of your cupboards!

I introduce you to the Instant Pot! Cute in size but powerful in nature, the Instant Pot can make even the worst at-home cookers into masterful chefs! This appliance gives you control of your kitchen and takes many tedious steps out of the cooking process for many types of meals.

Just like the name suggests, the Instant Pot will have your food ready incredibly fast! This is possible because an Instant Pot works by distributing heat quickly as well as evenly. It also features a unique, fully sealed cooking mechanism that keeps high pressure and the steam completely inside the pot. This process will not only cook the food faster, but it will keep it nutritious and tasty!

If you haven't noticed the Instant Pot is one of the most wanted kitchen appliances right now! Everyone from busy moms to at-home cooks have fallen in love with this wonderful little pot, and it's easy to see why. The Instant Pot happens to be just what you need when you have little time to cook a meal.

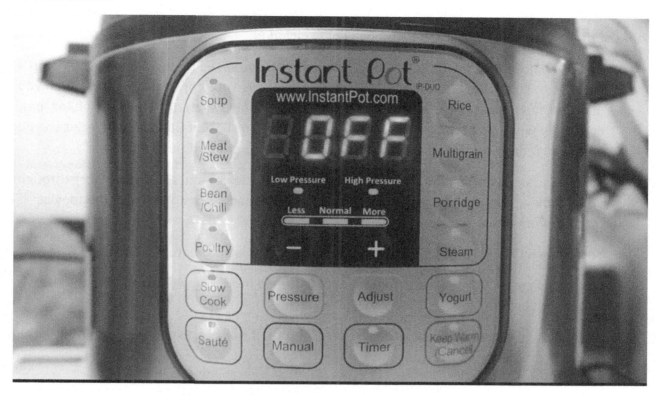

Whether you have already bought it or you are thinking about buying an instant pot, know that this revolutionary appliance will be the star of your kitchen and your new best friend. Why? Because it replaces 7 different kitchen gadgets. The Instant Pot cooker is a multi-tasking device that serves as a browning pan, warming pot, slow cooker, steamer, sauté pan, electric cooker, rice cooker, and yogurt maker. Even better, it is capable of all these different things at just the touch of a few buttons and often cooks food faster than a more traditional alternative, all without using any gimmicks or microwave technology. Just like with most modern slow cookers, it also offers the ability to set a delayed programmable start time.

The Instant Pot is safer, more convenient, and more dependable. You are in a position to switch it to slow cook if you leave the house to attend to some errands, or you may set to pressure cook if you in a situation you happen to be in a hurry. Or, you can also switch to steamer when you desire to reheat your leftover food!

The Most Outstanding Benefits of Instant Pot

Some of the advantages of the cooker you will enjoy include:

- You will enjoy convenience in cooking. Your time will be saved up to 70%, and you are in a position to select the cooking type you desire. Also saves your precious energy. When you use one, you don't have to stand around stirring and watching over a bubbling pot, especially when you're too busy or tired. An Instant Pot has all the bases covered so you create incredibly quick homemade meals without being stuck in the kitchen.

- You can accurately measure your ingredients using the device and seamlessly work through your cooking by use of simple buttons. This is made possible since the device is programmed.

- You enjoy easy timing of the food since the instant pot is automated.

- Nutritious meals. Original taste maintained. Softened food. Enjoy them all with the use of instant pot cooker.

- Your kitchen area remains clean since there is no food spillage. Expecting noise or smell? You won't experience any from the kitchen.

Helpful Tips for Using the IP

To use your Instant Pot effectively and optimize the use of this nifty kitchen device, get to understand the following tips:

- **Cook with at least ½ cup of water:** It is important to note that pressure is generated from steam; thus, you need at least ½ cup of water to generate steam that will, in turn, build the pressure within the inner pot.

- **Protect your counter from heat:** The heat generated by the Instant Pot can be so intense that your kitchen counter might get damaged. So, if your working surface is not heat-proof, place a cutting board between the Instant Pot and the surface to protect it from heat damage.

- **Never delay the timer especially when cooking meats:** The feature of the delay timer is very helpful especially if you want your meal to be ready by the time you get home. However, if you are cooking meats, don't use the delay timer as much as possible, because your meat might spoil after a few hours left at room temperature. If you really want to use the delay timer, make sure that you delay the timer for only a few minutes and never an hour.

- **If your recipe calls for stovetop cooking, reduce the cooking time with your Instant Pot:** If you are not using an Instant Pot cookbook to make your meals, you can still cook food perfectly if the recipe calls for conventional stovetop cooking. You simply reduce the cooking time indicated in the recipe to at least 1/3 as your pressure cooker cooks food faster than ordinary stovetop cooking.

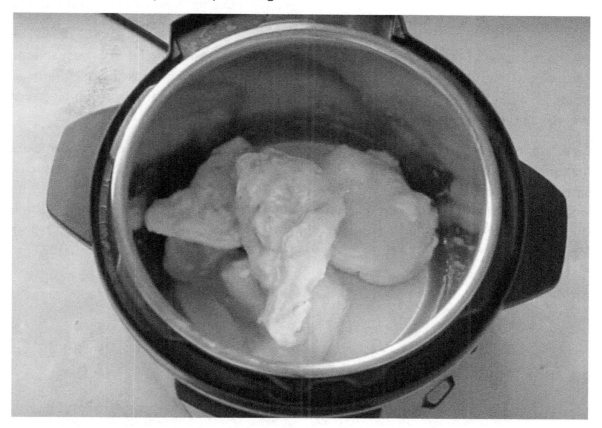

Efficient Cleaning Tips

Is it a necessity to clean the IP? To maintain the efficacy of your Instant Pot, it is crucial that you clean it after every use. Cleaning the Instant Pot is not difficult, but there are certain things that you need to be aware of so that you can clean this kitchen device properly.

- **Unplug from the power supply:** Before anything else, make sure the Instant Pot is unplugged from the power supply. When unplugging your Instant Pot from the power supply is also a good time to check there is no damage to the electrical cord.

- **Separate the lid, interior pot, and exterior body:** Separating all three components is very important as they require different cleaning methods. For the exterior housing, you can wipe it clean using a damp cloth. Make sure that you dry the housing with a dry kitchen towel afterward. Pay attention to the electrical wiring and circuit and don't wipe them with a damp towel so the electrical components are not damaged.

- **Thoroughly wash the interior pot:** The only washable component of the Instant Pot is the interior pot. Use warm soapy water to wash the interior pot and allow it to air dry or wipe it with a dry towel before placing it back in the exterior housing. Never place a wet interior pot in the housing as the moisture could damage the electrical components.

- **Take extra care in cleaning the lid:** The lid is made of washable and non-washable parts. Remove the washable parts, such as the floater valve and O-ring. Soak them in warm soapy water. For the other parts, carefully remove any stuck food particles. Completely wipe everything clean before re-assembling.

- **Do a "steam cleaning" at least once a week:** If you use your Instant Pot every day, make sure that you do a steam cleaning at least once a week. Steam cleaning removes any stuck food particles from the steam vent. To do this, pour one part vinegar and one part water in the inner pot and add a tablespoon of dishwashing soap. Set vent to "Sealing" while the lid is closed. Press the "Steam" button and let it run for 5 minutes. This will soften and dissolve the food particles in the steam vent.

ABOUT THE INSTANT POT

Whether you're hungry for a delicious roast or a comforting soup that's ready when you walk through the door, an Instant Pot is an appliance that will make that happen. In this wonderful guide, I avail to you a variety of recipes that you can easily prepare with the IP. Enjoy a variety of breakfast recipes, the delicious meat and poultry meals you will prepare using the simple steps described. Did I forget about the seafood and soup dishes? No, they are there. Even the admirable desserts, rice and pasta will give you the strength to carry out your day. Are you a vegetarian? You are not left out. There are plenty of recipes that will favor your taste. As one of the best-known multi-cookers on the market, the Instant Pot will be able to cook just about everything thanks to its many cooking techniques!

This does not mean that the device is not without a learning curve, however, as it is positively covered with buttons, many of which, on the surface, sound as if they have very similar functions. As such, this introduction has served to take you through the basics of using your Instant Pot to ensure you make the most of this extremely useful device. It is now the time to enter the kitchen and experiment with the recipes.

Instant Pot Breakfast Recipes

INSTANT POT BREAKFAST RECIPES

1. Wild West Style Omelet Quiche
(Servings:4, Cooking Time: 10 minutes)

Ingredients:

- 6 large eggs, well beaten
- 8 ounces Canadian Bacon, chopped
- 1/2 cup half and half
- 1/8 teaspoon salt
- 1/8 teaspoon ground black pepper
- 1/2 to 3/4 cup diced peppers, red, green and/or orange
- 3-4 organic spring onions, sliced in thin coins, reserving tops for garnish
- 3/4 cup shredded cheese

Directions for Cooking:

1. Lightly grease with cooking spray a soufflé dish that fits inside the Instant Pot.
2. Add 1 ½ cups of water in pot and place trivet.
3. In mixing bowl, whisk well eggs and milk. Season with pepper and salt.
4. In prepared soufflé dish, evenly spread bacon, peppers, and cheese.
5. Pour egg mixture over bacon mixture and mix well.
6. Cover top of dish with foil and place on a trivet.
7. Close Instant Pot, press manual, choose high pressure, and set time to 10 minutes.
8. Once done cooking, do a quick pressure release (QPR).
9. Carefully remove dish out of the Instant Pot, remove foil, and garnish with green onions.
10. Serve and enjoy.

Nutrition information:
Calories per serving: 365; Carbohydrates: 6.0g; Protein: 29.0g; Fat: 24.0g; Sugar: 2.0g; Sodium: 1151mg

---

2. Mini Frittata from Leftover Meat
(Servings:4, Cooking Time: 5 minutes)

Ingredients:

- 5 eggs
- ½ cup almond milk
- ¼ tsp salt
- ¼ tsp pepper
- 2 ½ tbsp shredded cheddar cheese
- 1 cup diced leftover meat
- 2 tbsp green onions, sliced

Directions for Cooking:

1. Lightly grease with cooking spray a soufflé dish that fits inside the Instant Pot.
2. Add 1 ½ cups of water in pot and place trivet.
3. In mixing bowl, whisk well eggs and milk. Season with pepper and salt.
4. In prepared soufflé dish, evenly spread bacon, peppers, and cheese.
5. Pour egg mixture over bacon mixture and mix well.
6. Cover top of dish with foil and place on a trivet.
7. Close Instant Pot, press manual, choose high pressure, and set time to 10 minutes.
8. Once done cooking, do a quick pressure release (QPR).
9. Carefully remove dish out of the Instant Pot, remove foil, and garnish with green onions.
10. Serve and enjoy.

Nutrition information:
Calories per serving: 168; Carbohydrates: 3.7g; Protein: 17.8g; Fat: 8.6g; Sugar: 3.1g; Sodium: 292.5mg

3. No-Crust Quiche with Spinach & Tomato

(Servings: 6, Cooking Time:30 minutes)

Ingredients:

- 12 large eggs
- 3 cups fresh baby spinach, roughly chopped
- 1 cup diced seeded tomato
- 3 large green onions, sliced
- 4 tomato slices for topping the quiche
- 1/2 cup milk
- 1/2 teaspoon salt
- 1/4 teaspoon fresh ground black pepper
- 1/4 cup shredded Parmesan cheese

Directions for Cooking:

1. Lightly grease with cooking spray a 1.5-quart round baking dish that fits in your Instant Pot.
2. Add 1 ½ cup of water in pot and place trivet.
3. Meanwhile, in a large mixing bowl whisk eggs. Stir in milk, salt, and pepper. Whisk thoroughly.
4. Evenly spread in layers in a prepared dish the tomato, spinach, and then green onions. Pour egg mixture over the veggies. Add the tomato slice for topping on top of the eggs, carefully. Sprinkle with cheese
5. Cover dish with foil, place on a trivet inside the pot.
6. Cover Instant Pot, press manual button, choose high pressure, and set time to 20 minutes.
7. Allow for 10-minutes natural pressure release and then do a quick release.
8. Remove from pot, serve and enjoy.

Nutrition information:
Calories per serving: 233; Carbohydrates: 14.1g; Protein: 18.4g; Fat: 11.9g; Sugar: 6.1g; Sodium: 482mg

---

4. Breakfast Egg Casserole Mexican Style

(Servings: 8, Cooking Time:26 minutes)

Ingredients:

- 8 large eggs, well-beaten
- 1-pound mild ground sausage
- 1/2 large red onion, chopped
- 1 red bell pepper, chopped
- 1 can black beans, rinsed
- 1/2 cup green onions
- 1/2 cup flour
- 1 cup Cotija cheese
- 1 cup mozzarella cheese
- sour cream, cilantro to garnish (optional)

Directions for Cooking:

1. Press the sauté button on Instant Pot and wait for it to get hot.
2. Once hot, add onion and sausage. Sauté for 6 minutes or until sausage is cooked. Press the cancel button.
3. Transfer cooked sausage into a round casserole dish that fits inside your Instant Pot and evenly spread. Add cheeses, beans and chopped veggies on top of sausage in an even layer.
4. Add 1 ½ cups of water in Instant Pot and place trivet.

5. Meanwhile, in a large bowl, whisk eggs. Add flour and whisk until thoroughly combined. Pour into dish. Cover dish with foil and place in pot.

6. Close Instant Pot, press pressure cook button, choose high settings and set time to 20 minutes.

7. Once done cooking, do a QPR.

8. Remove dish, slice into suggested servings, and enjoy.

Nutrition information:

Calories per serving: 334; Carbohydrates: 14.9g; Protein: 25.2g; Fat: 18.9g; Sugar: 1.7g; Sodium: 675.7mg

---

5. Egg Stuffed Bell Pepper Cup Open Faced-Wich
(Servings: 2, Cooking Time:5 minutes)

Ingredients:

- 2 slices of whole wheat bread, toasted
- 2 slices of Smoked Scamorza, Mozerella or Gouda
- 1 small bunch of arugula
- 2 Fresh Eggs, refrigerated
- 2 Bell Peppers, ends cut off deseeded

Hollandaise Sauce Ingredients:

- ½ teaspoons salt
- ⅔ cup mayonnaise, reduced fat made with olive oil
- 1 tablespoon white wine vinegar
- 1 teaspoon fresh lemon juice
- 1 teaspoon of Turmeric
- 1½ teaspoons Dijon mustard
- 3 tablespoons orange juice

Directions for Cooking:

1. Make the hollandaise sauce by mixing all ingredients in a medium bowl. Whisk until thoroughly combined. Cover bowl with Saran wrap and refrigerate until ready to use.

2. Break one egg inside each bell pepper cup. Wrap pepper in foil, making sure that the eggs don't spill out.

3. Add a cup of water in Instant Pot and place a trivet in the pot. Place bell pepper cup on a trivet.

4. Close Instant Pot, press pressure cook button, choose low settings and set time to 4 minutes.

5. Once done cooking, do a QPR.

6. Remove pepper cups and slice in half.

7. Stack toast, 1 slice of cheese, ½ of the arugula, 2 pepper cup halves, and then top with a dollop of the hollandaise sauce. Repeat process for the second sandwich.

8. Serve and enjoy.

Nutrition information:

Calories per serving: 301; Carbohydrates: 4.2g; Protein:0.7 g; Fat: 31.3g; Sugar: 2.1g; Sodium: 1246mg

6. Peppers, Cheese & Sausage Frittata
(Servings: 3, Cooking Time:15 minutes)

Ingredients:
- ¼ cup cheddar cheese, shredded
- ¼ tsp salt
- ¼ tsp white pepper
- ½ cup bell pepper, chopped
- ½ tsp Italian seasoning
- 1 ½ tsp heavy cream
- 1 cup Italian sausage, cooked
- 4 eggs

Directions for Cooking:

1. Lightly grease a 7-inch round pan with cooking spray. Add 1 ½ cups of water in Instant Pot and place trivet.
2. In a medium bowl whisk well salt, white pepper, Italian seasoning, heavy cream, and eggs.
3. In prepared pan, evenly spread in layers the sausage, bell pepper, and then followed by the cheese.
4. Pour in egg mixture. Cover pan with foil and place on a trivet.
5. Close Instant Pot, press manual button, choose high settings, and set time to 15 minutes.
6. Once done cooking, do a QPR.
7. Serve and enjoy.

Nutrition information:
Calories per serving: 237; Carbohydrates: 2.9g; Protein: 15.6g; Fat: 17.8g; Sugar: 1.0g; Sodium: 717mg

7. Decadent Eggs in Ramekins
(Servings:3, Cooking Time:2 minutes)

Ingredients:
- 1 Tablespoon chives
- 3 eggs
- 3 Tablespoons cream
- 3 tsp Butter, room temp
- sea salt and freshly ground pepper

Directions for Cooking:

1. Ready 3 pieces of ramekins and add a teaspoon of butter in each one. With a pastry brush, brush insides of the ramekin with the butter.
2. Add a tablespoon of cream in each ramekin.
3. Crack an egg in each of the ramekin. Season eggs with pepper and salt. And then evenly divide chives on each of the egg.
4. Close Instant Pot, press pressure cook button, choose low settings, and set time to 2 minutes.
5. Once done cooking, do a QPR.
6. Serve and enjoy.

Nutrition information:
Calories per serving: 116; Carbohydrates: 0.9g; Protein: 6.1g; Fat: 9.7g; Sugar: 0.7g; Sodium: 141.3mg

8. Hash Brown and Egg Casserole

(Servings: 4, Cooking Time: 30 minutes)

Ingredients:

- 6 eggs
- 2 cups frozen hash browns
- ¼ cup unsweetened almond milk
- ½ cup fat free shredded cheddar cheese
- 1 tsp sea salt
- 1 tsp pepper
- ½ onion, diced
- ½ green pepper, diced
- ½ red pepper, diced
- 1 stalk green onion, sliced for garnish

Directions for Cooking:

1. Press sauté button and lightly grease pot with cooking spray. When hot, sauté red pepper, green pepper, and onion for 6 minutes or until tender.
2. Press cancel button and stir in frozen hash browns and stir to separate and soften.
3. In a round casserole dish that fits inside the Instant pot, lightly grease insides with cooking spray.
4. Transfer hash brown mixture into prepared dish.
5. Add 1 ½ cup of water in Instant Pot and place trivet.
6. In a mixing bowl, whisk well pepper, salt, ¼ cup cheese, milk, and eggs. Pour over hash brown mixture. Stir a bit
7. Close Instant Pot, press manual button, choose high settings, and set time to 20 minutes.
8. Once done cooking, do a QPR.
9. Remove dish inside pot and sprinkle remaining cheese and the green onions.
10. Serve and enjoy.

Nutrition information:

Calories per serving: 267; Carbohydrates: 32.9g; Protein: 17.4g; Fat: 7.6g; Sugar: 9.4g; Sodium: 970mg

---

9. Walnut-Banana Oats

(Servings: 4, Cooking Time:10 minutes)

Ingredients:

- ¼ tsp cinnamon for topping
- ½ medium banana, peeled and sliced for topping
- 1 cup steel cut oats
- 1 cup unsweetened almond milk
- 1 large ripe banana, mashed
- 1 teaspoon ground cinnamon
- 1 teaspoon pure vanilla extract
- 1/4 cup walnuts, chopped fine
- 2 cups water
- 2 tablespoons chia seeds
- 2 tablespoons ground flaxseeds (flaxseed meal)
- 2 tablespoons pure maple syrup

Directions for Cooking:

1. Except for topping ingredients, add everything in Instant Pot and mix well.
2. Close Instant Pot, press manual button, choose high settings, and set time to 10 minutes.
3. Once done cooking, do a QPR.
4. Scoop into bowls and top with cinnamon, banana, and walnuts.
5. Serve and enjoy.

Nutrition information:

- 2 tbsp chopped and toasted walnuts for topping
- Pinch salt

Calories per serving: 332; Carbohydrates: 48.0g; Protein: 11.0g; Fat: 12.0g; Sugar: 11.0g; Sodium: 78mg

---

10. Breakfast Egg & Sausage Burrito
(Servings: 6, Cooking Time:25 minutes)

Ingredients:

- ¼ cup milk
- ¼ tsp freshly ground black pepper, divided
- ½ tsp crushed red pepper flakes
- 1 ½ cup water for the pressure cooker pot
- 1 tbsp water
- 1 tsp crushed fennel seed
- 1 tsp light brown sugar
- 1 tsp sage
- 1 tsp thyme
- 1/8 tsp nutmeg
- 2 tsp kosher salt, divided
- 6 burrito size tortilla shells
- 8 eggs
- 8-oz ground pork
- Chunky salsa for garnish (optional)
- olive oil, for brushing aluminum
- Shredded cheddar for garnish

Directions for Cooking:

1. Mix well 1 tbsp water, nutmeg, brown sugar, red pepper, fennel seed, thyme, sage, 1/8 tsp pepper, 1 tsp salt, and ground pork in a large bowl. Wrap in Saran wrap and place in fridge.
2. Brush sides of two aluminum foil and wrap tortillas with it. Seal all sides of foil.

3. In a heatproof bowl whisk well, the eggs. Stir in 1 tsp salt, 1/8 tsp pepper, and milk.
4. Add the ground meat in bowl of eggs and with a spatula break into pieces.
5. Cover heatproof bowl with foil.
6. Add 1 ½ cups of water in Instant Pot and place trivet. Place heatproof bowl on top of trivet. And then place foil wrapped tortilla on top of bowl.
7. Close Instant Pot, press manual button, choose high settings, and set time to 15 minutes.
8. Once done cooking, allow for a 10-minute natural release and then do a QPR.
9. Remove tortilla and eggs.
10. Slice eggs into 6 servings, place 1 egg serving in middle of tortilla, spread chunky salsa on top of egg, sprinkle cheese and roll like a burrito. Repeat process for remaining tortilla and eggs.
11. Serve and enjoy.

Nutrition information:
Calories per serving: 409; Carbohydrates: 28.5g; Protein: 27.7g; Fat: 20.1g; Sugar: 5.1g; Sodium: 1621mg

11. Creamy Oats with Peaches

(Servings: 8, Cooking Time:10 minutes)

Ingredients:

- 1 teaspoon ground cinnamon
- 1 teaspoon salt
- 1/3 cup sugar
- 3 1/2 cups milk
- 3 1/2 cups water
- 4 cups Old Fashioned Oats
- 4 peaches

Directions for Cooking:

1. Wash and peel peaches. Chop and then save ¼ for topping.
2. In Instant pot, add all ingredients as well as ¾ of the chopped peaches. Mix well.
3. Close Instant Pot, press multigrain button, and set time to 6 minutes.
4. Once done cooking, do a QPR.
5. Serve and enjoy with a sprinkling of fresh chopped peaches.

Nutrition information:

Calories per serving: 243; Carbohydrates: 51.9g; Protein: 12.2g; Fat: 7.0g; Sugar: 20.6g; Sodium: 341mg

---

12. Eggs & Ham Brekky Casserole

(Servings: 6, Cooking Time:25 minutes)

Ingredients:

- 1 cup chopped ham
- 1 cup milk
- 1 teaspoon pepper
- 1 teaspoon salt
- 1/2 onion, diced
- 10 large eggs
- 2 cups shredded cheddar cheese
- 4 medium red potatoes, peeled and diced

Directions for Cooking:

1. Add 2 cups of water in Instant Pot and place trivet.
2. In a heatproof bowl that fits inside your Instant Pot, crack eggs and whisk well.
3. Season with pepper and salt. Whisk thoroughly.
4. Stir in onions, ham, cheese, and milk. Mix thoroughly.
5. Add diced potatoes. Cover bowl securely with foil. Place bowl inside pot.
6. Close Instant Pot, press manual button, choose high settings, and set time to 25 minutes.
7. Once done cooking, do a QPR.
8. Serve and enjoy.

Nutrition information:

Calories per serving: 452; Carbohydrates: 28.0g; Protein: 28.3g; Fat: 25.1g; Sugar: 4.7g; Sodium: 1083mg

13. French Toast with Banana-Pecans

(Servings: 6, Cooking Time:30 minutes)

Ingredients:

- 1 tablespoon white sugar
- 1 teaspoon vanilla extract
- 1/2 teaspoon ground cinnamon
- 1/4 cup cream cheese
- 1/4 cup milk
- 1/4 cup pecans chopped
- 2 tablespoons brown sugar
- 2 tablespoons butter chilled and sliced
- 3 eggs
- 4 bananas sliced
- 6 slices French bread cut into 3/4-inch cubes
- Pure maple syrup optional

Directions for Cooking:

1. Lightly grease a round baking dish that fits in your Instant Pot.
2. Layer the following evenly in baking dish in the same order: ½ of sliced bread, ½ of banana slices, and 1 tbsp brown sugar.
3. Melt cream cheese in microwave for 30 seconds. Mix well and if needed, reheat in 15-second spurts. Spread on top of banana slices.
4. Repeat step two with the remaining half of the ingredients.
5. Whisk well cinnamon, vanilla, white sugar, milk and eggs in a mixing bowl. Whisk thoroughly.
6. Spread ½ of the pecans on top of the bread. And then pour egg mixture all over the bread. Cover top of dish with foil.
7. Add a cup of water in Instant Pot, place trivet, and place dish on top of trivet.
8. Close Instant Pot, press porridge button, and set time to 30 minutes.
9. Once done cooking, do a QPR.
10. Remove dish from pot, discard foil, and evenly divide into 6 servings
11. Serve and enjoy with a drizzle of maple syrup.

Nutrition information:

Calories per serving: 420; Carbohydrates: 35.8g; Protein: 19.4g; Fat: 22.6g; Sugar: 17.5g; Sodium: 351mg

14. Smoked Salmon & Eggs in Ramekins
(Servings: 4, Cooking Time:4minutes)

Ingredients:

- 4 Eggs
- 4 Slices of smoked salmon
- 4 Slices of Cheese
- 4 Fresh Basil leaves for garnish
- Olive Oil

Directions for Cooking:

1. Add a cup of water in Instant pot and place trivet on bottom.
2. Lightly grease each ramekin with a drop of olive oil each. Spread well.
3. Crack an egg in each ramekin. Place a slice of cheese, a slice of smoked salmon, and basil leaf in each ramekin.
4. Cover each ramekin with foil and place on trivet.
5. Close Instant Pot, press manual button, choose low settings, and set time to 4 minutes.
6. Once done cooking, do a QPR.
7. Serve and enjoy.

Nutrition information:

Calories per serving: 241; Carbohydrates: 0.9g; Protein: 17.5g; Fat: 18.3g; Sugar: 0.2g; Sodium: 433mg

---

15. Nutty-Strawberry Oatmeal
(Servings: 2, Cooking Time:10 minutes)

Ingredients:

- 1 ½ Cups Water
- 1 cup chopped strawberries, for topping
- 1 Cup Freshly Squeezed Orange Juice
- 1 Cup Steel Cut Oats
- 1 Tbsp Chopped Dried Apricots
- 1 Tbsp Dried Cranberries
- 1 Tbsp Raisins
- 1/4 Tsp Ground Cinnamon
- 1/8 Tsp Salt
- 2 Tbsp Butter
- 2 Tbsp Pure Maple Syrup
- 3 Tbsp Chopped Pecans, for topping

Directions for Cooking:

1. Lightly grease Instant Pot insert with cooking spray and then add all ingredients except for topping ingredients. Mix well.
2. Close Instant Pot, press manual button, choose high settings, and set time to 10 minutes.
3. Once done cooking, do a QPR.
4. Transfer to two bowl and evenly divide toppings on bowl.
5. Serve and enjoy.

Nutrition information:

Calories per serving: 422; Carbohydrates: 72.4g; Protein: 11.1g; Fat: 19.2g; Sugar: 30.0g; Sodium: 270mg

INSTANT POT BREAKFAST RECIPES

16. Vanilla-Latte Oatmeal
(Servings: 4, Cooking Time:20 minutes)

Ingredients:

- 1 cup milk
- 1 cup steel cut oats
- 1 teaspoon espresso powder
- 1/4 teaspoon salt
- 2 1/2 cups water
- 2 tablespoons sugar
- 2 teaspoon vanilla extract
- finely grated chocolate
- freshly whipped cream

Directions for Cooking:

1. Mix well salt, espresso powder, sugar, oats, milk, and water in Instant Pot.
2. Close Instant Pot, press manual button, choose high settings, and set time to 10 minutes.
3. Once done cooking, do a natural release for 10-minutes and then do a QPR.
4. Uncover pot and stir in vanilla extract. Spoon into 4 bowls.
5. Garnish with grated chocolate and whipped cream.
6. Serve and enjoy.

Nutrition information:
Calories per serving: 166; Carbohydrates: 27.6g; Protein: 6.5g; Fat: 6.8g; Sugar: 11.4g; Sodium: 177mg

17. Egg & Bacon Breakfast Risotto
(Servings: 2, Cooking Time:10 minutes)

Ingredients:

- 1 1/2 cups Chicken Broth
- 1/3 cup Chopped Onion
- 2 Eggs
- 2 tablespoons Grated Parmesan Cheese
- 3 slices Center Cut Bacon, chopped
- 3 tablespoons Dry White Wine
- 3/4 cup Arborio Rice
- Chives, for garnish
- Salt and Pepper, to taste

Directions for Cooking:

1. Press sauté button and cook bacon to a crisp, around 8 minutes.
2. Stir in onion and sauté for 3 minutes.
3. Add rice and sauté for a minute.
4. Pour in wine and deglaze pot. Continue sautéing until wine is completely absorbed by rice, around 5 minutes.
5. Stir in chicken broth.
6. Close Instant Pot, press manual button, choose high settings, and set time to 5 minutes.
7. Meanwhile, cook eggs sunny side up to desired doneness.
8. Once done cooking, do a QPR. Stir in pepper, salt, and parmesan.
9. Divide risotto evenly on to two plates, add egg, and sprinkle with chives.
10. Serve and enjoy.

Nutrition information:
Calories per serving: 292; Carbohydrates: 16.0g; Protein: 12.0g; Fat: 11.0g; Sugar: 1.0g; Sodium: 959mg

INSTANT POT BREAKFAST RECIPES

18. Breakfast Quinoa with Cinnamon-Apple
(Servings: 4, Cooking Time:9 minutes)

Ingredients:
- 1 ½ cups Water
- 1 Chopped Apple
- 1 cup Quinoa
- 1/2 tsp Vanilla
- 1/4 cup Gentle Sweet
- 1/4 tsp Mineral Salt
- 2 tbsp Cinnamon

Directions for Cooking:

1. Mix all ingredients in Instant Pot. Thoroughly combine.
2. Close Instant Pot, press manual button, choose high settings, and set time to 1 minute.
3. Once done cooking, do a natural release for 8-minutes and then do a QPR.
4. Serve and enjoy.

Nutrition information:

Calories per serving: 192; Carbohydrates: 37.0g; Protein: 6.3g; Fat: 2.7g; Sugar: 4.9g; Sodium: 150mg

---

19. Strawberry-Cheesecake Flavored Breakfast Quinoa
(Servings: 3, Cooking Time:11 minutes)

Ingredients:
- 1 1/2 cups uncooked quinoa
- 1/2 cup vanilla Greek yogurt
- 1/2 teaspoon vanilla
- 1/4 teaspoon sweet spice mix such as pumpkin pie spice
- 2 1/4 cups water
- 2 cups sliced strawberries
- 2 tablespoons raw honey

Directions for Cooking:

1. In Instant Pot, add all ingredients and mix well.
2. Close Instant Pot, press manual button, choose high settings, and set time to 1 minute.
3. Once done cooking, do a natural release for 10-minutes and then do a QPR.
4. Serve and enjoy.

Nutrition information:

Calories per serving: 405; Carbohydrates: 74.7g; Protein: 15.6g; Fat: 5.6g; Sugar: 17.2g; Sodium: 20mg

20. Cornmeal-Porridge Jamaican Style Brekky
(Servings: 4, Cooking Time:20 minutes)

Ingredients:

- 1 cup milk
- 1 cup yellow cornmeal, fine
- 1 tsp vanilla extract
- 1/2 cup sweetened condensed milk
- 1/2 tsp nutmeg, ground
- 2 sticks cinnamon
- 3 pimento berries
- 4 cups water separated

Directions for Cooking:

1. In a mixing bowl, whisk well cornmeal and a cup of water.

2. Add 1 cup milk and 3 cups water in Instant Pot. Stir in cornmeal mixture and mix well.
3. Stir in cinnamon sticks, berries, vanilla, and nutmeg. Mix well.
4. Close Instant Pot, press porridge button, and set time to 6 minutes.
5. Once done cooking, do a natural release all the way until it's safe to open pot.
6. Stir in condensed milk.
7. Serve and enjoy.

Nutrition information:

Calories per serving: 225; Carbohydrates: 42.0g; Protein: 6.1g; Fat: 3.9g; Sugar: 5.8g; Sodium: 49mg

21. Traditional Pancake in Instant Pot
(Servings:2, Cooking Time:40minutes)

Ingredients:

- 1 1/2 cups milk
- 2 1/2 tsp baking powder
- 2 cups all-purpose flour
- 2 large eggs
- 2 tbsp granulated white sugar
- 2 tbsp maple syrup

Directions for Cooking:

1. In a large mixing bowl, whisk well eggs. Stir in milk, baking powder, and white sugar. Mix thoroughly.

2. Add flour and mix well.
3. Grease Instant Pot with cooking spray on bottom and sides. Pour batter in pot.
4. Close Instant Pot, press multigrain button, choose low settings, do not seal vent and set time to 40 minutes.
5. Once done cooking, open pot no need to release pressure as there is no pressure.
6. Serve with syrup and enjoy.

Nutrition information:

Calories per serving: 746.5; Carbohydrates: 133.5g; Protein: 25.0g; Fat: 12.0g; Sugar: 34.4g; Sodium: 160.5mg

INSTANT POT BREAKFAST RECIPES

22. Oat, Millet & Apple Porridge
(Servings: 8, Cooking Time:35 minutes)

Ingredients:

- ¼ tsp salt
- ½ cup rolled oats
- ½ tsp ground ginger
- ¾ cup dry millet
- 1 tsp ground cinnamon
- 2 apples, cored and diced
- 3 cups water

Directions for Cooking:

1. Press brown button on Instant Pot and toast millet until fragrant and browned, around 5 to 10 minutes. Stir frequently.

2. Press cancel button and stir in remaining ingredients and mix well.
3. Close Instant Pot, press manual button, choose high settings, and set time to 10 minutes.
4. Once done cooking, allow for a 15-minute natural release and then do a QPR.
5. Serve and enjoy.

Nutrition information:
Calories per serving: 110; Carbohydrates: 24.2g; Protein: 3.2g; Fat: 1.3g; Sugar: 24.2g; Sodium: 76mg

---

23. Breakfast Burrito in Instant Pot
(Servings: 6, Cooking Time:30 minutes)

Ingredients:

- 1 avocado, pitted, peeled, and sliced thinly
- 1 cup salsa
- 1 diced jalapeno
- 1/2 tsp mesquite seasoning
- 1/2 tsp salt
- 1/4 cup chopped white or yellow onion
- 1/4 tsp chili powder
- 2-pound red potatoes, peeled and cubed
- 3/4 tsp taco seasoning
- 4 eggs
- 6 coconut flour tortillas
- 6-oz ham steak cubed
- hot sauce

Directions for Cooking:

1. Lightly grease a round casserole dish that fits in Instant Pot.
2. Add a cup of water into Instant Pot and place trivet.

3. In a mixing bowl, whisk eggs well. Stir in salt, mesquite seasoning, chili powder, and taco seasoning. Whisk well.
4. Stir in cubed potatoes, chopped onion, diced jalapeno, and cubed ham steak. Mix well and pour into prepared casserole dish.
5. Cover top of dish securely with foil and place dish on trivet in pot.
6. Close Instant Pot, press manual button, choose high settings, and set time to 13 minutes.
7. Once done cooking, do a natural release for 15 minutes and then do a QPR.
8. When ready, open pot.
9. Evenly divide casserole in middle of 6 tortillas. Top each evenly with salsa, avocado, and hot sauce if desired.
10. Serve and enjoy.

Nutrition information:
Calories per serving: 381; Carbohydrates: 50.0g; Protein: 17.6g; Fat: 13.2g; Sugar: 5.5g; Sodium: 1207mg

24. Breakfast Tacos with Green Chile
(Servings: 6, Cooking Time:2 hours)

Green Chile Ingredients:

- ¾ cup chicken broth
- 1 ½ tsp cumin
- 1 14-oz can roasted crushed tomatoes
- 1 onion, chopped
- 2-lbs pork shoulder
- 2 hot hatch green chiles
- 2 mild hatch green chiles
- 3 tbsp lard or bacon fat
- salt and pepper to taste

Breakfast Taco Ingredients:

- 1 avocado sliced
- 1 lime, sliced in wedges for garnish
- 3 tbsp chopped fresh cilantro
- 6 eggs, scrambled
- 6 Siete Foods Tortillas or any other paleo tortilla

Directions for Cooking:

1. Press browning button on Instant Pot and heat lard.
2. Season pork shoulder with salt, pepper, and cumin.
3. Once lard is heated, brown pork shoulder for 5 minutes per side. Then transfer to a plate.
4. Sauté onions until caramelized, around 8 minutes.
5. Add broth and deglaze pot. Stir in tomatoes and green chile, mix well.
6. Return pork to pot.
7. Close Instant Pot, press manual button, choose high settings, and set time to 90 minutes.
8. Meanwhile, cook scrambled eggs on a skillet on medium fire to desired doneness and set aside.
9. Once done cooking, do a QPR.
10. With 2 forks shred pork.
11. To assemble, place tortillas on a flat surface, evenly divide scrambled eggs, shredded pork, avocado slices, and cilantro. Roll to make a burrito.
12. Serve and enjoy with a side of lemon wedge.

Nutrition information:
Calories per serving: 546; Carbohydrates: 22.4g; Protein: 35.6g; Fat: 35.3g; Sugar: 5.2g; Sodium: 369mg

---

25. Hashed Sweet Potato
(Servings: 4, Cooking Time:20 minutes)

Directions for Cooking:

Ingredients:

- 6 large eggs
- 1 tablespoon Italian seasoning
- 1/2 teaspoon sea salt
- 1/2 teaspoon ground black pepper
- 1/2-pound ground pork sausage
- 1 large sweet potato, peeled and cubed
- 1 small onion, peeled and diced
- 2 cloves garlic, minced

1. Lightly grease a heatproof glass dish that fits in Instant Pot.
2. Add water in pot and place trivet.

3. In a medium mixing bowl, whisk well eggs. Season with pepper, salt, and Italian seasoning.

- 1 medium green bell pepper, seeded and diced
- 2 cups water

4. Add bell pepper, garlic, onion, sweet potato, and sausage in bowl and mix well. Pour into prepared dish and cover dish with foil.
5. Place on trivet in Pot.

Close Instant Pot, press manual button, choose high settings, and set time to 10 minutes.

6. Once done cooking, allow for a 10-minute natural release and then do a QPR.
7. Serve and enjoy.

Nutrition information:

Calories per serving: 546; Carbohydrates: 17.7g; Protein: 32.2g; Fat: 38.2g; Sugar: 7.2g; Sodium: 1785mg

26. Cheesy Eggs in Instant Pot
(Servings: 4, Cooking Time:35 minutes)

Ingredients:

- ¼ cup milk
- ½ teaspoon pepper
- 1 cup shredded cheddar cheese, divided
- 1 stalk green onions, chopped
- 1 teaspoon kosher salt
- 2 cups frozen hash browns
- 6 eggs
- 6 slices bacon, chopped

Directions for Cooking:

1. Press sauté button and sauté bacon until crisped, around 8 minutes.
2. Stir in hash browns and cook for 2 to 3 minutes until no longer frozen.
3. With cooking spray, lightly grease a round heatproof dish that fits in Instant Pot and whisk eggs. Stir in pepper, salt, ½ cup shredded cheese, and milk. Mix well.

4. Add hash browns and bacon into dish and mix well. Cover dish with foil.
5. Press cancel button, add water, and place trivet on bottom of Instant Pot. Add dish on top of trivet.
6. Close Instant Pot, press pressure cook button, choose high settings, and set time to 20 minutes.
7. Once done cooking, do a QPR.
8. Remove foil, sprinkle remaining cheese and chopped onions. Cover and let it sit in pot for 5 minutes more.
9. Serve and enjoy.

Nutrition information:

Calories per serving: 567; Carbohydrates: 22.4g; Protein: 28.0g; Fat: 40.5g; Sugar: 2.5g; Sodium: 1131mg

27. Baked Chicken-Potato Ranch Casserole
(Servings: 6, Cooking Time:60 minutes)

Ingredients:

- 16 oz skinless chicken breasts
- 3 slices uncured, nitrate-free bacon cooked and crumbled
- 6 red potatoes medium sized and cut into chunks
- 1/2 cup low-sodium chicken broth
- 1/2 cup unsweetened almond milk
- 1/2 cup plain, non-fat Greek yogurt
- 1 tbsp butter
- 1 tsp olive oil
- 1 cup reduced fat cheddar cheese shredded
- 1/2 cup part-skim mozzarella cheese shredded
- 2 tbsp green onions chopped
- 1 tsp chives
- 3/4 packet ranch seasoning
- 1 tsp paprika
- McCormick's Grill Mates Chicken Seasoning to taste
- salt and pepper to taste

Directions for Cooking:

1. Press sauté and add olive oil to pot.
2. While waiting for oil to heat up, with chicken seasoning, season chicken breasts and then brown each side for two minutes. Brown chicken in batches and place on a plate.
3. Once done browning, return chicken to pot and add chicken broth and potato chunks. Deglaze pot and stir to mix.
4. Close Instant Pot, press manual button, choose high settings, and set time to 10 minutes.
5. Once done cooking, do a 10-minute natural release and then do a QPR.
6. Transfer chicken to a plate and shred with two forks. And then mash the potatoes in the pot. Stir in ranch seasoning, chives, paprika, and ½ cup of cheese as well as the shredded chicken. Mix well. Season with pepper and salt.
7. Lightly grease a baking pan with cooking spray and preheat oven to 375°F.
8. Transfer the mixture from the Instant Pot to the prepared baking dish. Sprinkle remaining cheese on top and bake for 15 minutes.
9. Serve and enjoy.

Nutrition information:
Calories per serving: 354; Carbohydrates: 35.4g; Protein: 30.1g; Fat: 9.9g; Sugar: 5.3g; Sodium: 953mg

28. Simple Breakfast Hash
(Servings: 4, Cooking Time:10 minutes)

Ingredients:

- 6 eggs, beaten
- 1 cup shredded American cheese
- 1 cup chopped breakfast ham
- 6 small potatoes, shredded

Directions for Cooking:

1. Lightly grease Instant Pot insert with cooking spray and press sauté button.
2. In processor, shred the potatoes and squeeze excess moisture. Add to pot and cook for 5 minutes.
3. Whisk eggs in a bowl.
4. Shred meat and cheese in processor.
5. After 5 minutes, breakup the shredded potatoes and add ¼ cup of water. Mix well.
6. Stir in shredded meat and cheese. Mix well.
7. Pour in whisked eggs and lightly combine.
8. Close Instant Pot, press manual button, choose high settings, and set time to 1 minute.
9. Once done cooking, do a QPR.
10. Serve and enjoy.

Nutrition information:
Calories per serving: 502; Carbohydrates: 43.8g; Protein: 25.8g; Fat: 24.8g; Sugar: 6.3g; Sodium: 1864mg

---

29. Spinach, Sausage & Sweet Potato Hash
(Servings: 4, Cooking Time:15 minutes)

Ingredients:

- 3 large sweet potatoes, peeled and cut into 1-inch pieces
- 1 tablespoon olive oil, divided
- 1/2 teaspoon Kosher salt
- 12-ounces Italian sausage
- 1 small onion, finely chopped
- 2 cloves garlic, minced or put through a garlic press
- 1/2 teaspoon ground sage
- 1/4 teaspoon freshly ground black pepper
- 11-ounces baby spinach
- 4 large eggs, optional

Directions for Cooking:

1. Preheat oven to 425°F.
On a baking pan, add sweet potatoes and drizzle with salt and 2 teaspoons olive oil. Roast for 30 minutes or until fork tender.

1. Midway through roasting time, stir potatoes. Once done roasting turn oven off and set sweet potatoes aside.
2. Press sauté button on Instant Pot and heat remaining oil. Sauté sausage and crumble to pieces. Cook for 10 minutes.
3. Stir in pepper, sage, garlic, and onions. Sauté for three minutes.
4. Stir in spinach and sweet potatoes and mix well.
5. Break eggs on top of the mixture.
6. Close Instant Pot, press pressure cook button, choose low settings, and set time to 1 minute.
7. Once done cooking, do a QPR.
8. Serve and enjoy.

Nutrition information:
Calories per serving: 508; Carbohydrates: 29.2g; Protein: 26.6g; Fat: 31.9g; Sugar: 8.5g; Sodium: 1481mg

30. Loaded Potatoes Brekky Style
(Servings: 4, Cooking Time:30 minutes)

Ingredients:

- 4 russet potatoes, scrubbed
- 1-lb Butcher Box Pork Sausage
- 1/4 cup onion, diced
- 1 red bell pepper, diced
- 1 orange bell pepper, diced
- 1/2 teaspoon Primal Palate Meat & Potato Seasoning
- 1/2 teaspoon garlic powder
- pinch of sea salt & pepper
- handful of green onion, sliced
- Tessemae's Hot Buffalo Sauce
- 4 eggs
- 2 tablespoons apple cider vinegar

Directions for Cooking:

1. Add 4 cups of water in Instant Pot and place steamer rack. Add potatoes on steamer rack.
2. Close Instant Pot, press pressure cook button, choose high settings, and set time to 20 minutes.
3. Meanwhile, place a nonstick pan on medium-high fire and sauté onions for 5 minutes.
4. Stir in pork sausage, crumble and cook for 10 minutes or until browned completely.
5. Season with pepper, salt, garlic powder, plus meat & potato seasoning. Mix well.
6. Stir in Peppers and sauté for 3 minutes or until tender. Turn fire off and set aside.
7. Bring a small pot of water to a boil and add apple cider vinegar. Once boiling turn off fire, crack egg one at a time and carefully lower in boiling water. Cover and let it sit for 5 minutes. Remove eggs with a slotted spoon.
8. Once done cooking potatoes, do a QPR.
9. Remove potatoes from steamer rack, slice in half, and lightly scrape sides of potato with fork. Stuff potatoes evenly with the pork mixture and then top with the poached eggs.
10. Serve and enjoy.

Nutrition information:
Calories per serving: 534; Carbohydrates: 38.4g; Protein: 33.0g; Fat: 28.0g; Sugar: 3.8g; Sodium: 1027mg

INSTANT POT BREAKFAST RECIPES

31. Potato Hash with Spanish Chorizo
(Servings: 4, Cooking Time: 22 minutes)

Ingredients:

- Instant Pot Duo
- 6 Large Potatoes, peeled and diced
- 1 Chorizo Sausage, sliced thinly
- 4 Slices Bacon, sliced into chunks
- 1 Large Onion, peeled and diced
- 250 g Soft Cheese
- 2 Tbsp Greek Yoghurt
- 1 Tbsp Garlic Puree
- 1 Tbsp Olive Oil
- 200 ml Vegetable Stock
- 3 Tbsp Rosemary
- 3 Tbsp Basil
- Salt & Pepper

Directions for Cooking:

1. Press sauté button and heat oil. Once hot sauté garlic and onion for 5 minutes or until onions are soft.
2. Add sausages and potatoes. Sauté for 3 minutes.
3. Add bacon and cook for 3 minutes more.
4. Stir in stock. Mix well and then press cancel button.
5. Close Instant Pot, press soup button, and set time to 10 minutes.
6. Meanwhile, in a large shallow dish mix well soft cheese, yoghurt, rosemary, basil, salt, and pepper. Mix well and set aside.
7. Once done cooking, do a QPR.
8. Transfer pot mixture into shallow dish and toss well to coat in cheese mixture.
9. Serve and enjoy.

Nutrition information:

Calories per serving: 749; Carbohydrates: 99.0g; Protein: 29.6g; Fat: 27.2g; Sugar: 7.2g; Sodium: 1936mg

---

32. French Toast Casserole
(Servings: 4, Cooking Time: 30 minutes)

Ingredients:

- 3 eggs
- 1 cup half and half cream
- 1/2 cup milk
- 1 Tbsp cinnamon
- 1 tsp vanilla
- 1 loaf of French bread cubed
- 1/2 cup blueberries - more to taste

Directions for Cooking:

1. Lightly spray Instant Pot insert with cooking spray the bottom and sides.
2. Add cubed bread evenly in pot.
3. In a bowl, whisk well eggs, vanilla, cinnamon, cream, and milk. Pour over bread cubes. Toss bread to coat and soak up the milk mixture.
4. Sprinkle blueberries on top.
5. Close Instant Pot, press pressure cook button, choose high settings, and set time to 15 minutes.
6. Once done cooking, allow a complete natural release.
7. Serve and enjoy.

Nutrition information:

Calories per serving: 159; Carbohydrates: 20.0g; Protein: 7.7g; Fat: 5.4g; Sugar: 11.8g; Sodium: 162mg

33. Ranch Dressed Bacon-Potato Brekky

(Servings: 6, Cooking Time: 15 minutes)

Ingredients:

- 2-lb red potatoes, scrubbed and cubed into 1-inch pieces
- 3 bacon strips, sliced into small pieces
- 2 tsp dried parsley
- 1 tsp kosher salt
- 1 tsp garlic powder
- 4-oz. cheddar cheese, shredded
- 1/3 cup Ranch dressing, liquid

Directions for Cooking:

1. Press sauté button and cook bacon until crisped, around 8 minutes.
2. Stir in salt, garlic powder, dried parsley, and potatoes.
3. Stir in 1/3 cup of water.
4. Close Instant Pot, press manual button, choose high settings, and set time to 7 minutes.
5. Once done cooking, do a QPR.
6. Stir in cheese and ranch dressing.
7. Serve and enjoy.

Nutrition information:

Calories per serving: 248; Carbohydrates: 33.5g; Protein: 7.3g; Fat: 9.7g; Sugar: 3.2g; Sodium: 820mg

---

34. Banana Bread for Breakfast

(Servings: 16, Cooking Time:1 hour and 10 minutes)

Ingredients:

- 1 1/2 cup Steel Cut Oats
- 2 Ripe Bananas
- 4 Eggs
- 1/3 cup Raw Organic Honey
- 2 tsp Pure Vanilla Extract
- 1/2 tsp Baking Soda
- Pinch of Sea Salt
- 1/4 cup +2 tbsp Mini Dairy Free Chocolate Chips

Directions for Cooking:

1. In a high-powered blender, add all ingredients except for chocolate chips and blend on high until smooth and creamy.
2. Fold in ¼ cup chocolate chips and pour batter in a 7-inch springform pan. Sprinkle remaining chocolate chips on top of batter, Cover securely with foil.
3. Add 1 ½ cups of water in Instant pot and place trivet. Place pan on top of trivet.
4. Close Instant Pot, press manual button, choose high settings, and set time to 60 minutes.
5. Once done cooking, do a natural release for 10-minutes and then do a QPR.
6. Serve and enjoy.

Nutrition information:

Calories per serving: 87; Carbohydrates: 16.7g; Protein: 3.2g; Fat: 2.5g; Sugar: 9.0g; Sodium: 66mg

35. Slow Cooked Cinnamon-Oats
(Servings: 8, Cooking Time:4 hours)

Ingredients:

- 2 cups steel-cut oats
- 8 cups milk
- 2 tbsp butter
- 1/2 cup light brown sugar
- 1 tsp vanilla extract
- 1/2 tsp ground cinnamon
- 1/4 tsp ground nutmeg
- 1 tsp salt
- 1-pint blueberries
- 1 1/2 cups chopped, roasted, and unsalted cashews

Directions for Cooking:

1. Except for cashews and blueberries, mix all ingredients in Instant Pot insert.
2. Close Instant Pot, press slow cook button, keep vent on release position, choose low settings, and set time to 4 hours.
3. Once done cooking, open pot and stir in blueberries and cashews.
4. Serve and enjoy.

Nutrition information:

Calories per serving: 543; Carbohydrates: 53.0g; Protein: 19.0g; Fat: 31.0g; Sugar: 28.0g; Sodium: 405mg

---

36. Another Breakfast Burrito Recipe
(Servings:10, Cooking Time:35 minutes)

Ingredients:

- 1 cup diced ham (or protein of your choice)
- 1/2 cup shredded cheese
- 1/4 cup milk
- 1/4 cup sour cream
- 1/4 tsp salt
- 1/8 tsp pepper
- 10 tortilla
- 2 1/2 cups O'Brien hash browns
- 6 eggs

Directions for Cooking:

1. Add a cup of water in Instant pot and place trivet.
2. Lightly grease a heatproof dish that fits inside Instant Pot and evenly spread ham, followed by hash brown.
3. Whisk well salt, pepper, shredded cheese, sour cream, milk and eggs in a medium bowl. Pour over hash browns. Cover dish with foil securely.
4. Place dish on trivet in Instant Pot.
5. Close Instant Pot, press manual button, choose high settings, and set time to 25 minutes.
6. Once done cooking, do a QPR.
7. Remove foil and stir egg mixture.
8. Close Instant Pot, press manual button, choose high settings, and set time to 10 minutes.
9. Once done cooking, do a QPR.
10. Evenly divide into 6 tortilla and roll like a burrito.
11. Serve and enjoy.

Nutrition information:

Calories per serving: 276; Carbohydrates: 23.0g; Protein: 11.5g; Fat: 15.8g; Sugar: 1.1g; Sodium: 314mg

INSTANT POT BREAKFAST RECIPES

37. Easy-Cheesy Breakfast Egg Casserole
(Servings:4, Cooking Time:22 minutes)

Ingredients:

- 8 eggs
- Pinch salt and pepper
- 1/2 cup sausage, diced
- 1/2 cup diced bell pepper
- 1/2 cup diced onion
- 1/4 cup milk
- 1/4 tsp garlic salt
- 1/2-3/4 c cheese

Directions for Cooking:

1. Grease well a pan that fits inside your Instant Pot. As 1 ½ cups water in Instant Pot insert and place trivet.
2. Evenly spread layer sausage, bell pepper, onion, and cheese.
3. In a bowl whisk well eggs, salt and pepper. Stir in milk and then pour over sausage.
4. Cover top of dish securely with foil and place on trivet inside the Instant Pot.
5. Close Instant Pot, press pressure cook button, choose high settings, and set time to 12 minutes.
6. Once done cooking, do a natural release for 10 minutes and then do a QPR.
7. Serve and enjoy.

Nutrition information:
Calories per serving: 343; Carbohydrates: 12.0g; Protein: 20.0g; Fat: 23.0g; Sugar: 2.0g; Sodium: 474mg

38. Broccoli and Egg Casserole
(Servings: 6, Cooking Time:4 hours)

Ingredients:

- 1/2 teaspoon salt
- 1/3 cup all-purpose flour
- 1/4 cup butter, melted
- 2 cups shredded cheddar cheese
- 3 cups cottage cheese
- 3 cups frozen, chopped broccoli, thawed and drained
- 3 tablespoons finely chopped onion
- 6 eggs, lightly beaten
- Additional shredded cheddar cheese, optional

Directions for Cooking:

1. Lightly grease bottom and sides of Instant Pot Insert.
2. Evenly layer and spread broccoli and chopped onion in insert.
3. In a bowl, whisk eggs, melted butter, and salt. Stir in cottage cheese, cheddar cheese, and flour. Pour over broccoli.
4. Close Instant Pot, press slow cook button, choose high settings, and set time to 1 hour.
5. Once done, open pot and stir.
6. Close Instant Pot, press slow cook button, choose low settings and set time to 3 hours.
7. Once done cooking, open pot, serve and enjoy.

Nutrition information:
Calories per serving: 435; Carbohydrates: 13.0g; Protein: 29.0g; Fat: 30.0g; Sugar: 4.0g; Sodium: 730mg

39. Scotch Eggs in Pressure Cooker
(Servings: 4, Cooking Time: 25minutes)

Ingredients:

- 4 large eggs
- 1-lb country style ground sausage
- 1 tablespoon vegetable oil

Directions for Cooking:

1. Add a cup of water in Instant Pot, place eggs in a steamer basket and place inside pot.
2. Close Instant Pot, press pressure cook button, choose high settings, and set time to 6 minutes.
3. Once done cooking, do a 6-minute natural release and then do a QPR.
4. Remove eggs and place in an ice water bath. When cool enough to handle, peel eggs.
5. Evenly divide ground sausage into four parts. Use one part of sausage to cover one peeled egg. Repeat process to remaining eggs.
6. Discard water in Instant Pot. Press sauté button and once all water has evaporated, add vegetable oil. Sauté Scotch eggs for two minutes on fours ides. Transfer Scotch Eggs to a plate.
7. Add a cup of water in Instant Pot and place trivet. Place Scotch Eggs on trivet.
8. Close Instant Pot, press pressure cook button, choose high settings, and set time to six minutes.
9. Once done cooking, do a QPR.
10. Serve and enjoy.

Nutrition information:

Calories per serving: 491; Carbohydrates: 5.2g; Protein: 28.0g; Fat: 39.1g; Sugar: 1.2g; Sodium: 1440mg

40. Buckwheat Porridge in Instant Pot
(Servings: 4, Cooking Time:26 minutes)

Ingredients:

- 1 cup raw buckwheat groats
- 3 cups rice milk
- 1 banana sliced
- 1/4 cup raisins
- 1 tsp ground cinnamon
- 1/2 tsp vanilla

Directions for Cooking:

1. Rinse groats and place inside Instant Pot insert.
2. Stir in vanilla, cinnamon, raisins, banana, and milk.
3. Close Instant Pot, press pressure cook button, choose high settings, and set time to 6 minutes.
4. Once done cooking, do a 20-minute natural release and then do a QPR.
5. Serve and enjoy.

Nutrition information:

Calories per serving: 281; Carbohydrates: 53.3g; Protein: 9.4g; Fat: 3.5g; Sugar: 11.7g; Sodium: 547mg

41. Eggs Benedicta in a Casserole
(Servings: 6, Cooking Time:60 minutes)

Ingredients:

- 6 English muffins, split and cut into 1-inch pieces
- 1 tablespoon olive oil, plus more for greasing
- 1 large leek, dark green part removed, cut into 1/4-inch half moons
- 12-ounces Canadian bacon, chopped
- 6 large eggs, at room temperature
- 2 1/2 cups whole milk
- 1 1/2 teaspoon dried mustard
- 1 1/2 cup heavy cream
- 2 tablespoons fresh chives, plus more for garnish
- 1/2 teaspoon cayenne pepper
- Salt and pepper, to taste

Hollandaise Sauce Ingredients:

- 1 stick butter
- 8 egg yolks, at room temperature
- 1 tablespoon fresh lemon juice
- 1 teaspoon Dijon mustard
- 1/2 cup heavy cream
- 1/2 teaspoon salt
- 1/4 teaspoon cayenne pepper

Directions for Cooking:

1. Start the Casserole by preheating oven to 350°F.

2. Evenly layer English muffins on a baking sheet and bake for 10-15 minutes or until golden brown. Transfer to prepared baking dish.

3. On Instant Pot, press sauté button and heat oil. Stir in leeks and sauté for 2 minutes.

4. Add and brown bacon for 8 minutes until crisped. Transfer to a plate.

5. Press cancel button, add English muffins on bottom of pot and spread bacon on top.

6. Whisk eggs cayenne, chives, cream, dry mustard, milk, and eggs in a large bowl. Season with pepper and salt. Pour over mixture in Instant Pot.

7. Close Instant Pot, press pressure cook button, choose high settings, and set time to 10 minutes.

8. Meanwhile, make the Hollandaise sauce by microwaving butter until melted.

9. In double boiler, whisk cayenne, salt, cream, Dijon mustard, lemon juice, and egg yolks. Cook for 15 minutes until thick enough to coat back of spoon. Slowly whisk in melted butter. Set aside.

10. Once done cooking, do a natural release for 10-minutes and then do a QPR.

11. Serve and enjoy with a drizzle of Hollandaise sauce.

Nutrition information:
Calories per serving: 827; Carbohydrates: 38.0g; Protein: 31.0g; Fat: 63.0g; Sugar: 10.0g; Sodium: 950mg

INSTANT POT BREAKFAST RECIPES

42. Maple-Cranberry Oatmeal
(Servings: 9, Cooking Time:5 hours)

Ingredients:

- 8 cups water
- 2 cups steel-cut oats
- 2/3 cup dried cranberries, chopped
- 1/2 cup maple syrup
- 1 tbsp cinnamon
- 1/2 tsp salt
- 3 cups slivered almonds, toasted

Directions for Cooking:

1. Except for the almonds, mix all ingredients in Instant Pot.
2. Close Instant Pot, press slow cook button, choose low settings, and set time to 5 hours.
3. Once done cooking, open pot and stir in almonds.
4. Serve and enjoy.

Nutrition information:
Calories per serving: 287; Carbohydrates: 35.4g; Protein: 10.1g; Fat: 16.8g; Sugar: 14.5g; Sodium: 137mg

---

43. Pepper, Ham & Broccoli Frittata
(Servings: 4, Cooking Time:30 minutes)

Ingredients:

- 8 ounces ham cubed
- 1 cup sweet peppers sliced
- 2 cups frozen broccoli
- 4 eggs
- 1 cup half and half
- 1 cup shredded cheddar cheese
- 1 tsp salt
- 2 teaspoons ground pepper

Directions for Cooking:

1. Grease well a heatproof dish that fits inside your Instant Pot, add 2 cups of water in Instant Pot followed by a trivet.
2. Evenly spread and layer sweet peppers, cubed ham, and broccoli.
3. Whisk well pepper, salt, half and half, and eggs. Stir in cheese. Pour over mixture in Instant Pot. Cover securely with foil and place on trivet in Instant Pot.
4. Close Instant Pot, press pressure cook button, choose high settings, and set time to 20 minutes.
5. Once done cooking, do a 10-minute natural release and then do a QPR.
6. Remove dish from pot and flip on a plate after letting it cool for at least 10 minutes.
7. Serve and enjoy.

Nutrition information:
Calories per serving: 373; Carbohydrates: 14.4g; Protein: 29.7g; Fat: 22.3g; Sugar: 6.8g; Sodium: 1670mg

---

44. French Toast with Blueberry Syrup
(Servings: 12, Cooking Time:4 hours)

French Toast Ingredients:

- 8 large eggs
- 1/2 cup yogurt
- 1/3 cup sour cream
- 1 teaspoon vanilla extract
- 1/2 teaspoon ground cinnamon
- 1 cup milk
- 1/3 cup maple syrup
- 1-pound French bread, cubed
- 1 1/2 cup blueberries
- 12 ounces cream cheese, cubed

Blueberry Syrup Ingredients:

- 1 cup sugar
- 2 tablespoons cornstarch
- 1 cup cold water
- 3/4 cups blueberries
- 1 tablespoon butter
- 1 tablespoon lemon juice

Directions for Cooking:

1. Lightly grease sides and bottom of Instant Pot insert and evenly spread half of the cubed bread on bottom of insert followed by half of the blueberries and half of the cream cheese.

2. Whisk well cinnamon, vanilla, sour cream, yogurt, and eggs. Pour half of the mixture over the bread in insert.

3. Evenly layer the remaining bread, blueberries, and cream cheese in insert. And then pour remaining egg mixture over it. Cover insert with Saran wrap and refrigerate for a night.

4. Place at room temperature for at least 30 minutes before cooking.

5. Close Instant Pot, press slow cook button, choose low settings, and set time to 4 hours.

6. Meanwhile, make the syrup. On medium fire place a saucepan and whisk well cornstarch and sugar. Stir in water and mix well until smooth. Add ¼ cup of blueberries and cook until blueberries pot, around 5 minutes. Turn off fire and stir in remaining berries, lemon juice, and butter.

7. Once French Toast is done cooking, open pot.

8. Serve and enjoy with blueberry syrup.

Nutrition information:

Calories per serving: 397; Carbohydrates: 51.0g; Protein: 11.0g; Fat: 17.0g; Sugar: 29.0g; Sodium: 397mg

45. Carrot Cake Flavored Oatmeal
(Servings: 8, Cooking Time:20 minutes)

Ingredients:
- 4-1/2 cups water
- 1 can (20 ounces) crushed pineapple, undrained
- 2 cups shredded carrots
- 1 cup steel-cut oats
- 1 cup raisins
- 2 teaspoons ground cinnamon
- 1 teaspoon pumpkin pie spice

Directions for Cooking:

1. Grease Instant Pot insert.
2. Add all ingredients in pot and mix well.
3. Close Instant Pot, press manual button, choose high settings, and set time to 10 minutes.
4. Once done cooking, do a 10-minute natural release and then do a QPR.
5. Serve and enjoy.

Nutrition information:
Calories per serving: 91; Carbohydrates: 23.1g; Protein: 2.7g; Fat: 0.9g; Sugar: 13.3g; Sodium: 22mg

---

46. Cheese and Bacon Quiche
(Servings: 6, Cooking Time:4 hours)

Ingredients:
- 1 box refrigerated pie crusts
- 2 cups shredded Monterrey Jack cheese
- 1 cup cooked bacon
- 6 eggs
- 1 cup milk
- 1/4 teaspoon salt
- 1/4 teaspoon freshly ground pepper

Directions for Cooking:

1. Grease Instant Pot insert on bottom and sides. Press pie crust on bottom and up to 2-inches up on the sides of the pot. Overlap seams by ¼-inch.
2. Close Instant Pot, press slow cook button, choose high settings, and set time to 1 hour and 30 minutes.
3. Meanwhile, whisk eggs, milk, salt and pepper. And set aside
4. Once done cooking, open pot, pour in egg mixture, and top with cheese.
5. Close Instant Pot, press slow cook button, choose low settings and set time to 2 hours and 30 minutes.
6. Once done cooking, open pot.
7. Serve and enjoy.

Nutrition information:
Calories per serving: 524; Carbohydrates: 22.0g; Protein: 25.0g; Fat: 37.0g; Sugar: 2.0g; Sodium: 912mg

47. 6-Ingredient Breakfast Granola
(Servings: 4, Cooking Time:2 hours and 30 minutes)

Ingredients:

- 1 ½ cups old-fashioned oats
- 2 cups crisp brown rice cereal
- 2 large egg whites, room temperature
- ¼ cup honey
- ¼ cup chopped cashews
- ¼ cup pecan halves

Directions for Cooking:

1. Line a rimmed baking pan with foil and coat lightly with cooking spray you Instant Pot insert.
2. Toss well to mix in a large bowl the oats and rice cereal.
3. In another bowl, whisk well eggs. Stir in honey and mix well. Pour over bowl of cashews and mix well using a spatula. Transfer to Instant Pot.
4. Close Instant Pot, press slow cook button, do not seal vent, choose high settings, and set time to 2 hours and 30 minutes.
5. Once done cooking, open pot, and spread on prepared pan.
6. Once cooled completely, mix in cashews and pecan halves. Toss well to coat.
7. Serve and enjoy.

Nutrition information:

Calories per serving: 361; Carbohydrates: 69.3g; Protein: 12.4g; Fat: 11.0g; Sugar: 19.0g; Sodium: 33mg

---

48. Simple Cinnamon French Toast
(Servings: 6, Cooking Time:2 hours and 30 minutes)

Ingredients:

- 1 loaf of crusty bread, cut into 1inch cubes
- 1/3 cup golden raisins
- 4 eggs
- 2 cups milk
- 1/4 cup pure maple syrup
- 1 teaspoon vanilla extract
- 1 teaspoon ground cinnamon

Directions for Cooking:

1. Grease well Instant Pot insert on bottom and sides.
2. Evenly spread sliced bread in Pot.
3. Sprinkle raisins over the bread.
4. Whisk well cinnamon, vanilla, maple syrup, milk, and eggs in a medium bowl.
5. Pour mixture over the bread in Pot.
6. With a fork, press down on the bread to soak the liquid.
7. Close Instant Pot, press slow cook button, choose high settings, and set time to 2 hours and 30 minutes.
8. Once done cooking, open pot.
9. Serve and enjoy.

Nutrition information:

Calories per serving: 323; Carbohydrates: 51.0g; Protein: 13.0g; Fat: 7.0g; Sugar: 21.0g; Sodium: 403mg

INSTANT POT BREAKFAST RECIPES

49. No-Crust Crab Quiche in Instant Pot
(Servings: 4, Cooking Time: 50 minutes)

Ingredients:

- 4 eggs
- 1 cup half and half
- 1/2 tsp salt
- 1 teaspoon pepper
- 1 teaspoon sweet smoked paprika
- 1 teaspoon Herb de Provence
- 1 cup shredded parmesan or swiss cheese
- 1 cup chopped green onions green and white parts
- 1 cup chopped imitation crab meat
- ½ cup real crab meat
- ½ cup chopped raw shrimp

Directions for Cooking:

1. Grease well a round baking dish that fits inside your Instant Pot. Add 2 cups of water in pot and place trivet.

2. Whisk well half and half and eggs in a large bowl. Stir in salt, pepper, paprika, and Herb de Provence. Mix well.

3. Add green onions, imitation crab meat, crab meat, and raw shrimp. Mix well. Pour into prepared round baking dish.

4. Sprinkle cheese on top and then cover securely with foil. Place on trivet inside pot.

5. Close Instant Pot, press pressure cook button, choose high settings, and set time to 40 minutes.

6. Once done cooking, do a 10-minute natural release and then do a QPR.

7. Serve and enjoy.

Nutrition information:
Calories per serving: 395; Carbohydrates: 19.0g; Protein: 22.0g; Fat: 25.0g; Sugar: 3.0g; Sodium: 526mg

---

50. Coconut-Rice Pudding in Instant Pot
(Servings: 5, Cooking Time:4 hours and 30 minutes)

Ingredients:

- 1 cup brown basmati rice
- 3 cups milk
- 1 13.5-ounce can light coconut milk
- 1/4 cup pure maple syrup
- 1 teaspoon vanilla extract
- 1/2 cup raisins

Directions for Cooking:

1. Place rice on a sieve and wash. Drain water completely and place rice in Instant Pot.

2. Stir in vanilla extract, maple syrup, coconut milk, and milk. Mix well.

3. Close Instant Pot, press slow cook button, choose low settings, and set time to 4 hours and 30 minutes.

4. Once done cooking, open pot and stir in raisins.

5. Serve and enjoy.

Nutrition information:
Calories per serving: 373; Carbohydrates: 59.0g; Protein: 8.0g; Fat: 11.0g; Sugar: 27.0g; Sodium: 85mg

51. An Extra-Ordinary Breakfast Casserole
(Servings: 12, Cooking Time: 8 hours)

Ingredients:

- 1 package (30 ounces) frozen shredded hash brown potatoes
- 1-pound Jones No Sugar Pork Sausage Roll, cooked and drained
- 1 medium onion, chopped
- 1 can (4 ounces) chopped green chilies
- 1-1/2 cups shredded cheddar cheese
- 12 large eggs
- 1 cup 2% milk
- 1/2 teaspoon salt
- 1/2 teaspoon pepper

Directions for Cooking:

1. Grease well the sides and bottom of Instant Pot and evenly spread in layers half of the potato, onion, chilies, and then followed by cheese. Repeat layering for the remaining half of the ingredients.
2. Whisk well pepper, salt, milk, and eggs in a large bowl. Pour into pot of potatoes.
3. Close Instant Pot, press slow cook button, choose low settings, and set time to 8 hours.
4. Once done cooking, do a QPR.
5. Serve and enjoy.

Nutrition information:

Calories per serving: 397; Carbohydrates: 23.6g; Protein: 17.7g; Fat: 26.4g; Sugar: 2.3g; Sodium: 578mg

---

52. Cornbread for Breakfast
(Servings: 8, Cooking Time:2 hours)

Ingredients:

- 2 tablespoons unsalted butter
- 1 1/2 cup cornmeal
- 1 1/2 cup all-purpose flour
- 2 tablespoons sugar
- 1 tablespoon baking powder
- 1 teaspoon kosher salt
- 1 teaspoon chili power
- 2 cups buttermilk
- 2 large eggs

Directions for Cooking:

1. Press sauté button and melt butter in Instant Pot. Once melted, press cancel and coat sides and bottom of Instant pot with the melted butter.
2. In a bowl whisk well, eggs and buttermilk. Stir in salt, chili powder, and baking powder and mix thoroughly.
3. Whisk in sugar, flour, and cornmeal. Mix thoroughly and then pour into greased pot.
4. Close Instant Pot, press slow cook button, choose high settings, and set time to 2 hours.
5. Once done cooking, open pot.
6. Serve and enjoy.

Nutrition information:

Calories per serving: 275; Carbohydrates: 48.0g; Protein: 8.0g; Fat: 5.0g; Sugar: 7.0; Sodium: 315mg

INSTANT POT BREAKFAST RECIPES

53. Delicata and Apple Porridge
(Servings: 3, Cooking Time:20 minutes)

Ingredients:

- 4 small or 2 large apples unpeeled, flesh cut from the cores
- 1 delicata squash washed and whole
- 1/2 cup bone broth with little fat, or water instead
- 3 Tablespoons slippery elm
- 3 Tablespoons gelatin
- 2 Tablespoons maple syrup
- 1/2 teaspoon cinnamon
- 1/8 teaspoon cloves
- 1/8 teaspoon ginger
- pinch sea salt

Directions for Cooking:

1. Place delicata squash and apple chunks in Instant Pot. Add bone broth, cinnamon, cloves, ginger, and salt.

2. Close Instant Pot, press manual button, choose high settings, and set time to 8 minutes.
3. Once done cooking, allow for a 10-minute natural release and then do a QPR.
4. Remove squash and let it cool enough to handle. Slice in half, scoop and discard.
5. Transfer pot content in a blender and scoop out squash meat and add to blender. Add maple syrup, gelatin, and slippery elm in blender and blend until smooth and creamy.
6. Serve and enjoy either hot or cold.

Nutrition information:
Calories per serving: 228; Carbohydrates: 59.0g;
Protein: 2.0g; Fat: 0.7g; Sugar: 46.6g; Sodium: 71mg

54. Ham, Tomatoes, and Spinach Frittata
(Servings: 8, Cooking Time:5 hours)

Ingredients:

- 8 eggs, beaten
- 2 cloves garlic
- 2 cups spinach, chopped
- 1 cup ham, diced
- 1 small onion, chopped
- ½ cup canned coconut milk
- 1 teaspoon coconut oil
- 1 teaspoon sea salt
- ½ teaspoon pepper

Directions for Cooking:

1. Press sauté button and heat coconut oil in Instant Pot.

2. Once hot stir in garlic and onion and sauté for 5 minutes.
3. Stir in ham and cook while you whisk pepper, salt, coconut milk, and eggs in a medium bowl. Press cancel button.
4. Stir in spinach and sauté for a minute. Pour egg mixture and mix well.
5. Close Instant Pot, press slow cook button, choose low settings, and set time to 5 hours.
6. Once done cooking, open pot.
7. Serve and enjoy.

Nutrition information:
Calories per serving: 152; Carbohydrates: 3.0g;
Protein: 11.0g; Fat: 11.0g; Sugar: 0.6g; Sodium: 364mg

55. Breakfast Fajita Casserole
(Servings: 2, Cooking Time:10 minutes)

Ingredients:

- 1/2 cup onion (sliced)
- 1 1/2 cup sliced bell peppers (green, red, and orange)
- 1 tbsp olive oil
- 4 eggs
- A sprinkle of salt and pepper
- For optional garnish: cilantro, avocado, and limes
- 2 whole wheat bread, toasted

Directions for Cooking:

1. Press sauté and heat olive oil.
2. Sauté bell peppers, onions, and garlic for 5 minutes. Press cancel button.
3. Transfer veggies into a heatproof dish that fits inside Instant pot and crack eggs on top. Securely cover dish with foil.
4. Add a cup of water in Instant Pot, place trivet, and place casserole dish on trivet.
5. Close Instant Pot, press pressure cook button, choose high settings, and set time to 2 minutes.
6. Once done cooking, do a QPR.
7. Serve and enjoy with sliced limes, cilantro, avocados and toasted bread.

Nutrition information:

Calories per serving: 478; Carbohydrates: 49.1g; Protein: 19.8g; Fat: 24.4g; Sugar: 6.4g; Sodium: 418mg

---

56. Slow Cooked Oats the Irish Way
(Servings: 8, Cooking Time:3 hours)

Ingredients:

- Cooking spray
- 4 cups vanilla soy milk
- 1 ¾ cups steel-cut oats
- ½ cup dried cherries or raisins
- ½ cup plus 3 tablespoons pure maple syrup
- ½ teaspoon salt
- ¼ teaspoon ground allspice
- 4 cups water, plus more as needed
- ½ cup blueberries, for garnish
- 1/3 cup chopped pecans, for garnish

Directions for Cooking:

1. Grease Instant Pot insert on sides and bottom with cooking spray.
2. In pot, add and thoroughly mix oats, cherries, salt, allspice, ½ cup maple syrup, and water.
3. Close Instant Pot, press slow cook button, choose high settings, and set time to 3 hours.
4. Once done cooking, open pot and stir in remaining maple syrup, pecans, and blueberries.
5. Serve and enjoy.

Nutrition information:

Calories per serving: 231; Carbohydrates: 45.1g; Protein: 7.4g; Fat: 6.3g; Sugar: 26.8g; Sodium: 210mg

INSTANT POT BREAKFAST RECIPES

57. Meat Lovers No-Crust Quiche
(Servings: 4, Cooking Time: 40 minutes)

Ingredients:

- 6 large eggs, well beaten
- 1/2 cup milk
- 1/4 teaspoon salt
- 1/8 teaspoon ground black pepper
- 4 slices bacon, cooked and crumbled
- 1 cup cooked ground sausage
- 1/2 cup diced ham
- 2 large green onions, chopped
- 1 cup shredded cheese

Directions for Cooking:

1. Lightly grease a soufflé dish that fits inside your Instant Pot.
2. Add a cup of water and trivet in pot.
3. Whisk well pepper, salt, milk and eggs in a large mixing bowl.
4. In prepared soufflé dish, evenly spread bacon, sausage, ham, cheese, and green onions. Pour egg mixture over and cover securely with foil. Place on top of trivet in pot.
5. Close Instant Pot, press pressure cook button, choose high settings, and set time to 30 minutes.
6. Once done cooking, do a 10-minute natural release and then do a QPR.
7. Serve and enjoy.

Nutrition information:

Calories per serving: 460; Carbohydrates: 10.0g; Protein: 29.5g; Fat: 33.4g; Sugar: 5.4g; Sodium: 784mg

58. Quiche the Mexican Way
(Servings: 8, Cooking Time:4 hours)

Ingredients:

- 4 green onions, chopped
- Refrigerated pie crust
- 6 eggs, whisked
- 1 cup salsa
- 1/4 teaspoon freshly ground pepper
- 1/4 teaspoon chili powder
- 2 cups shredded cheddar cheese
- 1 cup cooked cannellini beans
- 1 refrigerated pie crust

Directions for Cooking:

1. Grease bottom and sides of Instant Pot and press pie crust halves in bottom and overlap seams by at least ¼-inch.
2. Close Instant Pot, press slow cook button, choose high settings, and set time to 1 hour and 30 minutes.
3. Once done cooking, open pot.
4. Spread beans and onions evenly on top of crust. Pour salsa on top.
5. In a bowl, whisk eggs and pour over salsa. Gently toss around.
6. Top with chili powder and cheese.
7. Close Instant Pot, press slow cook button, choose low settings, and time for 2 hours and 30 minutes.
8. Open pot, serve and enjoy.

Nutrition information:

Calories per serving: 436; Carbohydrates: 26.4g; Protein: 17.3g; Fat: 29.3g; Sugar: 3.4g; Sodium: 788mg

59. Zucchini-Choco Breakfast Cake

(Servings:12, Cooking Time:25 minutes)

Ingredients:

- 2 organic or pastured eggs
- 3/4 cup evaporated cane juice
- 1/2 cup coconut oil
- 2 teaspoons vanilla extract
- 1 tablespoon butter melted
- 3 tablespoons cocoa powder
- 1 cup sprouted einkorn flour learn how to sprout your grains
- 1/2 teaspoon baking soda
- 1/4 teaspoon sea salt
- 3/4 teaspoon ground cinnamon
- 1 cups zucchini or squash grated
- 1/3 cup chocolate chips
- 1 cup water

Directions for Cooking:

1. In blender, blend vanilla extract, coconut oil, sweetener, and eggs.
2. Add melted butter and cocoa. Blend well.
3. Add cinnamon, sea salt, baking soda, and flour. Blend well.
4. Remove blender from stand and fold in chocolate chips and grated zucchini.
5. Grease a baking dish that fits inside the Instant Pot and pour in batter. Cover top securely with foil.
6. Add a cup of water in Instant pot, place a trivet, and put dish with batter on top of trivet.
7. Close Instant Pot, press pressure cook button, choose low settings, and set time to 10 minutes.
8. Once done cooking, do a 15-minute natural release and then do a QPR.
9. Serve and enjoy.

Nutrition information:

Calories per serving: 163; Carbohydrates: 12.7g; Protein: 2.51g; Fat: 11.8g; Sugar: 3.2g; Sodium: 122mg

60. Creamy potato Hash Breakfast Casserole

(Servings: 8, Cooking Time: 3 hours)

Ingredients:

- 6 potatoes, shredded
- 1 can cream of chicken soup
- 1 stick butter, melted
- 1/2 cup chopped onion
- 2 cups grated Cheddar cheese

Directions for Cooking:

1. Lightly grease sides and bottom of Instant Pot.
2. Add potatoes in pot and season with pepper and salt.
3. Mix well melted butter, cream of chicken soup, and onions in a bowl. Pour over potatoes.
4. Sprinkle cheese on top.
5. Close Instant Pot, press slow cook button, choose low settings, and set time to 3 hours.
6. Once done cooking, open pot.
7. Serve and enjoy.

Nutrition information:

Calories per serving: 379; Carbohydrates: 32.0g; Protein: 11.0g; Fat: 23.0g; Sugar: 2.0g; Sodium: 451mg

61. Frittata the Spanish Way

(Servings: 4, Cooking Time:35 minutes)

Ingredients:

- 6 large Eggs
- 4 oz French Fries (defrosted) (or Hash Browns or Raw Potatoes)
- 1 tablespoon Butter melted
- 1/4 cup Spanish Onions, Scallions or Onions, diced
- 1/2 teaspoon Sea Salt, or to taste
- 1/4 teaspoon Freshly Ground Black Pepper or to taste
- 1 teaspoon Fox Point Seasoning or other seasoning
- 1 clove Fresh Garlic minced
- 1/4 cup Milk
- 1 teaspoon Tomato Paste
- 4 oz Cheese grated, any kind or a combination
- 1-1/2 cups Water

Directions for Cooking:

1. Soak French fries for 20-minutes in water.
2. Whisk salt, pepper, seasoning, and eggs in a mixing bowl until frothy.
3. Add garlic and onion. Mix well.
4. Grease thoroughly a casserole dish that fits in your Instant Pot.
5. Drain French Fries and pat dry with paper towel. Transfer to prepared dish. Pour melted butter and toss fries to coat.
6. Pour egg mixture over fries.
7. Add water to Instant Pot, put trivet on pot bottom, and place casserole dish uncovered on trivet.
8. Close Instant Pot, press pressure cook button, choose high settings, and set time to 20 minutes.
9. Once done cooking, do a 10-minutes natural release and then do a QPR.
10. Sprinkle cheese on top, cover and let it sit for another 5 minutes or until cheese has melted.
11. Serve and enjoy.

Nutrition information:

Calories per serving: 300; Carbohydrates: 10.4g; Protein: 18.0g; Fat: 20.5g; Sugar: 1.6g; Sodium: 750mg

62. Frittata the Provencal Way
(Servings: 6, Cooking Time: 55 minutes)

Ingredients:

- 1 tablespoon olive oil
- 1 medium Yukon Gold potato, peeled and sliced
- 1 small onion, thinly sliced
- 1/2 teaspoon smoked paprika
- 1 cup water
- 12 large eggs
- 1 teaspoon minced fresh thyme or 1/4 teaspoon dried thyme
- 1 teaspoon hot pepper sauce
- 1/2 teaspoon salt
- 1/4 teaspoon pepper
- 1 log (4 ounces) crumbled fresh goat cheese, divided
- 1/2 cup chopped sun-dried tomatoes (not packed in oil)

Directions for Cooking:

1. Lightly grease bottom and sides of soufflé dish and set aside.

2. Press sauté button and heat oil. Once hot, sauté onion and potato for 7 minutes or until lightly browned. Stir in paprika and sauté for a minute. Transfer to prepared soufflé dish.

3. Press cancel button, add a cup of water in pot, and place trivet on bottom.

4. Whisk well eggs, thyme, pepper sauce, salt, and pepper. Pour over potatoes.

5. Evenly top with tomatoes and sprinkle cheese. Cover dish with foil and place on trivet inside pot.

6. Close Instant Pot, press manual button, choose high settings, and set time to 35 minutes.

7. Once done cooking, do a 10-minute natural release and then do a QPR.

8. Serve and enjoy.

Nutrition information:
Calories per serving: 245; Carbohydrates: 12.0g; Protein: 15.0g; Fat: 14.0g; Sugar: 4.0g; Sodium: 12mg

63. Nutella-Raspberry Breakfast Porridge
(Servings: 6, Cooking Time: 17 minutes)

Ingredients:

- 1 sliver butter (or 1/2 tsp of your favorite oil if you're vegan)
- 1 cup quinoa
- 1 can coconut milk
- 1/3 cup milk of your choice
- 1 tbsp cocoa powder the darkest you can find
- 1/2 tsp hazelnut extract
- 1-2 tbsp maple syrup depending on your preferred level of sweetness
- 1 ½ cups raspberry

Directions for Cooking:

1. Press sauté button and melt butter. Once melted add quinoa and sauté until toasted, around 10 minutes.

2. Add the remaining ingredients except for the raspberry and mix well.
3. Press cancel button.
4. Close Instant Pot, press manual button, choose high settings, and set time to 2 minutes.
5. Once done cooking, do a 5-minute natural release and then do a QPR.
6. Serve and enjoy with ¼ cup of raspberry per serving.

Nutrition information:

Calories per serving: 249; Carbohydrates: 23.0g; Protein: 5.0g; Fat: 15.0g; Sugar: 2.0g; Sodium: 16mg

64. Crisped Apple and Sweet Potato Brekky
(Servings: 4, Cooking Time: 35 minutes)

Ingredients:

- 3 cups peeled cubed fresh sweet potatoes
- 2 cups chopped apples not peeled
- 1/4 cup chopped dates
- 1/4 cup maple syrup
- 1 tbsp cinnamon
- 1/4 tsp pumpkin pie spice
- 1/4 cup coconut flour
- 1/4 tsp sea salt
- 2 tbsp vegan butter, melted

Directions for Cooking:

1. Add a cup of water in Instant Pot and place trivet on bottom.
2. On a mixing cup, mix well maple syrup, flour, cinnamon, pumpkin pie spice, and melted butter.

3. Lightly grease a heatproof dish that fits in Instant pot and place cubed sweet potatoes, chopped apples, and chopped dates. Pour in maple syrup mixture and toss well to coat and mix. Cover dish with foil and place on trivet in pot.
4. Close Instant Pot, press pressure cook button, choose high settings, and set time to 10 minutes.
5. Once done cooking, do a QPR.
6. Remove foil cover and mix the mixture well.
7. Close Instant Pot, press cancel, press pressure cook button, choose high settings, and set time to 5 minutes.
8. Allow for a complete natural release.
9. Serve and enjoy.

Nutrition information:

Calories per serving: 351; Carbohydrates: 73.4g; Protein: 4.0g; Fat: 6.3g; Sugar: 38.0g; Sodium: 857mg

65. Broccoli-Bacon Frittata

(Servings: 4, Cooking Time: 45 minutes)

Ingredients:

- 2 tbsp grass-fed butter or ghee
- 1 small yellow onion, diced
- 4 fresh garlic cloves, grated or finely minced
- 1 cup chopped broccoli florets, cut into smaller bite-size pieces
- 4 pastured eggs
- 1/4 cup milk of choice (coconut milk)
- 1 tsp sea salt
- Zest of 1 lemon
- 1 tbsp chopped fresh Italian parsley
- 1 tsp chopped fresh thyme
- 1 1/2 cups shredded cheddar cheese
- 6-8 slices of pre-cooked crispy organic or pastured turkey bacon, crumbled
- 1 cup water

Directions for Cooking:

1. Press sauté and heat oil. Once hot, sauté garlic and onions until caramelized, around 7 minutes. Add broccoli and sauté for 4 minutes. Press cancel button.
2. Lightly grease a heatproof dish that fits in your Instant pot.
3. Whisk milk and eggs in a large mixing bowl.
4. Whisk in thyme, parsley, lemon zest, and salt.
5. Stir in broccoli mixture, bacon, and cheddar cheese. Pour into prepared dish. Cover securely with foil. Place on trivet in pot.
6. Close Instant Pot, press manual button, choose high settings, and set time to 23 minutes.
7. Once done cooking, do a 10-minute natural release and then do a QPR.
8. Serve and enjoy with a sprinkle of crumbled turkey bacon.

Nutrition information:

Calories per serving: 372; Carbohydrates: 6.1g; Protein: 21.2g; Fat: 29.4g; Sugar: 2.8g; Sodium: 1217mg

Instant Pot Meat Recipes

66. Instant Spare Ribs and Rice
(Servings: 4, Cooking time: 35 minutes)

Ingredients:

- 1-pound pork spare ribs, cut into pieces
- 1 ½ tablespoon black bean sauce
- 1 tablespoon regular soy sauce
- 1 tablespoon Shaoxing wine
- 1 tablespoon grated ginger
- 3 cloves of garlic, minced
- 1 teaspoon sugar
- 1 teaspoon sesame oil
- 1 teaspoon fish sauce
- 1 tablespoon oil
- 1 ½ cups Jasmine rice, rinsed
- 1 ½ cup cold water
- Chopped green onions for garnish

Directions for Cooking:

1. Marinate the spare ribs by putting the first nine ingredients in a mixing bowl. Allow to marinate for at least 2 hours in the fridge.
2. Press the Sauté button on the Instant Pot and heat the oil. Place the spare ribs and try to sauté for at least 5 minutes. Put in the remaining juices from the marinade.
3. Add Jasmine rice on top and pour cold water.
4. Close Instant Pot, press the Manual button, choose high settings, and set time to 35 minutes.
5. Once done cooking, do a QPR.
6. Garnish with chopped green onions.
7. Serve and enjoy.

Nutrition information:
Calories per serving: 354; Carbohydrates: 38g; Protein: 12g; Fat: 15g; Sugar: 10.2g; Sodium: 291mg

---

67. Cuban Pulled Pork Sandwiches
(Servings: 10, Cooking time: 25 minutes)

Ingredients:

- 5 pounds pork shoulder butt roast
- 2 teaspoons salt
- 2 teaspoons pepper
- 1 tablespoon olive oil
- 1 cup orange juice
- ½ cup lime juice
- 12 cloves of garlic, minced
- 2 tablespoons spiced rum
- 2 tablespoons ground coriander
- 2 teaspoons white pepper
- 1 teaspoon cayenne pepper
- 2 loaf of French bread, cut into 20 slices
- Yellow mustard
- 1 ½ pounds deli ham, cut into 10 slices
- 1 ½ pounds Swiss cheese, cut into 10 slices

Directions for Cooking:

1. Season the pork butt roast with salt and pepper.
2. Press the Sauté button on the Instant Pot and heat the oil. Sear the seasoned pork butt on all sides for at least 5 minutes. Add the orange juice, lime juice, garlic, spiced rum, coriander, white pepper, and cayenne pepper. Add more salt if desired.
3. Close Instant Pot, press Manual button, choose high settings, and set time to 20 minutes. Once done cooking, do a QPR. Take the meat out and shred using two forks.
4. Assemble the sandwiches by slathering mustard on slices of French bread. Put pulled pork, deli ham, Swiss cheese, and a

- 10 dill pickle slices

Nutrition information:
Calories per serving: 573; Carbohydrates: 35g;
Protein: 45g; Fat: 28g; Sugar: 5g; Sodium: 1240mg

pickle on to before adding another slice of French bread.

5. Serve and enjoy.

---

68. Sweet and Sour Pork Chops
(Servings: 4, Cooking time: 35 minutes)

Ingredients:

- 1 tablespoon olive oil
- 2 pounds pork chops, pounded
- 1 onion, chopped
- 3 cloves of garlic minced
- 2/3 cup pineapple chunks
- 1 green bell pepper, chopped
- ¾ cup water
- ¼ cup ketchup
- ¼ cup white vinegar
- 1 ½ teaspoons white sugar
- 1 tablespoon soy sauce
- 1 tablespoon tomato paste
- 1 teaspoon Worcestershire sauce
- 2 tablespoons cornstarch + 3 tablespoons water

Directions for Cooking:

1. Press the Sauté button in the Instant Pot and heat the oil. Sear the pork chops on both sides for 5 minutes and Add the onions and garlic until fragrant.
2. Stir in the rest of the ingredients except for the cornstarch and water.
3. Close Instant Pot, press the Manual button, choose high settings, and set time to 30 minutes.
4. Once done cooking, do a QPR.
5. Press the Sauté button and stir in the cornstarch. Allow to simmer for a minute to thicken the sauce.
6. Serve and enjoy.

Nutrition information:
Calories per serving:493; Carbohydrates:35 g;
Protein: 46g; Fat: 9g; Sugar: 24g; Sodium: 931mg

INSTANT POT MEAT RECIPES

69. Instant Pot Pork Carnitas
(Servings: 12, Cooking time: 90 minutes)

Ingredients:

- 6 pounds pork butt roast
- 1 ½ tablespoons salt
- 1 tablespoon dried oregano
- 2 teaspoons ground cumin
- 1 teaspoon black pepper
- ½ teaspoon chili powder
- ½ teaspoon ground paprika
- 2 tablespoons olive oil
- 1 cup orange juice
- ¼ cup water
- 1 onion, chopped
- 4 cloves of garlic, minced

Directions for Cooking:

1. Season the pork butt roast with salt, oregano, cumin, black pepper, chili powder, and paprika. Allow to marinate in the fridge for at least 3 hours.

2. Press the Sauté button on the Instant Pot and heat the oil. Place the pork butt roast and allow to sear on all sides for 5 minutes.
3. Add the rest of the ingredients.
4. Close Instant Pot, press Manual button, choose high settings, and set time to 90 minutes.
5. Once done cooking, do a QPR.
6. Remove meat from the pressure cooker and shred the meat.
7. Serve with sauce and enjoy.

Nutrition information:

Calories per serving:190; Carbohydrates: 2.4g; Protein: 11.8g; Fat: 14.5g; Sugar: 0.5g; Sodium: 471mg

70. Pork Tenderloin in Garlic Herb Rub
(Servings: 4, Cooking time: 20 minutes)

Ingredients:

- 1 cup chicken broth
- 1 tablespoon balsamic vinegar
- 2 pounds pork tenderloin
- 1 teaspoon garlic powder
- 1 teaspoon dried parsley
- ½ teaspoon salt
- ¼ teaspoon onion powder
- ¼ teaspoon black pepper
- 3 tablespoons honey
- 1 tablespoon ketchup
- 1 tablespoon cornstarch + 1 tablespoon water

Directions for Cooking:

1. Pour chicken broth and balsamic vinegar in the Instant Pot. Place a trivet on top.

3. Arrange in the trivet. Close Instant Pot, press Steam button, choose high settings, and set time to 20 minutes.
4. Once done cooking, do a QPR.
5. Remove the cooked pork and set aside. Remove the trivet as well.
6. Press the Sauté button and to the chicken broth, stir in honey, ketchup and cornstarch slurry.
7. Allow to simmer until the sauce thickens.
8. Pour over the steamed pork chops.
9. Serve and enjoy.

Nutrition information:

Calories per serving: 478; Carbohydrates: 16.1g; Protein: 72.6g; Fat: 12.3g; Sugar: 3.2g; Sodium: 708mg

2. Season the pork tenderloin with garlic powder, dried parsley, salt, onion powder, and black pepper.

---

71. Instant Pot Gumbo
(Servings: 6, Cooking time: 15 minutes)

Ingredients:

- 1 tablespoon olive oil
- 1 onion, diced
- 6 cloves of garlic, minced
- 2 ribs celery, diced
- 1 ¾ pounds bone-in chicken thighs
- ½ pound Andouille sausage, cut into ¼" slices
- 1-pound fresh okra, chopped into ½" thick
- 1 bell pepper, diced
- 4 cups chicken stock
- 1 tablespoon Worcestershire sauce
- 1 tablespoon fish sauce
- 3 bay leaves
- 1 teaspoon cayenne pepper
- 1 teaspoon smoked paprika
- A pinch of thyme
- Salt to taste

Directions for Cooking:

1. Press the Sauté button on the Instant Pot and heat the oil. Sauté the onion and garlic until fragrant. Add the celery and cook for another minute.
2. Stir in the chicken and sausages and continue cooking for three more minutes.
3. Pour in the rest of the ingredients. Close Instant Pot, press the Manual button, choose high settings, and set time to 10 minutes.
4. Once done cooking, do a QPR.
5. Serve and enjoy.

Nutrition information:
Calories per serving: 662; Carbohydrates: 38.3g; Protein: 37.9g; Fat: 41.2g; Sugar: 5g; Sodium: 1911mg

72. Hearty Pork Black Bean Nachos
(Servings: 10, Cooking time: 40 minutes)

Ingredients:

- 4-oz beef jerky, chopped
- 3 pounds pork spare ribs, cut into 2-rib sections
- 4 cans black beans, rinsed and drained
- 1 cup chopped onion
- 4 teaspoons minced garlic
- 1 teaspoon crushed red pepper flakes
- 4 cups beef broth
- Salt and pepper to taste
- Tortilla chips
- 6 strips of bacon, cooked and crumbled

Directions for Cooking:

1. Dump the beef jerky ribs, black bins, onions, garlic, red pepper flakes, and beef broth. Season with salt and pepper to taste.
2. Close Instant Pot, press the Manual button, choose high settings, and set time to 20 minutes.
3. Once done cooking, do a QPR.
4. Remove and discard the bones.
5. Serve with tortilla chips and crumbled bacon.
6. Enjoy.

Nutrition information:

Calories per serving:469; Carbohydrates: 27g; Protein:33 g; Fat: 24g; Sugar: 3g; Sodium: 1055mg

---

73. Instant Korean Ribs
(Servings: 4, Cooking time: 35 minutes)

Ingredients:

- 2 pounds baby back ribs
- 1 Asian pear, peeled and grated
- 1 bulb garlic, minced
- 1 onion, minced
- ½ teaspoon grated garlic
- 1 teaspoon ground black pepper
- ½ cup soy sauce
- 2 tablespoons honey
- 2 tablespoons brown sugar
- 2 tablespoons rice vinegar
- 2 tablespoons sesame oil

Directions for Cooking:

1. Place all ingredients in the Instant Pot and mix all ingredients.
2. Close Instant Pot, press the Manual button, choose high settings, and set time to 35 minutes.
3. Once done cooking, do a QPR.
4. Serve and enjoy.

Nutrition information:

Calories per serving: 722; Carbohydrates: 25.6g; Protein: 47.7g; Fat: 48.3g; Sugar: 20g; Sodium: 619mg

74. Barbecue Pulled Pork

(Servings: 8, Cooking time: 1 hour and 40 minutes)

Ingredients:

- 2 teaspoons hot paprika
- 3 tablespoons light brown sugar
- 1 teaspoon mustard powder
- ½ teaspoon ground cumin
- Salt and pepper to taste
- 4 pounds pork shoulder
- 2 teaspoons vegetable oil
- ½ cup apple cider vinegar
- 3 tablespoons tomato paste

Directions for Cooking:

1. Place all ingredients in the Instant Pot and mix all ingredients.
2. Close Instant Pot, press the Manual button, choose high settings, and set time to 1 hour and 40 minutes.
3. Once done cooking, do a QPR.
4. Shred the meat using fork and serve.

Nutrition information:

Calories per serving: 637; Carbohydrates: 5g; Protein: 57.3g; Fat: 41.4g; Sugar: 3.7g; Sodium: 144mg

---

75. Spare Ribs and Black Bean Sauce

(Servings: 4, Cooking time: 35 minutes)

Ingredients:

- 1-pound pork spare ribs, cut into large cubes
- 1 tablespoon black bean sauce
- 1 tablespoon soy sauce
- 1 tablespoon Shaoxing wine
- 1 tablespoon grated ginger
- 3 cloves of garlic, minced
- 1 teaspoon sesame oil
- 1 teaspoon sugar
- 1 tablespoon oil
- 1 tablespoon cornstarch + 2 tablespoon water
- Chopped green onions for garnish

Directions for Cooking:

1. In a mixing bowl, combine the pork spare ribs, black bean sauce, soy sauce, Shaoxing wine, grated ginger, garlic, sesame oil, and sugar. Allow to marinate in the fridge for at least 2 hours.
2. Press the Sauté button on the Instant Pot. Heat the oil and sear the pork on all sides for 3 minutes. Put in the sauce and add water if needed.
3. Close Instant Pot, press the Manual button, choose high settings, and set time to 35 minutes.
4. Once done cooking, do a QPR.
5. Press the Sauté button again and stir in cornstarch slurry. Allow to simmer until the sauce thickens.
6. Garnish with green onions.
7. Serve and enjoy.

Nutrition information:

Calories per serving: 242; Carbohydrates: 9.2g; Protein: 25.9g; Fat: 10.9g; Sugar: 5.6g; Sodium: 538mg

76. Instant Pot Mesquite Ribs

(Servings: 8, Cooking time: 40 minutes)

Ingredients

- 1 cup water
- 2 tablespoons cider vinegar
- 1 tablespoon soy sauce
- 4 pounds baby back ribs
- 2 tablespoons mesquite seasoning
- ¾ cup barbecue sauce, divided

Directions for Cooking:

1. Mix all ingredients in the Instant Pot. Make sure that you only put half of the barbecue sauce. Reserve it for later.

2. Close Instant Pot, press the Manual button, choose high settings, and set time to 35 minutes.
3. Once done cooking, do a QPR.
4. Press the Sauté button and pour in the remaining amount of barbecue sauce.
5. Allow to simmer for 5 minutes.
6. Serve and enjoy.

Nutrition information:

Calories per serving: 329; Carbohydrates: 10g; Protein: 23g; Fat: 21g; Sugar: 8g; Sodium: 678mg

---

77. Ginger Pork Shogayaki

（Servings: 2 , Cooking time: 55 minutes）

Ingredients

- 1-pound pork shoulder
- 2 tablespoons ginger root, grated
- 1 clove of garlic, minced
- 1 onion, chopped
- 1 tablespoon soy sauce
- ½ tablespoon white miso paste
- 2 tablespoons Japanese cooking sake
- 2 tablespoons mirin
- ¼ cup water
- 1 tablespoon peanut oil
- ½ head romaine lettuce

Directions for Cooking:

1. Place the pork shoulder, ginger root, garlic, onion soy sauce, miso paste, sake, mirin, and water in the Instant Pot. Give a good stir.
2. Close Instant Pot, press the Manual button, choose high settings, and set time to 55 minutes.
3. Once done cooking, do a QPR.
4. Before serving drizzle with peanut oil.
5. Serve with lettuce and enjoy.

Nutrition information:

Calories per serving: 772; Carbohydrates: 16.4g; Protein: 60.5g; Fat: 48.9g; Sugar: 3.7g; Sodium: 433mg

78. Apple Cider Pork Chops

(Servings: 6, Cooking time: 40 minutes)

Ingredients

- 2 tablespoons canola oil
- 1 ½ pounds pork chops
- 6 medium russet potatoes, peeled and quartered
- 1 ½ cups chicken broth
- ¼ cup whole milk
- Salt and pepper to taste
- 2 cups carrots, peeled and cut into 2-inch pieces
- 1 ½ cups apple cider
- ¼ cup packed brown sugar
- 1 tablespoon mustard
- 2 tablespoons cornstarch + 3 tablespoons water

Directions for Cooking:

1. Press the Sauté button and heat the canola oil. Sear the pork chops for 3 minutes until lightly brown on all sides. Set aside.
2. Place the potatoes, chicken broth, and milk in the Instant Pot. Season with salt and pepper to taste.
3. Place a trivet on top. Place the carrots on the trivet. Arrange the pork chop on top of the carrots.
4. Close Instant Pot, press the Manual button, choose high settings, and set time to 35 minutes.
5. Once done cooking, do a QPR.
6. Take the carrots and pork out. Remove the trivet.
7. Press the Sauté button and Add the apple cider vinegar, sugar, mustard, and cornstarch slurry. Allow to simmer until the sauce thickens.
8. Pour the sauce over the steamed pork and carrots.
9. Serve and enjoy.

Nutrition information:

Calories per serving: 757; Carbohydrates: 88.2g; Protein: 50.8g; Fat: 22.2g; Sugar: 20.7g; Sodium: 492mg

---

79. Instant Pot Hoisin Meatballs

(Servings: 6, Cooking time: 10 minutes)

Ingredients:

- 1 cup beef broth
- 3 tablespoons hoisin sauce
- 2 tablespoons soy sauce
- 1 large egg, beaten
- 4 green onions, chopped
- ¼ cup chopped onion
- ¼ cup fresh cilantro, minced
- 2 cloves of garlic, minced
- Salt and pepper to taste
- 1-pound ground beef
- 1-pound ground pork
- ¼ cup sesame seeds

Directions for Cooking:

1. In a mixing bowl, combine all ingredients and form 12 balls using your hands.
2. Place inside the fridge to set.
3. Carefully place the meatballs inside the Instant Pot.
4. Close Instant Pot, press the Manual button, choose high settings, and set time to 10 minutes.
5. Once done cooking, do a QPR.
6. Serve and enjoy.

Nutrition information:

Calories per serving:78; Carbohydrates: 1g; Protein: 6g; Fat: 5g; Sugar: 1; Sodium: 156mg

80. Instant Pot Pork Roast
(Servings: 8, Cooking time: 35 minutes)

Ingredients:

- 2 pounds pork loin roast
- Salt and pepper to taste
- 2 tablespoons butter
- 1 onion, diced
- 4 cloves of garlic, minced
- 2 carrots, peeled and chopped
- 2 stalks of celery, chopped
- ½ cup broth
- 2 tablespoons Worcestershire sauce
- 1 tablespoon brown sugar
- 1 teaspoon yellow mustard
- 2 teaspoons herbs of choice
- 1 tablespoon cornstarch + ¼ cup water

Directions for Cooking:

1. Season the pork loin roast with salt and pepper to taste.

2. Press the Sauté button on the Instant Pot and add the butter. Sear the pork loin roast for 3 minutes on all sides. Stir in the onion and garlic until fragrant.

3. Add the carrots and celery. Pour in the broth and season with Worcestershire sauce, brown sugar, mustard, and herbs.

4. Close Instant Pot, press the Manual button, choose high settings, and set time to 29 minutes.

5. Once done cooking, do a QPR.

6. Press the Sauté button and stir in the cornstarch slurry. Allow to simmer until the sauce thickens.

7. Serve and enjoy.

Nutrition information:
Calories per serving: 268; Carbohydrates: 5.2g; Protein: 30.8g; Fat: 13.1g; Sugar: 2.5g; Sodium: 188mg

81. Instant Pot Pork Chops and Onions
(Servings: 4 , Cooking time: 25 minutes)

Ingredients:

- 4 boneless pork chops, cut into 1 ½ inches thick
- 1 tablespoon soy sauce
- 1 tablespoon Shaoxing wine
- ¼ teaspoon salt
- ½ teaspoon sugar
- ¼ teaspoon white pepper
- ¼ teaspoon sesame oil
- 1 tablespoon olive oil
- 1 onion, sliced
- 1 tablespoon balsamic vinegar
- 1 teaspoon sugar
- ¾ cup chicken stock
- Salt to taste
- 1 ½ tablespoons cornstarch + 2 tablespoons water

2. Press the Sauté button on the Instant Pot and heat the oil.

3. Stir in the onion and sauté until fragrant. Add the marinated pork and cook for 3 minutes.

4. Pour in the balsamic vinegar, sugar, and chicken stock. Season with salt to taste.

5. Close Instant Pot, press the Manual button, choose high settings, and set time to 19 minutes.

6. Once done cooking, do a QPR.

7. Once the lid is open, press the Sauté button and stir in the cornstarch slurry. Allow to simmer until the sauce thickens.

8. Serve and enjoy.

Directions for Cooking:

1. In a large bowl, place the pork chops and Add the soy sauce, Shaoxing wine, salt, sugar, white pepper, and sesame oil. Allow to marinate in the fridge for at least 2 hours.

Nutrition information:

Calories per serving: 294; Carbohydrates:9 g; Protein:39 g; Fat: 13g; Sugar: 4g; Sodium: 769mg

---

82. Beer-Braised Pulled Ham
(Servings: 16, Cooking time: 25 minutes)

Ingredients:

- 2 bottles of beer
- ¾ cup Dijon mustard
- ½ teaspoon ground pepper
- 1 fully cooked ham, bone-in
- 4 fresh rosemary sprigs
- 16 pretzel hamburger buns, split
- Dill pickle slices

Directions for Cooking:

1. Put the beer, mustard, pepper, ham, and rosemary sprigs in the Instant Pot.
2. Close Instant Pot, press the Manual button, choose high settings, and set time to 25 minutes.
3. Once done cooking, do a QPR.
4. Slice the ham and put in between hamburger buns. Garnish with pickle slices.
5. Serve and enjoy.

Nutrition information:

Calories per serving: 378; Carbohydrates: 40g; Protein: 25g; Fat: 9g; Sugar: 4g; Sodium: 1246mg

---

83. Pork Chops with HK Mushroom Gravy
(Servings: 4, Cooking time: 35 minutes)

Ingredients:

- 4 bone-in pork loin chops
- 1 onion, chopped
- 3 cloves of garlic, minced
- 10 large cremini mushrooms, sliced
- A dash of sherry wine
- 1 cup chicken stock
- 1 tablespoon Worcestershire sauce
- 1 tablespoon soy sauce
- 2 tablespoons peanut oil
- ¼ cup heavy cream
- Salt and pepper to taste

Directions for Cooking:

1. Press the Sauté button on the Instant Pot. Place the pork chops and sear on all sides for 5 minutes each. Stir in the onion and garlic until fragrant.
2. Add the mushrooms, sherry wine, chicken stock, Worcestershire sauce, soy sauce, peanut oil and cream. Season with salt and pepper to taste.
3. Close Instant Pot, press the Manual button, choose high settings, and set time to 20 minutes.

- 2 tablespoons cornstarch + 2 tablespoons water

Nutrition information:

Calories per serving:482; Carbohydrates: 10.4g; Protein: 44.6g; Fat: 28.9g; Sugar:5.3g; Sodium: 282mg

4. Once done cooking, do a QPR.
5. Once the lid is open, press the Sauté button and stir in cornstarch slurry. Allow to simmer until the sauce thickens.
6. Serve and enjoy.

84. Pork Chops in Apple Sauce
(Servings: 4, Cooking time: 16 minutes)

Ingredients:

- 4 pork loin chops, scored on the surface
- 1 tablespoon olive oil
- 1 onion, sliced
- 3 cloves of garlic, minced
- 2 apples, cored and sliced thinly
- 2 pieces whole cloves
- 1 teaspoon cinnamon powder
- 1 tablespoon honey
- ½ cup chicken stock
- 2 tablespoons soy sauce
- 1 tablespoon butter
- Salt and pepper to taste
- 1 tablespoon cornstarch + 2 tablespoon water

Nutrition information:

Calories per serving: 879; Carbohydrates: 22.4g; Protein: 73.2g; Fat: 54.2g; Sugar: 16.8g; Sodium: 386mg

Directions for Cooking:

1. Press the Sauté button on the Instant Pot and brown the pork chops on each side for 3 minutes each.
2. Add the olive oil and sauté the onion and garlic until fragrant.
3. Stir in the apples, cloves, cinnamon powder, honey, chicken stock, soy sauce and butter. Season with salt and pepper to taste.
4. Close Instant Pot, press the Manual button, choose high settings, and set time to 10 minutes.
5. Once done cooking, do a QPR.
6. Once the lid is open, press the Sauté button and Add the cornstarch slurry. Allow to simmer until the sauce thickens.
7. Serve and enjoy.

85. Chinese Pork Bone Soup

（Servings: 4, Cooking time:　1 hour and 20 minutes ）

Ingredients:

- 2 ½ pounds pork bones
- 2 large carrots, roughly chopped
- 2 corn on the cob, chopped
- 1 thumb-size ginger, sliced
- 2 dried dates
- 4 cups water
- Salt to taste

Directions for Cooking:

1. Place all ingredients in the Instant Pot.
2. Close Instant Pot, press the Manual button, choose high settings, and set time to 1 hour and 20 minutes.
3. Once done cooking, do a QPR.
4. Serve and enjoy.

Nutrition information:

Calories per serving:62; Carbohydrates: 14g;
Protein:1 g; Fat: 7g; Sugar:6g; Sodium: 28mg

---

86. Shrimp Pork Dumplings (Humai)

(Servings: 4, Cooking time: 10 minutes)

Ingredients:

- ½ pound tiger prawns or shrimps, finely chopped
- 2 tablespoons cornstarch
- ¼ teaspoon salt
- ¼ teaspoon oil
- ½ pound ground pork
- 2 tablespoons chicken stock
- 1 tablespoon Shaoxing wine
- 2 teaspoons soy sauce
- 1 teaspoon fish sauce
- 1 teaspoon sesame oil
- ½ teaspoon white pepper
- ½ teaspoon sugar
- 20 wonton wrappers

Directions for Cooking:

1. Place a trivet in the Instant Pot and add a cup of water.
2. In a mixing bowl, combine all ingredients except for the wonton wrappers.
3. Use your hands to mix everything.
4. Place a tablespoon of the mixture on the center of the wonton wrappers. Fold the wanton wrappers and pinch the edges to close.
5. Place gently on the trivet.
6. Close Instant Pot, press the Steam button, choose high settings, and set time to 10 minutes.
7. Once done cooking, do a QPR.
8. Serve and enjoy.

Nutrition information:

Calories per serving:793; Carbohydrates: 97.6g;
Protein: 45.3g; Fat: 22.3g; Sugar: 1g; Sodium: 1302mg

87. Sweet Balsamic Pork
(Servings: 3, Cooking time: 45 minutes)

Ingredients

- 1 ½ pound pork tenderloin cut into four pieces
- 3 cloves of garlic, minced
- ¼ cup brown sugar
- ¼ cup balsamic vinegar
- 1 tablespoon olive oil
- ¼ cup water
- 1 tablespoon soy sauce
- 1 tablespoon chopped rosemary
- 1 tablespoon cornstarch + 2 tablespoons water

Directions for Cooking:

1. In a mixing bowl, combine the pork tenderloin, garlic, brown sugar, and balsamic vinegar. Allow to marinate in the fridge for at least 2 hours.

2. Press the Sauté button on the Instant Pot. Heat the oil and sauté the marinate pork mixture for 5 minutes. Do not include the marinade.
3. Add the marinade, water, soy sauce, and rosemary.
4. Close Instant Pot, press Manual button, choose high settings, and set time to 30 minutes.
5. Once done cooking, do a QPR.
6. Once the lid is open, press the Sauté button and pour in the cornstarch slurry. Allow to simmer until the sauce thickens.
7. Serve and enjoy.

Nutrition information:
Calories per serving: 498; Carbohydrates: 24.1g; Protein: 61.7g; Fat: 15.3g; Sugar: 22.2g; Sodium: 1294mg

---

88. Instant Pot Korean Beef
(Servings: 10, Cooking time: 25 minutes)

Ingredients:

- ½ cup beef broth
- 1/3 cup soy sauce
- 1/3 cup brown sugar
- 4 cloves of garlic, minced
- 1 tablespoon sesame oil
- 1 tablespoon rice wine
- 1 tablespoon grated ginger
- 1 teaspoon Sriracha sauce
- ½ teaspoon onion powder
- ½ teaspoon white pepper
- 3 ½ pounds boneless beef chuck roast, cut into chunks
- 2 tablespoons cornstarch + 3 tablespoons water
- 1 teaspoon sesame seeds
- 2 green onion, chopped

Nutrition information:

Directions for Cooking:

1. Place the soy sauce, brown sugar, garlic, sesame oil, rice wine, ginger, Sriracha sauce, onion powder, white pepper, and beef in the Instant Pot. Stir to combine.
2. Close Instant Pot, press the Manual button, choose high settings, and set time to 20 minutes.
3. Once done cooking, do a QPR.
4. Open the lid and press the Sauté button. Pour in the cornstarch slurry and allow to simmer for 5 minutes until the sauce thickens.
5. Garnish with sesame seeds and green onions.
6. Serve and enjoy.

Calories per serving: 370; Carbohydrates: 12.8g; Protein: 43.4g; Fat: 16.6g; Sugar: 3.2g; Sodium: 278mg

---

89. Instant Pot Mongolian Beef
(Servings: 3, Cooking time: 20 minutes)

Ingredients:

- 1 ½ pounds flank steak, sliced thinly
- 1 tablespoon cornstarch
- 1 tablespoon olive oil
- 10 cloves of garlic, minced
- 1 tablespoon grated ginger
- ½ cup brown sugar
- ½ cup soy sauce
- 1 cup water
- 1 tablespoon rice wine
- 1 teaspoon red pepper flakes
- 2 tablespoons cornstarch + 3 tablespoons water

Nutrition information:

Calories per serving: 654; Carbohydrates: 55.3g; Protein: 52.9g; Fat: 24.2g; Sugar: 44g; Sodium: 778mg

Directions for Cooking:

1. In a bowl, dust the flank steak with cornstarch. Set aside.Press the Sauté button on the Instant Pot and heat the oil.
2. Stir-fry the beef for 3 minutes then add garlic and ginger until fragrant.
3. Stir in the sugar, soy sauce, water rice wine, and red pepper flakes. Season with salt and pepper to taste.
4. Close Instant Pot, press the Manual button, choose high settings, and set time to 16 minutes.
5. Once done cooking, do a QPR.
6. Open the lid and press the Sauté button. Pour in the cornstarch slurry and allow to simmer until the sauce thickens.
7. Serve and enjoy.

INSTANT POT MEAT RECIPES

90. Instant Pot Barbacoa Beef

(Servings: 7, Cooking time: 1 hour and 25 minutes)

Ingredients:

- 1 tablespoon olive oil
- 4 cloves of garlic, minced
- 1 small onion, chopped
- ¼ teaspoon ground cloves
- 1 tablespoon ground cumin
- 1 tablespoon Mexican oregano
- 3 pounds beef chuck roast, cut into chunks
- 2 teaspoons salt
- 1 teaspoon black pepper
- 2/3 cup water
- 2 chipotles in adobo sauce
- 1 can green chilies
- ¼ cup fresh lime juice
- 2 tablespoons apple cider vinegar
- 3 bay leaves

Directions for Cooking:

1. Press the Sauté button on the Instant Pot and heat the oil. Sauté the garlic, onion, cloves, cumin, and oregano until fragrant. Stir in the beef and sauté for 3 minutes. Season with salt and pepper to taste.
2. Close Instant Pot, press the Manual button, choose high settings, and set time to 1 hour and 25 minutes.
3. Once done cooking, do a QPR.
4. Serve and enjoy.

Nutrition information:

Calories per serving: 388; Carbohydrates: 3.4g; Protein: 52.3g; Fat: 18.6g; Sugar: 1.1g; Sodium: 823mg

---

91. Instant Pot Beef and Broccoli

(Servings: 6, Cooking time: 15 minutes)

Ingredients:

- 1 ½ pounds boneless beef chuck roast, trimmed and cut into strops
- Salt and pepper to taste
- 2 teaspoons olive oil
- 1 onion, chopped
- 4 cloves of garlic, minced
- ¾ cup beef broth
- ½ cup soy sauce
- 1/3 cup brown sugar
- 2 tablespoons sesame oil
- 1/8 teaspoon red pepper flakes
- 1-pound broccoli flowers
- 3 tablespoons cornstarch + 3 tablespoons water
- Toasted sesame seeds for garnish

Directions for Cooking:

1. Season the beef with salt and pepper to taste. Set aside.
2. Press the Sauté button on the Instant Pot and heat the oil. Sauté the onion and garlic until fragrant. Stir in the beef and allow to brown for 3 minutes while stirring constantly.
3. Add the beef broth, soy sauce, brown sugar, sesame oil and red pepper flakes.
4. Close Instant Pot, press the Manual button, choose high settings, and set time to 10 minutes.
5. Once done cooking, do a QPR.
6. Open the lid and press the Sauté button, stir in the broccoli flowers and cornstarch slurry. Allow to simmer until the vegetables are half-cooked and the sauce thickens.
7. Garnish with toasted sesame seeds.
8. Serve and enjoy.

Nutrition information:

Calories per serving: 415; Carbohydrates: 26.9g; Protein: 34.7g; Fat: 19.8g; Sugar: 17g; Sodium: 477mg

92. Instant Pot Roast Potatoes
(Servings: 6, Cooking time: 1 hour and 20 minutes)

Ingredients:

- 3 pounds beef chuck roast
- 1 tablespoon oil
- 1 teaspoon salt
- 1 teaspoon onion powder
- 1 teaspoon garlic powder
- ½ teaspoon black pepper
- ½ teaspoon smoked paprika
- 1-pound baby red potatoes, scrubbed clean
- 4 large carrots, chopped
- 1 onion, chopped
- 4 cups beef broth
- 2 tablespoons Worcestershire sauce
- ¼ cup water
- 2 tablespoons cornstarch + 3 tablespoons water

Nutrition information:

Calories per serving: 584; Carbohydrates: 34.2g; Protein: 63.9g; Fat: 21.9g; Sugar: 4.7g; Sodium: 886mg

Directions for Cooking:

1. Season the chuck roast with oil, salt, onion powder, garlic powder, black pepper, and smoked paprika. Rub the entire surface of the roast and allow to marinate inside the fridge for at least 3 hours.
2. Place the marinated beef in the Instant Pot and arrange the potatoes, carrots, and onions on one side. Pour in the broth, Worcestershire sauce and water. Season with more salt and pepper if desired.
3. Close Instant Pot, press the Manual button, choose high settings, and set time to 1 hour and 20 minutes.
4. Once done cooking, do a QPR.
5. Open the lid and press the Sauté button. Stir in the cornstarch slurry and allow to simmer until the sauce thickens.
6. Serve and enjoy.

93. Instant Pot Beef Tips
(Servings: 4, Cooking time: 15 minutes)

Ingredients:

- 3 tablespoons olive oil
- 1-pound beef sirloin steak, cut into cubes
- Salt and pepper to taste
- 1/3 cup dry red wine
- ½ pounds baby Portobello mushrooms, sliced
- 1 onion, sliced
- 2 cups beef broth
- 1 tablespoon Worcestershire sauce

Nutrition information:

Calories per serving: 378; Carbohydrates: 15.1g; Protein: 26.3g; Fat: 23.2g; Sugar: 2.3g; Sodium: 270mg;

Directions for Cooking:

1. Press the Sauté button and heat the oil.
2. Stir in the beef cubes and season with salt and pepper to taste. Continue stirring for 3 minutes to brown the beef.
3. Add the rest of the ingredients.
4. Close Instant Pot, press the Manual button, choose high settings, and set time to 12 minutes.
5. Once done cooking, do a QPR.
6. Serve and enjoy.

94. Sesame Beef Asparagus Salad
(Servings:6, Cooking time: 15 minutes)

Ingredients:

- 1-pound beef round steak, sliced
- 3 tablespoons soy sauce
- 2 tablespoons sesame oil
- 1 tablespoon rice vinegar
- ½ teaspoon ginger root, grated
- 4 cups steamed asparagus, cut into 2-inch pieces
- Sesame seeds for garnish
- 1 head lettuce leaves, washed and torn
- 1 carrot, peeled and julienned
- 1 radish, peeled and julienned

Directions for Cooking:

1. In the Instant Pot, place the steak slices, soy sauce, sesame oil, rice vinegar, and ginger root.
2. Close Instant Pot, press the Manual button, choose high settings, and set time to 15 minutes.
3. Once done cooking, do a QPR.
4. Open the lid and take the beef slices out. Allow to cool before making the salad.
5. In a salad mix the rest of the ingredients. Give a toss.
6. Serve and enjoy.

Nutrition information:

Calories per serving: 211; Carbohydrates: 12.5g; Protein: 20.9g; Fat: 9.4g; Sugar: 7.6g; Sodium: 201mg

---

95. Persian Beef Stew
(Servings: 3, Cooking time: 50 minutes)

Ingredients:

- 2 tablespoons vegetable oil
- 2 onions, chopped
- 2 cloves of garlic, minced
- 1 ½ pounds beef stew meat, cut into chunks
- 1 tablespoon ground cumin
- ½ teaspoon saffron threads
- ½ teaspoon turmeric
- ¼ teaspoon ground cinnamon
- ¼ teaspoon ground allspice
- Salt and pepper to taste
- ¼ cup tomato paste
- 1 can split peas, rinsed and drained
- 3 cups bone broth
- 1 can crushed tomatoes
- 4 tablespoon lemon juice, freshly squeezed

Directions for Cooking:

1. Press the Sauté button on the Instant Pot. Heat the oil and sauté the onion and garlic until fragrant. Add cumin, saffron, turmeric, cinnamon, and allspice. Stir in the beef and brown for 3 minutes. Season with salt and pepper to taste.
2. Pour in the rest of the ingredients.
3. Close Instant Pot, press the Manual button, choose high settings, and set time to 50 minutes.
4. Once done cooking, do a QPR.
5. Serve and enjoy.

Nutrition information:

Calories per serving: 472; Carbohydrates: 36g; Protein: 49g; Fat: 14g; Sugar: 7g; Sodium: 197mg

INSTANT POT MEAT RECIPES

96. Instant Pot Beef Curry
(Servings: 4, Cooking time: 30 minutes)

Ingredients:

- 2 tablespoons coconut oil
- 1 onion, chopped
- 5 cloves of garlic, minced
- 1-pound beef stew meat, cut into chunks
- 3 large potatoes, peeled and cubed
- 6 carrots, roughly chopped
- 1 cup coconut milk
- ½ cup bone broth
- 1 ½ tablespoon curry powder
- Salt and pepper to taste
- ¼ teaspoon paprika

Directions for Cooking:

1. Press the Sauté button on the Instant Pot and heat the oil. Sauté the onion and garlic until fragrant.
2. Stir in the beef and brown on all sides for 5 minutes. Add the rest of the ingredients.
3. Close Instant Pot, press the Manual button, choose high settings, and set time to 30 minutes.
4. Once done cooking, do a QPR.
5. Serve and enjoy.

Nutrition information:

Calories per serving:363; Carbohydrates: 12g; Protein: 27g; Fat: 23g; Sugar: 4g; Sodium:565 mg

---

97. Instant Pot Beef Stew Bourguignon
(Servings: 4, Cooking time: 50 minutes)

Ingredients:

- 1-pound steak flank, cut into large strips
- ½ pound bacon tips
- 1 onion, sliced
- 2 cloves of garlic, minced
- 5 carrots, cut into sticks
- Salt and pepper to taste
- 2 tablespoons dried thyme
- 2 tablespoons parsley
- 1 cup red wine
- ½ cup beef broth
- 2 large sweet potatoes, peeled and cubed
- 1 tablespoon maple syrup

Directions for Cooking:

1. Press the Sauté button on the Instant Pot and add the steak and bacon. Allow the meat and bacon to render their fat before stirring in the onions and garlic.
2. Stir in the carrots and the rest of the ingredients.
3. Close Instant Pot, press the Manual button, choose high settings, and set time to 50 minutes.
4. Once done cooking, do a QPR.
5. Serve and enjoy.

Nutrition information:

Calories per serving:489; Carbohydrates:37.8 g; Protein: 33.5g; Fat: 22.7g; Sugar: 13g; Sodium: 1023mg

98. Instant Pot Salisbury Steak with Mushroom Gravy
(Servings: 6, Cooking time: 15 minutes)

Ingredients:

- 1 ½ pounds ground beef
- 3 tablespoons whole milk
- 1 tablespoon Worcestershire sauce
- 1 clove of garlic, minced
- 1/3 cup panko bread crumbs
- A pinch of salt and pepper to taste
- 1 tablespoon ghee or butter
- 8 ounces baby Portobella mushrooms, sliced
- 1 onion, sliced
- 2 cups beef broth
- 1 tablespoon tomato paste
- 1 tablespoon Dijon mustard
- 2 tablespoons parsley, minced
- 3 tablespoons cornstarch + 3 tablespoons water

Nutrition information:

Calories per serving: 367; Carbohydrates: 11.6g; Protein: 30.1g; Fat: 20.7g; Sugar: 2.7g; Sodium: 208mg

Directions for Cooking:

1. In a mixing bowl, combine the first seven ingredients. Mix until well combined and form patties using the mixture. Place in the fridge and allow to set for at least 2 hours.
2. Press the Sauté button on the Instant Pot. Gently place the patties and allow to brown for 3 minutes on each side.
3. Put in the mushrooms, onion, beef broth, tomato paste, and mustard on top.
4. Close Instant Pot, press the Manual button, choose high settings, and set time to 15 minutes.
5. Once done cooking, do a QPR.
6. Once the lid is open, stir in the parsley and the cornstarch slurry. Allow to simmer until the sauce thickens.
7. Serve and enjoy.

99. Instant Pot Meatloaf
(Servings: 6, Cooking time: 30 minutes)

Directions for Cooking:

Ingredients:

- 2 pounds ground beef
- 2 ½ cups bread crumbs
- 1 cup parmesan cheese
- 4 large eggs, beaten
- 1 tablespoon minced garlic
- 1 teaspoon steak seasoning
- Salt and pepper to taste
- 5 teaspoons brown sugar
- 2/3 cup ketchup
- 1 tablespoon mustard
- 2 teaspoons Worcestershire sauce

1. Place a trivet in the Instant Pot and pour a cup of beef broth.
2. In a mixing bowl, mix together the beef, bread crumbs, cheese, eggs, garlic, and steak seasoning. Season with salt and pepper to taste.
3. Pour meat mixture in a heat-proof pan and place on top of the trivet.
4. Close Instant Pot, press the Steam cook button, choose high settings, and set time to 30 minutes.
5. While waiting for the meatloaf to cook, combine in a saucepan the sugar, ketchup, mustard, and Worcestershire sauce. Mix until the sauce becomes thick.

Nutrition information:
Calories per serving:581; Carbohydrates: 23.2g; Protein: 46.6g; Fat: 32.7g; Sugar: 10g; Sodium: 682mg

6. Once done cooking, do a QPR.
7. Remove the meatloaf from the Instant Pot and allow to cool.
8. Serve with sauce and enjoy.

100. Instant Pot Shredded Beef
(Servings: 6, Cooking time: 1 hour and 10 minutes)

Ingredients:

- 3 pounds beef chuck roast
- 2 tablespoons olive oil
- 1 chipotle in adobo sauce, chopped
- 1 tablespoon adobo sauce
- 2 teaspoons dried cumin
- 2 teaspoons dried oregano
- Salt and pepper to taste
- ½ teaspoon chili powder
- 1 onion, peeled and quartered
- 1 green bell pepper, chopped
- 1 cup water

Directions for Cooking:

1. Place all ingredients in the Instant Pot. Give a good stir.
2. Close Instant Pot, press the Manual button, choose high settings, and set time to 1 hour and 20 minutes.
3. Once done cooking, do a QPR.
4. Take the beef out and shred using forks.
5. Serve with chopped cilantro and enjoy.

Nutrition information:
Calories per serving: 473; Carbohydrates: 3.9g; Protein: 61.2g; Fat: 23.9g; Sugar: 1.7g; Sodium: 213mg;

101. Chili Lime Steak Bowl
(Servings: 4, Cooking time: 15 minutes)

Ingredients:

- 2 pounds beef steak, cut into cubes
- 1 tablespoon water
- 1 teaspoon minced garlic
- 1 tablespoon chili powder
- 2 teaspoons lime juice
- Salt and pepper to taste
- 2 avocados, diced
- 1 cup tomato, diced
- 1 cup chopped cilantro

Nutrition information:
Calories per serving: 498; Carbohydrates: 12.6g; Protein: 50.3g; Fat: 27.6g; Sugar: 2.4g; Sodium: 201mg;

Directions for Cooking:

1. Place the beef steak slices, water, garlic, chili powder, and lime juice in the Instant Pot. Season with salt and pepper to taste.
2. Close Instant Pot, press the Manual button, choose high settings, and set time to 15 minutes.
3. Once done cooking, do a QPR.
4. Assemble the steak bowl by putting in a bowl the meat and garnishing with fresh avocado, tomatoes, and cilantro on top.
5. Serve and enjoy.

102.   Italian Beef Dinner
(Servings: 6, Cooking time: 45 minutes)

Ingredients:

- 3 pounds beef chuck roast, cut into cubes
- 3 pounds red potatoes, scrubbed and peeled
- 3 cups carrots, roughly chopped
- ¼ cup water
- 1 can tomato sauce
- 1 teaspoon Italian herb seasoning mix

Directions for Cooking:

1. Place all ingredients in the Instant Pot and give a good stir.
2. Close Instant Pot, press the Manual button, choose high settings, and set time to 45 minutes.
3. Once done cooking, do a QPR.
4. Serve and enjoy.

Nutrition information:

Calories per serving: 457; Carbohydrates: 34g; Protein: 36g; Fat: 19g; Sugar: 6g; Sodium: 480mg

103.   Instant Pot Beef Gyros
(Servings: 6, Cooking time: 10 minutes)

Ingredients:

- 4 tablespoons olive oil
- 3 cloves of garlic, minced
- 1 onion, sliced
- 2 pounds beef roast, sliced thinly
- 1 tablespoon dried parsley
- ½ cup vegetable broth
- 1 tablespoon lemon juice
- 1 tablespoon apple cider vinegar
- Salt and pepper to taste
- 6 flat pita bread
- Sliced carrots
- Sliced onions
- Sliced cucumber
- 1 cup plain Greek yogurt

Directions for Cooking:

1. Press the Sauté button on the Instant Pot and heat the oil. Heat the oil and sauté the garlic and onions until fragrant. Add the beef roast slices, parsley, vegetable broth, lemon juice, and apple cider vinegar. Season with salt and pepper to taste.
2. Close Instant Pot, press the Manual button, choose high settings, and set time to 10 minutes.
3. Once done cooking, do a QPR.
4. Remove the meat from the Instant Pot and discard the sauce. Allow to cool.
5. Serve the beef slices on pita bread and serve with carrots, onions, and cucumber. Drizzle with Greek yogurt on top.
6. Serve and enjoy.

Nutrition information:

Calories per serving: 535; Carbohydrates:17.9 g; Protein: 43.1g; Fat: 22.2g; Sugar: 1.4g; Sodium: 391mg;

INSTANT POT MEAT RECIPES

104.   Instant Pot Beef Burritos

（Servings: 6， Cooking time: 15 minutes）

Ingredients:

- 2 tablespoons vegetable oil
- 1 onion, diced
- 3 cloves of garlic, minced
- 1-pound lean ground beef
- 1 tablespoon chili powder
- 2 teaspoons cumin powder
- 1 Salt and pepper to taste
- 1/4 cup beef broth
- 1 can black beans, rinsed and drained
- 1 can corn kernels, rinsed and drained
- 1 cup diced tomatoes
- 6 flour tortillas

Nutrition information:

Calories per serving: 381; Carbohydrates: 18g;
Protein: 17g; Fat: 8g; Sugar: 2g; Sodium: 318

Directions for Cooking:

1. Press the Sauté button on the Instant Pot and heat the oil. Sauté the onions and garlic until fragrant.
2. Stir in the ground beef until brown and add the chili powder and cumin powder. Season with salt and pepper to taste.
3. Pour in the broth, black beans, corn, and tomatoes.
4. Close Instant Pot, press the Manual button, choose high settings, and set time to 15 minutes.
5. Once done cooking, do a QPR.
6. Once the lid is open, ladle onto flour tortillas.
7. Serve and enjoy.

105.   Instant Pot Picadillo

(Servings: 3, Cooking time: 20 minutes)

Ingredients:

- 1 ½ pounds lean ground beef
- ½ onion, chopped
- 2 cloves of garlic, minced
- 1 tomato, chopped
- Salt and pepper to taste
- ½ red bell pepper, chopped
- 2 tablespoons cilantro
- ½ can tomato sauce
- 1 teaspoon ground cumin
- 2 bay leaves
- 2 tablespoons capers

Nutrition information:

Calories per serving: 516; Carbohydrates: 6.7g;
Protein: 61.9g; Fat: 25.5g; Sugar: 0.9g; Sodium:
572mg;

Directions for Cooking:

1. Press the Sauté button on the Instant Pot and stir in the lean ground beef. Stir until the fat has lightly rendered. Stir in the onions and garlic until fragrant.
2. Add the tomatoes and season with salt and pepper. Stir in the rest of the ingredients.
3. Close Instant Pot, press the Manual button, choose high settings, and set time to 20 minutes.
4. Once done cooking, do a QPR.
5. Serve and enjoy.

106.   Instant Pot Beef Pot Pie
(Servings: 6, Cooking time: 30 minutes)

Ingredients:

- 4 tablespoons butter
- 1 cup diced onion
- 1 cup diced celery
- 4 cloves of garlic, minced
- 1-pound beef
- 1 teaspoon dried thyme
- 2 cups potatoes, diced
- 1 cup carrots, diced
- 1 cup frozen peas
- 2 cups beef broth
- 1/3 cup milk
- 2 tablespoons cornstarch + 3 tablespoons water
- 1 box puff pastry
- 2 egg whites

Nutrition information:

Calories per serving: 325; Carbohydrates: 26.6g; Protein: 20.8g; Fat: 15.3g; Sugar: 10.4g; Sodium: 307mg

Directions for Cooking:

1. Press the Sauté button on the Instant Pot and heat the butter. Sauté the onion, celery and garlic until fragrant. Add the beef and brown for 5 minutes.
2. Stir in the thyme, potatoes, carrots, frozen peas, beef broth and milk.
3. Close Instant Pot, press Manual cook button, choose high settings, and set time to 10 minutes.
4. Once done cooking, do a QPR.
5. Ladle into ramekins and cover the top of the ramekins with puff pastry. Brush the top with egg whites.
6. Place in a 350⁰F preheated oven for 15 minutes.
7. Serve and enjoy.

---

107.   Tex Mex Beef Stew
(Servings: 6, Cooking time: 28 minutes)

Ingredients:

- 1 tablespoon chili powder
- 2 teaspoons cumin powder
- 1 teaspoon ground coriander
- ¼ teaspoon smoked paprika
- 2 pounds beef stew meat
- Salt and pepper to taste
- 1 tablespoon olive oil
- 1 onion, chopped
- 4 cloves of garlic, minced
- 1 can diced tomatoes
- 1 tablespoon apple cider vinegar
- 1 cup chopped cilantro
- 1 cup shredded cheddar cheese

Directions for Cooking:

1. In a mixing bowl, combine the chili powder, cumin, coriander, paprika and beef stew meat. Allow to marinate in the fridge for 2 hours.
2. Press the Sauté button on the Instant Pot and heat the oil. Sauté the onion and garlic until fragrant. Add the marinated beef and allow to brown for 3 minutes.
3. Stir in the tomatoes and apple cider vinegar. Adjust the seasoning and water.
4. Close Instant Pot, press the Manual cook button, choose high settings, and set time to 25 minutes.
5. Once done cooking, do a QPR.

Nutrition information:
Calories per serving: 434; Carbohydrates:5.8 g; Protein: 60.6g; Fat: 17.7g; Sugar: 2.4g; Sodium: 775mg

6. Before serving, garnish with cilantro and cheddar cheese.
7. Serve and enjoy.

---

108. Instant Pot Beef Tips
(Servings: 4, Cooking time: 20 minutes)

Ingredients:

- 4 tablespoons olive oil
- 2 pounds sirloin beef tips
- ¼ cup diced onions
- 3 tablespoons flour
- ½ teaspoon garlic salt
- ½ teaspoon black pepper
- 1 cup beef broth
- ½ cup red wine
- 1 can cream of mushroom soup

Directions for Cooking:

1. Press the Sauté button on the Instant Pot and heat the oil. Add the sirloin beef tips and onions. Stir until meat is lightly brown.
2. Add the rest of the ingredients.
3. Close Instant Pot, press the Manual cook button, choose high settings, and set time to 20 minutes.
4. Once done cooking, do a QPR.
5. Serve and enjoy.

Nutrition information:
Calories per serving: 563; Carbohydrates: 14.2g; Protein: 49.9g; Fat: 32.4g; Sugar: 3.9g; Sodium: 221mg

---

109. Simple Instant Pot Beef Stew
(Servings: 6, Cooking time: 60 minutes)

Ingredients:

- 2 pounds beef stew meat
- 4 cups water
- 5 potatoes, peeled and chopped
- 1 cup carrot, chopped
- 1 onion, chopped
- 4 stalks of celery
- Salt and pepper to taste

Directions for Cooking:

1. Place all ingredients in the Instant Pot.
2. Close Instant Pot, press pressure cook button, choose high settings, and set time to 60 minutes.
3. Once done cooking, do a QPR.
4. Serve and enjoy.

Nutrition information:
Calories per serving: 554; Carbohydrates:58.2g; Protein: 60.9g; Fat: 7.8g; Sugar: 5g; Sodium: 599mg

110.   Instant Pot Mediterranean Beef
(Servings: 4, Cooking time: 60 minutes)

Ingredients:

- 3 tablespoons all-purpose flour
- ½ dried oregano
- Salt and pepper to taste
- 2 pounds beef chuck roast
- 2 tablespoon olive oil
- 1 onion, chopped
- 4 shallots, chopped
- ½ cup beef broth
- ¼ cup red wine
- ¼ cup balsamic vinegar
- ½ cup Medjool dates, pitted and chopped

Nutrition information:

Calories per serving: 555; Carbohydrates: 17.4g; Protein: 62.2g; Fat: 26.1g; Sugar: 3.8g; Sodium: 230mg

Directions for Cooking:

1. In a mixing bowl, rub all-purpose flour, oregano, salt and pepper on the beef chuck roast.
2. Press the Sauté button on the Instant Pot and heat the oil.
3. Place the roast and brown on all sides for at least 5 minutes.
4. Add the onion and shallots and stir until fragrant.
5. Stir in the rest of the ingredients.
6. Close Instant Pot, press the Manual cook button, choose high settings, and set time to 1 hour.
7. Once done cooking, do a QPR.
8. Serve and enjoy.

111.   Instant Pot Taco Meat
(Servings: 4, Cooking time: 13 minutes)

Ingredients:

- 2 pounds ground beef
- 2 onions, diced
- 3 bell peppers (any color), diced
- 2 packets of taco seasoning
- 1 cup water

Nutrition information:

Calories per serving:612; Carbohydrates: 8.3; Protein: 58.6g; Fat: 36.8g; Sugar: 2.6g; Sodium: 158mg;

Directions for Cooking:

1. Press the Sauté button on the Instant Pot and stir in the beef and ground onions.
2. Allow to brown for 3 minutes while stirring constantly.
3. Add the rest of the ingredients.
4. Close Instant Pot, press the Manual cook button, choose high settings, and set time to 10 minutes.
5. Once done cooking, do a QPR.
6. Serve and enjoy.

INSTANT POT MEAT RECIPES

112.   Beef Cheesy Potatoes
(Servings: 6, Cooking time: 25 minutes)

Ingredients:

- 1 ½ pounds ground beef
- 6 large potatoes, peeled and chopped
- 2 cups cheddar cheese, shredded
- ¾ cup chicken broth
- 1 tablespoon Italian seasoning mix
- Salt and pepper to taste

Directions for Cooking:

1. Press the Sauté button on the Instant Pot and stir in the beef. Brown the meat until some of the oil has rendered.
2. Add the rest of the ingredients.
3. Close Instant Pot, press the Manual button, choose high settings, and set time to 20 minutes.
4. Once done cooking, do a QPR.
5. Serve and enjoy.

Nutrition information:

Calories per serving: 806; Carbohydrates: 66.8g; Protein: 53.4g; Fat: 35.6g; Sugar: 3.5g; Sodium: 609mg;

113.   Sweet Potato Chili Recipe
(Servings: 5, Cooking time: 25 minutes)

Ingredients:

- 1 teaspoon olive oil
- 1 onion, diced
- 3 cloves of garlic, minced
- ½ pound ground pork
- 1-pound ground beef
- 1 large sweet potato, peeled and cut into ½" pieces
- 3 celery stalks, sliced
- 3 ½ cups crushed tomatoes
- 1 tablespoon Worcestershire sauce
- 1 teaspoon cumin
- 1 teaspoon chili powder
- Salt and pepper to taste

Directions for Cooking:

1. Press the Sauté button on the Instant Pot and heat the olive oil. Sauté the onion and garlic until fragrant.
2. Stir in the pork and beef and allow to brown for 5 minutes.
3. Add the rest of the ingredients.
4. Close Instant Pot, press the Manual button, choose high settings, and set time to 20 minutes.
5. Once done cooking, do a QPR.
6. Serve and enjoy.

Nutrition information:

Calories per serving:447; Carbohydrates: 16.4g; Protein: 36.9g; Fat: 25.9g; Sugar: 4.1g; Sodium: 172mg;

INSTANT POT MEAT RECIPES

114.   Instant Pot Stuffed Peppers
(Servings: 8, Cooking time: 25 minutes)

Ingredients:

- ½ pound ground beef
- 1/3 cup diced onions
- 1 ½ cup spaghetti sauce
- ½ teaspoon garlic salt
- 2 cups cooked rice
- 8 bell peppers, cut the top and remove the seeds
- 1 cup mozzarella cheese, shredded

Directions for Cooking:

1. Press the Sauté button on the Instant Pot and Add the beef and onions. Stir constantly.
2. Stir in the spaghetti sauce and season with garlic salt.
3. Close Instant Pot, press the Manual cook button, choose high settings, and set time to 10 minutes.
4. Once done cooking, do a QPR.
5. Transfer into a bowl and add the cooked rice. Stir to combine. Pack the mixture into hollow bell peppers and top with mozzarella cheese.
6. Place a trivet in the Instant Pot and pour water. Place the stuffed bell peppers on the trivet and close the lid. Press the Steam button and cook for 10 minutes.
7. Serve and enjoy.

Nutrition information:
Calories per serving: 265; Carbohydrates: 32g; Protein: 12g; Fat: 9; Sugar: 10g; Sodium: 930mg

---

115.   Braised Brisket
(Servings: 4, Cooking time: 60 minutes)

Ingredients:

- 2 pounds beef brisket, cut into 4 pieces
- Salt and pepper to taste
- 2 cups sliced onion
- ½ cup water
- 2 tablespoons tomato paste
- 2 tablespoons Worcestershire sauce
- 2 teaspoons liquid smoke

Directions for Cooking:

1. Put all ingredients in the Instant Pot. Mix all ingredients to combine everything.
2. Close Instant Pot, press pressure cook button, choose high settings, and set time to 60 minutes.
3. Once done cooking, do a QPR.
4. Serve and enjoy.

Nutrition information:
Calories per serving: 490; Carbohydrates: 9.9g; Protein: 34.5g; Fat: 33.9g; Sugar: 4.8g; Sodium: 885mg

---

116.   Instant Pot Corned Beef and Cabbages

(Servings: 5, Cooking time: 60 minutes)

Ingredients:

- 6 cloves of garlic, chopped
- 1 onion, quartered
- 2 ½ pounds corned beef brisket, cut in large slices
- 12-oz. beer
- 2 cups water
- 3 carrots, roughly chopped
- 2 potatoes, chopped
- 1 head cabbage, cut into four pieces

Nutrition information:

Calories per serving:758; Carbohydrates: 45.8g; Protein: 43.1g; Fat: 44.7g; Sugar: 8.7g; Sodium: 940mg;

Directions for Cooking:

1. In the Instant Pot, place the garlic, onion, corned beef brisket, beer, and water. Season with salt and pepper to taste.
2. Close Instant Pot, press the Manual button, choose high settings, and set time to 50 minutes.
3. Once done cooking, do a QPR.
4. Open the lid and take out the meat. Shred the meat using fork and place it back into the Instant Pot.
5. Stir in the vegetables.
6. Close the lid and seal the vent and press the Manual button. Cook for another 10 minutes. Do QPR.
7. Serve and enjoy.

---

117.   Instant Pot Beef Vindaloo

(Servings: 2, Cooking time: 50 minutes)

Ingredients:

- 1-pound beef shin, cut into chunks
- ½ teaspoon ground cinnamon
- ¼ teaspoon ground cloves
- 1 teaspoon dried mango powder
- 1 teaspoon ground turmeric
- ½ teaspoon ground cumin
- 3 cloves of garlic, minced
- 1 tablespoon lemon juice
- 1 teaspoon honey
- 12 cardamom pods, bashed
- Salt and pepper to taste
- 2 tablespoons ghee
- 1 cup onions, cut into wedges
- 2 green chilies, sliced
- 2 tomatoes, chopped
- 1 cup water

Directions for Cooking:

1. In a mixing bowl, combine the first 11 ingredients and allow to marinate in the fridge for at least 2 hours.
2. Press the Sauté button on the Instant Pot and Add the ghee. Stir in the marinated beef and brown on all sides for at least 5 minutes.
3. Stir in the rest of the ingredients.
4. Close Instant Pot, press the Manual button, choose high settings, and set time to 45 minutes.
5. Once done cooking, do a QPR.
6. Serve and enjoy.

Nutrition information:

Calories per serving: 590; Carbohydrates: 19.3g; Protein: 51.5g; Fat: 20g; Sugar: 10g; Sodium: 531mg;

INSTANT POT MEAT RECIPES

118.   Instant Pot Guinness Beef Stew Recipe
(Servings: 8, Cooking time: 40 minutes)

Ingredients:

- 2 tablespoons olive oil
- 1 tablespoon butter
- 1 cup bacon, chopped
- 1 cup shallots, chopped
- 1 ½ pounds braising steak, cubed
- Salt and pepper to taste
- 1 cup button mushrooms, sliced
- 1 cup wild mushrooms, sliced
- 2 carrots, peeled and sliced
- 2 tablespoons tomato paste
- 1 tablespoon Worcestershire sauce
- 1 tablespoon soy sauce
- 1 ½ cups Guinness beer

Directions for Cooking:

1. Press the Sauté button on the Instant Pot and heat the olive oil and butter. Stir in the bacon and shallots until fragrant.
2. Stir in the steak and season with salt and pepper to taste.
3. Add the rest of the ingredients.
4. Close Instant Pot, press the Manual button, choose high settings, and set time to 35 minutes.
5. Once done cooking, do a QPR.
6. Serve and enjoy.

Nutrition information:

Calories per serving: 503; Carbohydrates: 10g; Protein: 33g; Fat: 36g; Sugar: 4g; Sodium: 433mg

119.   Ethiopian Beef Stew
(Servings: 3, Cooking time: 55 minutes)

Ingredients:

- 1 ½ pounds beef stew meat, cut into chunks
- ¼ teaspoon turmeric powder
- 1 tablespoon garam masala
- 1 tablespoon coriander powder
- 1 teaspoon cumin
- ¼ teaspoon ground nutmeg
- 2 teaspoons smoked paprika
- ¼ teaspoon black pepper
- 3 tablespoons ghee
- 1 onion, chopped
- 1 tablespoon ginger, grated
- 2 cloves of garlic, grated
- 1 tablespoon onions
- 3 tablespoons tomato paste
- ½ teaspoon sugar
- Salt and pepper to taste
- 1 cup water

Directions for Cooking:

1. In a mixing bowl, combine the first 8 ingredients and allow to marinate in the fridge for at least 4 hours.
2. Press the Sauté button and heat the oil. Sauté the onion, ginger, and garlic until fragrant. Stir in the marinated beef and allow to brown for 3 minutes.
3. Stir in the rest of the ingredients.
4. Close Instant Pot, press the Manual button, choose high settings, and set time to 50 minutes.
5. Once done cooking, do a QPR.
6. Serve and enjoy.

Nutrition information:

Calories per serving: 591; Carbohydrates: 11.5g; Protein: 83.5g; Fat: 23.4g; Sugar: 3.2g; Sodium: 940mg

120.   Easy Instant Pot Beef
(Servings: 4, Cooking time: 35 minutes)

Ingredients:

- 1 tablespoon butter
- 1-pound beef chunks
- Salt and pepper to taste
- 1 cup onions, chopped
- 1 tablespoon garlic, minced
- 2 carrots, sliced diagonally
- ½ cup chopped celery
- ¾ cup mushrooms, halved
- 3 potatoes, peeled and quartered
- 2 tablespoons Worcestershire sauce
- 2 tablespoons tomato paste
- 1 cup chicken broth
- 2 tablespoons all-purpose flour + 2 tablespoons water

Nutrition information:

Calories per serving: 565; Carbohydrates: 61.3g; Protein:43.9g; Fat: 13.1g; Sugar: 6.4g; Sodium: 682mg;

Directions for Cooking:

1. Turn on the Sauté button on the Instant Pot and melt the butter. Brown the beef chunks and season with salt and pepper to taste. Add the onions and garlic until fragrant.
2. Stir in the carrots, celery, mushrooms and potatoes.
3. Add the Worcestershire sauce, tomato paste, and chicken broth. Season with more salt and pepper to taste.
4. Close Instant Pot, press the Manual cook button, choose high settings, and set time to 30 minutes.
5. Once done cooking, do a QPR.
6. Open the lid and press the Sauté button. Stir in the all-purpose flour and allow to simmer until the sauce thickens.
7. Serve and enjoy.

121.   Instant Pot Ghormeh Sabzi
(Servings: 5, Cooking time: 55 minutes)

Ingredients:

- 1 tablespoon olive oil
- 1 ½ pounds lamb meat, cubed
- 1 onion, chopped
- 4 bunches parsley, chopped
- 1 bunch cilantro, chopped
- 4 leeks, chopped
- 1 tablespoon dried fenugreek, sliced
- 4 tablespoons lemon juice, freshly squeezed
- 1 tablespoon turmeric
- 1 cup dark red kidney beans, rinsed and drained
- 1 cup water
- Salt and pepper to taste

Directions for Cooking:

1. Turn the Instant Pot and press the Sauté button. Heat the olive oil and brown the lamb meat.
2. Add the onion, parsley, cilantro, leeks, fenugreek, lemon juice, and turmeric.
3. Stir in kidney beans and water. Season with salt and pepper to taste.
4. Close Instant Pot, press the Manual button, choose high settings, and set time to 50 minutes.
5. Once done cooking, do a QPR.
6. Serve and enjoy.

Nutrition information:

Calories per serving:530; Carbohydrates: 27g; Protein: 26g; Fat: 35.2g; Sugar: 5g; Sodium: 186mg;

INSTANT POT MEAT RECIPES

122.   BBQ Instant Pot Ribs
(Servings: 3, Cooking time: 45 minutes)

Ingredients:

- 1 rack baby back ribs
- ¼ cup commercial BBQ sauce
- Salt and pepper to taste
- 1 tablespoon liquid smoke

Nutrition information:

Calories per serving: 1163; Carbohydrates: 3.9g; Protein:103.2g; Fat: 81.9g; Sugar:0.4g; Sodium: 461mg;

Directions for Cooking:

1. Place all ingredients in the Instant Pot. Give a good stir.
2. Close Instant Pot, press the Manual button, choose high settings, and set time to 45 minutes.
3. Once done cooking, do a QPR.
4. Serve and enjoy.

---

123.   Instant Pot Adovado
(Servings: 10, Cooking time: 1 hour and 25 minutes)

Ingredients:

- 1 tablespoon canola oil
- 4 pounds pork shoulder, cut into cubes
- 1 onion, diced
- 6 cloves of garlic, minced
- 2 chipotle peppers in adobo sauce
- 1 tablespoon apple cider vinegar
- ½ teaspoon dried oregano
- ¼ teaspoon ground cumin
- 2 cups chicken broth
- 8 dried Mexican chilies, chopped
- Salt and pepper to taste

Directions for Cooking:

1. Press the Sauté button on the Instant Pot. Heat the canola oil and sear the pork shoulders on all sides.
2. Add the onion and garlic and sauté until fragrant.
3. Stir in the rest of the ingredients.
4. Close Instant Pot, press the Manual button, choose high settings, and set time to 1 hour and 25 minutes.
5. Once done cooking, do a QPR.
6. Serve and enjoy.

Nutrition information:

Calories per serving:217; Carbohydrates: 4.1g; Protein: 21.3g; Fat: 12.6g; Sugar: 0.9g; Sodium: 288mg

INSTANT POT MEAT RECIPES

124.　　Asian Pot Roast
(Servings: 6, Cooking time: 50 minutes)

Ingredients:

- 3 pounds beef pot roast
- 1 tablespoon Chinese five-spice powder
- ¼ cup soy sauce
- ¼ cup black bean sauce
- 2-star anise
- 3 bay leaves
- 1 cup water
- 1 onion, diced
- 3 cloves of garlic, minced
- Sesame seeds for garnish

Directions for Cooking:

1. Place all ingredients in the Instant Pot except for the sesame seeds.
2. Close Instant Pot, press pressure cook button, choose high settings, and set time to 50 minutes.
3. Once done cooking, do a QPR.
4. Garnish with sesame seeds.
5. Serve and enjoy.

Nutrition information:

Calories per serving:352; Carbohydrates: 6.5; Protein: 51.9g; Fat: 13.3g; Sugar: 3.1g; Sodium: 419mg;

125.　　Instant Pot Nikujaga
(Servings: 4, Cooking time: 40 minutes)

Ingredients:

- 1 tablespoon oil
- 1 onion, chopped
- 1-pound beef rib eye, sliced
- 1 teaspoon sugar
- 1 cup dashi
- 3 tablespoons mirin
- 2 tablespoons sake
- 3 tablespoons soy sauce
- 2 carrots, chopped
- 2 potatoes, peeled and quartered
- Salt and pepper to taste
- 2 cups water
- 1 package shirataki noodles, washed and drained
- ½ cup green beans, pre-boiled

Directions for Cooking:

1. Press the Sauté button on the Instant Pot and sauté the onion and beef slices. Stir to turn slightly golden.
2. Stir in the sugar, dashi, mirin, sake, and soy sauce.
3. Add the carrots and potatoes. Season with salt and pepper to taste. Pour in water.
4. Close Instant Pot, press the Manual cook button, choose high settings, and set time to 35 minutes.
5. Once done cooking, do a QPR.
6. Open the lid and press the Sauté button. Stir in the shirataki noodles and green beans until cooked.
7. Serve and enjoy.

Nutrition information:

Calories per serving: 442; Carbohydrates: 43.6g; Protein:29.3g; Fat: 14.6g; Sugar: 7.6g; Sodium: 309mg;

126.   Apple Bacon BBQ Pulled Pork
(Servings: 10, Cooking time: 40 minutes)

Ingredients:

- 4 slices of bacon, chopped
- 1 ½ cup onion, chopped
- 1 medium apple, chopped
- 1 ½ cup ketchup
- 3 tablespoon brown sugar
- 1/3 cup Worcestershire sauce
- 3 tablespoon apple cider vinegar
- 2 teaspoon salt
- 2-pounds pork tenderloin

Nutrition information:

Calories per serving: 244; Carbohydrates: 19.0g;
Protein: 25.7g; Fat: 7.4g; Sugar: 14.3g; Sodium:
983mg

Directions for Cooking:

1. Press the sauté button on the Instant Pot and drop the chopped bacons. Cook until the bacon has rendered its fat. Set aside.
2. Sauté the onions and apples for a minute. Add the ketchup, brown sugar, Worcestershire sauce, and apple cider vinegar. Season with salt.
3. Add the pork tenderloin.
4. Close the lid and press the manual button. Cook on high for 35 minutes.
5. Do natural pressure release.
6. Remove the pork from the pot and shred using a fork.
7. Garnish with crispy bacon.

127.   Balsamic-Honey Pork Roast
(Servings: 8, Cooking time: 35 minutes)

Ingredients

- 2-pound pork roast, bones and fat removed
- ½ teaspoon garlic powder
- Salt and pepper to taste
- 1/3 cup balsamic vinegar
- 1/3 cup vegetable broth
- ¼ cup liquid aminos
- 1 tablespoon raw honey
- 1 ½ cup water

Directions for Cooking:

1. Place the pork roast in the Instant Pot and sprinkle with garlic powder, salt, and pepper. Rub the spices on the pork.
2. Add the rest of the ingredients.
3. Close the lid and select the manual button. Cook on high for 35 minutes.
4. Do QPR.
5. Serve and enjoy.

Nutrition information:

Calories per serving: 256; Carbohydrates: 5.2g;
Protein: 30.4g; Fat: 11.8g; Sugar: 4.3g; Sodium: 80mg

128. Apple Barbecue Ribs
(Servings: 6, Cooking time: 35 minutes)

Ingredients:

- 4 cups apple juice
- ½ cup apple cider vinegar
- 1 tablespoon salt
- 3-pounds rack of ribs
- ½ tablespoon garlic powder
- ½ tablespoon black pepper
- 1 cup Southern apple cider barbecue sauce
- ½ cup water

Nutrition information:

Calories per serving:477; Carbohydrates: 29.8g; Protein: 52.9g; Fat: 14.9g; Sugar: 24.2g; Sodium: 1600mg

Directions for Cooking:

1. Place all ingredients in the pot.
2. Make sure that the pork is coated with the sauce.
3. Close the lid and press the manual button. Adjust the cooking time by pressing the "+" "-" button to 25 minutes.
4. Do quick release. Remove the ribs from the pot and set it on a baking pan. Cover the baking pan with aluminum foil and place the ribs in the oven. Cook for 10 minutes at 400°F.
5. Serve and enjoy.

129. Pork Tenderloin Green Chili
(Servings: 6, Cooking time: 25 minutes)

Ingredients:

- 2 cups kale, chopped
- 2 15-ounce cannellini beans, drained
- 2 cups chicken broth
- 1 4 ounce diced green chilies, drained
- 1 cup salsa verde
- 1 cup chopped green bell pepper
- 2 cups onion, chopped
- 1 tablespoon chili powder
- 1 tablespoon garlic, minced
- 1 teaspoon ground cumin
- 1 dried bay leaf
- ½ teaspoon dried oregano
- 12-ounces pork tenderloin, boneless and fat trimmed
- ½ cup cilantro, chopped

Directions for Cooking:

1. In a blender, mix together kale, half of the cannellini beans and broth. Blend until smooth.
2. Transfer this mixture into the slow cooker and add the rest of the ingredients except the cilantro.
3. Close the lid and press the manual button. Cook on high for 25 minutes.
4. Do quick pressure release to open the lid.
5. Remove the bay leaf and transfer the pork in another bowl. Shred with fork.
6. Garnish with cilantro.

Nutrition information:

Calories per serving: 287; Carbohydrates: 16.3g; Protein: 35.5g; Fat: 9.0g; Sugar: 4.8g; Sodium: 723mg

130.   Teriyaki Pork Tenderloin
(Servings: 6, Cooking time: 25 minutes)

Ingredients:

- 2 tablespoon olive oil
- 2-pounds pork tenderloin, cut into strips
- 4 cloves of garlic, minced
- ½ large onion, chopped
- 3 red chili pepper, chopped
- ¼ teaspoon black pepper
- ½ cup teriyaki sauce
- 1 cup chicken broth
- ¼ cup brown sugar

Nutrition information:

Calories per serving: 393; Carbohydrates: 16.9g; Protein: 50.3g; Fat: 12.7g; Sugar: 14.0g; Sodium: 683mg

Directions for Cooking:

1. Press the sauté button on the Instant Pot.
2. Heat the oil and add the tenderloins. Stir constantly for 5 minutes or until they become brown.
3. Add in garlic, onion, red chili pepper and black pepper.
4. Add the remaining ingredients.
5. Close the lid and press the stew button. Adjust the cooking time to 20 minutes.
6. Do natural pressure release.
7. Serve with rice.

131.   Southwestern Pork Chops
(Servings: 4, Cooking time: 20 minutes)

Ingredients:

- 4 4-ounces lean pork loin chop, boneless and fat trimmed
- 1 tbsp vegetable oil
- 1/3 cup salsa
- 2 tablespoon lime juice
- 1 cup water
- ¼ cup fresh cilantro

Nutrition information:

Calories per serving: 274; Carbohydrates: 2.1g; Protein: 29.4g; Fat: 16.0g; Sugar: 1.0g; Sodium: 215mg

Directions for Cooking:

1. Flatten the pork chops with your hand.
2. Add oil to the Instant Pot set at the sauté setting. Place the pork chops and cook for one minute on each side.
3. Pour the salsa and lime juice over the pork chops.
4. Add in the water.
5. Close the lid and press the stew setting. Press the "+" "-" button and adjust the time to 15 minutes.
6. Do natural pressure release.
7. Sprinkle with cilantro on top.

132. Tropical Beef with Peppers and Pineapple
(Servings: 4, Cooking time: 20 minutes)

Ingredients:

- 1 tablespoon olive oil
- 1 large onion, chopped
- 2-pounds round steak, cut into chunks
- ½ teaspoon salt
- 1/8 teaspoon pepper
- 1 can pineapple chunks
- 2 large green peppers, chopped
- 1 can mild green chilies
- 1 can diced tomatoes
- 1 ½ tablespoon Greek seasoning
- 1 cup water
- 2 tablespoon cornstarch + 1 tablespoon water

Nutrition information:

Calories per serving: 583; Carbohydrates: 23.5g; Protein: 71.0g; Fat: 21.2g; Sugar: 17.6g; Sodium: 785mg

Directions for Cooking:

1. Press the Sauté button and heat the oil. Sauté the onion until tender. Keep on stirring to avoid the onions from burning.
2. Season the round steak with salt and pepper. Add to the pot and brown for another five minutes.
3. Add the pineapples, green pepper, chilies and diced tomatoes. Season with Greek seasoning. Add water.
4. Close the lid and press the stew button for 15 minutes.
5. Meanwhile, mix together the cornstarch and water in a bowl.
6. Do a quick release to open the lid. Add the cornstarch slurry and press the sauté button. Simmer until the sauce thickens.
7. Enjoy.

---

133. Herb-Crusted Beef
(Servings: 6, Cooking time: 35 minutes)

Ingredients:

- 1-pound lean beef roast
- ½ teaspoon black pepper, ground
- 1 ½ teaspoon salt
- ¼ cup Dijon mustard
- 1 ½ teaspoon prepared horseradish
- 2 tablespoon low-calorie mayonnaise
- 2 cloves of garlic, minced
- 1 ½ cup water
- 1/3 cup fresh parsley, chopped
- 2 tablespoon thyme, chopped
- 2 tablespoon dill, chopped

Directions for Cooking:

1. Mix all ingredients in the Instant Pot.
2. Close the lid and press the manual button. Cook on high for 35 minutes.
3. Do natural pressure release.
4. Check if the meat is done and tender.
5. Serve and enjoy.

Nutrition information:

Calories per serving: 166; Carbohydrates: 3.2g; Protein: 11.4g; Fat: 8.0g; Sugar: 0.4g; Sodium: 770mg

134.   Instant Pot Beef Lasagna

(Servings: 6, Cooking time: 20 minutes)

Ingredients:

- 1 pound lean ground beef
- 1 clove of garlic, minced
- 1 onion, chopped
- 1 can tomato sauce
- 1 can tomato, crushed
- 1 teaspoon salt
- 1/2 teaspoon dried basil
- 1 teaspoon dried oregano
- 1/4 teaspoon red pepper flakes
- 1 1/2 cup low-fat mozzarella cheese, grated
- 1 cup part-skim ricotta cheese
- 6 lasagna noodles
- ½ cup water
- 1/2 cup parmesan cheese, grated

Directions for Cooking:

1. Press the Sauté button on the Instant Pot and add the ground beef, garlic and onions. Stir constantly to avoid browning at the bottom and also to break up large pieces of the beef.

2. Add in the tomato sauce and crushed tomatoes. Season with salt, dried basil, oregano, and red pepper flakes. Set aside to assemble the lasagna.

3. Prepare the cheese sauce by mixing the 1 cup of mozzarella with ricotta.

4. Break the lasagna noodles and stir in the pot.

5. Place ¾ cup of the meat mixture at the bottom of the pot then drizzle with the cheese sauce. Add a layer of lasagna noodles. Do this alternately until all ingredients are placed inside the pot. Pour over water.

6. Close the lid and press the manual button. Cook on high for 15 minutes.

7. Do natural release to open the lid.

8. Sprinkle with parmesan cheese for garnish.

9. Serve and enjoy.

Nutrition information:

Calories per serving: 458; Carbohydrates: 25.4g; Protein: 38.3g; Fat: 21.5g; Sugar: 7.0g; Sodium: 1594mg

135. Caribbean Pineapple Filet Mignon

(Servings: 1, Cooking time: 35 minutes)

Ingredients:

- 1 filet mignon
- ½ cup pineapple, chopped
- 1-piece bacon
- ¼ teaspoon jalapeno pepper
- 2 tablespoon red onions, chopped
- 2 cloves of garlic, minced
- 2 tablespoon coconut aminos or soy sauce
- 3 tablespoon honey
- ½ of a lime, juiced
- 1 tablespoon apple cider vinegar
- ¼ teaspoon ground ginger
- 1 teaspoon thyme
- ¼ teaspoon cinnamon
- 1/8 teaspoon ground cloves
- 1/8 teaspoon ground nutmeg
- Salt and pepper to taste

Directions for Cooking:

1. Place all ingredients in the Instant Pot and mix well.
2. Close the lid and press the manual button. Cook on high for 35 minutes.
3. Do natural pressure release to open the lid.
4. Serve and enjoy.

Nutrition information:

Calories per serving: 656; Carbohydrates: 85.4g; Protein: 45.5g; Fat: 18.4g; Sugar: 75.1g; Sodium: 1263mg

Instant Pot Poultry Recipes

136.   Thai Green Chicken Curry
(Servings: 6 , Cooking time: 15 minutes)

Ingredients:

- 3 tablespoons Thai green curry paste
- 1 cup coconut milk
- 1 teaspoon coriander powder
- ½ teaspoon cumin powder
- 1-pound chicken breasts, bones removed and cut into chunks
- ¼ cup chicken broth
- 2 tablespoons fish sauce
- 1 tablespoon brown sugar
- 1 tablespoon lime juice
- 4 lime leaves, crushed
- ½ cup bamboo shoots, sliced
- ½ cup onion, cubed
- Salt and pepper to taste
- 1 cup green bell pepper
- 1 cup zucchini, sliced
- ¼ cup Thai basil leaves

Nutrition information:

Calories per serving: 211; Carbohydrates:9 g;
Protein:16 g; Fat: 12g; Sugar: 7g; Sodium: 970mg

Directions for Cooking:

1. Press the Sauté button on the Instant Pot. Place the Thai green curry paste and the coconut milk. Stir until the mixture bubbles. Stir in the coriander and cumin powder and cook for 30 seconds.
2. Stir in the chicken and coconut broth. Season with fish sauce, brown sugar, lime juice, bamboo shoots, lime leaves, and onion. Season with salt and pepper to taste.
3. Close Instant Pot, press the Manual button, choose high settings, and set time to 10 minutes.
4. Once done cooking, do a QPR. Open the lid and press the Sauté button. Stir in the green bell pepper, zucchini, and basil leaves. Allow to simmer for at least 5 minutes to cook the vegetables.
5. Serve and enjoy.

---

137.   Chinese Take-out General Tso's Chicken
(Servings: 6, Cooking time: 15 minutes)

Ingredients:

- 3 pounds chicken breasts, cut into chunks
- 1 cup potato starch
- 2 eggs, beaten
- 2 tablespoons peanut oil
- 2 tablespoons sesame seeds
- 1 tablespoon grated ginger root
- 1 tablespoon garlic, minced
- ½ cup chicken stock
- ¼ cup rice vinegar
- ¼ cup brown sugar
- ¼ cup Shaoxing wine
- ¼ cup soy sauce
- 1 teaspoon pure sesame oil
- 2 teaspoon sambal oelek

Directions for Cooking:

1. In a plastic bag, place the chicken and potato starch. Dip the chicken into the egg mixture then set aside.
2. Press the Sauté button on the Instant Pot and add oil. Place the dredged chicken pieces and sear until the chicken becomes lightly brown and puffy. Stir in the sesame seeds.
3. Stir in the rest of the ingredients and give a good stir.
4. Close Instant Pot, press the button, choose high settings, and set time to 10 minutes.
5. Once done cooking, do a QPR.
6. Serve with rice and enjoy.

Nutrition information:

Calories per serving: 549; Carbohydrates: 18.2g; Protein: 52.7g; Fat: 33.3g; Sugar: 11g; Sodium: 373mg

---

138.   Best Instant Pot Chicken Breast

(Servings: 4, Cooking time: 10 minutes)

Ingredients:

- 1 teaspoon dried Italian herb mix
- ½ teaspoon paprika
- ½ teaspoon ground coriander
- ½ teaspoon ground ginger
- ½ teaspoon ground garlic powder
- Salt and pepper to taste
- 2 pounds chicken breast
- 2 tablespoons olive oil
- 1 cup chicken stock

Directions for Cooking:

1. In a mixing bowl, combine the Italian herb mix, paprika, coriander, ginger, garlic, salt and pepper. Sprinkle over the chicken breasts.

2. Press the Sauté button on the Instant Pot and heat the oil. Sauté the chicken breasts for 3 minutes on each side until lightly brown. Set aside.

3. Place a trivet or a steamer in the Instant Pot and pour the chicken stock. Place the chicken back on the steamer.

4. Close Instant Pot, press the Steam button, choose high settings, and set time to 5 minutes.

5. Once done cooking, do natural pressure release.

6. Serve and enjoy.

Nutrition information:

Calories per serving:282; Carbohydrates: 2g; Protein: 35g; Fat: 13g; Sugar: 0.3g; Sodium: 202mg

---

139.   Hawaiian Chicken Instant Pot

(Servings: 9, Cooking time: 15 minutes)

Ingredients:

- 2 tablespoons coconut oil
- 4 ½ pounds boneless chicken thighs
- 2 cups chopped onion
- 4 cloves of garlic, minced
- 2 cups red bell pepper, chopped
- 1 cup pineapple chunks
- 1 ¼ cup pineapple juice
- ¾ cup soy sauce
- 2 tablespoons apple cider vinegar
- 1 cup dark brown sugar
- 2 tablespoons cornstarch + 3 tablespoons water

Directions for Cooking:

1. Press the Sauté button on the Instant Pot and heat the oil.

2. Stir in the chicken, onion, and garlic. Continue stirring until the chicken turns lightly golden.

3. Add the bell pepper, pineapple chunks, pineapple juice, soy sauce, apple cider vinegar, and dark sugar.

4. Close Instant Pot, press the Manual button, choose high settings, and set time to 10 minutes.

5. Once done cooking, do a QPR.

Nutrition information:
Calories per serving:703; Carbohydrates: 32.1g; Protein: 52.9g; Fat: 40.1g; Sugar: 12.4g; Sodium: 1293mg

6. Open the lid and press the Sauté button. Pour the cornstarch slurry and stir until the sauce thickens.
7. Serve and enjoy.

140. Honey Bourbon Chicken
(Servings: 9, Cooking time: 15 minutes)

Ingredients:

- 1 tablespoon oil
- ¾ cup onion, chopped
- 3 cloves of garlic, minced
- 2 pounds chicken, cut into bite-sized pieces
- 3 tablespoons tomato paste
- ½ cup honey
- 1/3 cup soy sauce
- ¼ cup water
- ½ teaspoon smoked paprika
- ½ teaspoon pepper
- 2 tablespoons cornstarch + 3 tablespoons water

Nutrition information:
Calories per serving:326; Carbohydrates: 20.4; Protein: 19.1g; Fat: 18.4g; Sugar: 8.2g; Sodium: 289mg

Directions for Cooking:

1. Press the Sauté button on the Instant Pot and heat the oil. Sauté the onion and garlic until fragrant.
2. Stir in the chicken until lightly golden. Add the tomato paste, honey, soy sauce, water, paprika, and pepper.
3. Close Instant Pot, press the Manual button, choose high settings, and set time to 10 minutes.
4. Once done cooking, do a QPR.
5. Open the lid and press the Sauté button. Stir in the cornstarch slurry and allow to simmer until the sauce thickens.
6. Serve and enjoy.

141. Creamy Tuscan Garlic Chicken
(Servings: 4, Cooking time: 15 minutes)

Ingredients:

- 2 tablespoons olive oil
- 2 pounds skinless chicken breasts, halved and pounded
- 4 cloves of garlic, minced
- 1 tablespoon Italian seasoning
- 1 teaspoon salt
- 3/4 cup chicken stock
- ¾ cup heavy cream
- ¾ cup parmesan cheese

Directions for Cooking:

1. Press the Sauté button on the Instant Pot and sear the chicken breasts on all sides.
2. Stir in the garlic, Italian seasoning, and salt.
3. Pour in the chicken stock and the rest of the ingredients.
4. Close Instant Pot, press the Manual button, choose high settings, and set time to 10 minutes.

- ½ cup sun-dried tomato

Nutrition information:
Calories per serving: 533; Carbohydrates: 10.8g;
Protein: 59.9g; Fat: 26.5g; Sugar: 4g; Sodium:
1267mg

5. Once done cooking, do a QPR.
6. Serve and enjoy.

---

142. Chili Lime Chicken Thighs
(Servings: 4, Cooking time: 20 minutes)

Ingredients:

- 2 tablespoons olive oil
- 3 cloves of garlic, minced
- 1 teaspoon cumin
- 1 teaspoon chili powder
- 4 chicken thighs
- Juice from 1 lime
- 1 cup chicken stock
- Salt and pepper to taste
- 2 tablespoons cornstarch + 3 tablespoons water
- ¼ cup fresh cilantro, chopped

Nutrition information:
Calories per serving: 523; Carbohydrates: 5.9g;
Protein: 34.2g; Fat: 39.7g; Sugar: 1.8g; Sodium:
264mg

Directions for Cooking:

1. Press the Sauté button on the Instant Pot and heat the oil. Sauté the garlic, cumin, and chili powder until fragrant.
2. Stir in the chicken thighs and continue stirring until all sides are lightly golden.
3. Add the lime juice and chicken stock. Season with salt and pepper to taste.
4. Close Instant Pot, press the Manual button, choose high settings, and set time to 10 minutes.
5. Once done cooking, do a QPR.
6. Open the lid and stir in the cornstarch slurry and cilantro. Allow to simmer until the sauce thickens.
7. Serve and enjoy.

---

143. One Pot Peruvian Chicken
(Servings: 9 , Cooking time: 20 minutes)

Ingredients:

- 3 pounds chicken
- 3 tablespoons paprika
- 2 tablespoons ground cumin
- 1 ½ tablespoons minced garlic
- 2 tablespoons lime juice
- 4 tablespoons canola oil
- Salt and pepper to taste
- ¼ cup chopped cilantro
- ½ cup water
- 5 jalapenos, chopped
- 1 tablespoon lime juice

Directions for Cooking:

1. Place all ingredients in the Instant Pot. Mix all ingredients until well-combined.
2. Close Instant Pot, press the Manual button, choose high settings, and set time to 20 minutes.
3. Once done cooking, do a QPR.
4. Serve and enjoy.

Nutrition information:

Calories per serving: 397; Carbohydrates: 3.2g;
Protein: 28.9g; Fat: 29.6g; Sugar: 0.6g; Sodium:
111mg

144. Whole 30 Chicken Cacciatore
(Servings: 4 , Cooking time: 15 minutes)

Ingredients:

- 1 tablespoon oil
- 1 ¼ pounds chicken thighs, cut into large chunks
- 1 onion, diced
- 3 teaspoons garlic, minced
- 1 tablespoon Italian seasoning
- 2 bell peppers, cut into strips
- 1 can crushed tomatoes
- Salt and pepper to taste

Nutrition information:

Calories per serving: 199; Carbohydrates: 6g;
Protein: 28g; Fat: 6g; Sugar: 3g; Sodium: 711mg

Directions for Cooking:

1. Press the Sauté button on the Instant Pot and stir in the chicken, onion, and garlic until fragrant.
2. Add the Italian seasoning and the rest of the ingredients.
3. Close Instant Pot, press the Manual button, choose high settings, and set time to 10 minutes.
4. Once done cooking, do a QPR.
5. Serve and enjoy.

145. Instant Pot Chicken and Dumplings
(Servings: 4 , Cooking time: 20 minutes)

Ingredients:

- 2 pounds chicken breasts, cut into cubes
- 2 cloves of garlic, minced
- 1 cup chopped onion
- 1 cup chopped celery
- 1 teaspoon dried thyme
- 1 tablespoon bouillon
- 2 cups frozen vegetables (peas and carrots)
- 3 cups chicken stock
- 2 cans cream of chicken
- Salt and pepper to taste
- 1 can Southern Homestyle biscuits
- ¼ cup parsley, chopped

Nutrition information:

Calories per serving:739; Carbohydrates: 51.2g;
Protein: 63.8g; Fat: 29.6g; Sugar: 8.3g; Sodium:
1165mg

Directions for Cooking:

1. Press the Sauté button on the Instant Pot and stir in the chicken, garlic, onion, celery, and thyme. Stir constantly and allow the onions to sweat.
2. Stir in bouillon, vegetables, stock, and cream of chicken. Stir in the cream of chicken and season with salt and pepper to taste. Allow to simmer for a few minutes.
3. Add the biscuits on top.
4. Close Instant Pot, press the Manual button, choose high settings, and set time to 15 minutes.
5. Once done cooking, do a QPR.
6. Garnish with parsley.
7. Serve and enjoy.

INSTANT POT POULTRY RECIPES

146.   Instant Pot Mississippi Chicken
(Servings: 6, Cooking time: 20 minutes)

Ingredients:

- 3 pounds chicken thighs
- ½ cup chicken broth,
- ½ jar pepperoncini, not drained
- 1 packet brown gravy mix
- 1 packet ranch dressing
- ½ stick butter
- Salt and pepper to taste
- 1 cup rice
- 2 cups water

Nutrition information:

Calories per serving: 714; Carbohydrates: 13.1g; Protein: 46.7g; Fat: 54.3g; Sugar: 0.6g; Sodium: 571mg

Directions for Cooking:

1. Place all ingredients in the Instant Pot except for the rice and water. Give a good stir.
2. Place a trivet on top of the chicken. In a heat-proof dish, place the rice and water. Place the bowl on the trivet.
3. Close Instant Pot, press the Manual button, choose high settings, and set time to 20 minutes.
4. Once done cooking, do a QPR.
5. Take the bowl of cooked rice and the trivet.
6. Ladle the chicken on to cooked rice.
7. Serve and enjoy.

---

147.   Instant Pot Butter Chicken
(Servings: 2, Cooking time: 20 minutes)

Ingredients:

- 4 ounces butter, cut into cubes
- 1-pound boneless chicken breast, cut into cubes
- 6 cloves of garlic, minced
- 2 teaspoons grated ginger
- 1 teaspoon turmeric powder
- ½ teaspoon cayenne pepper
- 1 teaspoon paprika
- 1 teaspoon garam masala
- 1 teaspoon ground cumin
- 1 can diced tomatoes
- 4 ounces heavy cream
- Salt to taste
- ¼ cup chopped cilantro

Directions for Cooking:

1. Press the Sauté button on the Instant Pot and heat the butter.
2. Stir in chicken breast, garlic, ginger, turmeric powder, cayenne pepper, paprika, garam masala, and cumin. Stir for 3 minutes until well-combined,
3. Add the diced tomatoes and heavy cream. Season with salt and pepper to taste.
4. Close Instant Pot, press the Manual button, choose high settings, and set time to 15 minutes.
5. Once done cooking, do a QPR.
6. Garnish with chopped cilantro
7. Serve and enjoy.

Nutrition information:

Calories per serving:918; Carbohydrates: 10.6g; Protein: 54.6g; Fat: 73.7g; Sugar: 4.4g; Sodium: 703mg

148.   Chinese Takeout Sweet and Sour Chicken
(Servings: 4, Cooking time: 15 minutes)

Ingredients:

- 2 pounds chicken breasts
- 1 cup potato starch
- ¼ teaspoon Chinese five-spice powder
- Salt and pepper to taste
- 3 tablespoons vegetable oil
- 2 cloves of garlic, minced
- 1 onion, chopped
- ½ cup water
- ¾ cup sugar
- ½ cup ketchup
- ¾ cup apple cider vinegar
- ¼ cup soy sauce

Nutrition information:

Calories per serving: 696; Carbohydrates: 46.8g; Protein: 50.7g; Fat: 34.5g; Sugar: 16.4g; Sodium: 663mg

Directions for Cooking:

1. In a mixing bowl, combine the chicken, potato starch, and Chinese five spice powder. Season with salt and pepper to taste.
2. Press the Sauté button on the Instant Pot and heat the oil. Fry the chicken on all sides until lightly brown.
3. Stir in the garlic and onion until fragrant.
4. Add the rest of the ingredients.
5. Close Instant Pot, press the Manual button, choose high settings, and set time to 10 minutes.
6. Once done cooking, do a QPR.
7. Serve and enjoy.

149.   Instant Pot Honey Garlic Chicken
(Servings: 3, Cooking time: 20 minutes)

Ingredients:

- 1 tablespoon olive oil
- 3 chicken breasts, cut into chunks
- Salt and pepper to taste
- 6 cloves of garlic, minced
- 1/3 cup honey
- 1 tablespoon soy sauce
- ¾ cup water
- 1 teaspoon lemon juice
- 1 tablespoon cornstarch + 2 tablespoons cold water

Nutrition information:

Calories per serving:683; Carbohydrates: 35.8g; Protein: 61.5g; Fat: 32.5g; Sugar: 21g; Sodium: 265mg

Directions for Cooking:

1. Press the Sauté button on the Instant Pot.
2. Heat the oil and stir in the chicken. Season with salt and pepper to taste and continue stirring until lightly golden. Add garlic until fragrant.
3. Stir in the honey, soy sauce, water, and lemon juice.
4. Close Instant Pot, press the Manual button, choose high settings, and set time to 15 minutes.
5. Once done cooking, do a QPR.
6. Open the lid and press the Sauté button. Stir in the cornstarch slurry and allow to simmer until the sauce thickens.
7. Serve and enjoy.

INSTANT POT POULTRY RECIPES

150.   Instant Pot Orange Chicken
(Servings: 4, Cooking time: 20 minutes)

Ingredients:

- 4 boneless chicken breasts, cubed
- ¼ cup water
- ½ cup orange juice
- ¼ cup brown sugar
- 1/3 cup soy sauce
- 2 tablespoons ketchup
- 1 tablespoon apple cider vinegar
- 2 cloves of garlic, minced
- ½ teaspoon ground ginger
- Salt and pepper to taste
- 2 tablespoons cornstarch + 3 tablespoons water

Directions for Cooking:

1. Place all ingredients in the Instant Pot except for the cornstarch mixture.
2. Close Instant Pot, press the Manual button, choose high settings, and set time to 20 minutes.
3. Once done cooking, do a QPR.
4. Open the lid and press the Sauté button. Stir in the cornstarch slurry and allow to simmer for the sauce to thicken.
5. Serve and enjoy.

Nutrition information:

Calories per serving: 431; Carbohydrates: 26.8g; Protein: 60.2g; Fat: 9.7g; Sugar: 12.6g; Sodium: 486mg

---

151.   One Pot Chicken Curry
(Servings: 6, Cooking time: 15 minutes)

Ingredients:

- 6 chicken drumsticks
- 1 onion, chopped
- 2 cloves of garlic, minced
- 1 thumb-size ginger
- 1 tablespoon curry powder or garam masala
- ½ cup chicken broth
- 1cup heavy cream

Directions for Cooking:

1. Place all ingredients in the Instant Pot and give a good stir.
2. Close Instant Pot, press the Manual button, choose high settings, and set time to 15 minutes.
3. Once done cooking, do a QPR.
4. Serve and enjoy.

Nutrition information:

Calories per serving: 270; Carbohydrates: 3.4g; Protein: 30.3g; Fat: 15.2g; Sugar: 1.4g; Sodium: 214mg

---

INSTANT POT POULTRY RECIPES

152.   Instant Pot Ranch Chicken
(Servings: 4, Cooking time: 17 minutes)

Ingredients:

- 1 tablespoon olive oil
- 2 pounds boneless chicken breasts
- 2 tablespoon taco seasoning
- 1 cup coconut cream
- ½ teaspoon garlic powder
- ½ teaspoon onion powder
- ½ teaspoon black pepper
- Salt and pepper to taste
- 1 tablespoon red wine vinegar
- ¾ cup chicken broth
- 1 cup parsley, chopped

Directions for Cooking:

1. Press the Sauté button on the Instant Pot and heat the oil.
2. Stir in the chicken and season with the taco seasoning. Keep stirring for 2 minutes.
3. Add the rest of the ingredients except for the parsley.
4. Close Instant Pot, press the Manual button, choose high settings, and set time to 15 minutes.
5. Once done cooking, do a QPR.
6. Garnish with chopped parsley.
7. Serve and enjoy.

Nutrition information:

Calories per serving:322; Carbohydrates: 3.5g; Protein: 28.6g; Fat: 20.9g; Sugar: 1.3g; Sodium: 229mg

---

153.   Instant Pot Gingered Orange Chicken
(Servings: 2, Cooking time: 20 minutes)

Ingredients:

- ¼ cup chicken broth
- 1/3 cup soy sauce
- ½ cup rice vinegar
- ½ cup honey
- 1 tablespoon ginger
- 1 teaspoon red pepper, crushed
- 2 cloves of garlic, minced
- 1 peeled orange, segmented and seeds removed
- A dash of orange zest
- 2 large chicken breasts

Directions for Cooking:

1. Place all ingredients in the Instant Pot and give a good stir.
2. Close Instant Pot, press the Manual button, choose high settings, and set time to 20 minutes.
3. Once done cooking, do a QPR.
4. Serve and enjoy.

Nutrition information:

Calories per serving: 1127; Carbohydrates: 97.1g; Protein: 103.2g; Fat: 34.9g; Sugar: 46.3g; Sodium: 891mg

---

154.   Instant Pot Cashew Chicken
(Servings: 2, Cooking time: 20 minutes)

Ingredients:

- 2 chicken breasts
- ½ cup chicken stock
- 2 tablespoons soy sauce
- 2 tablespoons rice vinegar
- 2 tablespoons hoisin sauce
- 1 tablespoon honey
- 2 teaspoons sesame oil
- 1 teaspoon fresh ginger, grated
- 1 clove of garlic, minced
- Salt and pepper to taste
- ½ red bell pepper, diced
- 1 ½ cups broccoli cut into florets
- 2 tablespoons cornstarch + 3 tablespoons water
- ½ cup whole cashews

Nutrition information:

Calories per serving:1090; Carbohydrates: 46g; Protein: 73.7g; Fat: 69.4g; Sugar: 24g; Sodium: 971mg

Directions for Cooking:

1. Place the chicken breasts, chicken stock, soy sauce, rice vinegar, hoisin sauce, honey, sesame oil, ginger, and garlic in the Instant Pot. Give a good stir.
2. Close Instant Pot, press the Manual button, choose high settings, and set time to 15 minutes.
3. Once done cooking, do a QPR.
4. Open the lid and press the Sauté button. Stir in the red peppers and broccoli florets. Allow to simmer until the vegetables are cooked through. Stir in the cornstarch slurry and stir until the sauce thickens.
5. Garnish with cashew nuts on top.
6. Serve and enjoy.

155.   Taiwanese Chicken San Bei Ji
(Servings: 4, Cooking time: 20 minutes)

Ingredients:

- ¼ cup sesame oil
- 5 dried chilies
- ¼ cup garlic, smashed
- 2 tablespoons sliced ginger
- 2 pounds chicken breasts, cut into half
- ¼ cup soy sauce
- ¼ cup rice wine
- Salt to taste
- ¼ cup chopped Thai basil
- 1 tablespoon cornstarch + 2 tablespoons water

Nutrition information:

Calories per serving: 596; Carbohydrates: 11.1g; Protein: 50.1g; Fat: 39.1g; Sugar: 5.2g; Sodium: 459mg

Directions for Cooking:

1. Place in the Instant Pot the sesame oil, dried chilies, garlic, ginger, chicken, soy sauce, and rice wine.
2. Close Instant Pot, press the Manual button, choose high settings, and set time to 15 minutes.
3. Once done cooking, do a QPR.
4. Open the lid and press the Sauté button. Stir in the Thai basil and cornstarch slurry and allow to simmer until the sauce thickens.
5. Serve and enjoy.

INSTANT POT POULTRY RECIPES

156. Instant Pot Teriyaki Chicken
(Servings: 4 , Cooking time: 25 minutes)

Ingredients:

- 1 cup soy sauce
- 1 cup brown sugar
- ½ cup ketchup
- 1 teaspoon ground ginger
- 2 pounds chicken breasts
- 1 tablespoon cornstarch + 2 tablespoons water

Nutrition information:

Calories per serving:816; Carbohydrates: 78.3g; Protein: 52.5g; Fat: 32.5g; Sugar: 25.2g; Sodium: 1395mg

Directions for Cooking:

1. Place the soy sauce, brown sugar, ketchup, ginger, and chicken breasts in the Instant Pot and give a good stir.
2. Close Instant Pot, press the Manual button, choose high settings, and set time to 20 minutes.
3. Once done cooking, do a QPR.
4. Open the lid and press the Sauté button. Stir in the cornstarch slurry and allow to simmer until the sauce thickens.
5. Serve and enjoy.

157. Honey Sesame Chicken
(Servings: 6, Cooking time: 16 minutes)

Ingredients:

- 2 tablespoons olive oil
- 1 onion, diced
- 4 cloves of garlic, minced
- 3 pounds chicken breasts
- 2/3 cup soy sauce
- 1/3 cup ketchup
- 1 tablespoon sesame oil
- 2/3 cup honey
- ½ teaspoon red pepper flakes
- 2 tablespoons cornstarch + 3 tablespoons water
- Green onions for garnish
- 2 tablespoons sesame seeds for garnish

Nutrition information:

Calories per serving: 707; Carbohydrates: 49.1g; Protein: 50.9g; Fat: 34.6g; Sugar: 26.3g; Sodium: 702mg

Directions for Cooking:

1. Press the Sauté button on the Instant Pot and heat the oil. Stir in the onion and garlic until fragrant.
2. Add the chicken breasts. Allow to sear on all sides for three minutes.
3. Stir in the soy sauce, ketchup, sesame oil, honey, and red pepper flakes.
4. Close Instant Pot, press the Manual button, choose high settings, and set time to 10 minutes.
5. Once done cooking, do a QPR.
6. Open the lid and press the Sauté button. Stir in the cornstarch slurry and allow to simmer until the sauce thickens.
7. Garnish with green onions and sesame seeds last.
8. Serve and enjoy.

158.   Spicy Chicken Rice Meal
(Servings: 6, Cooking time: 25 minutes)

Ingredients:

- 1 tablespoon oil
- 1 tablespoon minced garlic
- 1 onion, chopped
- 2 chicken breasts, cut into cubes
- 1 tablespoon chili powder
- 1 teaspoon cayenne pepper
- 1 cup long grain rice
- 2 cups prepared salsa
- 1 ½ cups water
- Salt and pepper to taste
- 1 can beans
- 1 cup corn
- cilantro

Directions for Cooking:

1. Press the Sauté button on the Instant Pot and heat the oil. Stir in the garlic and onions and cook until fragrant. Add n the chicken breasts and season with chili powder and cayenne powder.
2. Stir in the rice, salsa, and water. Season with salt and pepper to taste.
3. Close Instant Pot, press the Manual button, choose high settings, and cook for 20 minutes.
4. Once done cooking, do a QPR.
5. Open the lid and stir in the beans, corn, and cilantro.
6. Serve and enjoy.

Nutrition information:

Calories per serving: 444; Carbohydrates: 53.9g;
Protein: 27.1g; Fat: 13.8g; Sugar: 5g; Sodium: 759mg

---

159.   Instant Pot Chicken and Corn Soup
(Servings: 2, Cooking time: 15 minutes)

Ingredients:

- 1 tablespoon oil
- 2 chicken breasts, cut in half
- 1 tablespoon garlic, minced
- 1 tablespoon chili powder
- Salt and pepper to taste
- 1 cup corn
- 4 cups chicken broth
- 1 cup cilantro, chopped

Directions for Cooking:

1. Press the Sauté button on the Instant Pot and heat the oil.
2. Stir in the chicken, garlic, and chili powder. Stir to combine everything.
3. Season with salt and pepper to taste.
4. Add the corn and chicken broth.
5. Close Instant Pot, press the Manual button, choose high settings, and set time to 15 minutes.
6. Once done cooking, do a QPR.
7. Open the lid and stir in the cilantro.
8. Serve and enjoy.

Nutrition information:

Calories per serving: 1649; Carbohydrates: 71.1g;
Protein: 173.5g; Fat: 71.3g; Sugar: 2g; Sodium:
2309mg

INSTANT POT POULTRY RECIPES

160. Instant Pot Hawaiian Chicken
(Servings: 9, Cooking time: 15 minutes)

Ingredients:

- 2 tablespoons coconut oil
- 4 cloves of garlic, minced
- 1 onion, chopped
- 4 ½ pounds skinless chicken thighs
- 2 cups yellow corn, cut
- 2 cups red bell pepper, chopped
- 2 cups yellow bell pepper, chopped
- 1 can pineapple chunks
- 1 ¼ cups pineapple juice
- ¾ cup soy sauce
- 2 tablespoons apple cider vinegar
- 1 cup dark brown sugar
- 2 tablespoons cornstarch + 3 tablespoons water

Nutrition information:

Calories per serving: 855; Carbohydrates: 76.8g; Protein: 57.8g; Fat: 35.6g; Sugar: 28g; Sodium: 1306mg

Directions for Cooking:

1. Press the Sauté button and heat the oil. Stir the garlic and onion until fragrant.
2. Stir in the chicken for three minutes until lightly golden.
3. Stir in the corn, bell peppers, pineapple chunks, pineapple juice, soy sauce, apple cider vinegar, and sugar.
4. Close Instant Pot, press the Manual button, choose high settings, and set time to 10 minutes.
5. Once done cooking, do a QPR.
6. Open the lid and press the Sauté button. Stir in the cornstarch slurry and allow to simmer until the sauce thickens.
7. Serve and enjoy.

---

161. Greek Chicken Rice
(Servings: 4 , Cooking time: 20 minutes)

Ingredients:

- 1 ½ cups uncooked white rice
- 1 cup chicken stock
- A dash of lemon zest
- 4 chicken breasts, cubed
- ½ cup chicken stock
- 1 tablespoon oregano
- ½ teaspoon rosemary
- ½ teaspoon thyme
- 3 cloves of garlic, minced
- Juice from 1 lemon, freshly squeezed

Nutrition information:

Calories per serving: 432; Carbohydrates: 60g; Protein: 31g; Fat: 4g; Sugar: 1g; Sodium: 264mg

Directions for Cooking:

1. Prepare the rice by placing the rice, chicken stock, and lemon zest in a heat-proof dish that will fit inside the Instant Pot. Set aside.
2. Press the Sauté button on the Instant Pot and Add the rest of the ingredients.
3. Place a trivet on top of the chicken and place the dish with the prepared rice.
4. Close Instant Pot, press the Manual button, choose high settings, and set time to 20 minutes.
5. Once done cooking, do a QPR.
6. Serve rice with chicken and enjoy.

162. Instant Pot Butter Chicken

(Servings: 4, Cooking time: 15 minutes)

Ingredients:

- 2 tablespoons coconut oil
- 4 teaspoon garlic paste
- 5 teaspoon tomato paste
- 1 cup tomato pasta
- 4 tablespoons garam masala
- ½ teaspoon coriander
- ½ teaspoon cumin
- 1 tablespoon smoked paprika
- 1 teaspoon turmeric
- 2-pound chicken thighs
- 1 cup chicken stock
- 1 cup milk
- 2 tablespoons cornstarch + 3 tablespoons water

Directions for Cooking:

1. Press the Sauté button on the Instant Pot and heat the oil.
2. Stir in the garlic paste, tomato paste, pasta, garam masala, coriander, cumin, smoked paprika, and turmeric. Toast for a minute until fragrant.
3. Place the chicken and stir for 2 minutes.
4. Add the chicken stock and milk.
5. Close Instant Pot, press the Manual button, choose high settings, and set time to 10 minutes.
6. Once done cooking, do a QPR.
7. Open the lid and stir in the cornstarch slurry. Allow to simmer until the sauce thickens.
8. Serve and enjoy.

Nutrition information:

Calories per serving: 678; Carbohydrates: 17.8g; Protein: 43.1g; Fat: 47.8g; Sugar: 7.4g; Sodium: 464mg

---

163. Honey Mustard Curry Chicken

(Servings: 4 , Cooking time: 20 minutes)

Ingredients:

- 1 tablespoon olive oil
- 4 tablespoons butter
- 1 teaspoon onion, minced
- 4 boneless skinless chicken breasts
- Salt and pepper to taste
- ½ cup honey
- ¼ cup Dijon mustard
- 1 ½ teaspoon curry powder
- ½ cup water

Directions for Cooking:

1. Press the Sauté button on the Instant Pot and heat the oil and butter.
2. Sauté the onion until fragrant and add the chicken. Season with salt and pepper to taste.
3. Stir in the rest of the ingredients.
4. Close Instant Pot, press the Manual button, choose high settings, and set time to 15 minutes.
5. Once done cooking, do a QPR.
6. Serve and enjoy.

Nutrition information:

Calories per serving:586; Carbohydrates: 43.6g; Protein: 54.9g; Fat: 21.9g; Sugar: 38g; Sodium: 891mg

INSTANT POT POULTRY RECIPES

164.   Instant Pot Simple Chicken Dinner
(Servings: 4, Cooking time: 15 minutes)

Ingredients:

- 1 can crushed pineapple
- 2 pounds boneless chicken breasts
- 3 cans fire-roasted tomatoes
- Salt and pepper to taste

Nutrition information:

Calories per serving: 396; Carbohydrates: 29.9g; Protein: 53.1g; Fat: 6.3g; Sugar: 13.2g; Sodium: 391mg

Directions for Cooking:

1. Place all ingredients in the Instant Pot. Give a good stir.
2. Close Instant Pot, press the Manual button, choose high settings, and set time to 15 minutes.
3. Once done cooking, do a QPR.
4. Serve and enjoy.

---

165.   Instant Pot Chicken Pot Pie
(Servings: 4, Cooking time: 20 minutes)

Ingredients:

- 4 chicken breasts
- 1 can cream of chicken soup
- 1 cup milk
- 1 cup chicken broth
- ½ onion, chopped
- 4 potatoes, peeled and diced
- 1 bag frozen mixed vegetables
- ½ cup celery, chopped
- ¼ teaspoon poultry seasoning
- Salt and pepper to taste
- Canned biscuits

Directions for Cooking:

1. In the Instant Pot, place the chicken, chicken soup, milk, chicken broth, onion, potatoes, vegetables, celery, and poultry seasoning. Season with salt and pepper to taste.
2. Close Instant Pot, press the Manual button, choose high settings, and set time to 20 minutes.
3. Once done cooking, do a QPR.
4. Open the lid and serve with biscuits on top.
5. Serve and enjoy.

Nutrition information:

Calories per serving:1028; Carbohydrates: 80.9g; Protein: 85.7g; Fat: 38.8g; Sugar: 7g; Sodium: 1086mg

---

INSTANT POT POULTRY RECIPES

166. Creamy Salsa Chicken
(Servings: 5, Cooking time: 15 minutes)

Ingredients:

- 2 ½ pounds chicken breasts
- ½ cup chicken broth
- 4-ounce cream cheese
- ½ cup cottage cheese
- 1 cup salsa
- 2 teaspoon taco seasoning
- ¼ cup shredded cheese

Nutrition information:

Calories per serving: 559; Carbohydrates: 5.8g; Protein: 58.8g; Fat: 32.1g; Sugar: 3.5g; Sodium: 906mg

Directions for Cooking:

1. Place all ingredients in the Instant Pot except for the cheese.
2. Close Instant Pot, press the Manual button, choose high settings, and set time to 15 minutes.
3. Once done cooking, do a QPR.
4. Open the lid and garnish with cheese on top.
5. Serve and enjoy.

167. Spicy Chicken Korma
(Servings: 2, Cooking time: 20 minutes)

Ingredients:

- 2 tablespoons ghee
- ½ cup onion, chopped
- ¼ cup red pepper, chopped
- 2 tablespoons garlic, minced
- 1 ½ chicken breasts
- 2 tablespoons chili paste
- 2 tablespoons spicy red curry paste
- 2 tablespoons paprika
- 1 tablespoon garam masala
- ½ tablespoon coriander
- 3 cardamom pods
- 1 can diced tomatoes
- 1 cup Greek yogurt
- Salt and pepper to taste
- Fresh cilantro for garnish

Directions for Cooking:

1. Press the Sauté button on the Instant Pot and heat the ghee. Stir in the onion red pepper, and garlic until fragrant. Stir in chicken breasts.
2. Stir in the rest of the ingredients except for the cilantro.
3. Close Instant Pot, press the Manual button, choose high settings, and set time to 15 minutes.
4. Once done cooking, do a QPR.
5. Open the lid and garnish with cilantro.
6. Serve and enjoy.

Nutrition information:

Calories per serving: 488; Carbohydrates: 22.8g; Protein: 50.8g; Fat: 34.9g; Sugar: 8.6g; Sodium: 580mg

INSTANT POT POULTRY RECIPES

168. Balsamic Ginger Chicken
(Servings: 8, Cooking time: 15 minutes)

Ingredients:

- 8 chicken thighs
- 1/3 cup balsamic vinegar
- 3 tablespoons mustard
- 2 tablespoons ginger garlic paste
- 4 cloves of garlic, minced
- 2-inches fresh ginger root
- 4 tablespoons honey
- Salt and pepper to taste

Directions for Cooking:

1. Place all ingredients in the Instant Pot. Stir to combine everything.
2. Close Instant Pot, press the Manual button, choose high settings, and set time to 15 minutes.
3. Once done cooking, do a QPR.
4. Serve and enjoy.

Nutrition information:
Calories per serving: 477; Carbohydrates:12.5g; Protein: 32.4g; Fat: 32.9g; Sugar: 10.5g; Sodium: 244mg

---

169. Buffalo Chicken Wings
(Servings: 8, Cooking time: 20 minutes)

Ingredients:

- 4 pounds chicken wings
- 2 teaspoon salt
- ½ teaspoon garlic powder
- 1 teaspoon black pepper
- ½ teaspoon cayenne pepper
- 1 tablespoon smoked paprika
- 1 cup red hot sauce
- 1 stick butter

Nutrition information:
Calories per serving:439; Carbohydrates: 2.1g; Protein: 51.2g; Fat: 23.8g; Sugar: 0.8g; Sodium: 908mg

Directions for Cooking:

1. In a mixing bowl, combine the chicken wings, salt, garlic powder, black pepper, cayenne pepper, and paprika. Place in the fridge to marinate for at least 2 hours.
2. Press the Sauté button on the Instant Pot and stir in the chicken. Cook for at least 3 minutes until the chicken lightly turns golden.
3. Stir in the hot sauce and butter.
4. Close Instant Pot, press the Manual button, choose high settings, and set time to 15 minutes.
5. Once done cooking, do a QPR.
6. Serve and enjoy.

170. Instant Pot Coq Au Vin Blanc
(Servings: 20, Cooking time: 6 minutes)

Ingredients:

- 6 chicken drumsticks
- Salt and pepper to taste
- 4 strips of bacon, diced
- 1 tablespoon minced garlic
- 2 cups leeks, diced
- 1 ½ cups baby carrots
- 2 cups mushrooms, slice
- 1 tablespoon tomato paste
- ¼ cup brandy
- 1 cup dry white wine
- 1 cup chicken broth
- 1 cup pearl onions
- Salt and pepper to taste
- 3 tablespoons butter
- 3 tablespoons cornstarch + 4 tablespoons water

Nutrition information:

Calories per serving:445; Carbohydrates: 14g;
Protein: 31g; Fat: 18g; Sugar: 6g; Sodium: 315mg

Directions for Cooking:

1. Season the chicken with salt and pepper to taste.
2. Press the Sauté button on the Instant Pot and cook the bacon until the fat has rendered and it crispy. Take out from the Instant Pot and set aside.
3. Place the chicken in the Instant Pot including the garlic and leeks and sauté for three minutes.
4. Stir in carrots, mushrooms, tomato paste, brandy, white wine, chicken broth, and pearl onions. Season with salt and pepper to taste.
5. Close Instant Pot, press the Manual button, choose high settings, and set time to 15 minutes.
6. Once done cooking, do a QPR. Open the lid and press the Sauté button. Stir in the butter until it melts. Stir in the cornstarch slurry and allow to simmer until the sauce thickens.
7. Serve and enjoy.

171. Instant Pot Burrito Bowl
(Servings: 6, Cooking time: 20 minutes)

Ingredients:

- ½ cup uncooked brown rice
- ½ cup dry black beans
- 1 can tomatoes, drained
- 2 chicken breasts, sliced into 6 pieces
- 2 tablespoons garlic
- 2 tablespoons cumin
- 1 tablespoon onion powder
- 2 tablespoon chili powder
- 1 ½ cups chicken stock
- Salt and pepper
- 1 head Romaine lettuce
- 1 cup cheddar cheese
- 1 big avocado, pitted and sliced

Directions for Cooking:

1. In a heat-proof dish, place the brown rice, and black beans. Place a cup of water. Set aside.
2. In the instant pot, place the tomatoes, chicken breasts, garlic, cumin, onion powder, chili powder, and chicken stock. Season with salt and pepper to taste.
3. Place a trivet on the Instant Pot and place the bowl of rice on top.
4. Close Instant Pot, press the Manual button, choose high settings, and set time to 20 minutes.

- 1 cup green salsa

Nutrition information:
Calories per serving: 545; Carbohydrates: 43.1g;
Protein: 40.5g; Fat: 24.6g; Sugar: 12g; Sodium:
1646mg

5. Once done cooking, do a QPR.
6. Open the lid and take the bowl of rice. Remove the trivet.
7. Serve the rice with chicken, romaine lettuce, cheddar cheese, avocado, and green salsa.
8. Serve and enjoy.

---

172.   Instant Pot Korean Chicken
(Servings: 4, Cooking time: 25 minutes)

Ingredients:

- ½ cup gochujang paste
- ¼ cup hoisin sauce
- ¼ cup ketchup
- ¼ cup mirin
- ¼ cup soy sauce
- ¼ cup rice wine
- 1 tablespoon rice vinegar
- 2 pounds chicken thighs
- 2 tablespoons vegetable oil
- 1 tablespoon minced garlic
- 1 onion, chopped
- 1 cup chicken broth
- 2 teaspoons cornstarch + 3 teaspoons water

Nutrition information:
Calories per serving:817; Carbohydrates: 29.3g;
Protein: 55.1g; Fat: 53.7g; Sugar: 51.3g; Sodium:
1140mg

Directions for Cooking:

1. In a mixing bowl, combine the gochujang paste, hoisin sauce, ketchup, mirin, soy sauce, rice wine, rice vinegar, and chicken thighs. Allow to marinate overnight.
2. Press the Sauté button and heat the oil. Sauté the garlic and onion. Stir in the chicken and cook for 3 minutes. Stir in the chicken broth.
3. Close Instant Pot, press the Manual button, choose high settings, and set time to 15 minutes.
4. Once done cooking, do a QPR.
5. Open the lid and Add the cornstarch slurry. Press the Sauté button and allow the sauce to thicken.
6. Serve and enjoy.

---

173.   Chipotle Chicken Tacos
(Servings: 4, Cooking time: 20 minutes)

Ingredients:

- 2 pounds chicken breasts, chopped
- Salt and pepper to taste
- 1 tablespoon avocado oil
- 2 cloves of garlic, minced
- 1 onion, chopped
- 1 teaspoon oregano
- 1 tablespoon chipotle pepper
- ¼ cup chicken broth

Directions for Cooking:

1. Season the chicken breasts with salt and pepper to taste.
2. Press the Sauté button on the Instant Pot and heat the oil.
3. Sauté the garlic and onion until fragrant. Add the chicken breasts. Stir for 3 minutes

- ¼ cup lime juice
- 4 cassava tortillas
- 1 avocado, peeled and sliced
- 2 roman tomatoes, chopped
- 1 can black olives

Nutrition information:

Calories per serving: 657; Carbohydrates: 29.6g; Protein: 55.9g; Fat: 35.1g; Sugar: 4g; Sodium: 456mg

and add the oregano and chipotle pepper. Stir in the chicken broth and lime juice.

4. Close Instant Pot, press the Manual button, choose high settings, and set time to 15 minutes.
5. Once done cooking, do a QPR. Open the lid and take the chicken out.
6. Assemble the taco by placing the chicken on the tortillas. Garnish with avocado slices, tomatoes, and black olives.
7. Serve and enjoy.

---

174.   Chicken Tikka Masala
(Servings: 6 , Cooking time: 20 minutes)

Ingredients:

- 1 tablespoon butter
- 1 onion, chopped
- 4 cloves of garlic, minced
- 2 teaspoon grated ginger
- 1 teaspoon cumin
- 2 teaspoon turmeric
- ½ teaspoon garam masala
- ¼ teaspoon Indian chili powder
- ¼ teaspoon cardamom
- 1 ½ pounds chicken breasts, sliced
- 1 can diced tomatoes
- 3 cups chickpeas
- 2 carrots, peeled and sliced
- 1 can coconut milk

Directions for Cooking:

1. Press the Sauté button on the Instant Pot and melt the butter. Sauté the onion and garlic until fragrant. Add the cumin, turmeric, garam masala, chili powder, and cardamom. Toast until fragrant and Add the chicken breasts. Stir until the chicken is lightly brown. Stir in the rest of the ingredients.
2. Close Instant Pot, press the Manual button, choose high settings, and set time to 15 minutes.
3. Once done cooking, do a QPR.
4. Garnish with chopped green onions.
5. Serve and enjoy.

Nutrition information:

Calories per serving: 795; Carbohydrates: 72g; Protein: 46.7g; Fat: 37.8g; Sugar: 15g; Sodium: 165mg

175.   BBQ Pulled Chicken Sliders
(Servings: 6, Cooking time: 35 minutes)

Ingredients:

- 2 tablespoons butter
- 2 cloves of garlic
- 3 chicken breasts
- 1 cup chicken broth
- 1 cup BBQ sauce
- 24 slider buns, sliced

Directions for Cooking:

1. Press the Sauté button on the Instant Pot and melt the butter. Sauté the garlic until fragrant and stir in the chicken breasts until lightly golden. Stir in the chicken broth and BB sauce.
2. Close Instant Pot, press the Manual button, choose high settings, and set time to 30 minutes.
3. Once done cooking, do a QPR.
4. Open the lid and take the chicken out. Shred the chicken using forks.
5. Serve chicken on slider buns and add the sauce.
6. Serve and enjoy.

Nutrition information:
Calories per serving:573; Carbohydrates: 43.1g; Protein: 46.7g; Fat: 22.8g; Sugar: 6.2g; Sodium: 984mg

---

176.   Instant Pot Salsa Verde Chicken
(Servings: 6, Cooking time: 20 minutes)

Ingredients:

- 3 pounds boneless chicken breasts
- 1 teaspoon salt
- 1 cup commercial salsa Verde

Nutrition information:
Calories per serving: 287; Carbohydrates: 2.5g; Protein: 51.4g; Fat: 6.3g; Sugar: 1.4g; Sodium: 839mg

Directions for Cooking:

1. Place all ingredients in the Instant Pot.
2. Close Instant Pot, press the Manual button, choose high settings, and set time to 20 minutes.
3. Once done cooking, do a QPR.
4. Serve and enjoy.

INSTANT POT POULTRY RECIPES

177.   Instant Pot Ginger Garlic Drumsticks
(Servings: 8, Cooking time: 20 minutes)

Ingredients:

- 8 chicken drumsticks
- ¼ cup water
- ½ cup soy sauce
- 2 tablespoons honey
- 2 tablespoons brown sugar
- 2 tablespoons rice wine vinegar
- 2 cloves of garlic, minced
- 1 teaspoon minced ginger
- 1 onion, chopped

Directions for Cooking:

1. Place all ingredients in the Instant Pot.
2. Close Instant Pot, press the Manual button, choose high settings, and set time to 20 minutes.
3. Once done cooking, do a QPR.
4. Serve and enjoy.

Nutrition information:

Calories per serving: 288; Carbohydrates: 12.3g; Protein: 24.8g; Fat: 14.6g; Sugar: 4.3g; Sodium:381 mg

---

178.   Instant Pot Whole Chicken
(Servings: 6, Cooking time: 40 minutes)

Ingredients:

- 3 pounds whole chicken
- ½ tbsp butter, melted
- Salt and pepper to taste
- ½ teaspoon smoked paprika
- ½ teaspoon onion powder
- ½ teaspoon garlic powder
- ¼ teaspoon dried oregano
- 1 cup water
- 1 lemon, sliced

Nutrition information:

Calories per serving: 470; Carbohydrates: 46.3g; Protein: 36.8g; Fat: 15.8g; Sugar: 8.7g; Sodium: 835mg

Directions for Cooking:

1. In a small bowl, mix together butter, paprika, onion powder, garlic powder, oregano, pepper and salt.
2. Rub butter and spice mixture all over the chicken.
3. Pour water into the instant pot and place trivet into the pot.
4. Place chicken on the trivet.
5. Close Instant Pot, press the Manual button, choose high settings, and set time to 40 minutes.
6. Once done cooking, do a QPR.
7. Garnish with lemon slices
8. Serve and enjoy.

INSTANT POT POULTRY RECIPES

179.   Instant Pot Chicken Adobo
(Servings: 4, Cooking time: 35 minutes)

Ingredients:

- 2 pounds boneless chicken thighs
- 1/3 cup white vinegar
- ½ cup water
- 1/3 cup soy sauce
- 1 head garlic, peeled and smashed
- 3 bay leaves
- ½ teaspoon pepper
- 1 tablespoon oil

Nutrition information:

Calories per serving: 805; Carbohydrates: 3.2g; Protein: 43.9g; Fat: 58.3g; Sugar: 0.8g; Sodium: 892mg

Directions for Cooking:

1. Place all ingredients in the Instant Pot.
2. Close Instant Pot, press the Manual button, choose high settings, and set time to 30 minutes.
3. Once done cooking, do a QPR.
4. Open the lid and press the Sauté button. Allow the sauce to reduce so that the chicken is fried slightly in its oil.
5. Serve and enjoy.

180.   Instant Pot Kung Pao Chicken
(Servings: 5, Cooking time: 20 minutes)

Ingredients:

- 1 tablespoon olive oil
- 3 cloves of garlic, minced
- 1 teaspoon grated ginger
- 1 teaspoon crushed red pepper
- 1 onion, chopped
- 2 pounds chicken breasts, cut into bite-sized pieces
- ½ cup soy sauce
- ¼ cup honey
- ¼ cup hoisin sauce
- 1 zucchini, diced
- 1 red bell pepper, chopped

Nutrition information:

Calories per serving:506; Carbohydrates: 29.4g; Protein: 40.7g; Fat: 24.5g; Sugar: 15.3g; Sodium: 918mg

Directions for Cooking:

1. Press the Sauté button on the Instant Pot and heat the oil. Sauté the garlic, ginger, red pepper, and onion until fragrant.
2. Add the chicken breasts and stir for 3 minutes until lightly golden.
3. Stir in the soy sauce, honey, and hoisin sauce.
4. Close Instant Pot, press Manual button, choose high settings, and set time to 10 minutes.
5. Once done cooking, do a QPR.
6. Open the lid and press the Sauté button. Stir in the zucchini and bell pepper. Allow to simmer until the vegetables are cooked.
7. Serve and enjoy.

181.　　Instant Pot Shredded Buffalo Chicken

(Servings: 4, Cooking time: 20 minutes)

Ingredients:

- 4 chicken breasts
- 4 tablespoons butter
- ½ bottle buffalo wing sauce
- 2 tablespoons honey
- 2 teaspoons cider vinegar
- 2 tablespoons Tabasco sauce

Nutrition information:

Calories per serving: 695; Carbohydrates: 23.2g;
Protein: 61g; Fat: 38.6g; Sugar: 20g; Sodium: 852mg

Directions for Cooking:

1. Place all ingredients in the Instant Pot.
2. Close Instant Pot, press the Manual button, choose high settings, and set time to 20 minutes.
3. Once done cooking, do a QPR.
4. Once cooked, take the chicken out and shred using forks.
5. Serve and enjoy.

182.　　Instant Pot Chicken Saag

(Servings: 2, Cooking time: 18 minutes)

Ingredients:

- 1-pound chicken breasts, cut into 3 pieces
- Salt and pepper to taste
- 1 tablespoon oil
- ½ teaspoon cumin seeds
- 1-inch ginger, chopped
- 6 cloves of garlic, minced
- 2 onion, chopped
- ¼ cup water
- ¼ teaspoon turmeric
- ½ teaspoon red chili powder
- 2 teaspoon coriander powder

Nutrition information:

Calories per serving: 327; Carbohydrates: 10g;
Protein: 21g; Fat: 22g; Sugar: 2g; Sodium: 732mg

Directions for Cooking:

1. Season the chicken with salt and pepper to taste.
2. Press the Sauté button and heat the oil. Toast the cumin, ginger, garlic, and onion until fragrant.
3. Stir in the chicken and sauté for at least 3 minutes until lightly golden.
4. Add the rest of the ingredients.
5. Close Instant Pot, press the Manual button, choose high settings, and set time to 15 minutes.
6. Once done cooking, do a QPR.
7. Garnish with chopped green onions.
8. Serve and enjoy.

INSTANT POT POULTRY RECIPES

183.   Instant Pot Chicken Tacos
(Servings: 6 , Cooking time: 20 minutes)

Ingredients:

- 6 chicken breasts
- 1 tablespoon chili powder
- 1 cup salsa
- ½ cup Pico de gallo
- Salt and pepper to taste
- Corn tortillas
- Diced avocado
- Mexican cheese, shredded

Nutrition information:

Calories per serving:683; Carbohydrates: 16.9g; Protein: 67.4g; Fat: 37.8g; Sugar: 8.3g; Sodium: 700mg

Directions for Cooking:

1. In the Instant Pot, place the chicken, chili powder, salsa, and Pico de gallo. Season with salt and pepper to taste.
2. Close Instant Pot, press the Manual button, choose high settings, and set time to 20 minutes.
3. Once done cooking, do a QPR.
4. Serve with corn tortillas, avocado and Mexican cheese
5. Serve and enjoy.

184.   Coconut Chicken Curry
(Servings: 3, Cooking time: 20 minutes)

Ingredients:

- 1 tablespoon olive oil
- 1 ½ pound chicken breasts
- 1 onion, diced
- 2 cloves of garlic, minced
- 5 tablespoons red curry paste
- ½ inch fresh ginger, minced
- 2 tablespoon fish sauce
- Salt and pepper to taste
- 1 cup coconut milk
- ¾ cup bone broth
- 2 red bell peppers, sliced
- 3 carrots, chopped
- 1 ½ cup green beans, chopped
- Juice from ½ lime

Directions for Cooking:

1. Press the Sauté button on the Instant Pot and heat the oil.
2. Stir in the chicken breasts, onion, garlic, red curry paste, ginger, and fish sauce.
3. Season with salt and pepper to taste.
4. Add the coconut milk and water. Stir in the rest of the ingredients.
5. Close Instant Pot, press the Manual button, choose high settings, and set time to 15 minutes.
6. Once done cooking, do a QPR.
7. Serve and enjoy.

Nutrition information:

Calories per serving: 732; Carbohydrates: 28.4g; Protein: 54.1g; Fat: 46.6g; Sugar: 10g; Sodium: 1156mg

185.   One-Pot Thai Red Curry
(Servings: 3, Cooking time: 20 minutes)

Ingredients:

- 3 tablespoon Thai red curry paste
- 1 can coconut milk
- 1-pound chicken breasts, sliced into chunks
- ¼ cup chicken broth
- 2 tablespoon fish sauce
- 2 teaspoon brown sugar
- 1 tablespoon lime juice
- 1 cup red and green bell pepper
- 1 cup carrots, peeled and sliced
- ½ cup cubed onion
- ½ cup bamboo shoots, sliced
- 4 lime leaves
- 12 Thai Basil leaves

Directions for Cooking:

1. Place all ingredients in the Instant Pot and give a good stir.
2. Close Instant Pot, press the Manual button, choose high settings, and set time to 20 minutes.
3. Once done cooking, do a QPR.
4. Serve and enjoy.

Nutrition information:

Calories per serving:733; Carbohydrates: 26.1g; Protein: 42.5g; Fat: 54.3g; Sugar: 12.1g; Sodium:553mg

---

186.   Jamaican Chicken Curry
(Servings: 2, Cooking time: 25 minutes)

Ingredients:

- 2 tablespoons oil
- 1 tablespoon minced garlic
- 1 cup chopped onion
- 1 ½ tablespoon Jamaican curry powder
- 1 scotch bonnet pepper, sliced
- ½ teaspoon ground allspice
- 3 sprigs of thyme
- 1-pound boneless chicken thighs, chunked
- Salt and pepper to taste
- 1 large potato, cut into chunks
- 1 cup water

Directions for Cooking:

1. Press the Sauté button on the Instant Pot and sauté the garlic, onion, curry powder, scotch bonnet pepper, allspice, and thyme until fragrant.
2. Stir in the chicken thighs and cook until lightly golden. Season with salt and pepper to taste.
3. Add the potatoes and water.
4. Close Instant Pot, press the Manual button, choose high settings, and set time to 20 minutes.
5. Once done cooking, do a QPR.
6. Serve and enjoy.

Nutrition information:

Calories per serving: 1084; Carbohydrates: 78.5g; Protein: 48.6g; Fat: 65.6g; Sugar: 6.3g; Sodium: 1866mg

INSTANT POT POULTRY RECIPES

187.   Instant Pot Chicken Tetrazzini
(Servings: 6, Cooking time: 15 minutes)

Ingredients:

- 3 tablespoons butter
- 3 tablespoons flour
- ½ cup heavy cream
- 1 cup parmesan cheese
- ¼ cup cheddar cheese
- 4 chicken thighs, boneless and sliced
- 2 cups chicken broth
- Salt and pepper to taste
- ½ box spaghetti, cooked according to package instructions

Nutrition information:

Calories per serving:737; Carbohydrates: 32.7g; Protein: 50.5g; Fat: 43.6g; Sugar: 14.2g; Sodium: 929mg

Directions for Cooking:

1. Press the Sauté button on the Instant Pot and melt the butter. Whisk in the flour until it dissolves. Stir in the heavy cream, parmesan cheese, and cheddar cheese. Stir until melted. Set aside and clean the Instant Pot.
2. Still with the Sauté button on, stir in the chicken thighs and allow to sear until lightly golden. Season with salt and pepper to taste. Stir in chicken broth and spaghetti.
3. Pour over the cheese sauce.
4. Close Instant Pot, press the Manual button, choose high settings, and set time to 10 minutes.
5. Once done cooking, do a QPR.
6. Serve and enjoy.

---

188.   Instant Pot Chicken Shawarma
(Servings: 4, Cooking time: 20 minutes)

Ingredients:

- ¼ teaspoon coriander
- ¼ teaspoon cumin
- ½ teaspoon paprika
- 1 teaspoon cardamom
- ½ teaspoon cinnamon powder
- ¼ teaspoon cloves
- ¼ teaspoon nutmeg
- ¼ cup lemon juice
- ¼ cup yogurt
- 2 tablespoons garlic, minced
- 2 pounds boneless chicken breasts, cut into strips
- 2 bay leaves
- Salt and pepper to taste
- 4 pita bread
- ¼ cup Greek yogurt
- For garnish: tomatoes, lettuce, and cucumber

Directions for Cooking:

1. Place in the Instant Pot the coriander, cumin, paprika, cardamom, cinnamon powder, cloves, nutmeg, lemon juice, yogurt, garlic, and chicken breasts. Add the bay leaves and season with salt and pepper to taste.
2. Close Instant Pot, press the button, choose high settings, and set time to 20 minutes.
3. Once done cooking, do a QPR.
4. Place the chicken in the pita bread and drizzle with Greek yogurt. Garnish with tomatoes, lettuce, and cucumber.
5. Serve and enjoy.

Nutrition information:

Calories per serving: 383; Carbohydrates: 21.8g; Protein: 55.1g; Fat: 7.1g; Sugar: 2.5g; Sodium: 262mg

189.   One-Pot Mediterranean Chicken Paste
(Servings: 6, Cooking time: 15 minutes)

Ingredients:

- 3 skinless chicken breasts
- 1 cup chicken broth
- 2 cups marinara sauce
- 1 can diced tomatoes
- 1 tablespoon roasted peppers, chopped
- ½ cup sun-dried tomatoes
- ½ cup kalamata olives
- 9-ounce penne pasta

Directions for Cooking:

1. Place all ingredients in the Instant Pot. Mix to combine everything.
2. Close Instant Pot, press the Manual button, choose high settings, and set time to 15 minutes.
3. Once done cooking, do a QPR.
4. Garnish with chopped green onions.
5. Serve and enjoy.

Nutrition information:

Calories per serving: 483; Carbohydrates: 24.1g; Protein: 38.6g; Fat: 8.8g; Sugar: 7.5g; Sodium: 398mg

---

190.   Creamy Garlic Tuscan Chicken Pasta
(Servings: 10, Cooking time: 20 minutes)

Ingredients:

- 2 tablespoons olive oil
- 4 tablespoons butter
- 1 onion, divided
- 6 cloves of garlic, minced
- 3 chicken breasts, sliced into strips
- 1 tablespoon paprika
- Salt and pepper to taste
- ¼ cup white wine
- 1 jar sun-dried tomatoes
- 2 teaspoons Italian seasoning
- 4 cups chicken broth
- 1 cup milk
- 3 ½ cups dry elbow macaroni pasta
- 1 cup parmesan cheese, grated
- 1 cup mozzarella cheese, grated
- 1 ½ cup half and half
- Fresh basil leaves for garnish

Directions for Cooking:

1. Press the Sauté button on the Instant Pot and heat the oil and butter. Sauté the onion and garlic until fragrant. Add the chicken and stir until lightly golden. Season with salt and pepper to taste.
2. Stir in the rest of the ingredients. Give a stir to combine.
3. Close Instant Pot, press the Manual button, choose high settings, and set time to 15 minutes.
4. Once done cooking, do a QPR.
5. Serve and enjoy.

Nutrition information:

Calories per serving: 609; Carbohydrates: 37.1g; Protein: 52.3g; Fat: 26.7g; Sugar: 5.1g; Sodium: 782mg

INSTANT POT POULTRY RECIPES

191.   Instant Pot Chicken Soup
(Servings: 12, Cooking time: 25 minutes)

Ingredients:

- 2 tablespoons olive oil
- 2 cups chopped onion
- 2 tablespoons minced garlic
- 1 cup chopped celery
- 1 tablespoon turmeric
- 1 tablespoon Italian seasoning
- 1 4-pound whole chicken, cut into pieces
- Salt and pepper to taste
- 2 cups carrots
- 3 cups baby red potatoes
- 4 cups chicken broth

Directions for Cooking:

1. Press the Sauté button on the Instant Pot and heat the oil. Sauté the onion, garlic, and celery until fragrant. Add the turmeric, Italian seasoning.
2. Stir in the chicken and season with salt and pepper to taste.
3. Add the carrots, potatoes, and chicken broth.
4. Close Instant Pot, press the button, choose high settings, and set time to 20 minutes.
5. Once done cooking, do a QPR.
6. Serve and enjoy.

Nutrition information:
Calories per serving: 506; Carbohydrates:41.8g; Protein: 43.6g; Fat: 18.5g; Sugar: 7.4g; Sodium: 981mg

---

192.   Instant Pot Chicken Chowder
(Servings: 4, Cooking time: 20 minutes)

Ingredients:

- 1-pound chicken thighs, cut into bite-sized pieces
- 6 strips of bacon, chopped
- ½ cup diced onions
- ½ cup chopped celery
- 2 teaspoons minced garlic
- ½ teaspoon dried thyme
- ½ teaspoon dried oregano
- 4 cups chicken stock
- 1 cup heavy cream
- Salt and pepper to taste
- 2 cups spinach

Directions for Cooking:

1. Press the Sauté button on the Instant Pot and stir in the chicken and bacon. Add the onions, celery, garlic, thyme, and oregano until fragrant.
2. Add the stock and heavy cream. Season with salt and pepper to taste.
3. Close Instant Pot, press the Manual button, choose high settings, and set time to 15 minutes.
4. Once done cooking, do a QPR.
5. Open the lid and stir in the spinach last.
6. Serve and enjoy.

Nutrition information:
Calories per serving: 482; Carbohydrates: 13.9g; Protein: 27.2g; Fat: 35.6g; Sugar: 6.1g; Sodium:709mg

193.   Instant Pot Chicken and Rice Soup
(Servings: 6, Cooking time: 20 minutes)

Ingredients:

- 1-pound chicken breast
- 1 cup carrots, peeled and diced
- 1 cup chopped celery
- 1 box wild rice
- 1 cup chopped onion
- 3 cups chicken broth
- 1 cup water
- 2 bay leaves
- 2 teaspoons butter
- 2 teaspoons minced garlic
- 3 cups light cream
- Salt and pepper to taste

Directions for Cooking:

1. Place all ingredients in the Instant Pot and give a good stir.
2. Close Instant Pot, press the Manual button, choose high settings, and set time to 20 minutes.
3. Once done cooking, do a QPR.
4. Serve and enjoy.

Nutrition information:

Calories per serving: 874; Carbohydrates: 70.3g; Protein: 57.4g; Fat: 40.7g; Sugar: 8.6g; Sodium: 845mg

---

194.   Instant Pot White Chicken Chili
(Servings: 6 , Cooking time: 20 minutes)

Ingredients:

- 3 tablespoons olive oil
- 1 onion, chopped
- 4 cloves of garlic, minced
- 2 stalks of celery, chopped
- 4 chicken breasts, cubed
- 1 tablespoon cumin
- 2 teaspoon chili powder
- 1 teaspoon oregano
- 2 teaspoon coriander
- Salt and pepper to taste
- 1 can diced chilies
- 1 can diced tomatoes
- 1 ½ cups salsa Verde
- 1 can white beans, rinsed and drained
- 4 cups chicken broth
- ½ cup cilantro, chopped
- 1 tablespoon fresh lime juice

Directions for Cooking:

1. Press the Sauté button on the Instant Pot and sauté the onion, garlic, and celery until fragrant. Stir in the chicken and season with cumin, chili powder, oregano, coriander, salt and pepper.
2. Add the chilies, tomatoes, salsa Verde, beans, and chicken broth.
3. Close Instant Pot, press the Manual button, choose high settings, and set time to 15 minutes.
4. Once done cooking, do a QPR.
5. Open the lid and garnish with cilantro and lime juice.
6. Serve and enjoy.

Nutrition information:

Calories per serving: 807; Carbohydrates:30.9 g; Protein: 84.5g; Fat: 37.2g; Sugar: 8g; Sodium: 1217mg

INSTANT POT POULTRY RECIPES

195. Instant Pot Chicken Fajita Soup
(Servings: 3, Cooking time: 20 minutes)

Ingredients:

- 1 tablespoon butter
- 1 cup onion, minced
- 1 tablespoon minced garlic
- 1-pound chicken breasts, chopped
- 1 jalapeno, diced
- 1 cup red bell pepper
- 1 cup green bell pepper
- 4 tomato, diced
- 2 cups chicken broth
- 1 tablespoon lemon juice
- 2 tablespoons sour cream

Directions for Cooking:

1. Press the Sauté button on the Instant Pot.
2. Heat the butter and sauté the onion and garlic until fragrant.
3. Stir in the chicken breasts until lightly golden.
4. Add the rest of the ingredients.
5. Close Instant Pot, press the Manual button, choose high settings, and set time to 20 minutes.
6. Once done cooking, do a QPR.
7. Garnish with chopped green onions.
8. Serve and enjoy.

Nutrition information:

Calories per serving:620; Carbohydrates: 15.8g; Protein: 69.1g; Fat: 30.2g; Sugar: 5.3g; Sodium: 803mg

---

196. Instant Pot Chicken Stock
(Servings: 4, Cooking time: 30 minutes)

Ingredients:

- 1 chicken carcass
- 1 onion, quartered
- 2 bay leaves
- 15 whole peppercorns
- 2 tablespoons apple cider vinegar
- Salt and pepper to taste
- Veggie scraps
- 4 cups water

Directions for Cooking:

1. Place all ingredients in the Instant Pot and give a good stir.
2. Close Instant Pot, press the Manual button, choose high settings, and set time to 30 minutes.
3. Once done cooking, do a QPR.
4. Serve and enjoy.

Nutrition information:

Calories per serving: 284; Carbohydrates: 4.5g; Protein: 49.2g; Fat: 6.5g; Sugar: 0.6g; Sodium: 623mg

---

197. White Bean Chicken Chili

(Servings: 9, Cooking time: 40 minutes)

Ingredients:

- 3 tablespoons coconut oil
- 2 cups chopped onions
- 4 cloves of garlic, minced
- 6 boneless chicken breasts, cubed
- 2 teaspoons chili powder
- 1 teaspoon ground cumin
- ½ teaspoon ground coriander
- ½ teaspoon dried oregano
- 1-pound dried great northern beans, soaked overnight then drained
- Salt and pepper to taste
- 1 can diced tomatoes
- 7 ounces diced green chilies
- 4 cups chicken broth

Directions for Cooking:

1. Press the Sauté button on the Instant Pot and heat the oil. Sauté the onions and garlic until fragrant.
2. Stir in the chicken for 3 minutes until lightly golden.
3. Add the chili powder, cumin, coriander, and oregano.
4. Stir in the rest of the ingredients.
5. Close Instant Pot, press the Manual button, choose high settings, and set time to 35 minutes.
6. Once done cooking, do a QPR.
7. Garnish with chopped green onions.
8. Serve and enjoy.

Nutrition information:

Calories per serving: 402; Carbohydrates: 37.3g; Protein: 34.9g; Fat: 12.7g; Sugar: 2.4g; Sodium: 442mg

198. Low Carb Poblano Chicken Soup

（Servings: 5， Cooking time: 40 minutes ）

Ingredients:

- ½ cup navy beans, soaked in hot water
- 1 cup onion, diced
- 3 poblano peppers, chopped
- 5 cloves of garlic, minced
- 1 cup cauliflower, diced
- 1 ½ pounds chicken breasts, cut into chunks
- 1 teaspoon ground coriander
- 1 teaspoon ground cumin
- 1 ½ cups water
- Salt and pepper to taste
- 1 cup cream cheese

Directions for Cooking:

1. Place all ingredients in the Instant Pot except for the cream cheese.
2. Close Instant Pot, press the Manual button, choose high settings, and set time to 40 minutes.
3. Once done cooking, do a QPR.
4. Open the lid and stir in the cream cheese. Press the Sauté button and allow to simmer until the cheese is dissolved.
5. Serve and enjoy.

Nutrition information:

Calories per serving: 208; Carbohydrates: 13g; Protein: 22g; Fat: 5g; Sugar: 2g; Sodium: 423mg

199.   Instant Pot Chicken Curry Soup
(Servings: 6, Cooking time: 20 minutes)

Ingredients:

- 2 tablespoons butter
- 1 cup onion, chopped
- 2 tablespoons garlic, minced
- 2 tablespoons ginger, chopped
- 1 jalapeno, sliced
- 2 tablespoons curry powder
- 2 pounds boneless chicken thighs
- Salt and pepper to taste
- 4 cups chicken broth
- 1 cup diced tomatoes
- 1 cup coconut milk
- 3 cups fresh spinach, chopped
- ¼ cup cilantro, chopped

Nutrition information:

Calories per serving: 920; Carbohydrates: 32.4g; Protein: 65.4g; Fat: 58.9g; Sugar: 4g; Sodium: 1914mg

Directions for Cooking:

1. Press the Sauté button on the Instant Pot and heat the butter. Sauté the onion, garlic, and ginger until fragrant. Add the jalapeno and curry powder. Stir in the chicken and season with salt and pepper to taste.
2. Stir in the chicken broth, tomatoes, and coconut milk.
3. Close Instant Pot, press the Manual button, choose high settings, and set time to 15 minutes.
4. Once done cooking, do a QPR.
5. Open the lid and press the Sauté button. Add the spinach and cilantro.
6. Serve and enjoy.

200.   Instant Pot Chicken Taco Soup
(Servings: 5, Cooking time: 40 minutes)

Ingredients:

- 2 boneless chicken breasts
- 1 onion, chopped
- 2 can diced tomatoes, undrained
- 1 can corn, drained
- 1 can black beans, drained and rinsed
- 1 can great northern beans, drained and rinsed
- 1 can tomato paste
- 1 tablespoon taco seasoning
- 2 tablespoons dry Ranch seasoning
- 2 teaspoons cumin

Directions for Cooking:

1. Place all ingredients in the Instant Pot and mix everything.
2. Close Instant Pot, press the Manual button, choose high settings, and set time to 40 minutes.
3. Once done cooking, do a QPR.
4. Serve and enjoy.

Nutrition information:

Calories per serving: 473; Carbohydrates: 47.6g; Protein: 47.5g; Fat: 11.4g; Sugar: 10.5g; Sodium: 1094mg

201. Healthy Chicken Stew
(Servings: 6, Cooking time: 20 minutes)

Ingredients:

- 2 pounds boneless chicken thighs
- ¾ cup water
- 1 cup carrot, peeled and chopped
- 1 cup chopped onion
- 1 cup bell pepper, sliced
- ¼ cup soy sauce

Directions for Cooking:

1. Place all ingredients in the Instant Pot.
2. Close Instant Pot, press the Manual button, choose high settings, and set time to 20 minutes.
3. Once done cooking, do a QPR.
4. Serve and enjoy.

Nutrition information:

Calories per serving: 392; Carbohydrates: 13g; Protein: 27g; Fat: 25g; Sugar: 6g; Sodium: 696mg

---

202. Paleo Buffalo Chicken Chili
（Servings: 5 ，Cooking time: 20 minutes ）

Ingredients:

- 1 ½ pounds boneless chicken breasts
- 1 onion, chopped
- 5 cloves of garlic, minced
- 2 stalks of celery, chopped
- 2 carrots, chopped
- 1 tablespoon tomato paste
- 1 teaspoon chili powder
- 1 teaspoon cumin
- 1 teaspoon coriander
- 1 teaspoon onion powder
- Salt and pepper to taste
- 3 cups bone broth
- 1 can diced tomatoes
- ¼ cup hot sauce

Directions for Cooking:

1. Place all ingredients in the Instant Pot. Mix until well-combined.
2. Close Instant Pot, press the Manual button, choose high settings, and set time to 20 minutes.
3. Once done cooking, do a QPR.
4. Serve and enjoy.

Nutrition information:

Calories per serving:229; Carbohydrates: 9.9g; Protein: 35.1g; Fat: 4.9g; Sugar: 2.1g; Sodium: 918mg

203.   Instant Pot Keema Matar
(Servings: 2, Cooking time: 25 minutes)

Ingredients:

- 2 tablespoon oil
- 1 tablespoon garlic paste
- 1 tablespoon ginger paste
- 1 onion, chopped
- 1-pound ground chicken
- 2 teaspoon coriander powder
- 1 teaspoon cayenne pepper
- 1 teaspoon garam masala
- ½ teaspoon ground cumin
- Salt and pepper to taste
- 2 tomato, diced
- ½ cup green peas
- ¼ cup water
- 1 tablespoon lemon juice
- ½ cup mint leaves

Directions for Cooking:

1. Press the Sauté button on the Instant Pot and heat the oil and sauté the garlic and ginger paste. Add the onion and sauté until fragrant.
2. Stir the chicken and season with coriander powder, cayenne pepper, garam masala, and cumin. Season with salt and pepper to taste. Stir for 3 minutes.
3. Add the tomato, green peas, water, and lemon juice.
4. Close Instant Pot, press the Manual button, choose high settings, and set time to 20 minutes.
5. Once done cooking, do a QPR.
6. Garnish with chopped mint leaves.
7. Serve and enjoy.

Nutrition information:

Calories per serving: 546; Carbohydrates:20.7g; Protein: 44.8g; Fat: 33.1g; Sugar: 8.4g; Sodium: 851mg

---

204.   Buffalo Chicken Meatballs
（Servings: 5， Cooking time: 15 minutes）

Ingredients:

- 1 ½ pounds ground chicken
- ¾ cup almond meal
- 1 teaspoon salt
- 2 cloves of garlic, minced
- 2 green onions, sliced thinly
- 2 tablespoons ghee
- 4 tablespoons coconut oil, melted
- ½ cup water
- 6 tablespoons hot sauce
- Salt and pepper to taste
- 1 tablespoon cornstarch + 2 tablespoons water

Directions for Cooking:

1. Place all ingredients in the mixing bowl except for the hot sauce and coconut oil.
2. Mix until well combined and form small balls using your hands. Allow to set in the fridge for at least 3 hours.
3. Press the Sauté button on the Instant Pot and heat the oil. Slowly add the meatballs and allow to sear on all sides. Add water, hot sauce, salt and pepper.
4. Close Instant Pot, press the Manual button, choose high settings, and set time to 10 minutes.
5. Once done cooking, do a QPR.

Nutrition information:

Calories per serving: 357; Carbohydrates: 3g; Protein: 23g; Fat: 28g; Sugar: 0.8g; Sodium: 867mg

6. Open the lid and press the Sauté button. Stir in the cornstarch slurry and allow to simmer until the sauce thickens.
7. Serve and enjoy.

---

205.   Instant Pot Frozen Chicken
（Servings: 10， Cooking time: 50 minutes）

Ingredients:

- 5 pounds whole chicken, frozen
- 1 cup chicken broth
- 2 cloves of garlic, minced
- 1 onion, chopped
- Salt and pepper to taste

Nutrition information:

Calories per serving: 508; Carbohydrates: 46.3g; Protein: 42.1g; Fat: 17.5g; Sugar: 8.8g; Sodium: 923mg

Directions for Cooking:

1. Place all ingredients in the Instant Pot.
2. Close Instant Pot, press the Manual button, choose high settings, and set time to 50 minutes.
3. Once done cooking, do a QPR.
4. Garnish with chopped green onions.
5. Serve and enjoy.

Instant Pot Seafood Recipes

206. Miso & BokChoy on Sesame-Ginger Salmon
(Servings: 1, Cooking Time:6 minutes)

Ingredients:

- 1 tablespoon toasted sesame oil
- 1 tablespoons rice vinegar
- 2 tablespoons brown sugar
- 1/2 cup Shoyu (soy sauce)
- 1 garlic clove, pressed
- 1 tablespoon freshly grated ginger
- 1 tablespoon toasted sesame seed
- 2 green onions, sliced reserve some for garnish
- 1 7-oz Salmon filet
- 2 baby Bok Choy washed well
- 1 teaspoon Miso paste mixed with a 1/2 cup of water

Directions for Cooking:

1. On a loaf pan that fits inside your Instant Pot, place salmon with skin side down.
2. In a small bowl whisk well sesame oil, rice vinegar, brown sugar, shoyu, garlic, ginger, and sesame seed. Pour over salmon.
3. Place half of sliced green onions over salmon. Securely cover pan with foil.
4. On a separate loaf pan, place Bok Choy. In a small bowl, whisk well water and miso paste. Pour over Bok choy and seal pan securely with foil.
5. Add water to Instant Pot and place trivet. Place pan of salmon side by side the Bok choy pan on trivet.
6. Close Instant Pot, press manual button, choose high settings, and set time to 6 minutes.
7. Once done cooking, do a QPR.
8. Serve and enjoy.

Nutrition information:

Calories per serving:610; Carbohydrates: 30.4g; Protein: 56.0g; Fat: 29.2g; Sugar: 19.3g; Fiber: 2.9g; Sodium: 4872mg

207. Chipotle Shrimp Soup
(Servings: 5, Cooking Time:25 minutes)

Ingredients:

- 3 slices bacon, chopped
- 1 cup onion, diced
- 3/4 cup celery, chopped
- 1 tsp garlic
- 1 Tbsp flour
- 1/4 cup dry white wine
- 1 1/2 cups chicken or vegetable broth
- 1/2 cup whole milk
- 1 1/2 cups potatoes, cut into small (1/3-inch) cubes
- 1 cup frozen corn kernels
- 2 tsp diced canned chipotle peppers in adobo sauce
- 3/4 tsp salt (or to taste)

Directions for Cooking:

1. Press sauté and cook bacon until crisped, around 5 minutes.
2. Stir in garlic, celery, and onions. Cook for 3 minutes
3. Add flour and sauté for a minute. Press cancel.
4. Immediately stir in wine and deglaze pot.
5. Mix in thyme, black pepper, salt, Chipotle, corn, potatoes, and milk.
6. Close Instant Pot, press pressure cook button, choose high settings, and set time to 1 minute.
7. Once done cooking, do a QPR.

- 1/2 tsp ground black pepper
- 1/2 tsp dried thyme
- ½-lb shrimp, peeled and deveined
- 1/4 cup heavy cream

8. Stir in cream and shrimp.
9. Cover and let it sit for 10 minutes.
10. Serve and enjoy.

Nutrition information:
Calories per serving:314; Carbohydrates: 38.0g;
Protein: 17.0g; Fat: 9.0g; Sugar: 8.0g; Fiber: 4.0g;
Sodium: 579mg

---

208.   Seafood Stew in Instant Pot
(Servings: 6, Cooking Time:35 minutes)

Ingredients:

- 1/4 cup vegetable oil
- 14.5 ounces canned fire-roasted tomatoes
- 1 cup diced onion
- 1 cup chopped carrots, or 1 cup chopped bell pepper
- 1 cup water
- 1 cup white wine or broth
- 2 bay leaves
- 1 tablespoon tomato paste
- 2 tablespoons minced garlic
- 2 teaspoons fennel seeds toasted and ground
- 1 teaspoon dried oregano
- 2 teaspoons salt
- 1 teaspoon red pepper flakes
- 4 cups mixed seafood such as fish chunks, shrimp, bay scallops, mussels and calamari rings, defrosted
- 1-2 tablespoons fresh lemon juice

Directions for Cooking:

1. Press sauté button on Instant Pot and heat oil. Once hot, stir in onion and garlic. Sauté for 5 minutes. Stir in tomatoes, bay leaves, tomato paste, oregano, salt, and pepper flakes. Cook for 5 minutes. Press cancel.
2. Stir in bell pepper, water, wine, and fennel seeds. Mix well.
3. Close Instant Pot, press pressure cook button, choose high settings, and set time to 15 minutes.
4. Once done cooking, do a QPR.
5. Stir in defrosted mixed seafood. Cover and let it cook for 10 minutes in residual heat.
6. Serve and enjoy with a dash of lemon juice.

Nutrition information:
Calories per serving:241; Carbohydrates: 10.0g;
Protein: 18.0g; Fat: 10.0g; Sugar: 4.0g; Sodium: 1299mg

209. Easy Shrimp Pasta
(Servings: 6, Cooking Time: 7 minutes)

Ingredients:

- 1-pound dried spaghetti
- 3 cloves garlic, minced
- 1 teaspoon coconut oil
- 4 1/4 cup water
- 1-pound raw deveined jumbo shrimp
- 3/4 cup light mayonnaise
- 3/4 cup Thai sweet chili sauce
- 1/4 cup lime juice
- 1+ tablespoon sriracha sauce
- 1/2 cup chopped scallions
- Salt and pepper

Directions for Cooking:

1. Break the spaghetti noodles in half and place in the Instant Pot. Add the garlic, coconut oil, 1 teaspoon salt, and water.

2. Close Instant Pot, press pressure cook button, choose high settings, and set time to 4 minutes.

3. Meanwhile, mix well sriracha, lime juice, Thai sweet chili sauce, and mayonnaise in a medium bowl and set aside.

4. Once done cooking, do a QPR.

5. Press sauté button.

6. Mix in the sriracha sauce, scallions, and shrimps. Mix thoroughly. And cook for 3 minutes.

7. Serve and enjoy.

Nutrition information:

Calories per serving:485; Carbohydrates: 63.6g; Protein: 24.5g; Fat: 13.7g; Sugar: 14.1g; Sodium: 562mg

---

210. Yummy Shrimp and Grits
(Servings: 4, Cooking Time: 45 minutes)

Shrimp Ingredients:

- 1-lb shrimp, peeled and deveined
- 2 tsp Old Bay seasoning
- 3 strips smoked bacon, diced
- 1/3 cup onion, chopped
- 1/2 cup bell peppers, chopped
- 1 Tbsp garlic, minced
- 2 Tbsp dry white wine
- 1 1/2 cups canned diced tomatoes
- 2 Tbsp lemon juice
- 1/4 cup chicken broth
- 1/4 tsp tabasco sauce or hot sauce (or to taste)
- 1/2 tsp salt (or to taste)
- 1/4 tsp freshly ground black pepper
- 1/4 cup heavy cream

Directions for Cooking:

1. Dry shrimps with paper towel, season with Old Bay seasoning and set aside.

2. Press sauté button and cook bacon for 5 minutes or until crisped. Transfer to a plate.

3. Stir in bell peppers and onions and cook for 3 minutes until soft.

4. Stir in garlic and sauté for a minute. Press cancel button.

5. Add wine to pot and deglaze pot.

6. Mix in pepper, salt, hot sauce, broth, lemon juice, and tomatoes. Mix well.

7. Add trivet inside pot.

8. In a bowl that fits inside pot, mix well grits ingredients and cover with foil. Place on top of trivet in pot.

- 1/4 cup scallions, sliced thin (green parts only)

Grits Ingredients:

- 1/2 cup grits
- 1 cup milk
- 1 cup water
- salt and pepper, to taste
- 1 Tbsp butter

9. Close Instant Pot, press pressure cook button, choose high settings, and set time to 10 minutes.
10. Once done cooking, do a complete natural release for 15 minutes and then do a QPR.
11. Open pot, remove bowl of grits and stir in shrimps. Close pot and let it continue to cook for another 5 minutes.
12. Serve and enjoy.

Nutrition information:

Calories per serving:292; Carbohydrates: 18.0g; Protein: 30.0g; Fat: 9.0g; Sugar: 10.0g; Fiber: 3.0g; Sodium: 1178mg

---

211. Cajun Corn, Sausage & Shrimp Boil
(Servings: 4, Cooking Time: 10 minutes)

Ingredients:

- 1/2 pounds smoked sausage, cut into four pieces
- 4 ears corn
- 2 red potatoes, cut in half
- 1 tablespoon Louisiana Shrimp and Crab Boil
- 1/2 pounds raw shrimp

Sauce Ingredients:

- 6 tablespoons butter
- 1 tablespoon garlic, minced
- 1/8 teaspoon Cajun seasoning
- 1/4 teaspoons Old Bay seasoning
- 3-5 shakes hot sauce, such as Louisiana Hot sauce or Tabasco
- 1/8 teaspoon lemon pepper
- 1/2 lemon, juiced

Directions for Cooking:

1. In pot, add all ingredients except for the shrimp. Add water until all ingredients are just covered. Mix well.

2. Close Instant Pot, press pressure cook button, choose high settings, and set time to 4 minutes.
3. Meanwhile, make the sauce by sautéing butter and garlic in large pan on medium high fire. Sauté for 5 minutes. Stir in Cajun seasoning, Old Bay seasoning, hot sauce, lemon pepper, and lemon juice. Mix well and lower fire to low to keep sauce warm.
4. Once done cooking, do a QPR.
5. Stir in shrimps, cover and let it sit for 5 minutes.
6. Transfer shrimp, corn, and sausage in pan with sauce and mix well to coat.
7. Serve and enjoy.

Nutrition information:

Calories per serving:459; Carbohydrates: 18.0g; Protein: 22.0g; Fat: 33.0g; Sugar: 1.0g; Fiber: 1.0g; Sodium: 990mg

INSTANT POT SEAFOOD RECIPES

212. Salmon Quickie
(Servings: 4, Cooking Time: 10 minutes)

Ingredients:

- 3 medium lemon
- 3/4 cup water
- 4 4-oz salmon fillet
- 1 bunch dill weed, fresh
- 1 tablespoon butter, unsalted
- 1/4 teaspoon salt
- 1/4 teaspoon black pepper, ground

Directions for Cooking:

1. Place 1/4 cup fresh lemon juice, plus 3/4 cup water in the bottom of the Instant Pot. Add the metal steamer insert.
2. Place the (Sockeye) salmon fillets, frozen, on top of the steamer insert.
3. Sprinkle fresh dill on top of the salmon, then place one slice of fresh lemon on top of each one.
4. Close Instant Pot, press manual button, choose high settings, and set time to 5 minutes.
5. Meanwhile, in a Pyrex measuring cup, melt butter in microwave. Mix in pepper, salt, excess lemon, and excess dill.
6. Once done cooking, do a QPR.
7. Serve and enjoy with a drizzle of the butter lemon sauce.

Nutrition information:

Calories per serving:530; Carbohydrates: 49.0g; Protein: 45.0g; Fat: 16.0g; Sugar: 3.0g; Sodium: 1119mg

---

213. Alaskan Crab Legs in Instant Pot
(Servings: 3, Cooking Time: 5 minutes)

Ingredients:

- 2 pounds frozen crab legs
- 1 cup water
- 1/2 tablespoon salt
- 1 stick butter, melted for serving
- 1 medium lemon, for serving

Directions for Cooking:

1. Add a cup of water and salt in Instant Pot.
2. Place steamer basket in pot and add crab legs.
3. Close Instant Pot, press manual button, choose high settings, and set time to 4 minutes.
4. Meanwhile in a Pyrex measuring cup, melt butter in microwave. Juice the lemon and stir in melted butter. Keep warm.
5. Once done cooking, do a QPR.
6. Serve and enjoy with lemon butter sauce.

Nutrition information:

Calories per serving:578; Carbohydrates: 66.4g; Protein: 10.4g; Fat: 31.5g; Sugar: 60.6g; Fiber: 0g; Sodium: 1523mg

---

214. Shrimp Paella in Instant Pot
(Servings: 4, Cooking Time: 5minutes)

Ingredients:

- 1-lb jumbo shrimp, shell and tail on frozen
- 1 cup Jasmine rice
- 4 Tbsp butter
- 1 onion chopped
- 4 cloves garlic chopped
- 1 red pepper chopped
- 1 cup chicken broth
- 1/2 cup white wine
- 1 tsp paprika
- 1 tsp turmeric, 1/2 tsp salt
- 1/4 tsp black pepper
- 1 pinch saffron thread
- 1/4 tsp red pepper flakes
- 1/4 cup cilantro optional

Directions for Cooking:

1. Press sauté button and melt butter. Add onions and sauté for 5 minutes. Add garlic and sauté for a minute.
2. Stir in saffron thread, red pepper flakes, black pepper, salt, turmeric, and paprika. Cook for a minute.
3. Stir in red peppers and rice. Cook for 2 minutes.
4. Pour in wine and chicken broth mix well.
5. Close Instant Pot, press manual button, choose high settings, and set time to 4 minutes.
6. Once done cooking, do a QPR.
7. Add shrimp on top. Cover and set aside for 5 minutes.
8. Stir in cilantro, serve and enjoy.

Nutrition information:

Calories per serving:318; Carbohydrates: 47.8g; Protein: 26.4g; Fat: 13.2g; Sugar: 0.5g; Sodium: 790mg

215. Creamy Parmesan-Herb Sauce Over Salmon
(Servings: 4, Cooking Time: 10 minutes)

Ingredients:

- 4 frozen salmon filets
- 1/2 cup water
- 1 1/2 tsp minced garlic
- 1/2 cup heavy cream
- 1 cup parmesan cheese grated
- 1 tbsp chopped fresh chives
- 1 tbsp chopped fresh parsley
- 1 tbsp fresh dill
- 1 tsp fresh lemon juice
- Salt and pepper to taste

Directions for Cooking:

1. Add water and trivet in pot. Place fillets on top of trivet.
2. Close Instant Pot, press manual button, choose high settings, and set time to 4 minutes.
3. Once done cooking, do a QPR.
4. Transfer salmon to a serving plate. And remove trivet.
5. Press cancel and then press sauté button on Instant Pot. Stir in heavy cream once water begins to boil. Boil for 3 minutes. Press cancel and then stir in lemon juice, parmesan cheese, dill, parsley, and chives. Season with pepper and salt to taste. Pour over salmon.
6. Serve and enjoy.

Nutrition information:

Calories per serving:429; Carbohydrates: 6.4g; Protein: 43.1g; Fat: 25.0g; Sugar: 1.1g;Sodium: 1196 mg

216. New Orleans Seafood Gumbo
(Servings: 8, Cooking Time: 20 minutes)

Ingredients:

- 24-ounces sea bass filets patted dry and cut into 2" chunks
- 3 tablespoons ghee or avocado oil
- 3 tablespoons Cajun seasoning or Creole seasoning
- 2 yellow onions diced
- 2 bell peppers diced
- 4 celery ribs diced
- 28 ounces diced tomatoes
- 1/4 cup tomato paste
- 3 bay leaves
- 1 1/2 cups bone broth
- 2 pounds medium to large raw shrimp deveined
- sea salt to taste
- black pepper to taste

Directions for Cooking:

1. Press sauté button and heat oil.
2. Season fish chunks with pepper, salt, and half of Cajun seasoning. Once oil is hot, brown fish chunks for 3 minutes per side and gently transfer to a plate.
3. Stir in remaining Cajun seasoning, celery, and onions. Sauté for 2 minutes. Press cancel.
4. Stir in bone broth, bay leaves, tomato paste, and diced tomatoes. Mix well. Add back fish.
5. Close Instant Pot, press pressure cook button, choose high settings, and set time to 5 minutes.
6. Once done cooking, do a QPR.
7. Stir in shrimps. Cover and let it sit for 7 minutes. Open and mix well.
8. Serve and enjoy.

Nutrition information:
Calories per serving:270; Carbohydrates: 12.7g; Protein: 34.5g; Fat: 8.6g; Sugar: 3.7g; Sodium: 1432mg

---

217. Easy Steamed Mussels
(Servings: 4, Cooking Time: 10 minutes)

Ingredients:

- 2 Tablespoons butter
- 2 shallots chopped
- 4 garlic cloves minced
- 1/2 cup broth
- 1/2 cup white wine
- 2-lbs mussels cleaned
- Lemon optional for serving
- Parsley optional for serving

Directions for Cooking:

1. Press sauté button and melt butter.
2. Sauté garlic and shallots for 5 minutes.
3. Stir in broth and wine. Deglaze pot.
4. Add mussels.
5. Close Instant Pot, press pressure cook button, choose high settings, and set time to 5 minutes.
6. Once done cooking, do a QPR.
7. Discard unopened mussels.
8. Serve and enjoy.

Nutrition information:
Calories per serving: 189; Carbohydrates: 8.0g; Protein: 14.0g; Fat: 8.0g; Sugar: 1.0g; Sodium: 501mg

218. Easy Fish Tacos
(Servings: 2, Cooking Time:8 minutes)

Ingredients:

- 2 4-oz tilapia fillets
- 1 teaspoon canola oil
- 1 pinch of salt
- 2 tablespoons smoked paprika
- juice of one lime
- 1-2 sprigs of fresh cilantro
- 2 8-inch corn tortilla

Directions for Cooking:

1. Place tilapia in the middle of a large piece of parchment paper. Drizzle with canola oil, sprinkle with salt and paprika, squeeze lime juice on the tilapia and sprinkle with some cilantro. Fold your parchment paper into a packet, as not to let any air in.
2. Add 1 cup of water in pot and place trivet. Place packets on trivet.
3. Close Instant Pot, press pressure cook button, choose high settings, and set time to 8 minutes.
4. Once done cooking, do a QPR.
5. Warm tortilla in microwave for 10 seconds each. Place 1 packet of fish in each tortilla, add cilantro and dressing of choice.
6. Serve and enjoy.

Nutrition information:
Calories per serving: 206; Carbohydrates: 16.3g; Protein: 25.2g; Fat: 5.8g; Sugar: 1.3g; Sodium: 153mg

219. Mascarpone-Salmon Risotto
(Servings: 4, Cooking Time: 5 minutes)

Ingredients:

- 2 tbsp olive oil
- 1 onion finely chopped
- 1 garlic clove finely chopped
- 1 1/2 cups Arborio rice
- 3 1/2 cups gluten free chicken broth
- 1/2 tsp lemon zest
- 3 tbsp Italian parsley chopped
- 1/2 cup mascarpone cheese
- 4-oz smoked salmon chopped
- salt to taste
- pepper to taste
- lemon juice to taste

Directions for Cooking:

1. Press sauté button and heat oil.
2. Stir in garlic and onions. Sauté for 5 minutes. Press cancel.
3. Stir in rice and broth. Mix well.
4. Close Instant Pot, press pressure cook button, choose high settings, and set time to 5 minutes.
5. Once done cooking, do a QPR.
6. Stir in smoked salmon, mascarpone cheese, parsley, and lemon zest. Mix well.
7. Season with pepper and salt to taste.
8. Serve and enjoy.

Nutrition information:
Calories per serving: 503; Carbohydrates: 63.0g; Protein: 11.0g; Fat: 21.0g; Sugar: 1.0g; Sodium: 928mg

220.   Caper-Lemon Chimichurri on Salmon
(Servings: 4, Cooking Time: 30 minutes)

Ingredients:

- 2 tablespoons olive oil
- 1 teaspoon garlic, minced
- 2 anchovy fillets (optional) or 2 teaspoons anchovy paste
- 1/2 teaspoon crushed red pepper
- 1 tablespoon butter
- 1 cup loosely pack parsley
- juice and zest of 1 lemon
- 2 tablespoons capers
- 4 salmon portions
- sea salt
- ground pepper
- lemon slices

Rice Ingredients:

- 1 tablespoon olive oil
- 1 shallot, finely minced
- 1 cup long-grain rice
- 1 1/4 cups broth
- 1/4 cup lemon juice
- 1/2 cup white wine
- 1 teaspoon sea salt
- 1 tablespoon parsley, chopped
- zest of 1 lemon

Directions for Cooking:

1. Make the sauce by pressing the sauté function and melt heat oil. Stir in crushed red pepper, anchovy, garlic, and butter. Sauté for 4 minutes. Transfer to a bowl. Press cancel.
2. In food processor, process capers, zest of 1 lemon, and parsley. Add browned garlic mixture and pulse until chopped finely. Return to bowl and set aside.
3. Make the rice by pressing sauté button and heat oil. Add shallot and cook for 2 minutes. Stir in rice and cook for 2 minutes. Add pepper, salt, zest, parsley, broth, lemon juice, and white wine. Mix well.
4. Season salmon with pepper and salt. Place on Instant Pot steamer basket and top with lemon slices. Place basket on top of rice.
5. Close Instant Pot, press rice button.
6. Once done cooking, do a 5-minute natural release and then do a QPR.
7. Remove steamer basket. Fluff rice and transfer to serving plates. Add ¼ of salmon on each plate and pour ¼ of the sauce on each salmon.
8. Serve and enjoy.

Nutrition information:
Calories per serving: 498; Carbohydrates: 43.3g; Protein: 30.0g; Fat: 22.4g; Sugar: 2.4g; Sodium: 2108mg

221. Fish in Curried Coconut Sauce
(Servings: 4, Cooking Time: 15 minutes)

Ingredients:

- 1 ½-lbs Fish steaks or fillets, rinsed and cut into bite-size pieces
- 1 Tomato, chopped
- 2 Green Chiles, sliced into strips
- 2 Medium onions, sliced into strips
- 2 Garlic cloves, squeezed
- 1 Tbsp freshly grated Ginger
- 6 Bay Laurel Leaves
- 1 Tbsp ground Coriander
- 2 tsp ground Cumin
- ½ tsp ground Turmeric
- 1 tsp Chili powder
- ½ tsp Ground Fenugreek
- 2 cups unsweetened Coconut Milk
- Salt to taste
- Lemon juice to taste

Directions for Cooking:

1. Press sauté button and heat oil. Add garlic, sauté for a minute. Stir in ginger and onions. Sauté for 5 minutes. Stir in bay leaves, fenugreek, chili powder, turmeric, cumin, and coriander. Cook for a minute.
2. Add coconut milk and deglaze pot.
3. Stir in tomatoes and green chilies. Mix well.
4. Add fish and mix well.
5. Close Instant Pot, press pressure cook button, choose low settings, and set time to 5 minutes.
6. Once done cooking, do a QPR.
7. Adjust seasoning to taste.
8. Serve and enjoy with a squeeze of lemon.

Nutrition information:

Calories per serving: 418; Carbohydrates: 11.7g; Protein: 29.7g; Fat: 29.8g; Sugar: 5.4g; Sodium: 613mg

---

222. Shrimp Scampi in Instant Pot
(Servings: 6, Cooking Time: 15 minutes)

Ingredients:

- 2-pounds shrimp
- 2 tablespoons extra virgin olive oil
- 2 tablespoons pastured butter
- 1 tablespoon minced organic garlic
- 1/2 cup white wine
- 1/2 cup homemade chicken stock
- 1-pound gluten free pasta, cooked
- 1 tablespoon fresh squeezed lemon juice
- Sea salt and pepper, to taste
- Parsley, optional garnish

Directions for Cooking:

1. Press sauté button and heat oil.
2. Add garlic and sauté for a minute. Stir in butter and let it melt for a minute.
3. Stir in wine and stock. Mix well.
4. Stir in shrimps and cook for 5 minutes.
5. Add pasta and continue tossing well to coat and cooking for another 5 minutes or until heated through.
6. Adjust seasoning to taste.
7. Turn pot off.
8. Serve and enjoy.

Nutrition information:

Calories per serving: 308; Carbohydrates: 20.1g; Protein: 35.2g; Fat: 8.7g; Sugar: 0.3g; Sodium: 1458mg

223.   Salmon with Pepper-Lemon
(Servings: 4, Cooking Time: 10 minutes)

Ingredients:

- ¾ cup water
- A few sprigs of parsley dill, tarragon, basil or a combo
- 1-pound salmon filet skin on
- 3 teaspoons ghee or other healthy fat divided
- ¼ teaspoon salt or to taste
- ½ teaspoon pepper or to taste
- 1/2 lemon thinly sliced
- 1 zucchini julienned
- 1 red bell pepper julienned
- 1 carrot julienned

Directions for Cooking:

1. Add water and herb sprigs in Instant pot. Place trivet and add salmon with skin side down.
2. Season salmon with peppers, salt, and oil. Add lemon slices on top.
3. Close Instant Pot, press steam button, and set time to 3 minutes.
4. Once done cooking, do a QPR.
5. Remove salmon and trivet.
6. Add zucchini, pepper, and carrots in pot. Cover and let it sit for 5 minutes. Fish out the vegetables and place on serving tray. Add salmon on top.
7. Serve and enjoy.

Nutrition information:

Calories per serving: 202; Carbohydrates: 2.7g; Protein: 24.7g; Fat: 9.8g; Sugar: 1.3g; Sodium: 281mg

---

224.   Feta & Tomatoes on Shrimp
(Servings: 6, Cooking Time: 12 minutes)

Ingredients:

- 2 tablespoons Butter
- 1 tablespoon garlic
- 1/2 teaspoon red pepper flakes adjust to taste
- 1.5 cups chopped onion
- 1 14.5-oz can tomatoes
- 1 teaspoon oregano
- 1 teaspoons salt
- 1-pound frozen shrimp 21-25 count, shelled
- 1 cup crumbled feta cheese
- 1/2 cup sliced black olives
- 1/4 cup parsley

Directions for Cooking:

1. Press sauté button and melt butter. Add red pepper flakes and garlic. Sauté for a minute.
2. Stir in salt, oregano, tomatoes, and onions. Cook for 5 minutes.
3. Add shrimp. Mix well and press cancel.
4. Close Instant Pot, press pressure cook button, choose low settings, and set time to 1 minute.
5. Once done cooking, do a QPR.
6. Transfer to plates. Sprinkle feta cheese, olives and parsley.
7. Serve and enjoy.

Nutrition information:

Calories per serving: 211; Carbohydrates: 6.0g; Protein: 19.0g; Fat: 11.0g; Sugar: 2.0g; Sodium: 1468mg

---

INSTANT POT SEAFOOD RECIPES

225.   Salmon on Rice Pilaf
(Servings: 2, Cooking Time:5 minutes)

Ingredients:

- ½ cup Jasmine Rice
- ¼ cup dried vegetable soup mix
- 1 cup chicken bone-broth or water
- 1 tablespoon butter
- ¼ teaspoon sea salt
- 1 pinch saffron
- 2 4-6-ounce wild caught salmon filet FROZEN

Directions for Cooking:

1. Except for salmon, add all ingredients in Instant Pot and mix well.

2. Place steamer rack on top of ingredients.
3. Season salmon with pepper and salt. Place salmon on steamer rack.
4. Close Instant Pot, press pressure cook button, choose high settings, and set time to 5 minutes.
5. Once done cooking, do a QPR.
6. Serve and enjoy.

Nutrition information:

Calories per serving: 440; Carbohydrates: 40.6g; Protein: 32.2g; Fat: 15.3g; Sugar: 0.7g; Sodium: 860mg

---

226.   Lemon-Tahini Sauce over Salmon
(Servings: 2, Cooking Time: 3 minutes)

Ingredients:

- 1 tablespoon red wine vinegar
- 1 tablespoon freshly squeezed lemon juice (from ½ medium lemon)
- 1 clove garlic, minced
- ¼ teaspoon dried oregano
- ¼ teaspoon kosher salt
- ⅛ teaspoon freshly ground black pepper
- ¼ cup olive oil
- 1 tbsp feta cheese, crumbled
- 1lb salmon filets, fresh or frozen
- 2 sprigs fresh rosemary
- 2 slices of lemon

Directions for Cooking:

1. In a lidded jar, add vinegar, lemon juice, garlic, oregano, salt, pepper, feta cheese, and olive oil. Close jar and shake well until emulsified to make the lemon-tahini sauce. Set aside.

2. Add a cup of water in Instant Pot. Place trivet and add salmon on top. Season salmon with pepper and salt. Drizzle ¼ of the lemon-tahini sauce over salmon. Place lemon slices and rosemary sprigs on top of salmon.
3. Close Instant Pot, press manual button, choose low settings, and set time to 3 minutes.
4. Once done cooking, do a QPR.
5. Serve and enjoy with the remaining sauce drizzled over the salmon.

Nutrition information:

Calories per serving: 557; Carbohydrates: 4.9g; Protein: 47.5g; Fat: 38.2g; Sugar: 1.6g; Sodium: 506mg

227.   Crab Quiche without Crust

(Servings: 4, Cooking Time: 50 minutes)

Ingredients:

- 4 eggs
- 1 cup half and half
- 1/2 -1 tsp salt
- 1 teaspoon pepper
- 1 teaspoon sweet smoked paprika
- 1 teaspoon Simply Organic Herbs de Provence
- 1 cup shredded parmesan or swiss cheese
- 1 cup chopped green onions green and white parts
- 8 oz imitation crab meat about 2 cups OR
- 8 oz real crab meat, or a mix of crab and chopped raw shrimp

Directions for Cooking:

1. In a large bowl, beat together eggs and half-and-half with a whisk.
2. Add salt, pepper, sweet smoked paprika, Herb de Provence, and shredded cheese. Stir with a fork to mix.
3. Stir in chopped green onions.
4. Mix in crab meat with fork.
5. Lay out a sheet of aluminum foil that is cut bigger than the pan you intend to use. Place the springform pan on this sheet and crimp the sheet around the bottom.
6. Pour in the egg mixture into your spring form pan. Cover loosely with foil or a silicone lid.
7. Add 2 cups of water in Instant Pot and place a steamer rack inside.
8. Place the covered spring form pan on the trivet.
9. Close Instant Pot, press pressure cook button, choose high settings, and set time to 40 minutes.
10. Once done cooking, do a 10-minute natural release and then do a QPR.
11. Serve and enjoy.

Nutrition information:

Calories per serving: 395; Carbohydrates: 19.0g; Protein: 22.0g; Fat: 14.0g; Sugar: 3.0g; Sodium: 526mg

228.   Ginger-Orange Sauce over Salmon

(Servings: 4, Cooking Time: 15 minutes)

Ingredients:

- 1-pound salmon
- 1 tablespoon dark soy sauce
- 2 teaspoons minced ginger
- 1 teaspoon minced garlic
- 1 teaspoon salt
- 1 1/2 tsp ground pepper
- 2 tablespoons low sugar marmalade

Directions for Cooking:

1. In a heatproof pan that fits inside your Instant Pot, add salmon.
2. Mix all the sauce ingredients and pour over the salmon.

Allow it to marinate for 15-30 minutes. Cover pan with foil securely.
3. Put 2 cups of water in Instant Pot and add trivet.
4. Place the pan of salmon on trivet.
5. Close Instant Pot, press pressure cook button, choose low settings, and set time to 3 minutes.
6. Once done cooking, do a QPR.
7. Serve and enjoy.

Nutrition information:

Calories per serving: 179; Carbohydrates: 8.8g; Protein: 24.0g; Fat: 5.0g; Sugar: 6.9g; Sodium: 801mg

229. Clam Chowder
(Servings: 6, Cooking Time: 17 minutes)

Ingredients:

- 3 6.5-oz cans Chopped Clams (reserve the clam juice)
- Water
- 5 slices Bacon, chopped
- 3 Tbsp Butter
- 1 Onion, diced
- 2 stalks Celery, diced
- 2 sprigs Fresh Thyme
- 2 cloves Garlic, pressed or finely minced
- 1 1/4 tsp Kosher Salt or more
- 1/4 tsp Pepper
- 1 ½-lbs Potatoes, diced
- 1/2 tsp Sugar
- 1 1/3 cups Half and Half
- Chopped Chives, for garnish

Directions for Cooking:

1. Drain the clam juice into a 2-cup measuring cup. Add enough water to make 2 cups of liquid. Set the clams and juice/water aside.

2. Press sauté button and cook bacon for 3 minutes until fat has rendered out of it, but not crispy.

3. Add the butter, onion, celery, and thyme. Cook for 5 minutes while frequently stirring.

4. Add the garlic, salt, and pepper. Cook for 1 minute, stirring frequently.

5. Add the potatoes, sugar (if using) and clam juice/water mixture and deglaze pot. Press cancel.

6. Close Instant Pot, press pressure cook button, choose high settings, and set time to 4 minutes.

7. Once done cooking, do a natural release for 3 minutes and then do a QPR.

8. Mash the potatoes. Stir in half and half and the clams. Mix well.

9. Serve and enjoy garnished with chives.

Nutrition information:
Calories per serving: 384; Carbohydrates: 32.8g; Protein: 29.3g; Fat: 14.7g; Sugar: 5.0g; Sodium: 785mg

230. Salmon Casserole in Instant Pot
(Servings: 4, Cooking Time: 20 minutes)

Ingredients:

- 2 cups chicken broth
- 2 cups milk
- 2 frozen salmon pieces
- 1/4 cup olive oil
- ground pepper to taste
- 1 tsp of minced garlic
- 2 cups frozen vegetables
- 1 can of cream of celery soup
- ¼ tsp dill
- ¼ tsp cilantro
- 1 tsp Italian spice
- 1 tsp poultry seasoning
- 1 tbsp ground parmesan

Directions for Cooking:

1. Press sauté button and heat oil.

2. Add the salmon and cook until white on both sides and defrosted enough to split apart, around 2 minutes per side.

3. Add the garlic and just stir into the oil then deglaze the pot with the broth for 3 minutes.

4. Add the spices, milk, vegetables, noodles and stir.

5. Add the cream of celery soup on top and just gently stir so it is mixed in enough on top to not be clumpy.

Nutrition information:
Calories per serving: 434; Carbohydrates: 25.9g; Protein: 26.1g; Fat: 25.2g; Sugar: 10.0g; Sodium: 1024mg

6. Close Instant Pot, press pressure cook button, choose high settings, and set time to 8 minutes.
7. Once done cooking, do a QPR.
8. Serve and enjoy with a sprinkle of Parmesan.

---

231.   Salmon with Shoyu-Pineapple Sauce
(Servings: 1, Cooking Time: 6 minutes)

Ingredients:
- 1 6-oz Salmon filet
- 1/4 cup soy sauce
- 1/8 cup water
- 1/8 cup pineapple juice
- 3 slices of ginger julienned
- 1 clove of garlic chopped
- 5-6 pineapple chunks
- 1 cup broccoli florets
- ¼ cup carrots sliced thinly
- 1 small red onion peeled and quartered

Directions for Cooking:

1. Place salmon in a loaf pan that fits inside your Instant Pot.
2. Mix the soy sauce, pineapple juice and water in a small bowl then pour over the salmon. Sprinkle on the garlic and ginger and set aside.
3. Place all the veggies into a second pan that fits inside Instant Pot. Pour the water and soy sauce over the veggies then add the sesame oil. Season with salt and pepper to taste. Cover veggie pan tightly with foil.
4. Add 1 cup of water and the trivet to your pot.
5. Place your salmon pan on the trivet then stack the veggies pan on top.
6. Close Instant Pot, press pressure cook button, choose high settings, and set time to 6 minutes.
7. Once done cooking, do a QPR.
8. Serve and enjoy.

Nutrition information:
Calories per serving: 405; Carbohydrates: 32.8g; Protein: 47.0g; Fat: 10.1g; Sugar: 18.8g; Sodium: 4254mg

---

232.   Lobster Bisque
(Servings: 4, Cooking Time: 25 minutes)

Ingredients:
- 1 cup diced carrots
- 1 cup diced celery
- 29 oz canned petite diced tomatoes
- 2 Whole Shallots, Minced
- 1 Clove Garlic, Minced
- 1 Tbsp Butter
- 32-oz low-sodium chicken broth

Directions for Cooking:

1. Press sauté button and melt butter. Add garlic and shallots and sauté for a minute.
2. Stir in celery, carrots, and tomatoes. Sauté for 5 minutes. Press cancel.
3. Mix in spices, lobster, and chicken broth.

- 1 Tbsp Old Bay Seasoning
- 1 Tsp Dried Dill
- 1 Tsp Freshly Ground Black Pepper
- 1/2 Tsp Paprika
- 4 Lobster Tails, with fantail cut off
- 1 Pint Heavy Whipping Cream

Nutrition information:

Calories per serving: 331; Carbohydrates: 16.3g; Protein: 32.5g; Fat: 16.3g; Sugar: 8.4g; Sodium: 1007mg

4. Close Instant Pot, press pressure cook button, choose high settings, and set time to 4 minutes.
5. Once done cooking, do a 15-minute natural release and then do a QPR.
6. Remove the lobster tails, remove flesh from shell and return to pot.
7. With an immersion blender, puree bisque until smooth and creamy.
8. Serve and enjoy.

---

233. Fragrant Steamed Fish (Mok Pa)
(Servings: 6, Cooking Time: 35 minutes)

Ingredients:

- 2 pounds fish, white fish such as tilapia or catfish
- 3 tablespoons Lao sticky rice, soaked in water overnight and drained
- 1 stalk of lemongrass, thinly sliced, dry tough outer leaves removed
- 1 small shallot chopped
- 2 cloves garlic, peeled
- 1-3 Thai Bird chilies (Optional)
- 2 tablespoons water
- 10 Kaffir lime leaves, sliced thinly
- 2 tablespoons fish sauce
- 1 heaping tablespoon chopped green onion
- 1 cup fresh dill, not packed
- 1/2 cup cilantro leaves, not packed
- 2 cups quartered Thai eggplant

Directions for Cooking:

1. Cut fish into 1x2-inch cubes and place in a large bowl.
2. In a blender, puree Thai bird chili (if using), garlic, shallot, lemongrass, and soaked rice. Add water and puree some more. Add to bowl of fish and coat fish well with mixture.

3. Chop dill and cilantro roughly and add to bowl of fish.
4. Add Thai eggplant, green onion, fish sauce, and Kaffir leaves in bowl of fish. Mix well. Cover bowl with foil and marinate in the fridge for at least an hour.
5. Ready 6-pieces of 11x11-inch of foil. Evenly divide the fish mixture into the 6 foil packets and securely seal edges.
6. Add 2 cups of water in Instant Pot, place trivet, and add the fish packets on top of the trivet.
7. Close Instant Pot, press pressure cook button, choose high settings, and set time to 15 minutes.
8. Once done cooking, do a 20-minute natural release and then do a QPR.
9. Serve and enjoy.

Nutrition information:

Calories per serving: 185; Carbohydrates: 8.8g; Protein: 31.8g; Fat: 2.8g; Sugar: 1.6g; Sodium: 580mg

234. Shrimp Paella
(Servings: 4, Cooking Time: 15 minutes)

Ingredients:

- 1-lb jumbo shrimp, shell and tail on frozen
- 1 cup Jasmine rice
- 4 Tbsp butter
- 1 onion chopped
- 4 cloves garlic chopped
- 1 red pepper chopped
- 1 cup chicken broth
- 1/2 cup white wine
- 1 tsp paprika
- 1 tsp turmeric
- 1/2 tsp salt
- 1/4 tsp black pepper
- 1 pinch saffron threads
- 1/4 tsp red pepper flakes
- 1/4 cup cilantro optional

Directions for Cooking:

1. Press sauté button and melt butter.
2. Sauté onions for 5 minutes. Add garlic and sauté for a minute.
3. Stir in saffron threads, red pepper flakes, black pepper, salt, turmeric, and paprika. Sauté for a minute.
4. Add red peppers and rice. Sauté for a minute.
5. Stir in white wine and deglaze pot. Add chicken broth and mix well. Make sure that rice is fully covered in liquid.
6. Add shrimp on top. Press cancel.
7. Close Instant Pot, press manual button, choose high settings, and set time to 5 minutes.
8. Once done cooking, do a QPR.
9. Serve and enjoy with cilantro.

Nutrition information:

Calories per serving: 318; Carbohydrates: 47.8g; Protein: 26.4g; Fat: 13.2g; Sugar: 0.5g; Sodium: 790mg

235. Salmon Over Potatoes & Broccoli
(Servings: 1, Cooking Time: 10 minutes)

Ingredients:

- 3-oz Salmon Fillet
- 1 cup Broccoli florets
- 1 medium New Potatoes, cubed into ½-inch slices
- 1 tsp Rosemary, 1 tsp dill
- 1 tsp lemon juice
- 1 garlic clove, smashed
- 1 tbsp butter
- Pepper and salt to taste

Directions for Cooking:

1. In a heatproof dish that fits inside your Instant Pot, place potatoes on the sides and then the broccoli florets in the middle. Top with salmon fillet with skin side down.
2. Season salmon generously with salt and pepper. Season salmon with lemon juice, rosemary, dill, smashed garlic, and place butter on top of salmon. Securely cover top with foil.
3. Add a cup of water in Instant Pot, place trivet, and place dish of salmon on trivet.
4. Close Instant Pot, press pressure cook button, choose high settings, and set time to 5 minutes.
5. Once done cooking, do a 5-minute natural release and then do a QPR.
6. Serve and enjoy.

Nutrition information:

Calories per serving: 418; Carbohydrates: 41.1g; Protein: 23.8g; Fat: 18.4g; Sugar: 2.0g; Sodium: 487mg

236. Honeyed Salmon with Balsamic-Raspberry Sauce
(Servings: 1, Cooking Time: 6 minutes)

Ingredients:

- 1/2 cup Raspberry Balsamic Vinegar
- 2 Tablespoons Honey
- Pinch of Red Chili Pepper flakes
- 1 7-oz Salmon filet
- 4 medium Asparagus spears
- ½ red onion, sliced
- 5 cremini mushrooms
- 1 Red baby bell peppers, sliced
- 1 Yellow baby bell peppers, sliced
- 1/4 cup water
- Salt and Pepper to taste

Directions for Cooking:

1. In a loaf pan that fits inside your Instant Pot, mix well balsamic vinegar and honey. Add salmon and coat well with sauce. Add red pepper flakes on top of salmon. Securely cover with foil.

2. In another loaf pan, add water and all your veggies. Season with pepper and salt. Cover securely with foil.

3. Add a cup of water in Instant Pot, place trivet, and place pans on top of trivet.

4. Close Instant Pot, press pressure cook button, choose high settings, and set time to 6 minutes.

5. Once done cooking, do a QPR.

6. Serve and enjoy.

Nutrition information:

Calories per serving: 760; Carbohydrates: 77.6g; Protein: 48.4g; Fat: 27.7g; Sugar: 66.4g; Sodium: 167mg

237. Clams in Pale Ale
(Servings: 4, Cooking Time: 4minutes)

Ingredients:

- 1/4 cup olive oil
- 2 cloves garlic, peeled and minced
- 1/4 cup finely chopped fresh basil
- 2 cups pale ale
- 1 cup water
- 1/2 cup chicken broth
- 1/4 cup dry white wine
- 3 pounds fresh clams, scrubbed
- 2 tablespoons freshly squeezed lemon juice

Directions for Cooking:

1. Press sauté button and heat oil. Once oil is hot, sauté garlic until lightly browned around a minute.

2. Stir in basil and sauté for half a minute. Add pale ale, water, chicken broth, and white win. Mix well.

3. Add clams.

4. Close Instant Pot, press pressure cook button, choose high settings, and set time to 4 minutes.

5. Once done cooking, do a QPR.

6. Discard any unopened clams. Mix well.

7. Serve and enjoy with freshly squeezed lemon juice.

Nutrition information:

Calories per serving: 479; Carbohydrates: 24.1g; Protein: 51.6g; Fat: 18.3g; Sugar: 11.0g; Sodium: 2286mg

INSTANT POT SEAFOOD RECIPES

238.   Shrimps with Spiced Pineapples
(Servings: 4, Cooking Time: 12 minutes)

Ingredients:

- 1 large Red Bell Pepper cleaned and sliced
- 12-oz Calrose Rice or Quinoa
- 3/4 cup Unsweetened Pineapple Juice
- 1/4 cup Dry White Wine
- 2 Tablespoons Soy Sauce
- 2 Tablespoons Thai Sweet Chili Sauce
- 1 Tablespoon Sambal Oelek Ground Chili Paste
- 1-pound Large Shrimp, tails on frozen
- 4 Scallions chopped, White and Greens separated
- 1 1/2 cups Unsweetened Pineapple Chunks drained

Directions for Cooking:

1. Drain Juice from Pineapple and set Pineapple Chunks aside. Measure out 3/4 cup of Pineapple Juice.

2. Add Red Bell Peppers, Pineapple Juice, Wine, Chili Sauce, Soy Sauce, Sambal Oelek, Rice and chopped Scallions (the white part) to Pressure Cooker cooking pot. Place frozen Shrimp on top.
3. Close Instant Pot, press pressure cook button, choose high settings, and set time to 2 minutes.
4. Once done cooking, do a 10-minute natural release and then do a QPR.
5. Stir in green scallions and pineapple chunks.
6. Serve and enjoy.

Nutrition information:

Calories per serving: 282; Carbohydrates: 35.6g; Protein: 26.4g; Fat: 4.8g; Sugar: 27.9g; Sodium: 572mg

239.   Manhattan Clam Chowder
(Servings: 6, Cooking Time: minutes)

Ingredients:

- 4 strips Bacon chopped
- 3 large Carrots diced
- 3 stalks Celery finely diced
- 1 Red Pepper cleaned and diced
- 4 cloves Fresh Garlic minced
- 1 Tablespoon dried Oregano
- 1 teaspoon Sambal Oelek Ground Chili Paste or more to taste
- 1 1/2 teaspoons Ground Thyme
- 1 teaspoon Sea Salt
- 3/4 cup Fresh Leeks diced
- 6 ounces (3/4 cup) Turnip peeled and diced/cubed
- 10 Radishes trimmed and quartered
- 16 ounces Clam Juice
- 28-ounce Diced Tomatoes canned

Directions for Cooking:

1. Press sauté button and add bacon. Cook until browned, around 3 minutes. Sauté and cook for another 2 minutes.
2. Stir in peppers, carrots, and leeks. Cook for 5 minutes.
3. Stir in salt, thyme, oregano, Sambal Oelek chili paste, and garlic. Sauté for a minute.
4. Add tomato paste, crushed tomatoes, diced tomatoes, and clam juice. Deglaze pot.
5. Add bay leaves, turnips, and radishes.
6. Close Instant Pot, press pressure cook button, choose high settings, and set time to 5 minutes.
7. Once done cooking, do a 15-minute natural release and then do a QPR.
8. Stir in clams and parsley.

- 15-ounce Crushed Tomatoes (not puree)
- 1 1/2 Tablespoons Tomato Paste
- 2 Bay Leaves
- 3 6.5-oz cans Chopped Clams chopped, juice and solids separated
- 3 Tablespoons Fresh Flat Leaf Parsley chopped

9. Serve and enjoy.

Nutrition information:
Calories per serving: 357; Carbohydrates: 53.3g; Protein: 30.4g; Fat: 4.0g; Sugar: 23.5g; Sodium: 1170mg

---

240.   Seafood Stew
(Servings: 4, Cooking Time: 16 minutes)

Ingredients:

- 3 tablespoons extra-virgin olive oil, divided
- 2 bay leaves
- 2 teaspoons paprika
- 1 small onion thinly sliced
- 1 small green bell pepper thinly sliced
- 1 1/2 cups tomatoes diced
- 2 cloves garlic smashed
- sea salt to taste
- pepper freshly ground, to taste
- 1 cup Fish Stock
- 1 1/2 pounds meaty fish like cod or striped bass, cut into 2-inch chunks
- 1-pound Shrimp cleaned and deveined
- 12 Little Neck Clams
- 1/4 cup cilantro for garnish
- 1 tablespoon extra-virgin olive oil to add when serving

Directions for Cooking:

1. Press sauté button and heat 3 tbsp of olive oil.
2. Stir in paprika and bay leaves. Sauté for half a minute.
3. Stir in 2 tbsp cilantro, garlic, tomatoes, bell pepper, and onion. Sauté for 5 minutes.
4. Add fish stock and deglaze pot.
5. Add clams and shrimps. Place fish on top and season lightly with pepper and salt.
6. Close Instant Pot, press pressure cook button, choose high settings, and set time to 10 minutes.
7. Once done cooking, do a QPR.
8. Serve and enjoy with a drizzle of olive oil and a sprinkle of cilantro.

Nutrition information:
Calories per serving: 428; Carbohydrates: 8.2g; Protein: 58.1g; Fat: 17.0g; Sugar: 3.1g; Sodium: 1899mg

241.   Citrusy Salmon en Papilote
(Servings: 4, Cooking Time: 15 minutes)

Ingredients:

- 4 – 4 oz. salmon fillets
- Salt and pepper
- 1 tsp dill
- 1 orange, sliced thinly
- 1 lemon, sliced thinly
- 1 lime, sliced thinly
- 4 pieces foil
- 8 Asparagus spears, quartered
- 12 Cremini mushrooms, halved

Directions for Cooking:

1. Add a cup of water in Instant Pot and add trivet.
2. In each foil, place ¼ of Asparagus spears and mushrooms in each foil.
3. Top veggies with one salmon fillet and season generously with pepper and salt.
4. Add slices of orange, lemon, and lime on top of each salmon. Season with dill.
5. Securely seal foil packets and place on top of trivet.
6. Close Instant Pot, press pressure cook button, choose high settings, and set time to 5 minutes.
7. Once done cooking, do a 10-minute natural release and then do a QPR.
8. Serve and enjoy.

Nutrition information:

Calories per serving: 216; Carbohydrates: 18.3g; Protein: 26.0g; Fat: 5.4g; Sugar: 5.7g;Sodium: 131mg

---

242.   Oyster Sauce over Cod and Veggies
(Servings: 2, Cooking Time: 15 minutes)

Ingredients:

- 1 7-oz fresh or frozen Cod filet
- 1 heaping Tablespoon of Miso paste mixed with 3/4 cup of water plus 1 tablespoon soy sauce
- 1/4 cup Sake
- 1/4 cup mirin + 1 tbsp cornstarch to make a slurry
- 2 Tablespoons sugar
- 4 medium Asparagus spears, halved
- 1 small Red bell pepper, julienned
- 1 small Yellow bell pepper, julienned
- 1 small Red onion, julienned
- 2 Shiitake mushrooms, julienned
- 1/8 cup Oyster sauce mixed with 1/8 cup water

Directions for Cooking:

1. In a loaf pan that fits inside the Instant Pot, mix your miso sauce. Add cod and coat well in sauce. Cover securely with foil.
2. In another loaf pan, mix well oyster sauce and water. Add all sliced veggies and toss well to coat in sauce. Cover securely with foil.
3. Add a cup of water in Instant pot, place trivet, and stack the loaf pans on trivet.
4. Close Instant Pot, press pressure cook button, choose high settings, and set time to 6 minutes.
5. Once done cooking, do a QPR.
6. Remove loaf pans.
7. Transfer veggies and fish on to a plate.
8. Pour the sauce from the fish loaf pan in a small pot. Place on medium fire and stir in sake and sugar. Mix well. Once mixture is simmering, stir in the cornstarch slurry and continue whisking until thickened. Pour on top of fish.
9. Serve and enjoy.

Nutrition information:

Calories per serving: 211; Carbohydrates: 22.5g; Protein: 17.8g; Fat: 2.3g; Sugar: 14.2g; Sodium: 499mg

243.   Easy Sweet-Soy Salmon
(Servings: 2, Cooking Time: 8 minutes)

Ingredients:

- 2 8-oz salmon fillets
- ½ cup soy sauce
- ¼ cup water
- ¼ cup mirin (can substitute sake or sherry)
- 1 tablespoon sesame oil
- 2 teaspoons sesame seeds
- 1 clove garlic, minced
- 1 tablespoon freshly grated ginger
- 2 tablespoons brown sugar
- 2-3 green onions, minced, (reserve some for garnish)

Directions for Cooking:

1. In a heatproof casserole dish that fits inside the Instant Pot, mix well soy sauce, water, mirin, sesame oil, sesame seeds, garlic, ginger, brown sugar, and green onions.

2. Add salmon fillets and coat well in marinade. Keep in the fridge for at least an hour.
3. Cover dish with foil securely.
4. In Instant Pot, add a cup of water, place trivet, and put dish of salmon top of trivet.
5. Close Instant Pot, press pressure cook button, choose high settings, and set time to 8 minutes.
6. Once done cooking, do a QPR.
7. Serve and enjoy with a sprinkle of remaining green onions.

Nutrition information:

Calories per serving: 483; Carbohydrates: 16.0g; Protein: 53.3g; Fat: 18.7g; Sugar: 9.7g; Sodium: 2472mg

---

244.   Asparagus & Salmon with Buttered Garlic Sauce
(Servings: 3, Cooking Time: 4 minutes)

Ingredients:

- 1-lb Salmon Filet, divided equally into 3
- 1-lb Asparagus (small - medium stalks)
- 1/4 cup Lemon Juice
- 3 tbsp Butter
- 1 1/2 tbsp garlic (minced)
- Salt to taste
- Red Pepper Flakes

Directions for Cooking:

1. In a heatproof baking dish that fits in your Instant Pot, place asparagus. Season with salt.
2. Place salmon fillets on top of asparagus.

3. Season and drizzle with lemon juice, garlic, red pepper flakes. Season well with salt.
4. Cover dish securely with foil.
5. Add a cup of water in Instant Pot, place trivet, and add dish of salmon on trivet.
6. Close Instant Pot, press pressure cook button, choose high settings, and set time to 4 minutes.
7. Once done cooking, do a QPR.
8. Serve and enjoy.

Nutrition information:

Calories per serving: 360; Carbohydrates: 10.0g; Protein: 36.6g; Fat: 19.6g; Sugar: 4.2g; Sodium: 915mg

245.   Shrimp-Asiago Risotto

(Servings: 4, Cooking Time: 22 minutes)

Ingredients:

- 4 tablespoons butter, divided
- 1 small yellow onion, finely chopped
- 2 garlic cloves, minced
- 1 1/2 cups Arborio rice
- 2 tablespoons dry white wine
- 4 1/2 cups low-sodium chicken stock, divided
- Coarse salt and freshly ground pepper
- 1-pound large shrimp, thawed, peeled and deveined
- 3/4 cup grated Asiago cheese
- 1/4 cup tarragon and flat-leaf parsley, chopped

Directions for Cooking:

1. Press sauté button and melt 2 tbsp butter. Add garlic and onions and sauté for 5 minutes.

2. Stir in rice and cook for a minute. Pour in wine and cook for a minute while deglazing pot until wine is fully evaporated.
3. Stir in 3 cups chicken stock and then season with pepper and salt. Press cancel.
4. Close Instant Pot, press pressure cook button, choose high settings, and set time to 10 minutes.
5. Once done cooking, do a QPR.
6. Press cancel, press sauté, stir in shrimp, and remaining broth. Cook for 4 minutes.
7. Stir in remaining butter and cheese.
8. Add herbs, toss well to mix.
9. Serve and enjoy.

Nutrition information:
Calories per serving: 499; Carbohydrates: 29.7g; Protein: 38.4g; Fat: 30.9g; Sugar: 2.3g; Sodium: 3180mg

---

246.   Salmon Lau

(Servings: 3, Cooking Time: 40 minutes)

Ingredients:

- 9-oz salmon filets, cut in 3 equal pieces
- Taro leaves 2-3 for each Lau Lau
- Ti leaves, 2 for each Lau Lau
- 1 medium Carrot, Julienned
- 1 small Onion, Thin sliced
- 3 Shiitake mushrooms, sliced
- 3 tbsp Best Foods Mayo
- Hawaiian sea salt

Directions for Cooking:

1. Cut the stem off the taro leaves and chop into 2" pieces.
2. Wash and rinse the taro leaves well.
3. Wash and dry the Ti leaves, remove the thick ribs.

4. Rehydrate the mushrooms if using dried Shiitake mushrooms and slice them

5. Stack 3 taro leaves, place 1 piece of salmon in the middle, sprinkle with sea salt, add some julienned carrots, sliced onions a few stem pieces and some mushrooms. Add 1 tablespoon of mayo. Form the leaves into a bundle. Lay 1 Ti leaf on the table and place the salmon bundle on the end of the Ti leaf and roll tightly. Place the roll on the second Ti leaf and roll end to end. Split the long stem and tie the bundle together.
6. Add a cup of water in Instant Pot, place trivet, and add Lau Lau on trivet.

Nutrition information:

Calories per serving: 387; Carbohydrates: 9.4g; Protein: 41.4g; Fat: 20.0g; Sugar: 2.9g; Sodium: 1430mg

7. Close Instant Pot, press pressure cook button, choose high settings, and set time to 20 minutes.
8. Once done cooking, do a 20-minute natural release and then a QPR.
9. Serve and enjoy.

---

247.   Olive & Tuna Rigatoni
(Servings: 4, Cooking Time: 10 minutes)

Ingredients:

- 1 tablespoon olive oil
- 2 cloves garlic, minced
- 16 oz package rigatoni pasta
- 4 cups water
- 2 teaspoons salt
- 3 pouches Star-Kist Selects E.V.O.O. Yellow fin Tuna
- 1 cup cherry tomatoes, halved
- ¼ cup Kalamata olives, roughly chopped
- ¼ teaspoon black pepper
- ½ cup freshly grated Parmesan cheese

Directions for Cooking:

1. Press sauté button and heat oil.
2. Sauté garlic for a minute.
3. Stir in Salt, water, and rigatoni.
4. Close Instant Pot, press pressure cook button, choose high settings, and set time to 4 minutes.
5. Once done cooking, do a QPR.
6. Stir in Parmesan, black pepper, olives, tomatoes, and tuna. Mix well and let it rest for 5 minutes while covered.
7. Serve and enjoy.

Nutrition information:

Calories per serving: 267; Carbohydrates: 37.1g; Protein: 17.0g; Fat: 5.8g; Sugar: 0.4g; Sodium: 1363mg

248. Orange-Ginger Sauce over Fish
(Servings: 4, Cooking Time: 7 minutes)

Ingredients:

- 4 white fish fillets
- Juice and zest from 1 orange
- Thumb size piece of ginger, chopped
- 3 to 4 spring onions
- Olive oil
- Salt and pepper
- 1 cup of fish stock or white wine

Directions for Cooking:

1. Pat dry fish with paper towel and rub olive oil all over. Lightly season with pepper and salt. Place in steamer basket.
2. Add remaining ingredients in Instant Pot and add steamer basket.
3. Add a cup of water in Instant Pot, place trivet, and add dish of salmon on trivet.
4. Close Instant Pot, press pressure cook button, choose high settings, and set time to 7 minutes.
5. Once done cooking, do a QPR.
6. Serve and enjoy.

Nutrition information:

Calories per serving: 243; Carbohydrates: 7.1g; Protein: 21.7g; Fat: 14.1g; Sugar: 4.7g; Sodium: 123mg

249. Salmon Croquette
(Servings: 2, Cooking Time: 10 minutes)

Ingredients:

- 2 6-oz salmon filets
- 1/4 cup Chopped onion
- 2 stalks green onion, chopped
- 1 egg
- 1/2 cup Panko, place in bowl
- Salt and pepper
- 2 tablespoons of cooking oil

Directions for Cooking:

1. Add a cup of water in Instant Pot, place trivet, and salmon on trivet.
2. Close Instant Pot, press pressure cook button, choose high settings, and set time to 3 minutes.
3. Once done cooking, do a QPR.
4. Remove salmon and let it cool.
5. Meanwhile, in a large mixing bowl, whisk well egg. Stir in green onion and yellow onion.
6. With two forks shred salmon and add to bowl of eggs.
7. Place a medium skillet on medium high fire and heat oil.
8. Divide salmon mixture into two patties. Roll in bowl of Panko until thoroughly covered. Pan fry for 3 minutes per side or until golden brown.
9. Serve and enjoy.

Nutrition information:

Calories per serving: 433; Carbohydrates: 23.9g; Protein: 41.8g; Fat: 17.9g; Sugar: 4.4g; Sodium: 446mg

INSTANT POT SEAFOOD RECIPES

250. Pesto-Spinach on Salmon Pasta
(Servings: 6, Cooking Time: 10 minutes)

Ingredients:

- 16 ounces dry pasta
- 4 cups water
- 12 ounces smoked salmon, broken up in bite sized pieces
- 1 lemon
- salt and pepper
- 1 teaspoon grated lemon zest
- 1 teaspoon lemon juice
- 1/2 cup heavy cream

Pesto-Spinach Sauce Ingredients:

- 1/4 cup walnuts
- 2 cloves of garlic
- 1/2-pound baby spinach
- 1/3 cup olive oil
- 1 cup freshly grated Parmesan + more for serving/garnish
- kosher salt and black pepper to taste
- 1 tablespoon grated lemon zest
- 1 cup heavy cream

Directions for Cooking:

1. Make the sauce in blender by pulsing garlic and walnuts until chopped. Add ¼ tsp pepper, ¼ tsp salt, ½ cup Parmesan, oil, and 2/3s of spinach. Puree until smooth.
2. Add butter, water, and pasta in Instant Pot.
3. Close Instant Pot, press pressure cook button, choose high settings, and set time to 4 minutes.
4. Once done cooking, do a QPR.
5. Press cancel and then press sauté.
6. Stir in remaining Parmesan, remaining spinach, sauce, lemon juice, lemon zest, heavy cream, and smoked salmon. Mix well and sauté for 5 minutes.
7. Serve and enjoy.

Nutrition information:

Calories per serving: 457.3; Carbohydrates: 31.0g; Protein: 20.1g; Fat: 29.0g; Sugar: 2.0g; Sodium: 967mg

---

251. Dill & Lemon Salmon
(Servings: 2, Cooking Time: 5 minutes)

Ingredients:

- 2 3-oz salmon filets
- 1 tsp fresh dill chopped
- 1/2 tsp salt
- 1/4 tsp pepper
- 1 cup Water
- 2 tbsp lemon juice
- 1/2 lemon sliced

Directions for Cooking:

1. Place salmon fillets on a steamer rack. Season with dill, salt, and pepper.
2. Add a cup of water in Instant Pot. Place steamer rack on Instant Pot. Squeeze lemon juice over salmon fillets and add lemon slices on top.
3. Close Instant Pot, press pressure cook button, choose high settings, and set time to 5 minutes.
4. Once done cooking, do a QPR.
5. Serve and enjoy.

Nutrition information:

Calories per serving: 305; Carbohydrates: 3.0g; Protein: 51.9g; Fat: 10.0g; Sugar: 1.0g; Sodium: 628mg

252. Asian Style Salmon Soy-Free
(Servings: 2, Cooking Time: 7 minutes)

Ingredients:

- 2 6-oz salmon fillets
- 1 tbsp coconut oil
- 1 tbsp brown sugar
- 3 tbsp coconut aminos (soy-free alternative)
- 2 tbsp maple syrup
- 1 tsp paprika
- ¼ tsp ginger
- 1 tsp sesame seeds (optional)
- Fresh scallions

Directions for Cooking:

1. Press sauté and heat coconut oil. Add brown sugar and melt for 4 minutes.

2. Stir in maple, coconut aminos, ginger, and paprika. Cook for a minute.
3. Add frozen salmon fillets with skin side down. Season with pepper and salt.
4. Close Instant Pot, press pressure cook button, choose low settings, and set time to 2 minutes.
5. Once done cooking, do a 5-minute natural release and then do a QPR.
6. Serve and enjoy with a garnish of sesame seeds and fresh scallion.

Nutrition information:
Calories per serving: 396; Carbohydrates: 20.4g; Protein: 38.8g; Fat: 17.4g; Sugar: 16.9g; Sodium: 963mg

---

253. Easy Tuna Pasta Casserole
(Servings: 4, Cooking Time: 10 minutes)

Ingredients:

- 1 can cream-of-mushroom soup
- 3 cups water
- 2 1/2 cups macaroni pasta
- 2 cans tuna
- 1 cup frozen peas
- 1/2 t each salt and pepper
- 1 cup shredded cheddar cheese

Directions for Cooking:

1. Mix soup and water in pressure cooker.

2. Add remaining ingredients except for cheese. Stir.
3. Close Instant Pot, press pressure cook button, choose high settings, and set time to 4 minutes.
4. Once done cooking, do a QPR.
5. Stir in cheese and let it sit for 5 minutes.
6. Serve and enjoy.

Nutrition information:
Calories per serving: 382; Carbohydrates: 34.0g; Protein: 28.0g; Fat: 14.1g; Sugar: 2.2g; Sodium: 407mg

---

254.   Salmon Biryani
(Servings: 4, Cooking Time: 5 minutes)

Ingredients:

- 16 oz salmon fillet
- 3 cloves of diced garlic
- Juice of 1/2 lime
- Dash or salt and pepper
- 1 tablespoon of finely chopped mint leaves
- 1 tablespoon turmeric powder (or fresh if you can find it)
- 1 tablespoon red chili flakes
- 1-inch piece of grated ginger
- 1/2 tablespoon cumin
- 1/2 tablespoon crushed coriander seeds
- 1/2 tablespoon crushed cardamom seeds
- 1/2 teaspoon cinnamon powder
- 1/4 teaspoon cloves
- 1/4 teaspoon nutmeg grated
- 1 medium sized onion diced
- 2 cups Basmati rice
- 3 cups stock or water
- Fresh chopped cilantro for garnish

Directions for Cooking:

1. In a large shallow dish, mix well garlic, lime juice, pepper, salt, mint leaves, turmeric, chili flakes, ginger, cumin, coriander seeds, cardamom seeds, cinnamon powder, cloves nutmeg, and onions.
2. Add salmon and marinate for at least an hour.
3. After an hour, add basmati rice in Instant Pot insert and rinse until water is clear.
4. Drain rice completely.
5. Add salmon and marinade on top of rice.
6. Add 3 cups of stock.
7. Add a cup of water in Instant Pot, place trivet, and add dish of salmon on trivet.
8. Close Instant Pot, press pressure cook button, choose high settings, and set time to 5 minutes.
9. Once done cooking, do a QPR.
10. Serve and enjoy with a garnish of cilantro.

Nutrition information:
Calories per serving: 548; Carbohydrates: 81.5g; Protein: 32.8g; Fat: 9.7g; Sugar: 3.1g; Sodium: 239mg

255.   Mahi-Mahi in Sweet Spicy sauce
(Servings: 2, Cooking Time: 5 minutes)

Ingredients:

- 2 6-oz mahi-mahi fillets
- Salt, to taste
- black pepper, to taste
- 1-2 cloves garlic, minced or crushed
- 1" piece ginger, finely grated
- ½ lime, juiced
- 2 tablespoons honey
- 1 tablespoon Nanami Togarashi
- 2 tablespoons sriracha
- 1 tablespoon orange juice

Directions for Cooking:

1. In a heatproof dish that fits inside the Instant Pot, mix well orange juice, sriracha, nanami togarashi, honey lime juice, ginger, and garlic.
2. Season Mahi-mahi with pepper and salt. Place in bowl of sauce and cover well in sauce. Seal dish securely with foil.
3. Add a cup of water in Instant Pot, place trivet, and add dish of mahi-mahi on trivet.

Nutrition information:
Calories per serving: 201; Carbohydrates: 20.1g;
Protein: 28.1g; Fat: 0.8g; Sugar: 18.1g;Sodium: 442mg

4. Close Instant Pot, press pressure cook button, choose high settings, and set time to 5 minutes.
5. Once done cooking, do a QPR.
6. Serve and enjoy.

256.　　　Very Creamy Tuna Pasta Casserole #2
(Servings: 6, Cooking Time: 20 minutes)

Ingredients:

- 2 cups pasta, elbow mac
- 1 cup onion
- 1 cup celery
- 3 ½ cups chicken stock
- 2 tsp salt
- freshly ground black pepper
- 8-oz fresh tuna
- 3 tbsp butter
- 3 tbsp all-purpose flour
- ¼ cup heavy cream
- 1 cup frozen peas
- 1 cup buttery crackers, crushed
- 1 cup shredded cheddar

Directions for Cooking:

1. Press sauté and add chicken stock, celery, onion, and pasta. Season with pepper and salt.
2. Add tuna on top.

3. Press cancel, close Instant Pot, press pressure cook button, choose high settings, and set time to 5 minutes.
4. Meanwhile, in a sauté pan, heat the butter on medium-high fire. Stir in the flour and cook 2 minutes. Remove from heat and set aside.
5. Once done cooking, do a QPR. Remove tuna and set aside.
6. Press cancel, press sauté, and then stir in the butter mixture. Mix well. Cook until thickened, around 5 minutes.
7. Stir in heavy cream and mix well.
8. Add tuna and peas.
9. Cover top with crackers and then followed by cheese. Press cancel, cover pot, and let it stand for 5 minutes.
10. Serve and enjoy.

Nutrition information:
Calories per serving: 399; Carbohydrates: 40.6g;
Protein: 21.5g; Fat: 16.9g; Sugar: 3.5g; Sodium: 1181mg

257. Caramel Salmon Vietnamese Style
(Servings: 4, Cooking Time: 10 minutes)

Ingredients:

- 1 tablespoon extra-virgin olive oil
- 1/3 cup packed light brown sugar
- 3 tablespoons Asian fish sauce
- 1 1/2 tablespoons soy sauce or low-sodium soy sauce
- 1 teaspoon grated peeled fresh ginger
- Finely grated zest of 1 lime (about 2 teaspoons)
- Juice of 1/2 lime (about 1 tablespoon)
- 1/2 teaspoon freshly ground black pepper
- 4 8-oz salmon fillets
- Sliced scallions (white and green parts), for garnish
- Fresh cilantro leaves, for garnish

Directions for Cooking:

1. Press sauté and heat oil. Whisk in black pepper, lime juice, lime zest, ginger, soy sauce, fish sauce, brown sugar, and oil. Cook until it simmers, around 2 minutes. Press cancel.
2. Add fish with skin side down. Cover in sauce.
3. Close Instant Pot, press pressure cook button, choose low settings, and set time to 1 minute.
4. Once done cooking, do a 5-minute natural release and then do a QPR.
5. Remove fish and transfer to a plate.
6. Press cancel, press sauté, and the cook sauce until thick, around 3 minutes. Pour over fish.
7. Serve and enjoy.

Nutrition information:

Calories per serving: 426; Carbohydrates: 22.2g; Protein: 49.8g; Fat: 14.3g; Sugar: 19.9g; Sodium: 722mg

---

258. Tilapia with Basil-Tomato Dressing
(Servings: 4, Cooking Time: 4 minutes)

Ingredients:

- 4 (4 oz) tilapia fillets
- Salt and pepper
- 3 roma tomatoes, diced
- 2 minced garlic cloves
- 1/4 cup chopped basil (fresh)
- 2 Tbsp olive oil
- 1/4 tsp salt
- 1/8 tsp pepper
- Balsamic vinegar (optional)

Directions for Cooking:

1. Add a cup of water in Instant Pot, place steamer basket, and add tilapia in basket. Season with pepper and salt.
2. Close Instant Pot, press pressure cook button, choose high settings, and set time to 2 minutes.
3. Meanwhile, in a medium bowl toss well to mix pepper, salt, olive oil, basil, garlic, and tomatoes. If desired, you can add a tablespoon of balsamic vinegar. Mix well.
4. Once done cooking, do a QPR.
5. Serve and enjoy with the basil-tomato dressing.

Nutrition information:

Calories per serving: 170; Carbohydrates: 2.0g; Protein: 20.0g; Fat: 12.0g; Sugar: 0g; Sodium: 223mg

259. Old Bay Fish Tacos

(Servings: 6, Cooking Time: 5 minutes)

Ingredients:

- 2 large cod fillets (fresh or frozen)
- 1 tablespoon Old Bay Seasoning
- 1-2 tablespoons olive oil for frying
- 6 corn tortillas
- 1/2 cup quesadilla cheese

Pico de Gallo Ingredients:

- 1-2 ripe, medium tomatoes, seeded & diced
- 2-4 tablespoons finely chopped fresh cilantro
- 1/2 medium white onion, diced
- juice of 1 lime
- salt and pepper to taste

Chile-Cumin Guac Ingredients:

- 2 ripe, medium avocados, pitted
- juice of 1 lime
- 1 teaspoon ground cumin
- 2 tablespoons salsa Verde (green chile salsa)
- salt and pepper to taste

Directions for Cooking:

1. Add a cup of water in Instant Pot, place steamer basket, and add cod in basket. Season with Old bay seasoning.
2. Close Instant Pot, press steam button, choose high settings, and set time to 3 minutes.
3. Meanwhile, heat tortillas in microwave for 10 seconds each or to desired hotness.
4. Make the Pico de Gallo by mixing all ingredients in a bowl. Adjust seasoning to taste.
5. Mix all Chile-Cumin Guac Ingredients in a separate bowl. Adjust seasoning to taste.
6. Once done cooking, do a QPR.
7. Remove fish. Divide equally into 6 tortillas, top with Pico de gallo and guac.
8. Serve and enjoy.

Nutrition information:

Calories per serving: 259; Carbohydrates: 23.1g; Protein: 10.1g; Fat: 15.6g; Sugar: 2.7g; Sodium: 182mg

260. Sea Bass in Coconut Curry

(Servings: 3, Cooking Time: 3 minutes)

Ingredients:

- 1 (14.5 ounce) can coconut milk
- Juice of 1 lime
- 1 tablespoon red curry paste
- 1 teaspoon fish sauce
- 1 teaspoon coconut aminos
- 1 teaspoon honey
- 2 teaspoons Sriracha
- 2 cloves garlic, minced
- 1 teaspoon ground turmeric
- 1 teaspoon ground ginger
- 1/2 teaspoon sea salt
- 1/2 teaspoon white pepper
- 1-pound sea bass, cut into 1" cubes
- 1/4 cup chopped fresh cilantro
- 3 lime wedges

Directions for Cooking:

1. Whisk well pepper, salt, ginger, turmeric, garlic, sriracha, honey, coconut aminos, fish sauce, red curry paste, lime juice, and coconut milk in a large bowl.
2. Place fish in pot and pour coconut milk mixture over it.
3. Close Instant Pot, press pressure cook button, choose high settings, and set time to 3 minutes.
4. Once done cooking, do a QPR.
5. Serve and enjoy with equal amounts of lime wedge and cilantro.

Nutrition information:

Calories per serving: 519; Carbohydrates: 18.3g; Protein: 32.2g; Fat: 38.0g; Sugar: 8.0g; Sodium: 675mg

261. Mango-Salsa on Fish
(Servings: 2, Cooking Time: 5 minutes)

Ingredients:

- 1 cup coconut milk
- 1/2 to 1 tablespoon Thai green curry paste
- 1 tablespoon fish sauce
- zest of 1 lime and juice of 1/2 lime
- 2 teaspoons brown sugar
- 1 teaspoon garlic, minced
- 1 tablespoon fresh ginger, minced
- 2 6-oz fish portions
- 1 lime, cut in thin slices
- a sprinkle of cilantro leaves and chopped scallion

Mango Salsa Ingredients:

- 1 mango, peeled, seeded, and diced (about 3/4 cup small dice)
- 1 Fresno or jalapeno chiles, minced
- 1 scallion, finely chopped
- a handful of cilantro leaves, chopped
- juice of 1 lime

Directions for Cooking:

1. In a bowl, mix well coconut milk, Thai green curry paste, fish sauce, lime juice, lime zest, brown sugar, garlic, and ginger. Add fish and marinate for at least an hour.
2. Meanwhile, make the mango salsa by combining all ingredients in a separate bowl. Keep in the fridge.
3. Cut two 11x11-inch foils. Place one fish fillet in each foil. Top each equally with lime, scallion and cilantro. Seal foil packets.
4. Add a cup of water in Instant Pot, place trivet, and add foil packets on trivet.
5. Close Instant Pot, press pressure cook button, choose high settings, and set time to 5 minutes.
6. Once done cooking, do a QPR.
7. Serve and enjoy with mango salsa on top.

Nutrition information:
Calories per serving: 354; Carbohydrates: 28.5g; Protein: 29.3g; Fat: 15.6g; Sugar: 19.5g; Sodium: 1237mg

---

262. Cod the Mediterranean Way
(Servings: 6, Cooking Time: 15 minutes)

Ingredients:

- 6 pieces of frozen or fresh cod (about 1.5 pounds)
- 3 tablespoons butter
- 1 lemon, juiced
- 1 onion, sliced
- 1 teaspoon salt
- 1/2 teaspoon black pepper
- 1 teaspoon oregano
- 1- 28 oz. can diced tomatoes

Directions for Cooking:

1. Press sauté and melt butter. Stir in lemon juice, onion, salt, black pepper, oregano and diced tomatoes. Cook for 8 minutes.
2. Add fish and spoon sauce over it. Press cancel.
3. Close Instant Pot, press pressure cook button, choose high settings, and set time to 5 minutes.
4. Once done cooking, do a QPR.
5. Serve and enjoy.

Nutrition information:
Calories per serving: 145; Carbohydrates: 3.3g; Protein: 18.4g; Fat: 6.4g; Sugar: 2.0g; Sodium: 864mg

263. Cajun Gumbo
(Servings:8, Cooking Time: 25 minutes)

Ingredients:

- 1lb Chicken Breast, shredded
- 1lb Smoked Sausage
- 1lb Shrimp, raw, with no shell or tail
- 1/2- 1 jar of Roux
- 2 cups Onion, diced
- 1 large Green pepper, diced
- 3 celery stalks, diced
- 1 (12oz) bag of okra frozen
- 2 cloves of garlic
- 3 tsp of Tony Chachere seasoning
- pinch of thyme
- salt and pepper to your liking
- 3 cups of chicken broth
- 2 cups water
- 1 cup of rice

Directions for Cooking:

1. Mix well in Instant liner the chicken, sausage, roux, onions, green pepper, garlic, celery, Tony Chachere seasoning, thyme, and chicken broth.
2. In a heatproof dish that fits inside your Instant Pot, add rice and water.
3. Place a trivet on top of the Instant Pot Mixture and place dish of rice on trivet.
4. Close Instant Pot, press rice button, and set time to 15 minutes.
5. Once done cooking, do a QPR.
6. Remove rice.
7. Press cancel, press sauté and stir in shrimp and okra. Cook for 10 minutes.
8. Serve and enjoy with rice.

Nutrition information:
Calories per serving: 451.5; Carbohydrates: 38.1g; Protein: 42.9g; Fat: 14.8g; Sugar: 4.9g;Sodium: 1757mg

264. Shrimp Jambalaya
(Servings: 6, Cooking Time: 15 minutes)

Ingredients:

- 1-lb smoked sausage, 1/2-inch slices sliced on a bias
- 1-lb medium shrimp, peeled and deveined
- 1 medium onion, diced
- 3 stalks celery, diced
- 1 medium red pepper, diced
- 3 garlic cloves, minced
- 1 14.5-ounce can petite diced tomatoes, including juice
- 1 1/4 cup long grain white rice, rinsed
- 3/4 cup water
- 1 tsp Cajun seasoning, like Old Bay
- 1 t seasoned salt
- 1/2 tsp black pepper

Directions for Cooking:

1. Press sauté and once hot sauté sausage, garlic, red pepper celery, and onion for 5 minutes.
2. Stir in rice and sauté for 2 minutes.
3. Season with Cajun seasoning, pepper, salt, cayenne, and tabasco. Sauté for a minute.
4. Add water, shrimp, and tomatoes. Deglaze pot. Press cancel.
5. Close Instant Pot, press pressure cook button, choose high settings, and set time to 4 minutes.
6. Once done cooking, do a QPR.
7. Fluff rice and toss in scallions.
8. Serve and enjoy.

- 1/4 tsp cayenne or crushed red pepper, optional for spice
- 3-6 dashes tabasco, optional for spice
- 2 scallions, diced for garnish

Nutrition information:
Calories per serving: 420; Carbohydrates: 45.8g; Protein: 28.3g; Fat: 15.1g; Sugar: 3.8g; Sodium: 1583mg

---

265. Herby-Orange Salmon on Asparagus
(Servings: 3, Cooking Time: 10 minutes)

Ingredients:

- 1 cup filtered water
- 3 to 5 large sprigs dill, parsley, basil, thyme, or tarragon fresh
- 1 clove garlic fresh, crushed
- 1 pound wild-caught Alaskan salmon filet skin-on
- 1 tablespoon avocado oil + 2 tablespoons additional
- 1 teaspoon sea salt divided
- 1 teaspoon granulated garlic
- 1/2 teaspoon dried dill or parsley, basil, thyme, or tarragon
- 6 to 7 thin slices orange
- 1 small bunch asparagus woody ends removed, cut in half or sliced into 1-1/2" pieces, cut on the bias

Directions for Cooking:

1. Add a cup of water, crushed garlic, and fresh dill in Instant Pot, place trivet, and add salmon skin side down on trivet.
2. Drizzle salmon with 1 tbsp avocado oil. Season with dried dill, garlic granules, ¾ tsp salt.
3. Top evenly with Orange slices.
4. Close Instant Pot, press pressure cook button, choose high settings, and set time to 4 minutes.
5. Once done cooking, do a QPR.
6. Transfer fish to a serving plate and discard water from pot.
7. Press cancel, press sauté button and heat remaining oil.
8. Add asparagus and season with ¼ tsp salt. Sauté for 5 minutes.
9. Serve and enjoy with salmon.

Nutrition information:
Calories per serving: 284; Carbohydrates: 6.2g; Protein: 31.8g; Fat: 14.3g; Sugar: 3.6g; Sodium: 846mg

Instant Pot Vegetarian Recipes

266.   Instant Pot Black Bean Chili
(Servings: 4, Cooking time: 13 minutes)

Ingredients:

- 2 teaspoons olive oil
- 1 onion, diced
- 1 bell pepper, diced
- 1 teaspoon dried oregano
- 2 cloves of garlic, minced
- 2 tablespoons chili powder
- 2 teaspoons ground cumin
- 2 cans cooked black beans, drained
- 1 can tomatoes
- 1 jalapeno pepper, minced
- Salt and pepper to taste
- 1 cup water

Directions for Cooking:

1. Press the Sauté button on the Instant Pot and heat the olive oil.
2. Once hot, stir in the onion, bell pepper, oregano, and garlic until fragrant.
3. Stir in the rest of the ingredients.
4. Close Instant Pot, press the Manual button, choose high settings, and set time to 10 minutes.
5. Once done cooking, do a QPR.
6. Serve and enjoy.

Nutrition information:

Calories per serving: 294; Carbohydrates: 50.4g; Protein: 17.2g; Fat: 4.3g; Sugar: 4.1g; Sodium: 177mg

---

267.   Vegetarian Mushroom Bourguignon
(Servings: 2, Cooking time: 10 minutes)

Ingredients:

- 1 teaspoon oil
- 1 onion, chopped
- 3 cloves of garlic, minced
- 2 carrots, cut into thick strips
- 5 cups mushrooms, halved
- 1 cup red wine
- 4 tablespoons tomato paste
- 1 teaspoon dried marjoram
- 1 cup vegetable broth
- 3 teaspoons Italian herbs
- Salt and pepper to taste
- 1 tablespoon cornstarch + 2 tablespoons water

Directions for Cooking:

1. Press the Sauté button on the Instant Pot and heat the oil. Stir in the onion and garlic until fragrant.
2. Add the carrots and mushrooms and allow to soften. Stir in the rest of the ingredients except for the cornstarch slurry.
3. Close Instant Pot, press the Manual button, choose high settings, and set time to 5 minutes.
4. Once done cooking, do a QPR.
5. Open the lid and press the Sauté button. Stir in the cornstarch slurry and allow to simmer until the sauce thickens.
6. Serve and enjoy.

Nutrition information:

Calories per serving: 168; Carbohydrates: 25.1g; Protein: 10.2g; Fat: 3.3g; Sugar: 13g; Sodium: 323mg

268.   Vegetarian Fajita Pasta
(Servings: 6, Cooking time: 9 minutes)

Ingredients:

- 1 teaspoon oil
- 6 cloves of garlic, minced
- 1 cup chopped bell peppers
- 1 cup black beans, cooked
- 1 teaspoon taco seasoning mix
- 4 cups pasta, cooked according to package instruction
- 2 cups commercial enchilada sauce
- Salt and pepper to taste

Directions for Cooking:

1. vPress the Sauté button on the Instant Pot and heat the oil. Stir in the garlic and bell peppers and allow to wilt for 3 minutes.
2. Add the rest of the ingredients.
3. Close Instant Pot, press the Manual button, choose high settings, and set time to 6 minutes.
4. Once done cooking, do a QPR.
5. Serve and enjoy.

Nutrition information:

Calories per serving: 275; Carbohydrates: 52.1g; Protein: 10.4g; Fat: 3.5g; Sugar: 3.4g; Sodium: 257mg

269.   Instant Pot Tomato Soup
(Servings: 3, Cooking time: 9 minutes)

Ingredients:

- 2 tablespoons olive oil
- 1 onion, chopped
- 3 medium carrots, peeled and chopped
- 1 cans fire roasted tomatoes
- ¾ cup vegetable broth
- 2 teaspoons dried basil
- 1 teaspoon salt
- 2 teaspoons sugar
- 1 cup cashew nuts, soaked

Directions for Cooking:

1. Press the Sauté button on the Instant Pot and heat the oil.
2. Stir in the onions and carrots for 3 minutes
3. Add the rest of the ingredients.
4. Close Instant Pot, press the Manual button, choose high settings, and set time to 6 minutes.
5. Once done cooking, do a QPR.
6. Open the lid and transfer the contents into a blender. Pulse until smooth.
7. Serve and enjoy.

Nutrition information:

Calories per serving: 390; Carbohydrates: 27.7g; Protein: 8.8g; Fat: 29.9g; Sugar: 10g; Sodium: 1162mg

270. One-Pot Refried Black Beans
(Servings: 2, Cooking time: 40 minutes)

Ingredients:

- 1 ¼ cups dried black beans, soaked overnight
- 3 cups water
- 1 onion, chopped
- 2 cloves of garlic, minced
- ½ teaspoons ground cumin
- 2 tablespoons chilies, chopped
- Salt to taste

Directions for Cooking:

1. Place all ingredients in the Instant Pot.
2. Close Instant Pot, press the Manual button, choose high settings, and set time to 40 minutes.
3. Once done cooking, do a QPR.
4. Using potato masher mash beans until get desired consistency.
5. Serve and enjoy.

Nutrition information:

Calories per serving:465; Carbohydrates: 85.1g; Protein: 28.1g; Fat: 3.1g; Sugar: 5.5g; Sodium: 329mg

271. Pasta Mediterranean
(Servings: 3, Cooking time: 25 minutes)

Ingredients:

- 1 tablespoon olive oil
- 1 red onion, chopped
- 2 cloves of garlic, chopped
- 1 eggplant, chopped
- 1 can chopped tomatoes
- 1-pound pasta
- Enough vegetable broth to cover the pasta
- ¼ cup black olives, pitted and sliced
- Salt and pepper to taste

Directions for Cooking:

1. Press the Sauté button on the Instant Pot and heat the oil. Sauté the onions and garlic until fragrant before adding the eggplants Allow the eggplants to wilt before adding the rest of the ingredients.
2. Close Instant Pot, press the Manual button, choose high settings, and set time to 20 minutes.
3. Once done cooking, do a QPR.
4. Serve and enjoy.

Nutrition information:

Calories per serving: 399; Carbohydrates: 73g; Protein: 12g; Fat: 6g; Sugar: 8g; Sodium: 362mg

272.   Cilantro Lime Quinoa Salad
(Servings: 2, Cooking time: 15 minutes)

Ingredients:

- 1 cup quinoa, rinsed and drained
- 1 ¼ cups vegetable broth
- 2 tablespoons lime juice
- Zest from one lime, grated
- ½ cup chopped cilantro
- Salt to taste

Nutrition information:

Calories per serving: 108; Carbohydrates: 19g;
Protein: 4g; Fat: 1g; Sugar: 3.2g; Sodium: 197mg

Directions for Cooking:

1. In the Instant Pot, place the quinoa and vegetable broth.
2. Close Instant Pot, press the Manual button, choose high settings, and set time to 15 minutes.
3. Once done cooking, do a QPR.
4. Open the lid and fluff the quinoa using fork. Transfer to a bowl and let it cool.
5. Assemble the salad by adding into the quinoa the remaining ingredients.
6. Serve and enjoy.

273.   Mashed Cauliflower Casserole
(Servings: 3, Cooking time: 10 minutes)

Ingredients:

- 1 head of cauliflower, cut into florets
- 2 tablespoons salted butter, melted
- 4 ounces cream cheese
- ½ cup sour cream
- ½ cup heavy cream
- Salt to taste
- 2 cups cheddar cheese, grated

Directions for Cooking:

1. Place a trivet in the Instant Pot and pour a cup of water.
2. Place the cauliflower on the trivet.
3. Close Instant Pot, press the Steam button, choose high settings, and set time to 10 minutes.
4. Once done cooking, do a QPR.
5. Open the lid and transfer the cauliflower into a food processor.
6. Add in the rest of the ingredients. Pulse until a bit coarse.
7. Serve and enjoy.

Nutrition information:

Calories per serving:606 ; Carbohydrates: 10g;
Protein: 24.3g; Fat: 53.1g; Sugar: 1.3g; Sodium: 757mg

274.   Instant Pot Creamy Garlic and Veggies Pasta
(Servings: 6, Cooking time: 20 minutes)

Ingredients:

- 16-ounce ziti pasta
- 2 cups chopped zucchini
- 1 cup frozen peas
- 3 cloves of garlic, minced
- 1 cup white wine
- 2 cups chicken broth
- Salt and pepper to taste
- 1 cup mozzarella cheese, grated
- 1 cup milk

Directions for Cooking:

1. Place the pasta, zucchini, peas, garlic, white wine, and chicken broth in the Instant Pot. Season with salt and pepper to taste.
2. Close Instant Pot, press the Manual button, choose high settings, and set time to 15 minutes.
3. Once done cooking, do a QPR.
4. Open the lid then press the Sauté button. Stir in the cheese and milk. Allow to simmer for 5 minutes.
5. Serve and enjoy.

Nutrition information:

Calories per serving: 291; Carbohydrates: 27.7g; Protein: 26.9g; Fat: 7.5g; Sugar: 3.1g; Sodium: 491mg

275.   Instant Pot Black Bean Soup
(Servings: 5, Cooking time: 45 minutes)

Ingredients:

- 1 tablespoon olive oil
- 1 onion, chopped
- 3 cloves of garlic, minced
- 1 red pepper, diced
- 1 tablespoon cumin
- 2 tablespoons chili powder
- ½ teaspoon cayenne pepper
- 14 ounces dry black beans, soaked overnight
- 3 cups vegetable broth
- Juice and zest from 1 lemon
- Salt to taste

Directions for Cooking:

1. Press the Sauté button on the Instant Pot and heat the oil.
2. Sauté the onion and garlic until fragrant.
3. Stir in the rest of the ingredients.
4. Close Instant Pot, press the Manual button, choose high settings, and set time to 40 minutes.
5. Once done cooking, do a QPR.
6. Serve and enjoy.

Nutrition information:

Calories per serving: 165; Carbohydrates:27.4 g; Protein: 7.6g; Fat: 3.8g; Sugar: 4.5g; Sodium: 201mg

276. Cauliflower and Pasta Alfredo
(Servings: 6, Cooking time: 6 minutes)

Ingredients:

- 1 head cauliflower, cut into florets and boiled
- 2 tablespoons butter
- 4 cloves of garlic, minced
- 1 cup chicken broth
- ¼ cup half and half
- 1 teaspoon onion powder
- 2 teaspoons garlic powder
- Salt and pepper to taste
- 1 box fettuccini noodles, cooked according to package instructions

Directions for Cooking:

1. Place the cauliflower in the food processor and pulse until smooth. Set aside.
2. Press the Sauté button on the Instant Pot and heat the butter. Sauté the garlic until fragrant and add in the cauliflower puree.
3. Stir in the half and half, onion, and garlic. Season with salt and pepper to taste.
4. Close Instant Pot, press the Manual button, choose high settings, and set time to 6 minutes.
5. Once done cooking, do a QPR.
6. Open the lid and press the Sauté button and stir in the fettuccini noodles. Allow to simmer until the pasta is soaked with the sauce.
7. Serve and enjoy.

Nutrition information:
Calories per serving: 248; Carbohydrates: 29.4g; Protein: 16.1g; Fat: 7.7g; Sugar: 6.4g; Sodium: 523mg

277. Instant Pot Mushroom Risotto
(Servings: 3, Cooking time: 25 minutes)

Ingredients:

- 1 ½ tablespoons olive oil
- 2 tablespoons vegan butter, divided
- 1 onion, diced
- 3 cloves of garlic, minced
- 8 ounces cremini mushrooms, diced
- ¾ teaspoon dried thyme
- 1 ½ cups Arborio rice
- ½ cup dry white wine
- 4 cups vegetable broth
- Salt and pepper to taste
- 1 cup frozen peas, thawed

Directions for Cooking:

1. Press the Sauté button on the Instant Pot and heat the oil and half of the butter. Stir in the onions, garlic, mushrooms, and thyme until fragrant.
2. Add the rice and stir to coat well. Pour in the wine and allow to simmer for 2 minutes.
3. Pour in the rest of the ingredients.
4. Close Instant Pot, press the Manual button, choose high settings, and set time to 20 minutes.
5. Once done cooking, do a QPR.
6. Open the lid and stir in the remaining butter before serving.
7. Serve and enjoy.

Nutrition information:
Calories per serving:3 79; Carbohydrates: 59g; Protein:10 g; Fat: 9g; Sugar: 3g; Sodium: 646mg

278.   Instant Pot Pulled BBQ Jackfruit
(Servings: 6, Cooking time: 10 minutes)

Ingredients:

- 2 20-ounces cans young green jackfruit in water
- 1 can barbecue sauce
- 6 hamburger buns
- 1 head of cabbage, shredded

Directions for Cooking:

1. Mash or shred the jackfruit using fork.
2. Place the jackfruit and barbecue sauce in the Instant Pot.
3. Close Instant Pot, press the Manual button, choose high settings, and set time to 10 minutes.
4. Once done cooking, do a QPR.
5. Remove from the Instant Pot and allow to cool.
6. Serve on hamburger buns with shredded cabbage.
7. Serve and enjoy.

Nutrition information:

Calories per serving: 508; Carbohydrates: 72.4g; Protein: 20.7g; Fat: 16.9g; Sugar: 23.4g; Sodium: 1113mg

---

279.   Easy Autumn Soup
(Servings: 6, Cooking time: 15 minutes)

Ingredients:

- 2 cups vegetable stock
- 2 cloves of garlic, minced
- 1 carrot, diced
- 1 Granny Smith apple, cored and diced
- 1 medium squash, seeded and diced
- 1 onion, diced
- Salt and pepper to taste
- A pinch of ground cinnamon
- ½ cup canned coconut milk
- A pinch of paprika powder

Directions for Cooking:

1. In the Instant Pot, put in the vegetable stock, garlic, carrots, apples, and squash. Season with salt and pepper to taste and sprinkle with cinnamon.
2. Close Instant Pot, press the Manual button, choose high settings, and set time to 15 minutes.
3. Once done cooking, do a QPR.
4. Open the lid and press the Sauté button. Stir in the coconut milk.
5. Using an immersion blender, pulse until the mixture becomes smooth.
6. Sprinkle with paprika on top.
7. Serve and enjoy.

Nutrition information:

Calories per serving: 83; Carbohydrates: 9.7g; Protein: 1.4g; Fat: 4.9g; Sugar: 0.8g; Sodium: 12mg

280.   Veggie Spanish rice
(Servings: 12, Cooking time: 25 minutes)

Ingredients:

- 2 tablespoons olive oil
- 1 large onion, chopped
- 4 cloves of garlic, minced
- 4 cups rice, uncooked
- 1 can diced tomatoes with chilies
- Salt and pepper to taste
- 4 ½ cups rice

Directions for Cooking:

1. Press the Sauté button on the Instant Pot and heat the oil.

2. Sauté the onion and garlic for 5 minutes until the onions start to caramelize.
3. Place the rest of the ingredients and give a good stir.
4. Close Instant Pot, press the Manual button, choose high settings, and set time to 20 minutes.
5. Once done cooking, do a QPR.
6. Serve and enjoy.

Nutrition information:
Calories per serving:298; Carbohydrates: 44.8g; Protein: 11.7g; Fat: 19.7g; Sugar: 1.4g; Sodium: 166mg

---

281.   Instant Pot Steamed Cauliflower
(Servings: 2, Cooking time: 8 minutes)

Ingredients:

- 1 head of cauliflower, cut into florets
- Salt and pepper to taste

Directions for Cooking:

1. Place a trivet in the Instant Pot and pour a cup of water.
2. Place the cauliflower florets on the trivet.

3. Close Instant Pot, press the button, choose high settings, and set time to 8 minutes.
4. Once done cooking, do a QPR.
5. Place the cauliflower florets in a bowl and season with salt and pepper to taste.
6. Serve and enjoy.

Nutrition information:
Calories per serving: 42; Carbohydrates: 8.7g; Protein: 2.9g; Fat: 0.4g; Sugar: 0g; Sodium: 12mg

282.   Instant Pot Saag Tofu
(Servings: 6, Cooking time: 10 minutes)

Ingredients:

- 5 tablespoons vegetable oil
- 1 onion, diced
- 3 cloves of garlic, minced
- 1-inch ginger, minced
- 1 can diced tomatoes
- 1-pound extra-firm tofu, cut into cubes and fried
- 2 teaspoons garam masala
- ¼ cup water
- ¼ cup coconut milk
- Salt and pepper to taste
- ¼ teaspoon cayenne pepper
- 1 bag frozen spinach

Directions for Cooking:

1. Press the Sauté button on the Instant Pot and heat the oil.
2. Sauté the onion, garlic, and ginger until fragrant.
3. Stir in the tomatoes, fried tofu, garam masala water, and coconut milk. Season with salt and pepper to taste.
4. Close Instant Pot, press the Manual button, choose high settings, and set time to 6 minutes.
5. Once done cooking, do a QPR.
6. Open the lid and stir in the cayenne pepper and spinach. Press the Sauté button and allow spinach to cook.
7. Serve and enjoy.

Nutrition information:

Calories per serving:207; Carbohydrates: 6.1g; Protein: 8.4g; Fat: 18.2g; Sugar: g; Sodium: mg

---

283.   Lemon Butter Broccoli
(Servings: 3, Cooking time: 8 minutes)

Ingredients:

- 1 large head of broccoli, cut into florets
- 1 stick melted butter
- 1 teaspoon garlic powder
- 2 tablespoons lemon juice
- Salt and pepper to taste

Directions for Cooking:

1. Place a trivet in the Instant Pot and pour a cup of water.
2. Place the cauliflower florets on the trivet.
3. Close Instant Pot, press the button, choose high settings, and set time to 8 minutes.
4. Once done cooking, do a QPR.
5. Place the cauliflower florets in a bowl and stir in the rest of the seasonings.

Nutrition information:

Calories per serving: 32; Carbohydrates: 4.1g; Protein: 1.8g; Fat: 1.5g; Sugar: 1.2g; Sodium: 25mg

---

INSTANT POT VEGETARIAN RECIPES

284.   Sweet Potato Hash
(Servings: 8, Cooking time: 20 minutes)

Ingredients:

- 1 large sweet potato, sliced
- 3 cups butternut squash, cubed
- 1 cup water
- 2 tablespoons butter
- 4 cloves of garlic, minced
- 1 onion, sliced
- Salt and pepper to taste
- 1 teaspoon parsley, chopped

Directions for Cooking:

1. Place the potatoes and squash in the Instant Pot and pour in water.
2. Close Instant Pot, press the button, choose high settings, and set time to 15 minutes.
3. Once done cooking, do a QPR.
4. Open the lid and set the sweet potatoes and squash aside.
5. Remove the water from the Instant Pot.
6. Heat the Sauté button and melt the butter.
7. Sauté the garlic and onion until fragrant.
8. Add in the cooked vegetables and season with salt and pepper.
9. Garnish with parsley.
10. Serve and enjoy.

Nutrition information:

Calories per serving: 74; Carbohydrates: 11.9g;
Protein: 1.2g; Fat: 2.9g; Sugar: 2.9g; Sodium: 39mg

---

285.   Indian Green Bean Curried Potatoes
(Servings: 5, Cooking time: 15 minutes)

Ingredients

- 2 teaspoons cooking oil
- ½ teaspoon mustard seed
- ¼ teaspoon asofetida
- 3 cloves of garlic, minced
- ½ teaspoon ground turmeric
- ¼ teaspoon cayenne powder
- 2 ½ teaspoons ground coriander
- 2 cups long green beans
- 2 medium-sized potatoes, peeled and quartered
- ¼ cup water
- Juice from ½ lemon, freshly squeezed
- Salt and pepper to taste

Directions for Cooking:

1. Press the Sauté button on the Instant Pot and heat the oil.
2. Toast the mustard and asafetida until fragrant. Add in the garlic, turmeric, cayenne powder, and coriander. Toast for another minute.
3. Stir in the rest of the ingredients.
4. Close Instant Pot, press the Manual button, choose high settings, and set time to 10 minutes.
5. Once done cooking, do a QPR.
6. Serve and enjoy.

Nutrition information:

Calories per serving: 99; Carbohydrates: 14g; Protein: 6g; Fat: 2g; Sugar: 2.1g; Sodium: 1mg

286.   Easy Rustic Lentil Soup
(Servings: 6, Cooking time: 35 minutes)

Ingredients:

- 1 teaspoon olive oil
- 1 onion, diced
- 3 cloves of garlic, minced
- 3 stalks of celery, chopped
- 3 carrots, peeled and chopped
- 1 large potato, peeled and diced
- 2 teaspoons herbs de Provence
- 1 can diced tomatoes
- 6 cups vegetable broth
- 2 cups green lentils, soaked overnight
- Salt and pepper to taste
- 3 cups kale, torn

Directions for Cooking:

1. Press the Sauté button on the Instant Pot and heat the oil.
2. Sauté the onion, garlic, and celery until fragrant.
3. Stir in the carrots, potatoes, herbs, tomatoes, vegetable broth and lentils. Season with salt and pepper to taste.
4. Close Instant Pot, press the Manual button, choose high settings, and set time to 30 minutes.
5. Once done cooking, do a QPR.
6. Open the lid and stir in the kale while still hot.
7. Serve and enjoy.

Nutrition information:

Calories per serving: 326; Carbohydrates: 53g; Protein: 23g; Fat: 3g; Sugar: 3.1g; Sodium: 131mg

287.   Vegan Cauliflower Chickpea Curry
(Servings: 4, Cooking time: 9 minutes)

Ingredients:

- 1 tablespoon coconut oil
- 3 cloves of garlic, minced
- 1 onion, chopped
- ½ large red pepper, chopped
- 1 tablespoon yellow curry paste
- 1 can diced tomatoes
- 1 cup coconut milk
- 1 tablespoon soy sauce
- ½ tablespoon coconut sugar
- 1 can chickpeas, drained and rinsed
- 2 cups cauliflower, cut into florets
- Juice from 1 lemon
- Salt and pepper to taste
- Chopped cilantro for garnish

Directions for Cooking

1. Press the Sauté button on the Instant Pot and heat the oil. Sauté the garlic and onion for 30 seconds before adding the red peppers and yellow curry paste.
2. Stir in the rest of the ingredients except for the cilantro.
3. Close Instant Pot, press the Manual button, choose high settings, and set time to 8 minutes.
4. Once done cooking, do a QPR.
5. Garnish with cilantro on top.
6. Serve and enjoy.

Nutrition information:

Calories per serving: 579; Carbohydrates: 66.8g; Protein: 15.2g; Fat: 30.4g; Sugar: 12.8g; Sodium:1756 mg

288.   Organic Spinach Pasta
(Servings: 6, Cooking time: 9 minutes)

Ingredients:

- 1 tablespoon olive oil
- 4 cloves of garlic, minced
- 1-pound organic pasta
- 5 cups water
- Salt and pepper to taste
- 5 cups organic spinach
- 3 tablespoons butter

Directions for Cooking:

1. Press the Sauté button on the Instant Pot and heat the oil. Sauté the garlic until fragrant.

2. Add in the pasta and water. Season with salt and pepper to taste.
3. Close Instant Pot, press the Manual button, choose high settings, and set time to 6 minutes.
4. Once done cooking, do a QPR.
5. Open the lid and stir in the spinach and butter. Allow to simmer for additional 2 minutes.
6. Serve and enjoy.

Nutrition information:
Calories per serving: 137; Carbohydrates: 10.4g; Protein: 2.3g; Fat: 9.9g; Sugar: 3.1g; Sodium: 355mg

---

289.   Jackfruit and Potato Curry
(Servings: 8, Cooking time: 12 minutes)

Ingredients:

- 2 tablespoons coconut oil
- 1 cup onion, chopped
- 4 cloves of garlic, minced
- 1 teaspoon grated ginger
- 2 tablespoons curry powder
- 1 teaspoon paprika
- 1 teaspoon cumin
- 1 teaspoon turmeric powder
- 2 sprigs fresh thyme
- 1 can green jackfruit, drained and rinsed
- 4 medium potatoes, peeled and cubed
- 1 can coconut milk
- 2 cups vegetable broth
- 1 teaspoon cayenne pepper
- Salt and pepper to taste
- ¼ cup cilantro leaves

Directions for Cooking:

1. Press the Sauté button on the Instant Pot and heat the oil. Sauté the onion, garlic, and ginger until fragrant.
2. Stir in the rest of the ingredients.
3. Close Instant Pot, press the Manual button, choose high settings, and set time to 10 minutes.
4. Once done cooking, do a QPR.
5. Open the lid and stir in the cilantro leaves last.
6. Serve and enjoy.

Nutrition information:
Calories per serving: 267; Carbohydrates:27 g; Protein: 5g; Fat: 17g; Sugar: 3.6g; Sodium: 291mg

290. Vegan Pasta Puttanesca
(Servings: 4, Cooking time: 15 minutes)

Ingredients

- 1 tablespoon olive oil
- 3 cloves of garlic, minced
- 4 cups pasta sauce
- 3 cups water
- 4 cups penne pasta
- ¼ teaspoon crushed red pepper flakes
- 1 tablespoon capers
- ½ cup kalamata olives, sliced
- Salt and pepper to taste

Directions for Cooking:

1. Press the Sauté button on the Instant Pot and heat the oil.
2. Sauté the garlic until fragrant and add in the rest of the ingredients. Give a good stir.
3. Close Instant Pot, press the Manual button, choose high settings, and set time to 10 minutes.
4. Once done cooking, do a QPR.
5. Serve and enjoy.

Nutrition information:

Calories per serving: 504; Carbohydrates: 98g; Protein: 18g; Fat: 4g; Sugar: 13g; Sodium: 1620mg

---

291. Instant Pot Quinoa with Tofu
(Servings: 6, Cooking time: 10 minutes)

Ingredients

- 1 cup quinoa
- 1 10-ounce bag frozen peas
- 1 cup green beans
- 1 package firm tofu, cubed and fried
- 2 tablespoons soy sauce
- 1 teaspoon miso paste
- 1 tablespoon crushed garlic
- 1 tablespoon grated ginger
- 2 cups vegetable broth
- Salt and pepper to taste
- 1 tablespoon sesame oil
- Green onions for garnish

Directions for Cooking:

1. Add the quinoa, peas, green beans, tofu, soy sauce, miso pasta, garlic, ginger, and broth. Season with salt and pepper to taste.
2. Close Instant Pot, press the Manual button, choose high settings, and set time to 10 minutes.
3. Once done cooking, do a QPR.
4. Open the lid and fluff the quinoa mixture.
5. Stir in sesame oil and green onions.
6. Serve and enjoy.

Nutrition information:

Calories per serving: 276; Carbohydrates:29 g; Protein: 18g; Fat: 11g; Sugar: 3g; Sodium: 124mg

292.   Broccoli Macaroni and Cheese
(Servings: 5, Cooking time: 10 minutes)

Ingredients:

- 1-pound whole wheat macaroni pasta
- ¾ pounds broccoli, cut into florets
- 4 cups water
- 2 tablespoons unsalted butter
- 1 ½ cups whole milk
- 6 ounces cheddar cheese, grated
- 8 ounces provolone cheese, grated
- Salt and pepper to taste

Directions for Cooking:

1. Place all ingredients in the Instant Pot. Give a good stir.
2. Close Instant Pot, press the button, choose high settings, and set time to 10 minutes.
3. Once done cooking, do a QPR.
4. Open the lid and stir to combine everything.
5. Serve and enjoy.

Nutrition information:

Calories per serving:444; Carbohydrates: 40.9g; Protein: 25.7g; Fat: 21.3g; Sugar: 12g; Sodium: 447mg

---

293.   Vegan Lentil Gumbo
(Servings: 5, Cooking time: 6 minutes)

Ingredients:

- 1 tablespoon olive oil
- 1 ½ cups onion, sliced
- 1 teaspoon minced garlic
- 1 red bell pepper, chopped
- 2 celery ribs, chopped
- 1 tablespoon fresh thyme
- ½ teaspoon oregano
- ½ teaspoon Cajun mix spice
- 1 can lentils, rinsed and drained
- 1 can diced tomatoes
- 2 tablespoons tomato sauce
- 3 cups vegetable broth
- 2 cups okra, chopped roughly
- 1 cup cauliflower
- Salt and pepper to taste

Directions for Cooking:

1. Press the Sauté button on the Instant Pot and heat the oil. Sauté the onions and garlic until the onions start to caramelize.
2. Stir in the rest of the ingredients.
3. Close Instant Pot, press the Manual button, choose high settings, and set time to 6 minutes.
4. Once done cooking, do a QPR.
5. Serve and enjoy.

Nutrition information:

Calories per serving: 152; Carbohydrates: 17.2g; Protein: 10.4g; Fat: 5.6g; Sugar: 6g; Sodium: 494mg

---

294. Instant Pot Garlic Hummus

(Servings: 12, Cooking time: 50 minutes)

Ingredients:

- 1 ½ cups dried chickpeas, soaked overnight
- 6 cups water
- ½ cup tahini
- 2 cloves of garlic, minced
- 3 tablespoons lemon juice
- 1 ½ teaspoon salt to taste
- Crushed red pepper
- Chopped parsley
- Ground paprika

Directions for Cooking:

1. Place the chickpeas and water in the Instant Pot.
2. Close Instant Pot, press the Manual button, choose high settings, and set time to 50 minutes.
3. Once done cooking, do a QPR.
4. Open the lid and strain the chickpeas. Set aside.
5. In a food processor, place the chickpeas, tahini, garlic, and lemon juice. Season with salt and pepper to taste. Pulse until smooth. If the hummus is too thick, add water if necessary.
6. Garnish with crushed red pepper, parsley, and paprika.
7. Serve and enjoy.

Nutrition information:

Calories per serving: 159; Carbohydrates: 18.9g; Protein: 7.1g; Fat: 6.9g; Sugar: 3.1g; Sodium: 314mg

---

295. Cauliflower and Potato Soup

(Servings: 4, Cooking time: 7 minutes)

Ingredients:

- 1 head cauliflower, cut into florets
- 2 small red potatoes, peeled and sliced
- 4 cups vegetable stock
- 6 cloves of garlic, minced
- 1 onion, diced
- 1 cup heavy cream
- 2 bay leaves
- Salt and pepper to taste
- 2 stalks of green onions

Directions for Cooking:

1. Place the cauliflower, potatoes, vegetable stock, garlic, onion, heavy cream, and bay leaves in the Instant Pot. Season with salt and pepper to taste.
2. Close Instant Pot, press the Manual button, choose high settings, and set time to 6 minutes.
3. Once done cooking, do a QPR.
4. Open the lid and stir in the green onions.
5. Serve and enjoy.

Nutrition information:

Calories per serving: ; Carbohydrates: g; Protein: g; Fat: g; Sugar: g; Sodium: mg

---

296.   One-Pot Vegetarian Lentil Tortilla Soup
(Servings: 6, Cooking time: 40 minutes)

Ingredients:

- 1 cup diced onion
- 1 bell pepper, diced
- 1 jalapeno pepper, diced
- 2 ½ cups vegetable broth
- 1 can tomato sauce
- ½ cup salsa Verde
- 1 tablespoon tomato paste
- 1 can black beans, drained and rinsed
- 1 can pinto beans, drained and rinsed
- 1 cup fresh corn kernels
- ½ teaspoon chili powder
- ½ teaspoon garlic powder
- Salt and pepper to taste
- ¼ cup heavy cream

Directions for Cooking:

1. Place all ingredients in the Instant Pot except for the heavy cream and give a good stir.
2. Close Instant Pot, press the Manual button, choose high settings, and set time to 35 minutes.
3. Once done cooking, do a QPR.
4. Open the lid and press the Sauté button. Stir in the heavy cream and allow to simmer for 5 minutes.
5. Serve and enjoy.

Nutrition information:

Calories per serving:321 ; Carbohydrates: 48.7g; Protein: 8.6g; Fat: 12.4g; Sugar: 13.8g; Sodium: 496mg

---

297.   Chickpea and Sweet Potato Stew
(Servings: 6, Cooking time: 10 minutes)

Ingredients:

- 1 yellow onion, chopped
- 1 tablespoon garlic, minced
- 2 cans garbanzos beans, drained
- 1-pound sweet potatoes, peeled and chopped
- Salt and pepper to taste
- 1 teaspoon ground ginger
- 1 ½ teaspoon ground cumin
- 1 teaspoon ground coriander
- 1 teaspoon ground cinnamon
- 4 cups vegetable broth
- 4 cups spinach, torn

Directions for Cooking:

1. Place all ingredients in the Instant Pot except for the spinach.
2. Close Instant Pot, press the Manual button, choose high settings, and set time to 10 minutes.
3. Once done cooking, do a QPR.
4. Open the lid and stir in the spinach. Press the Sauté button and allow to simmer until the spinach wilts.
5. Serve and enjoy.

Nutrition information:

Calories per serving: 165; Carbohydrates: 32.3g; Protein: 6.3g; Fat: 1.1g; Sugar: 5.4g; Sodium: 751mg

298.   Vegan BBQ Meatballs
(Servings: 4, Cooking time: 10 minutes)

Ingredients:

- ¼ cup water
- 2 pounds frozen vegan meatballs
- 1 ½ cup barbecue sauce
- 1 can cranberry sauce
- Salt and pepper to taste

Directions for Cooking:

1. Place all ingredients in the Instant Pot and give a good stir.
2. Close Instant Pot, press the Manual button, choose high settings, and set time to 10 minutes.
3. Once done cooking, do a QPR.
4. Serve and enjoy.

Nutrition information:

Calories per serving: 347; Carbohydrates: 68.1g; Protein: 17.1g; Fat: 1.8g; Sugar: 23.1g; Sodium: 675mg

---

299.   Simple Garden Pasta
(Servings: 4, Cooking time: 10 minutes)

Ingredients:

- 1 onion, diced
- 2 cloves of garlic, minced
- 1 carrot, peeled and chopped
- 2 teaspoons dried basil
- ¾ teaspoon dried thyme
- 1 can diced tomatoes
- 2 tablespoons tomato paste
- 4 cups vegetable broth
- 1 medium zucchini, chopped
- ¼ cup shell pasta
- Salt and pepper to taste
- 1 cup baby spinach
- 1 teaspoon balsamic vinegar

Directions for Cooking:

1. Place all ingredients in the Instant Pot except for the spinach and balsamic vinegar.
2. Close Instant Pot, press the Manual button, choose high settings, and set time to 10 minutes.
3. Once done cooking, do a QPR.
4. Open the lid and press the Sauté button. Stir in the baby spinach and simmer until wilted.
5. Drizzle with balsamic vinegar.
6. Serve and enjoy.

Nutrition information:

Calories per serving:86 ; Carbohydrates: 18g; Protein: 4g; Fat: 1g; Sugar: 6g; Sodium: 678mg

300.   Vegan Lasagna Soup
(Servings: 3, Cooking time: 12 minutes)

Ingredients:

- 1 teaspoon oil
- ½ onion, chopped
- 4 cloves of garlic, minced
- 1 cup packaged vegetables
- ¼ cup red lentils, cooked
- 1 cup tomato puree
- 2 teaspoons Italian seasoning mix
- 2 cups veggie broth
- 5 ounces lasagna sheets, broken into small pieces
- Salt and pepper to taste
- 1 tablespoon nutritional yeast

Directions for Cooking:

1. Press the Sauté button on the Instant Pot and heat the oil. Sauté the onion and garlic until fragrant.
2. Stir in the rest of the ingredients.
3. Close Instant Pot, press the button, choose high settings, and set time to 10 minutes.
4. Once done cooking, do a QPR.
5. Serve and enjoy.

Nutrition information:

Calories per serving: 223; Carbohydrates: 35.3g; Protein: 11.4g; Fat: 4.8g; Sugar: 9.3g; Sodium: 472mg

---

301.   Vegan "Buttered" Chicken
(Servings: 3, Cooking time: 10 minutes)

Ingredients:

- 3 large ripe tomatoes, diced
- 4 cloves of garlic
- ½ inch ginger, minced
- 1 green chili, chopped
- ¾ cup water
- ½ teaspoon garam masala
- Salt and pepper to taste
- 1 cup cooked chickpeas
- 1 cup soy curls, rehydrated
- ½ teaspoon sugar
- Salt and pepper to taste

Directions for Cooking:

1. Place all ingredients in the Instant Pot and give a good stir.
2. Close Instant Pot, press the Manual button, choose high settings, and set time to 10 minutes.
3. Once done cooking, do a QPR.
4. Serve and enjoy.

Nutrition information:

Calories per serving: 191; Carbohydrates: 31.4g; Protein: 14.9g; Fat: 2.1g; Sugar: 14.2g; Sodium: 689mg

---

302.   One-Pot Cauliflower Cheddar Pasta
(Servings: 4, Cooking time: 10 minutes)

Ingredients:

- 1-pound pasta, dry
- 4 cups water
- 16 ounces cheddar cheese
- 1 cup frozen cauliflower
- 1 cup half and half
- Salt and pepper to taste
- A dash of paprika

Directions for Cooking:

1. Place all ingredients in the Instant Pot and give a good stir.
2. Close Instant Pot, press the button, choose high settings, and set time to 10 minutes.
3. Once done cooking, do a QPR.
4. Serve and enjoy.

Nutrition information:

Calories per serving:964 ; Carbohydrates: 90g; Protein: 45g; Fat: 46g; Sugar: 4g; Sodium: 755mg

---

303.   Instant Pot Tempeh Tajine
(Servings: 6, Cooking time: 15 minutes)

Ingredients:

- 1 teaspoon each of ground cumin, cinnamon, turmeric and ground ginger
- 2 packs tempeh, cubed
- 2 teaspoons soy sauce
- 4 cloves of garlic, minced
- 1 tablespoon oil
- 1 onion, chopped
- 2 carrots, peeled and chopped
- 1 sweet potato, peeled and chopped
- ½ cup prunes, pitted and chopped
- 1 can diced tomatoes
- 1 cup vegetable stock
- Salt and pepper to taste

Directions for Cooking:

1. In a mixing bowl, combine the herbs with the tempeh, soy sauce, and garlic. Allow to marinate in the fridge for at least 3 hours.
2. Press the Sauté button and heat the oil. Stir in the marinated tempeh and onions. Stir until lightly brown.
3. Stir in the rest of the ingredients.
4. Close Instant Pot, press the Manual button, choose high settings, and set time to 10 minutes.
5. Once done cooking, do a QPR.
6. Serve and enjoy.

Nutrition information:

Calories per serving: 242; Carbohydrates: 24.4g; Protein: 15.4g; Fat: 11.5g; Sugar: 3.4g; Sodium: 99mg

304. Veggie Shepherd's Pie

(Servings: 6, Cooking time: 4 hours and 5 minutes)

Ingredients:

- 4 red potatoes, boiled and peeled
- ¾ cup almond milk
- 4 tablespoons olive oil, divided
- ¼ cup nutritional yeast
- ½ teaspoon garlic powder
- Salt and pepper to taste
- 1 white onion, chopped
- 1 cup carrot, chopped
- 1 block extra firm tofu, chopped
- 1 bunch dinosaur kale, chopped
- ½ cup corn kernels
- ½ cup frozen peas
- ½ cup water

Directions for Cooking:

1. In a bowl, mash the potatoes, milk, half of the olive oil, nutritional yeast, and garlic powder. Season with salt and pepper to taste. Set aside.

2. Press the Sauté button on the Instant Pot and heat the remaining oil. Sauté the onion until fragrant and add in the carrots, tofu, kale, corn, and peas. Season with salt and pepper to taste.

3. Pour in water. Pack the vegetable mixture firmly and spread the potato mash on top.

4. Close Instant Pot but do not seal the vent.

5. Press the Slow Cook button and set time to 4 hours.

6. Serve and enjoy.

Nutrition information:

Calories per serving: 389; Carbohydrates: 51.4g; Protein: 16.2g; Fat: 14.5g; Sugar: 17.3g; Sodium: 446mg

305. Vegan Baked Beans

(Servings: 10, Cooking time: 50 minutes)

Ingredients:

- 1-pound dry navy beans
- 6 cups water
- ¾ cup molasses
- ½ cup brown sugar
- ¾ cup ketchup salt and pepper to taste
- 1 ½ tablespoon Worcestershire sauce
- 2 tablespoons apple cider vinegar
- 1 onion, chopped
- 3 cloves of garlic, minced
- 1 bay leaf

Directions for Cooking:

1. Place the beans and water in the Instant Pot.

2. Close Instant Pot, press the Manual button, choose high settings, and set time to 40 minutes.

3. Once done cooking, do a QPR.

4. Open the lid and strain the beans. Discard the water.

5. In the Instant Pot, place all ingredients including the beans.

6. Close the lid and seal the vent. Press the Manual button and set time to 10 minutes.

7. Serve and enjoy.

Nutrition information:

Calories per serving: 135; Carbohydrates: 34.1g; Protein: 0.7g; Fat: 0.2g; Sugar: 12.9g; Sodium: 42mg

306.   Simple Baked Beans
(Servings: 4, Cooking time: 50 minutes)

Ingredients:

- 1-pound dried navy beans
- 6 cups cold water
- 1 small onion, diced
- 6 cloves of garlic, chopped
- 1 ¾ cup cold water
- ¼ cup blackstrap molasses
- ¼ cup maple syrup
- 1 tablespoon soy sauce
- ¼ teaspoon salt
- 2 bay leaves
- 2 teaspoons Dijon mustard
- 1 teaspoon apple cider vinegar

Directions for Cooking:

1. Place the beans and water in the Instant Pot.
2. Close Instant Pot, press the Manual button, choose high settings, and set time to 40 minutes.
3. Once done cooking, do a QPR.
4. Open the lid and strain the beans. Discard the water.
5. Place all ingredients back in the Instant Pot.
6. Close the lid and seal the vent. Press the Manual button and set time to 10 minutes.
7. Serve and enjoy.

Nutrition information:

Calories per serving:522 ; Carbohydrates: 10.2g;
Protein: 26.5g; Fat: 2.4g; Sugar: 26.9g; Sodium: 337mg

---

307.   One-Pot Vegetable Barley Soup
(Servings: 3, Cooking time: 30 minutes)

Ingredients:

- 2 garlic cloves, minced
- 1 leek, sliced
- 3 carrots, peeled and sliced
- 3 stalks of celery, minced
- 8 ounces mushrooms, sliced
- 7 cups water
- 2 cubes of vegetable bouillon
- ½ cup dried pearled barley
- Salt and pepper to taste

Directions for Cooking:

1. Place all ingredients in the Instant Pot and give a good stir.
2. Close Instant Pot, press the button, choose high settings, and set time to 30 minutes.
3. Once done cooking, do a QPR.
4. Serve and enjoy.

Nutrition information:

Calories per serving:372; Carbohydrates:73.2g;
Protein: 11.5g; Fat: 1g; Sugar: 2.1g; Sodium: 47mg

308.   Creamy Tomato Soup
(Servings: 4, Cooking time: 12 minutes)

Ingredients:

- 4 tablespoons olive oil
- 1 onion, diced
- 2 cans crushed tomatoes
- 6 cups vegetable stock
- Salt and pepper to taste
- ½ cup fresh basil
- 1 ½ cups whole raw cashews

Directions for Cooking:

1. Press the Sauté button on the Instant Pot and heat the oil. Sauté the onion until slightly caramelized.
2. Stir in the rest of the ingredients.
3. Close Instant Pot, press the Manual button, choose high settings, and set time to 10 minutes.
4. Once done cooking, do a QPR.
5. Open the lid and use an immersion blender to smoothen the texture.
6. Serve and enjoy.

Nutrition information:

Calories per serving: 735; Carbohydrates: 36.1g; Protein: 13.1g; Fat: 64.7g; Sugar: 12.9g; Sodium: 395mg

---

309.   One-Pot Veggie Curry Dish
(Servings: 4, Cooking time: 7 minutes)

Ingredients:

- 3 potatoes, peeled and chopped
- 1 cup broccoli florets
- 1 cup cauliflower florets
- 1 red bell pepper, sliced
- ½ cup frozen corn
- ½ cup frozen peas
- 2 tablespoons green curry paste
- 1 teaspoon onion powder
- 1 teaspoon garlic powder
- 1 cup coconut milk
- 2 cups vegetable stock
- Salt to taste

Directions for Cooking:

1. Place all ingredients in the Instant Pot.
2. Close Instant Pot, press the Manual button, choose high settings, and set time to 7 minutes.
3. Once done cooking, do a QPR.
4. Serve and enjoy.

Nutrition information:

Calories per serving:410 ; Carbohydrates: 63g; Protein: 9.8g; Fat: 15.4g; Sugar: 6g; Sodium: 42mg

---

310. Vegan Carrot Ginger Soup

(Servings: 5, Cooking time: 8 minutes)

Ingredients:

- 1 ½ tablespoons olive oil
- 1 onion, diced
- 4 cloves of garlic, minced
- 1 ½ tablespoons fresh ginger, grated
- 1 teaspoon dried thyme
- ½ teaspoon ground coriander
- ½ teaspoon crushed red pepper
- 2 bay leaves
- 2 pounds carrots, chopped
- 4 cups vegetable broth
- Salt and pepper to taste
- 1 cup coconut milk
- 2 tablespoons lime juice

Directions for Cooking:

1. Press the Sauté button on the Instant Pot and heat the oil.
2. Sauté the onion and garlic until fragrant. Stir in the rest of the ingredients.
3. Close Instant Pot, press the Manual button, choose high settings, and set time to 6 minutes.
4. Once done cooking, do a QPR.
5. Serve and enjoy.

Nutrition information:

Calories per serving: 268; Carbohydrates: 26g; Protein: 7g; Fat: 16g; Sugar: 11g; Sodium: 584mg

---

311. Split Pea Soup

(Servings: 4, Cooking time: 40 minutes)

Ingredients:

- 1 tablespoon olive oil
- 1 onion, diced
- 2 stalks of celery, chopped
- 3 cloves of garlic, minced
- 3 carrots, sliced
- 2 teaspoons curry power
- 1 teaspoon ground cumin
- ½ teaspoon ground coriander
- 2 cups yellow split peas
- 4 cups vegetable broth
- 2 cups water
- Salt and pepper to taste

Directions for Cooking:

1. Press the Sauté button on the Instant Pot and sauté the onion, celery, and garlic until fragrant.
2. Stir in the carrots, curry powder, cumin, coriander, and peas.
3. Add in the rest of the ingredients.
4. Close Instant Pot, press the Manual button, choose high settings, and set time to 35 minutes.
5. Once done cooking, do a QPR.
6. Serve and enjoy.

Nutrition information:

Calories per serving: 383; Carbohydrates: 29g; Protein: 25g; Fat: 5g; Sugar: 13g; Sodium: 582mg

312.   Three Cheese Mushroom and Tortellini
(Servings: 8, Cooking time: 15 minutes)

Ingredients:

- 2 teaspoons butter
- 2 stalks of celery, chopped
- 3 cloves of garlic, minced
- 1 carrot, peeled and chopped
- 8 cups vegetable broth
- 5 ounces shiitake mushrooms, sliced
- 8 ounces baby Bella mushrooms, sliced
- 1 cup parmigiana Reggiano, grated
- 1 cup three cheese tortellini
- 1 cup mozzarella cheese, grated
- Salt to taste

Directions for Cooking:

1. Press the Sauté button on the Instant Pot and sauté the celery and garlic until fragrant.
2. Add in the rest of the ingredients. Stir to combine everything.
3. Close Instant Pot, press the Manual button, choose high settings, and set time to 15 minutes.
4. Once done cooking, do a QPR.
5. Serve and enjoy.

Nutrition information:

Calories per serving: 182; Carbohydrates: 19.5g; Protein: 10g; Fat: 12g; Sugar: 2.5g; Sodium: 605mg

---

313.   Instant Pot Vegan Burritos
(Servings: 8, Cooking time: 25 minutes)

Ingredients:

- 2 tablespoons olive oil
- 1 onion, chopped
- 3 cloves of garlic, minced
- 1 15-ounce can black beans, drained and rinsed
- 1 ½ cups brown rice
- 1 ½ cups corn
- 12 ounces commercial salsa
- 2 cups water
- 1 teaspoon ground cumin
- 2 teaspoons chili powder
- 1 teaspoon paprika
- Salt and pepper to taste
- 1 cup finely chopped kale
- 8 burrito tortillas
- 3 cups lettuce
- 2 avocados, sliced

Directions for Cooking:

1. Press the Sauté button on the Instant Pot and heat the oil and sauté the onions and garlic until fragrant.
2. Stir in the black beans, brown rice, corn, commercial salsa, water, cumin, chili powder, and paprika. Season with salt and pepper to taste.
3. Close Instant Pot, press the Manual button, choose high settings, and set time to 20 minutes.
4. Once done cooking, do a QPR.
5. Open the lid and stir in the chopped kale.
6. Assemble the burritos by placing the rice mixture, lettuce, and avocado. Roll into a burrito.Serve and enjoy.

Nutrition information:

Calories per serving:501; Carbohydrates: 78g; Protein: 14.5g; Fat: 15.8g; Sugar: 5.1g; Sodium: 392mg

314. Mushroom Bulgogi Lettuce Wraps
(Servings: 6, Cooking time: 18 minutes)

Ingredients:

- 1 tablespoon olive oil
- 1 onion, chopped
- 1 tablespoon minced ginger
- 1 tablespoon minced garlic
- 1-pound Portobello mushrooms, sliced
- ¼ cup soy sauce
- 2 tablespoons rice wine vinegar
- ¼ cup maple syrup
- 2 tablespoons hot sauce,¼ cup water
- 1 tablespoon sesame seeds
- 2 tablespoons toasted sesame oil
- 4 green onions, chopped
- 1 head butter lettuce, shredded
- Lime wedges

Directions for Cooking:

1. Press the Sauté button on the Instant Pot and heat the oil. Sauté the onion, ginger, garlic until fragrant.
2. Stir in the mushrooms and add the soy sauce, rice wine vinegar, maple syrup, hot sauce, and water.
3. Close Instant Pot, press the Manual button, choose high settings, and set time to 15 minutes.
4. Once done cooking, do a QPR.
5. Open the lid and stir in sesame seeds and sesame oil. Sprinkle with green onions.
6. Serve with butter and lime wedges.
7. Serve and enjoy.

Nutrition information:

Calories per serving: 182; Carbohydrates: 20.8g; Protein: 4.3g; Fat: 10.2g; Sugar: 14g; Sodium: 715mg

315. Curried Black Eyed Peas
(Servings: 5, Cooking time: 52 minutes)

Ingredients:

- 1 tablespoon olive oil
- 4 cloves of garlic, minced
- ½ onion, minced
- 1 cup dried black-eyed peas
- 2 cups water
- 3 dried curry leaves
- 1/8 teaspoon mustard seeds
- 2 ½ tablespoons tomato paste
- 1 teaspoon ground cumin
- 1 teaspoon ground coriander
- ¼ teaspoon ground turmeric
- 3 teaspoons brown sugar
- 2 teaspoons fresh lemon juice

Directions for Cooking:

1. Press the Sauté button on the Instant Pot and heat the oil.
2. Sauté the garlic and onion until fragrant. Stir in the rest of the ingredients.
3. Close Instant Pot, press the Manual button, choose high settings, and set time to 50 minutes.
4. Once done cooking, do a QPR.
5. Serve and enjoy.

Nutrition information:

Calories per serving:131; Carbohydrates: 24g; Protein: 8g; Fat: 3.2g; Sugar: 4g; Sodium: 753mg

316.   Quinoa Burrito Bowls
(Servings: 5, Cooking time: 33 minutes)

Ingredients:

- 1 teaspoon olive oil
- ½ red onion, diced
- 1 bell pepper, diced
- 1 teaspoon ground cumin
- 1 cup quinoa, rinsed
- 1 cup commercial salsa
- 1 cup water
- 1 ½ cups cooked black beans
- Salt and pepper to taste
- Avocado slices
- Fresh cilantro, chopped
- Lime wedges

Directions for Cooking:

Press the Sauté button and heat the oil. Sauté the onion until fragrant.

1.
2. Stir in the bell pepper, cumin, quinoa, commercial salsa, water, and black beans. Season with salt and pepper to taste.
3. Close Instant Pot, press the Manual button, choose high settings, and set time to 30 minutes.
4. Once done cooking, do a QPR.
5. Open the lid and ladle the mixture into bowls. Add in avocado slices, cilantro, and lime wedges.
6. Serve and enjoy.

Nutrition information:

Calories per serving: 296; Carbohydrates: 44.5g; Protein: 11.5g; Fat: 9.4g; Sugar: 3.8g; Sodium: 375mg

---

317.   Instant Pot Veggie Clear Soup
(Servings: 4, Cooking time: 10 minutes)

Ingredients:

- 1 onion, diced
- 2 cloves of garlic, minced
- 1 carrot, chopped
- 1 stalk of celery, chopped
- 2 teaspoons dried basil
- 1 teaspoon dried oregano
- ¾ teaspoon dried thyme
- 1 yellow zucchini, chopped
- 2 tablespoons nutritional yeast
- Salt and pepper to taste

Directions for Cooking:

1. Place all ingredients in the Instant Pot. Mix to combine.
2. Close Instant Pot, press the Manual button, choose high settings, and set time to 10 minutes.
3. Once done cooking, do a QPR.
4. Serve and enjoy.

Nutrition information:

Calories per serving: 62; Carbohydrates: 11.4g; Protein: 4.4g; Fat: 0.6g; Sugar: 2.4g; Sodium: 292mg

318. Cheesy Lentils and Brown Rice
(Servings: 5, Cooking time: 25 minutes)

Ingredients:

- 1 onion, diced
- 4 cloves of garlic, minced
- 1 red bell pepper, chopped
- ¾ cup brown rice
- ¾ cup brown lentils
- 2 ½ cups vegetable broth
- 1 can diced tomatoes
- 1 can diced green chilies
- 1 tablespoon taco seasoning
- Salt and pepper to taste
- 2 cups mozzarella cheese, shredded
- ¼ cup chopped cilantro

Directions for Cooking:

1. Place all ingredients except for the mozzarella cheese and cilantro.
2. Close Instant Pot, press the Manual button, choose high settings, and set time to 25 minutes.
3. Once done cooking, do a QPR.
4. Open the lid and stir in the mozzarella cheese and cilantro.
5. Serve and enjoy.

Nutrition information:

Calories per serving:530; Carbohydrates: 61g; Protein: 29g; Fat: 19g; Sugar: 6g; Sodium: 1125mg

---

319. Spicy Chili and Beer Macaroni
(Servings: 4, Cooking time: 15 minutes)

Ingredients:

- 3 ½ cups commercial chili
- 1 12-ounce beer
- ½ cup water
- 2 cups elbow pasta
- 1 cup coconut milk
- Salt and pepper to taste

Directions for Cooking:

1. Place all ingredients in the Instant Pot and give a good stir.
2. Close Instant Pot, press the Manual button, choose high settings, and set time to 15 minutes.
3. Once done cooking, do a QPR.
4. Serve and enjoy.

Nutrition information:

Calories per serving: 487; Carbohydrates: 47.8g; Protein: 14.2g; Fat: 28.5g; Sugar: 9g; Sodium: 1188mg

320. Vegetarian Quinoa Chili
(Servings: 9, Cooking time: 25 minutes)

Ingredients:

- 4 cups vegetable broth
- 2 cups canned crushed tomatoes
- 2 cups diced onions
- 1 green bell pepper, diced
- 1 red bell pepper, diced
- 1 cup corn
- 1 can spicy chili beans
- 1 cup cooked black beans
- 3 tablespoons chili powder
- 2 tablespoon cumin
- ½ cup quinoa
- ½ cup red lentils
- Salt and pepper to taste
- Avocado, sliced
- Cilantro for garnish
- Sour cream

Directions for Cooking:

1. Place the broth, tomatoes, onions, bell peppers, corn, chili beans, chili powder, cumin, quinoa, and red lentils. Season with salt and pepper to taste.
2. Close Instant Pot, press the Manual button, choose high settings, and set time to 25 minutes.
3. Once done cooking, do a QPR.
4. Open the lid and spoon into bowls. Top with avocado, cilantro, and sour cream.
5. Serve and enjoy.

Nutrition information:
Calories per serving: 241; Carbohydrates: 41.3g; Protein: 9.2g; Fat: 5.8g; Sugar: 4.1g; Sodium: 336mg

---

321. Instant Pot Acorn Squash
(Servings: 6, Cooking time: 25 minutes)

Ingredients:

- 1 tablespoon olive oil
- 1 shallot, chopped
- 3 large cloves of garlic, minced
- ½ cup wild rice, uncooked
- 8 ounces baby Bella mushrooms, chopped
- ½ teaspoon black pepper
- 1 can chickpeas, rinsed and drained
- 1/3 cup cranberries, chopped
- 1 tablespoon fresh thyme leaves, chopped
- Salt and pepper to taste
- 3 acorn squashes, halved and seeded
- ¼ cup pepitas, chopped

Nutrition information:
Calories per serving: 256; Carbohydrates: 47g; Protein: 7g; Fat: 4g; Sugar:3 g; Sodium: 253mg

Directions for Cooking:

1. Press the Sauté button on the Instant Pot and heat the oil. Sauté the shallot and garlic until fragrant. Stir in the rice, mushrooms, black pepper, chickpeas, cranberries, and thyme. Season with salt and pepper to taste.
2. Close Instant Pot, press the Manual button, choose high settings, and set time to 10 minutes.
3. Once done cooking, do a QPR.
4. Open the lid and spoon the quinoa into the hollows of the acorn squash. Sprinkle with pepitas on top.
5. Bake in a 350⁰F preheated oven for 15 minutes.
6. Serve and enjoy.

322.   Instant Pot Tomato Pasta Stew
(Servings: 4, Cooking time: 12 minutes)

Ingredients:

- 1 teaspoon oil
- 1 onion, chopped
- 4 cloves of garlic, minced
- 1 cup mixed vegetables
- ¼ cup cooked lentils
- 1 cup tomato puree
- 1 ½ cups diced tomatoes
- 2 cups veggie broth
- 1 tablespoon nutritional yeast
- A dash of red pepper flakes
- 1 cup shell pasta
- Salt and pepper to taste

Directions for Cooking:

1. Press the Sauté button on the Instant Pot and heat the oil. Sauté the onion and garlic until fragrant.
2. Stir in the rest of the ingredients.
3. Close Instant Pot, press the Manual button, choose high settings, and set time to 10 minutes.
4. Once done cooking, do a QPR.
5. Serve and enjoy.

Nutrition information:

Calories per serving:152 ; Carbohydrates:30.1 g;
Protein: 6.2g; Fat: 1.8g; Sugar: 8.2g; Sodium: 169mg

---

323.   Instant Pot Chickpea Gumbo
(Servings: 5, Cooking time: 12 minutes)

Ingredients:

- 1 tablespoon olive oil
- 1 teaspoon minced garlic
- 1 ½ cups chopped onion
- 2 celery ribs, chopped
- ½ tablespoon oregano
- ½ teaspoon cayenne pepper
- 1 cup cooked chickpeas
- 3 cups vegetable broth
- 2 cups frozen okra
- 1 red bell pepper, chopped
- 1 can diced tomatoes, drained
- 2 tablespoons apple cider vinegar
- ½ cups tomato sauce
- 1 cup cauliflower, cut into florets
- Salt and pepper to taste

Directions for Cooking:

1. Press the Sauté button on the Instant Pot and heat the oil. Sauté the garlic, onions, and celery until fragrant.
2. Stir in the rest of the ingredients.
3. Close Instant Pot, press the Manual button, choose high settings, and set time to 10 minutes.
4. Once done cooking, do a QPR.
5. Serve and enjoy.

Nutrition information:

Calories per serving: 221; Carbohydrates: 29.2g;
Protein: 13.2g; Fat: 6.3g; Sugar: 3.5g; Sodium: 768mg

324.   Instant Pot Pinto Beans
(Servings: 4, Cooking time: 42 minutes)

Ingredients:

- 1 tablespoon oil
- 1 onion, chopped
- 3 cloves of garlic, minced
- 1 cup dry pinto beans
- 4 cups water
- 1 teaspoon thyme
- Salt and pepper to taste

Directions for Cooking:

1. Press the Sauté button on the Instant Pot and heat the oil.

2. Sauté the onion and garlic until fragrant. Stir in the rest of the ingredients.
3. Close Instant Pot, press the Manual button, choose high settings, and set time to 40 minutes.
4. Once done cooking, do a QPR.
5. Serve and enjoy.

Nutrition information:

Calories per serving:111 ; Carbohydrates: 15.6g; Protein: 4.5g; Fat: 3.8g; Sugar: 1.9g; Sodium: 91mg

---

325.   Chickpea and Potato Soup
(Servings: 3, Cooking time: 15 minutes)

Ingredients:

- 1 tablespoon olive oil
- ½ onion, chopped
- 3 cloves of garlic, minced
- ½ cup chopped tomato
- 1/8 teaspoon fennel space
- ½ teaspoon onion powder
- ¼ teaspoon garlic powder
- ½ teaspoon oregano
- ¼ teaspoon cinnamon
- ½ teaspoon thyme
- 1 large potato, peeled and cubed
- ¾ cup carrots, chopped
- 1 ½ cups cooked chickpeas
- 1 cup water
- 1 cup almond milk
- 1 cup kale, chopped
- Salt and pepper to taste

Directions for Cooking:

1. Press the Sauté button on the Instant Pot and sauté the onion and garlic until fragrant.
2. Stir in the tomatoes, fennel, onion powder, garlic powder, oregano, cinnamon, and thyme. Stir until well-combined.
3. Add in the rest of the ingredients.
4. Close Instant Pot, press the Manual button, choose high settings, and set time to 10 minutes.
5. Once done cooking, do a QPR.
6. Serve and enjoy.

Nutrition information:

Calories per serving: 349; Carbohydrates: 60.7g; Protein: 11.8g; Fat: 8g; Sugar: 15g; Sodium: 97mg

326. Instant Pot Hearty Vegetable and Brown Rice Soup
(Servings: 8, Cooking time: 25 minutes)

Ingredients:

- 1 tablespoon olive oil
- 1 onion, chopped
- 3 cloves of garlic, minced
- 2 fresh ginger, minced
- 4 celery sticks, chopped
- 1 cup dry brown rice
- 1-pound red potatoes, peeled and chopped
- 3 carrots, peeled and chopped
- 2 ½ cups French green beans, cut into 2-inch pieces
- 2 tablespoons tomato paste
- 1 tablespoon dried basil
- 4 cups vegetable broth
- Salt and pepper to taste

Directions for Cooking:

1. Press the Sauté button on the Instant Pot and heat the oil.
2. Stir in the onions, garlic, ginger, and celery until fragrant.
3. Stir in the rice and sauté for 1 minute. Add in the rest of the ingredients.
4. Close Instant Pot, press the Manual button, choose high settings, and set time to 20 minutes.
5. Once done cooking, do a QPR.
6. Serve and enjoy.

Nutrition information:

Calories per serving: 193; Carbohydrates: 37.1g; Protein: 8.9g; Fat: 2.3g; Sugar: 16.3g; Sodium: 637

327. Portobello Pot Roast
(Servings: 6, Cooking time: 20 minutes)

Ingredients:

- 1 ½ pounds gold potatoes, cut into bite-sized pieces
- 1-pound baby Bella mushrooms
- 2 large carrots, peeled and chopped
- 2 cups frozen pearl onions
- 4 cloves of garlic, minced
- 3 sprigs fresh thyme
- 3 cups vegetable stock
- ½ cup white wine
- 3 tablespoons tomato paste
- Salt and pepper to taste

Directions for Cooking:

1. Place all ingredients in the Instant Pot and give a good stir.
2. Close Instant Pot, press the Manual button, choose high settings, and set time to 20 minutes.
3. Once done cooking, do a QPR.
4. Serve and enjoy.

Nutrition information:

Calories per serving: 376; Carbohydrates:91.1 g; Protein:12 g; Fat: 0.9g; Sugar: 7.9g; Sodium: 367mg

328. Creamy Parsnips and Chive Soup
(Servings: 10, Cooking time: 10 minutes)

Ingredients:

- 3 pounds parsnips, trimmed and peeled
- 3 cloves of garlic, minced
- ½ cup raw cashews
- 6 cups vegetable broth
- Juice from 1 lemon, freshly squeezed
- ¼ cup fresh chives
- Salt and pepper to taste

Nutrition information:
Calories per serving: 186; Carbohydrates: 29.9g;
Protein: 3.5g; Fat: 7.2g; Sugar: 9.3g; Sodium: 382mg

Directions for Cooking:

1. Place all ingredients in the Instant Pot
2. Close Instant Pot, press the Manual button, choose high settings, and set time to 10 minutes.
3. Once done cooking, do a QPR.
4. Open the lid and use the immersion blender to pulse everything until smooth.
5. Serve and enjoy.

---

329. Instant Pot Vegetable Korma
(Servings: 4, Cooking time: 25 minutes)

Ingredients:

- 2 tablespoons olive oil
- 7 black whole peppercorns
- 4 green cardamoms
- 4 whole cloves
- 1 bay leave
- ½ cup tomato puree
- 2 teaspoons coriander powder
- 1 teaspoon garam masala
- ¼ teaspoon red chili powder
- ½ teaspoon turmeric powder
- ½ cup water
- 1 cup coconut milk
- ½ teaspoon sugar
- 1 large potato, peeled and chopped
- Salt and pepper to taste
- Juice from ½ lemon
- 2 tablespoons chopped cilantro

Directions for Cooking:

1. Press the Sauté button on the Instant Pot and heat the oil.
2. Stir in the whole peppercorns, cardamoms, cloves, and bay leaf until fragrant.
3. Add in the tomato puree, coriander powder, garam masala, chili powder, and turmeric powder.
4. Stir in water, coconut milk, sugar and potatoes. Season with salt and pepper to taste.
5. Close Instant Pot, press the button, choose high settings, and set time to 20 minutes.
6. Once done cooking, do a QPR.
7. Open the lid and stir in the lemon juice and cilantro.
8. Serve and enjoy.

Nutrition information:
Calories per serving:248; Carbohydrates: 14g; Protein: 4g; Fat: 21g; Sugar: 4g; Sodium: 341mg

330.   Vegan Potato Corn Chowder

(Servings: 6, Cooking time: 10 minutes)

Ingredients:

- 1 cup diced onions
- 2 cloves of garlic, minced
- 1 cup diced carrots
- 1 cup diced celery
- 6 cups gold potatoes, peeled and quartered
- 1 bay leaf
- 1 teaspoon dried thyme
- 4 cups vegetable broth
- 2 cups frozen corns
- ½ cup coconut cream
- ½ cup water
- Salt and pepper to taste

Directions for Cooking:

1. Place all ingredients in the Instant Pot and mix until well combined.
2. Close Instant Pot, press the Manual button, choose high settings, and set time to 10 minutes.
3. Once done cooking, do a QPR.
4. Serve and enjoy.

Nutrition information:

Calories per serving: 243; Carbohydrates: 44g; Protein: 8g; Fat: 5g; Sugar: 4g; Sodium: 678mg

---

331.   Smoky Pecan Brussels sprouts

(Servings: 3, Cooking time: 6 minutes)

Ingredients:

- 2 cups small baby Brussels sprouts
- ¼ cup water
- ½ teaspoon liquid smoke
- ¼ cup chopped pecans
- 2 tablespoons maple syrup
- Salt and pepper to taste

Nutrition information:

Calories per serving:124 ; Carbohydrates: 16.7g; Protein: 3.1g; Fat: 6.2g; Sugar: 10.5g; Sodium: 18mg

Directions for Cooking:

1. Place the Brussels sprouts, water and liquid smoke into the Instant Pot.
2. Close Instant Pot, press the Manual button, choose high settings, and set time to 6 minutes.
3. Once done cooking, do a QPR.
4. Open the lid and press the Sauté button. Stir in the pecans, and maple syrup. Season with salt and pepper to taste.
5. Serve and enjoy.

332.   Maple Bourbon Sweet Potato Chili
(Servings: 4, Cooking time: 20 minutes)

Ingredients:

- 1 tablespoon cooking oil
- 1 onion, sliced thinly
- 3 cloves of garlic, minced
- 4 cups sweet potatoes, peeled and cubed
- 2 cups vegetable broth
- 1 ½ tablespoons chili powder
- 2 teaspoons cumin
- ½ teaspoon paprika
- 2 cans kidney beans, drained
- 1 can diced tomatoes
- ¼ cup bourbon
- 2 tablespoons maple syrup
- Salt and pepper to taste
- Green onions for garnish
- Tortillas, toasted and sliced

Directions for Cooking:

1. Press the Sauté button on the Instant Pot and heat the oil. Sauté the onion and garlic until fragrant.
2. Stir in the sweet potatoes, broth, chili powder, cumin, paprika, beans, tomatoes, bourbon, and maple syrup. Season with salt and pepper to taste.
3. Close Instant Pot, press the Manual button, choose high settings, and set time to 20 minutes.
4. Once done cooking, do a QPR.
5. Serve with green onions and tortillas.
6. Serve and enjoy.

Nutrition information:

Calories per serving: 239; Carbohydrates: 40g; Protein: 3g; Fat: 4g; Sugar: 13g; Sodium: 597mg

---

333.   Cauliflower Tikka Masala
(Servings: 4, Cooking time: 10 minutes)

Ingredients:

- 1 tablespoon olive oil
- 1 onion, diced
- 3 cloves of garlic, minced
- 1 tablespoon grated ginger
- 2 teaspoons dried fenugreek leaves
- 2 teaspoons garam masala
- 1 teaspoon turmeric
- ½ teaspoon ground chili
- ¼ teaspoon ground cumin
- 1 28-ounce crushed tomatoes
- 1 tablespoon maple syrup
- 1 cauliflower head, cut into florets
- Salt and pepper to taste
- ½ cup non-dairy yogurt
- ½ cup roasted cashews

Directions for Cooking:

1. Press the Sauté button on the Instant Pot and sauté the onion and garlic until fragrant.
2. Add in the ginger, fenugreek leaves, garam masala, turmeric, ground chili, cumin, tomatoes, and maple syrup.
3. Stir in the cauliflower florets and season with salt and pepper to taste.
4. Add water if necessary.
5. Close Instant Pot, press the Manual button, choose high settings, and set time to 10 minutes.
6. Once done cooking, do a QPR.
7. Garnish with yogurt and roasted cashews.
8. Serve and enjoy.

Nutrition information:

Calories per serving:331; Carbohydrates:32 g; Protein: 9.4g; Fat: 21.2g; Sugar: 12g; Sodium: 222mg

334.   Vegan Udon Noodles Bowl
(Servings: 3, Cooking time: 7 minutes)

Ingredients:

- 1-inch ginger, peeled
- 1 large carrot, peeled and sliced
- ½ cup water
- 1 teaspoon maple syrup
- 2 tablespoons miso paste
- 2 cups edamame, blanched
- ¾ cup green onions
- 2 ½ cups udon noodles, cooked

Directions for Cooking:

1. Place the ginger, carrots, water, maple syrup, and miso paste in the Instant Pot.

2. Close Instant Pot, press the Manual button, choose high settings, and set time to 7 minutes.
3. Once done cooking, do a QPR.
4. Open the lid and stir in the rest of the ingredients.
5. Serve and enjoy.

Nutrition information:

Calories per serving: 318; Carbohydrates: 51.1g; Protein: 15.3g; Fat: 6.4g; Sugar: 5.1g; Sodium: 582mg

---

335.   Basmati Rice Pilaf
(Servings: 4 , Cooking time: 20 minutes)

Ingredients:

- 1 tablespoon oil
- 1 onion, sliced
- 1 teaspoon turmeric
- 1 pinch cinnamon
- 1 pinch ground cumin
- 2 cups basmati rice
- 1 can chickpeas
- ½ cup raisins
- ½ cup dates, chopped
- 4 cups water
- Salt and pepper to taste

Directions for Cooking:

1. Press the Sauté button on the Instant and heat the oil. Sauté the onion until fragrant. Add the turmeric, cinnamon, and cumin until toasted.
2. Stir in the basmati rice for a minute and stir in the rest of the ingredients.
3. Close Instant Pot, press the Manual button, choose high settings, and set time to 15 minutes.
4. Once done cooking, do a QPR.
5. Serve and enjoy.

Nutrition information:

Calories per serving:487; Carbohydrates: 104g; Protein: 7g; Fat: 4g; Sugar: 12g; Sodium: 11mg

Instant Pot Soup Recipes

336.   Singaporean Prawn and Pork Ribs Noodle Soup
(Servings: 4, Cooking time: 40 minutes)

Ingredients:

- 3 pounds pork ribs
- 4 cloves of garlic, minced
- 3 cloves
- 1 star anise
- 1 tablespoon soy sauce
- 1 tablespoon sugar
- Salt and pepper to taste
- 6 cups water
- 1-pound Chinese yellow noodles, cooked
- 20 jumbo prawns, boiled and shelled
- 1 bunch water spinach, blanched
- 2 cups fresh bean sprouts
- 5 red chilies, chopped

Directions for Cooking:

1. In the Instant Pot, place the pork, garlic, cloves, star anise, soy sauce, sugar, salt, pepper, and water.
2. Close Instant Pot, press the Manual button, choose high settings, and set time to 40 minutes.
3. Once done cooking, do a QPR.
4. Assemble the noodles by place the noodles in a bowl and pouring in the beef and broth. Top with boiled prawns, spinach, and bean sprouts. Garnish with chilies on top.
5. Serve and enjoy.

Nutrition information:

Calories per serving: 600; Carbohydrates: 16.9g;
Protein: 79.7g; Fat: 23.4g; Sugar: 3.2g; Sodium: 684mg

337.   Chicken Wonton Soup
(Servings: 4, Cooking time: 20 minutes)

Ingredients

- 4 cups chicken stock
- 1 32-ounce pack frozen chicken wontons
- ½-inch ginger, peeled and sliced thinly
- 2 cloves of garlic, peeled and chopped
- 1 tablespoon rice vinegar
- 2 tablespoons soy sauce
- 1 tablespoon sambal oelek
- 1 teaspoon honey
- 1 tablespoon fish sauce
- 3 medium carrots, sliced
- 3 heads of Bok Choy
- ½ teaspoon sesame oil

1. In the Instant Pot, place the chicken stock, wonton, ginger, garlic, rice vinegar, soy sauce, sambal oelek, honey, fish sauce, and carrots.
2. Close Instant Pot, press the Manual button, choose high settings, and set time to 20 minutes.
3. Once done cooking, do a QPR.
4. Open the lid and press the Sauté button. Stir in the bok choy and allow to simmer until cooked.
5. Drizzle with sesame oil.
6. Serve and enjoy.

Directions for Cooking:

Nutrition information:

Calories per serving: 450; Carbohydrates: 12.9g;
Protein: 46.5g; Fat: 23.2g; Sugar: 7.1g; Sodium: 955mg

INSTANT POT SOUP RECIPES

338. Instant Pot Mexican Chicken Tomato Soup
(Servings: 5, Cooking time: 20 minutes)

Ingredients:

- 1 ½ cups tomatoes, crushed
- 1 cup chicken broth
- 1-ounce taco seasoning
- 1 red bell pepper, sliced
- 1 onion, sliced
- 1 ½ pounds chicken thighs
- Salt and pepper to taste

Directions for Cooking:

1. Place all ingredients in the Instant Pot.
2. Close Instant Pot, press the Manual button, choose high settings, and set time to 20 minutes.
3. Once done cooking, do a QPR.
4. Serve and enjoy.

Nutrition information:
Calories per serving: 411; Carbohydrates: 7.6g; Protein: 33.5g; Fat: 26.1g; Sugar: 2.7g; Sodium: 734mg

339. Instant Pot Chicken Rice Porridge
(Servings: 6, Cooking time: 40 minutes)

Ingredients:

- 1 tablespoon olive oil
- 1 onion, diced
- 3 cloves of garlic, minced
- 3 carrots, chopped
- 2 stalks of celery, chopped
- 2 chicken breasts, chopped
- 1 cup long grain rice
- 1 package button mushrooms
- 5 cups water
- Salt and pepper to taste

Directions for Cooking:

1. Press the Sauté button on the Instant Pot and heat the oil.
2. Sauté the onion and garlic until fragrant. Stir in the carrots, celery, and chicken breasts. Keep stirring for 2 minutes.
3. Add in the rest of the ingredients.
4. Close Instant Pot, press the Manual button, choose high settings, and set time to 35 minutes.
5. Once done cooking, do a QPR.
6. Serve and enjoy.

Nutrition information:
Calories per serving:328; Carbohydrates: 30.3g; Protein: 23.4g; Fat: 12.2g; Sugar: 3g; Sodium: 94mg

340.   New England clam chowder
(Servings: 5, Cooking time: 15 minutes)

Ingredients:

- 3 pieces of bacon
- 1 onion, peeled and diced
- 1 stalk of celery, diced
- 2 cups clam juice
- 4 potatoes, peeled and cubed
- 2 cups water
- 1 bay leaf
- 1 teaspoon thyme
- Salt and pepper to taste
- 1-pound clam meat
- 1 cup cream

Directions for Cooking:

1. Press the Sauté button on the Instant Pot and stir in the bacon. Cook the bacon until crispy. Set aside.

2. Use the bacon grease and sauté the onion and celery until fragrant. Add in the potatoes, water, bay leaf, and thyme. Season with salt and pepper to taste.

3. Close Instant Pot, press the Manual button, choose high settings, and set time to 10 minutes.

4. Once done cooking, do a QPR.

5. Open the lid and press the Sauté button. Stir in the clam meat and cream. Allow to simmer until the clam is cooked.

6. Garnish with sliced bacon on top.

7. Serve and enjoy.

Nutrition information:

Calories per serving:433 ; Carbohydrates: 77.1g; Protein: 9.6g; Fat: 10.8g; Sugar: 11.7g; Sodium: 692mg

---

341.   Vegan Ginger Noodle Soup
(Servings: 4, Cooking time: 23 minutes)

Ingredients:

- 2 tablespoons olive oil
- ¼ cup chopped onions
- 1 cup chopped celery
- 4 cloves of garlic, minced
- 1 cup kohlrabi, peeled and diced
- 1 cup sliced carrots
- 1 teaspoon of your favorite dried herbs
- 2 tablespoons fresh ginger, grated
- 3 bay leaves
- 8 cups vegetable broth
- 8 ounces fusilli noodles
- ¼ cup white wine
- Salt and pepper to taste

Directions for Cooking:

1. Press the Sauté button on the Instant Pot and heat the oil.

2. Stir in the onions, celery, and garlic until fragrant.

3. Add in the rest of the ingredients and give a good stir.

4. Close Instant Pot, press the Manual button, choose high settings, and set time to 20 minutes.

5. Once done cooking, do a QPR.

6. Serve and enjoy.

Nutrition information:

Calories per serving: 331; Carbohydrates: 53.1g; Protein: 9.4g; Fat: 8.5g; Sugar: 7.6g; Sodium: 1143mg

342. Instant Pot Salmon Tortellini Soup
(Servings: 4, Cooking time: 15 minutes)

Ingredients:

- 2 strips of bacon, diced
- 2/3 cup diced onions
- 2 cloves of garlic, minced
- 16 ounces boneless salmon, sliced
- 1 10-ounce packaged vegetables
- 10 ounces frozen tortellini
- 4 cups chicken broth
- 1 teaspoon Old Bay seasoning
- Salt and pepper to taste
- 3 handfuls of baby spinach

Directions for Cooking:

1. Press the Sauté button on the Instant Pot and stir in the bacon until the fat has rendered.
2. Sauté the onions and garlic until fragrant.
3. Add in the salmon, vegetables, tortellini, and chicken broth. Season with old bay seasoning, salt and pepper.
4. Close Instant Pot, press the Manual button, choose high settings, and set time to 15 minutes.
5. Once done cooking, do a QPR.
6. Open the lid and press the Sauté button. Stir in the baby spinach and allow to cook.
7. Serve and enjoy.

Nutrition information:
Calories per serving: 711; Carbohydrates: 30.6g; Protein: 80.2g; Fat: 28.2g; Sugar: 4.2g; Sodium: 1587mg

---

343. Instant Pot Chicken Ramen
(Servings: 3, Cooking time: 25 minutes)

Ingredients:

- 3 boneless, chicken breasts
- ½ onion, chopped
- 1 cup celery, chopped
- 1 cup carrots, chopped
- Salt and pepper to taste
- ¼ teaspoon thyme
- ½ teaspoon salt
- 1 teaspoon garlic
- 4 cups chicken broth
- 1 cup water
- 3 cups ramen noodles

Directions for Cooking:

1. Place all ingredients in the Instant Pot except for the ramen noodles.
2. Close Instant Pot, press the Manual button, choose high settings, and set time to 20 minutes.
3. Once done cooking, do a QPR.
4. Open the lid and press the Sauté button. Stir in the noodles and allow to simmer for additional 5 more minutes.
5. Serve and enjoy.

Nutrition information:
Calories per serving: 598; Carbohydrates: 11.3g; Protein: 76.6g; Fat: 24.1g; Sugar: 4.2g; Sodium: 884mg

INSTANT POT SOUP RECIPES

344.   Instant Pot Summer Soup
(Servings: 5, Cooking time: 25 minutes)

Ingredients:

- 1 tablespoon olive oil
- 1-pound chicken breasts
- 2 stalks of celery, chopped
- 3 cloves of garlic, minced
- 1 28-ounce can crushed tomatoes
- 4 carrots, peeled and chopped
- ½ cup farro
- 1 teaspoon basil
- ½ teaspoon onion powder
- 1 zucchini, chopped
- 6 cups chicken broth
- Salt and pepper to taste

Directions for Cooking:

1. Press the Sauté button on the Instant Pot and heat the oil. Stir in the chicken breasts, celery, and garlic. Keep stirring for 3 minutes.

2. Add in the tomatoes, carrots, farro, basil, onion powder, zucchini and chicken stock. Season with salt and pepper to taste.
3. Close Instant Pot, press the Manual button, choose high settings, and set time to 20 minutes.
4. Once done cooking, do a QPR.
5. Top with yogurt or parmesan cheese if desired.
6. Serve and enjoy.

Nutrition information:

Calories per serving:433 ; Carbohydrates: 9.4g;
Protein: 52.2g; Fat: 19.7g; Sugar: 3.8g; Sodium: 845mg

---

345.   Lebanese Chicken Soup
(Servings: 2, Cooking time: 6 minutes)

Ingredients:

- 2 large carrots, diced
- 1 onion, chopped
- 3 stalks of celery, diced
- 1 15-ounce can of chickpeas, drained
- 2 chicken breasts, sliced
- 1 teaspoon cinnamon
- 1 teaspoon garlic powder
- Salt and pepper to taste
- ¼ cup lemon juice
- 8 cups chicken broth
- 8 cups baby spinach

Directions for Cooking:

1. Place all ingredients in the Instant Pot except for the spinach.
2. Close Instant Pot, press the Manual button, choose high settings, and set time to 20 minutes.
3. Once done cooking, do a QPR.
4. Open the lid and press the Sauté button. Add in the spinach and allow to simmer.
5. Serve and enjoy.

Nutrition information:

Calories per serving: 236; Carbohydrates: 28g;
Protein: 27.8g; Fat: 3.7g; Sugar: 7.1g; Sodium: 992mg

INSTANT POT SOUP RECIPES

346. Pho Ga Noodle Soup
(Servings: 4 , Cooking time: 35 minutes)

Ingredients:

- 1 teaspoon black pepper corns
- 2 star anise
- 1 teaspoon fennel seeds
- 3 cloves
- 2 small cinnamon sticks
- 1 onion, peeled and quartered
- 3 pounds chicken, chopped
- 6 cups water
- 2 tablespoons fish sauce
- 1 tablespoon sugar
- 3-inch piece ginger, sliced thinly
- Salt to taste
- 1-pound thin rice noodles, blanched
- 1 ½ cups bean sprouts, rinsed
- ½ cup basil leaves
- 1 cup chopped coriander
- 1 lime, cut into wedges

Directions for Cooking:

1. Press the Sauté button on the Instant Pot and toast the peppercorns, anise, fennel seeds, cloves, cinnamon stick, and onion for 2 minutes. Place the toasted spices in a large tea bag or cloth.
2. In the Instant Pot, place the chicken, water, fish sauce, sugar, and ginger. Add in the cloth with the spices and season with salt and pepper.
3. Close Instant Pot, press the Manual button, choose high settings, and set time to 30 minutes.
4. Once done cooking, do a QPR. Open the lid and remove the bag of spices.
5. Assemble the pho by placing the bowl the blanched rice noodles. Pour over the soup and garnish with bean sprouts, basil leaves, coriander, and lime. Add sriracha if desired.
6. Serve and enjoy.

Nutrition information:

Calories per serving: 553; Carbohydrates: 37.6g; Protein: 75.3g; Fat: 9.9g; Sugar: 4.3g; Sodium: 999mg

347. Fish and Potato Chowder
(Servings: 5, Cooking time: 23 minutes)

Ingredients:

- 2/3 pounds tilapia fillet, sliced
- 1 cup Yukon gold potatoes, peeled and quartered
- ½ cups diced celery
- ¾ cup diced onions
- Salt and pepper to taste
- 1 cup chicken broth
- 2 cups water
- 2 tablespoons diced bacon
- 2 tablespoons butter
- 1 1/3 cups cream

Nutrition information:

Calories per serving: 346; Carbohydrates: 10.9g; Protein: 25.7g; Fat: 22.4g; Sugar: 3.9g; Sodium:357mg

Directions for Cooking:

In the Instant Pot, place the tilapia fillets, potatoes, celery, and onions.

Season with salt and pepper to taste before pouring in the chicken broth and water.

1. Close Instant Pot, press the Manual button, choose high settings, and set time to 20 minutes.
2. Once done cooking, do a QPR.
3. Open the lid and press the Sauté button. Stir in the bacon, butter, and cream and allow to simmer for another 3 minutes.
4. Serve and enjoy.

348. Bacon Cheeseburger Soup
(Servings: 4, Cooking time: 30 minutes)

Ingredients:

- 6 ounces bacon, chopped
- 1 ½ pounds hamburger, chopped
- 1 onion, diced
- 2 large carrots, diced
- 2 stalks celery, diced
- Salt to taste
- 4 cups cauliflower, chopped
- 4 cups beef broth
- 4 ounces cream cheese
- 1 cup cheddar cheese, shredded

Directions for Cooking:

1. Press the Sauté button on the Instant Pot and stir in the bacon. Cook the bacon until fried and crispy. Set aside.
2. Using the bacon fat, stir in the hamburger and sauté together with the onions, carrots, celery, and cauliflower. Season with salt to taste.
3. Add the cauliflower and beef broth.
4. Close Instant Pot, press the Manual button, choose high settings, and set time to 25 minutes.
5. Once done cooking, do a QPR.
6. Open the lid and press the Sauté button. Stir in the cream cheese and cheddar and allow to simmer for 3 minutes.
7. Garnish with bacon bits.
8. Serve and enjoy.

Nutrition information:

Calories per serving: 607; Carbohydrates: 10g; Protein: 33g; Fat: 47g; Sugar: 4g; Sodium: 535mg

349. Chicken and Chayote Soup
(Servings: 4, Cooking time: 20 minutes)

Ingredients:

- 1-pound chicken breasts, cut into large chunks
- 1 onion, chopped
- 1-inch ginger, sliced
- 3 cloves of garlic, minced
- Salt to taste
- 1 teaspoon whole peppercorns
- 2 chayote, peeled and sliced
- 3 tomatoes, chopped
- 4 cups water
- 1 bok choy

Directions for Cooking:

1. Press the Sauté button on the Instant Pot and stir in the chicken, onion, ginger, and garlic. Season with salt and pepper to taste. Stir for at least 3 minutes until the chicken has rendered some of its fats and the spices become fragrant.
2. Add in the peppercorns, chayote, and tomatoes. Pour in water.
3. Close Instant Pot, press the Manual button, choose high settings, and set time to 15 minutes.
4. Once done cooking, do a QPR.
5. Open the lid and press the Sauté button. Stir in the bok choy and allow to simmer until cooked.
6. Serve and enjoy.

Nutrition information:

Calories per serving: 247; Carbohydrates: 11.6g; Protein: 25.7g; Fat: 10.8g; Sugar: 2g; Sodium: 87mg

INSTANT POT SOUP RECIPES

350. Zuppa Toscana
(Servings: 5, Cooking time: 13 minutes)

Ingredients:

- 2 tablespoons olive oil
- 1 onion, chopped
- 3 cloves of garlic, minced
- 1-pound Italian sausages, sliced
- 3 large potatoes, peeled and cut into chunks
- 5 cups chicken broth
- 2 teaspoons dried basil
- 1 teaspoon dried fennel
- 2 cups fresh kale
- ½ cup heavy cream
- 1 tablespoon crushed red pepper
- Salt and pepper to taste

Directions for Cooking:

1. Press the Sauté button on the Instant Pot and heat the oil.
2. Sauté the onion and garlic until fragrant.
3. Stir in the Italian sausages, potatoes, and chicken broth.
4. Add in the rest of the ingredients.
5. Close Instant Pot, press the Manual button, choose high settings, and set time to 10 minutes.
6. Once done cooking, do a QPR.
7. Serve and enjoy.

Nutrition information:

Calories per serving: 974; Carbohydrates: 45.9g; Protein: 70.4g; Fat: 55.2g; Sugar: 3.7g; Sodium: 1674mg

351. Seattle Seafood Chowder
(Servings: 6, Cooking time: 15 minutes)

Ingredients:

- 2 tablespoons butter
- 2 cloves of garlic, minced
- 1 onion, chopped
- 2 stalks of celery, minced
- 1 teaspoon sage
- 4 cups vegetable broth
- 1 large potato, peeled and cubed
- 1 cup canned corn
- ½ pound frozen salmon
- Salt and pepper to taste
- 1 cup squid, cleaned and sliced
- 10 prawns, shelled and deveined
- 2 cups half-and half

Directions for Cooking:

1. Press the Sauté button on the Instant Pot and heat the butter.
2. Sauté the garlic, onion, celery, and sage until fragrant. Add in the broth, potatoes, and salmon. Season with salt and pepper to taste.
3. Close Instant Pot, press the Manual button, choose high settings, and set time to 10 minutes.
4. Once done cooking, do a QPR.
5. Open the lid and press the Sauté button. Stir in the rest of the ingredients and allow to simmer until cooked through.
6. Serve and enjoy.

Nutrition information:

Calories per serving: 444; Carbohydrates: 58.1g; Protein: 21.3g; Fat: 14.3g; Sugar: 6.5g; Sodium: 744mg

INSTANT POT SOUP RECIPES

352.   Chicken and Corn Chowder
(Servings: 4, Cooking time: 25 minutes)

Ingredients:

- 1-pound boneless chicken breasts, cut into cubes
- 1 cup frozen whole kernel corn
- ½ cup carrots, diced
- 3 stalks of celery, chopped
- 4 cups vegetable broth
- 1 can cream of chicken soup
- 1 tablespoon garlic powder
- 1 tablespoon onion powder
- 1 teaspoon dried parsley flakes
- Salt and pepper to taste

Directions for Cooking:

1. Place all ingredients in the Instant Pot and give a good stir.
2. Close Instant Pot, press the Manual button, choose high settings, and set time to 25 minutes.
3. Once done cooking, do a QPR.
4. Serve and enjoy.

Nutrition information:

Calories per serving: 285; Carbohydrates: 23.5g; Protein: 30.3g; Fat: 7.8g; Sugar: 2.1g; Sodium: 1284mg

---

353.   Butternut Squash Apple Soup
(Servings: 4, Cooking time: 15 minutes)

Ingredients:

- 1 teaspoon olive oil
- 1 onion, diced
- 2 cloves of garlic, minced
- 1 butternut squash, peeled and cubed
- 1 large apple, peeled and cubed
- Salt and pepper to taste
- 2 cups chicken broth
- ¼ cup heavy cream
- 1 tablespoon maple syrup

Directions for Cooking:

1. Press the Sauté button on the Instant Pot and heat the oil. Sauté the onion and garlic until fragrant. Add in the rest of the ingredients.
2. Close Instant Pot, press the button, choose high settings, and set time to 10 minutes.
3. Once done cooking, do a QPR.
4. Open the lid and transfer the contents in a blender or food processor. Pulse until smooth.
5. Serve and enjoy.

Nutrition information:

Calories per serving: 301; Carbohydrates: 20.4g; Protein: 27.2g; Fat: 12.3g; Sugar: 11.5g; Sodium: 508mg

INSTANT POT SOUP RECIPES

354.   Spicy Tomato Chicken Soup
(Servings: 3, Cooking time: 20 minutes)

Ingredients:

- 3 boneless chicken breasts
- 2 teaspoons chili powder
- Salt and pepper to taste
- 1 28-ounce can diced tomatoes
- 3 cups chicken broth
- 1 tablespoon lime juice
- Salt and pepper to taste
- ¾ cup green onions, sliced

1. Place all ingredients in the Instant Pot except for the green onions.
2. Close Instant Pot, press the Manual button, choose high settings, and set time to 20 minutes.
3. Once done cooking, do a QPR.
4. Garnish with green onions.
5. Serve and enjoy.

Directions for Cooking:

Nutrition information:
Calories per serving:349 ; Carbohydrates: 14.3g;
Protein: 56.3g; Fat: 7.2g; Sugar: 9.1g; Sodium:467mg

---

355.   Instant Pot Chicken Gnocchi Soup
(Servings: 6, Cooking time: 30 minutes)

Ingredients:

- 6 slices of bacon, chopped
- 2 tablespoons butter
- 1 onion, chopped
- 3 cloves of garlic, minced
- 3 chicken breasts
- 3 carrots, chopped
- 1 bay leaf
- 2 stalks of celery, chopped
- 1 sprig rosemary
- ½ teaspoon each of basil, thyme, and poultry seasoning
- Salt and pepper to taste
- 4 cups chicken broth
- 16 ounces gnocchi
- 1 cup spinach leaves
- 1 cup heavy cream
- ½ cup parmesan cheese, grated

Directions for Cooking:

1. Press the Sauté button on the Instant Pot and stir in the bacon. Cook the bacon until fried and crispy. Set aside.
2. To the Instant Pot, melt the butter and sauté the onions and garlic until fragrant. Stir in the chicken breasts, carrots, bay leaf, celery, rosemary, and herbs seasonings. Season with salt and pepper to taste before pouring in the broth and gnocchi.
3. Close Instant Pot, press the Manual button, choose high settings, and set time to 20 minutes.
4. Once done cooking, do a QPR.
5. Open the lid and press the Sauté button. Stir in the spinach leaves and heavy cream and allow to simmer for another 5 minutes.
6. Garnish with parmesan cheese on top.
7. Serve and enjoy.

Nutrition information:
Calories per serving: 874; Carbohydrates: 22.3g;
Protein: 73.6g; Fat: 53.1g; Sugar: 4.2g; Sodium: 968mg

INSTANT POT SOUP RECIPES

356.   Chicken Zoodle Soup
(Servings: 6, Cooking time: 25 minutes)

Ingredients:

- 1 tablespoon olive oil
- 1 onion, diced
- 2 cloves of garlic, minced
- 1-pound chicken breasts, sliced
- 3 carrots, sliced
- 3 stalks of celery, sliced
- 1 jalapeno pepper, dice
- Salt and pepper to taste
- 1 bay leaf
- 6 cups chicken broth
- 2 tablespoons apple cider vinegar
- 4 zucchinis, spiralized

Nutrition information:

Calories per serving: 164; Carbohydrates: 10g;
Protein: 19g; Fat: 5g; Sugar: 6g; Sodium: 1065mg

Directions for Cooking:

1. Press the Sauté button on the Instant Pot and heat the oil. Sauté the onion and garlic until fragrant. Add in the chicken breasts, carrots, celery, and jalapeno pepper. Stir for a minute. Season with salt and pepper to taste.
2. Add the bay leaf, chicken broth, and apple cider vinegar.
3. Close Instant Pot, press the Manual button, choose high settings, and set time to 20 minutes.
4. Once done cooking, do a QPR.
5. Open the lid and press the Sauté button. Stir in the spiralized zucchini and allow to simmer for another 3 minutes.
6. Serve and enjoy.

---

357.   Buffalo Chicken Soup
(Servings: 4, Cooking time: 25 minutes)

Ingredients:

- 1 tablespoon olive oil
- 1 onion, diced
- ½ cup celery, chopped
- 4 cloves of garlic, minced
- 1-pound chicken, shredded
- 4 cups chicken broth
- 3 tablespoons buffalo sauce
- Salt and pepper to taste
- 6 ounces cream cheese
- ½ cup heavy cream

Directions for Cooking:

1. Press the Sauté button on the Instant Pot and heat the oil. Sauté the onion, celery, and garlic until fragrant before adding the chicken. Keep stirring for another minute.

2. Pour in the chicken broth and buffalo sauce. Season with salt and pepper to taste.
3. Close Instant Pot, press the Manual button, choose high settings, and set time to 20 minutes.
4. Once done cooking, do a QPR.
5. Open the lid and press the Sauté button. Stir in the cream cheese and heavy cream and allow to simmer for another 5 minutes.
6. Serve and enjoy.

Nutrition information:

Calories per serving: 756; Carbohydrates: 13.9g;
Protein:79.1g; Fat: 40.3g; Sugar: 8.1g; Sodium: 1402mg

INSTANT POT SOUP RECIPES

358.   Broccoli Cheese Soup
(Servings: 5, Cooking time: 18 minutes)

Ingredients:

- 2 tablespoons butter
- 1 onion, chopped
- 2 cloves of garlic, minced
- 1 ½ teaspoon dry mustard
- 4 cups broccoli florets
- 4 cups chicken broth
- 2 cups spinach
- Salt and pepper to taste
- 1 cup cheddar cheese, shredded
- ½ cup parmesan cheese, shredded

Directions for Cooking:

1. Press the Sauté button on the Instant Pot and melt the butter. Sauté the onions and garlic until fragrant.

2. Add in the dry mustard, broccoli, chicken broth, and spinach. Season with salt and pepper to taste.
3. Close Instant Pot, press the Manual button, choose high settings, and set time to 15 minutes.
4. Once done cooking, do a QPR.
5. Open the lid and transfer contents into a blender. Blend until smooth.
6. Garnish with cheddar and parmesan cheese on top.
7. Serve and enjoy.

Nutrition information:
Calories per serving: 518; Carbohydrates: 7.9g; Protein: 52.6g; Fat: 29.9g; Sugar: 1.6g; Sodium: 1216mg

359.   Instant Pot Vegetable Beef Soup
(Servings: 6, Cooking time: 45 minutes)

Ingredients:

- 2 tablespoons olive oil
- 2 pounds beef stew meat, cut into chunks
- 1 tablespoon onion powder
- 1 tablespoon garlic powder
- Salt and pepper to taste
- 1 can tomato paste
- 1 can green beans
- 2 cans sliced carrots
- 1 can sweet corn
- 2 cups diced potatoes
- 5 cups beef broth

Directions for Cooking:

1. Press the Sauté button on the Instant Pot and heat the oil.

2. Stir in the beef and season with onion powder, garlic powder, salt, and pepper. Stir until the beef turns lightly golden.
3. Add in the rest of the ingredients.
4. Close Instant Pot, press the Manual button, choose high settings, and set time to 40 minutes.
5. Once done cooking, do a QPR.
6. Serve and enjoy.

Nutrition information:
Calories per serving: 371; Carbohydrates: 51.1g; Protein: 5.8g; Fat: 17.9g; Sugar: 8.3g; Sodium: 897mg

360. Peasant Chicken and Veggie Soup
(Servings: 6, Cooking time: 25 minutes)

Ingredients:

- 1 tablespoon olive oil
- 1 onion, chopped
- 2 cloves of garlic, minced
- 1-pound chicken breasts, sliced
- 1 sweet potato, peeled and cubed
- 1 carrot, peeled and cubed
- 1 head cauliflower, cut into florets
- 1 can diced tomatoes
- 6 cups chicken stock
- Salt and pepper to taste

Directions for Cooking:

1. Press the Sauté button on the Instant Pot. Heat the oil and sauté the onion, garlic, and chicken until the chicken turns lightly golden.
2. Pour in the rest of the ingredients.
3. Close Instant Pot, press the Manual button, choose high settings, and set time to 20 minutes.
4. Once done cooking, do a QPR.
5. Serve and enjoy.

Nutrition information:

Calories per serving: 271; Carbohydrates: 16.1g; Protein: 23.5g; Fat: 12.4g; Sugar: 7.1g; Sodium: 449mg

---

361. Cabbage Soup with Ground Beef
(Servings: 6, Cooking time: 35 minutes)

Ingredients:

- 1 tablespoon avocado oil
- 1 onion, chopped
- 1-pound ground beef
- ½ teaspoon garlic powder
- Salt and pepper to taste
- 1 can diced tomatoes
- 6 cups bone broth
- 2 bay leaves
- 1-pound shredded cabbage

Directions for Cooking:

1. Press the Sauté button on the Instant Pot and heat oil.
2. Sauté the onion and beef. Season with garlic powder, salt and pepper. Stir for 2 minutes.
3. Add in the diced tomatoes, bone broth, bay leaves and cabbages.
4. Close Instant Pot, press the Manual button, choose high settings, and set time to 30 minutes.
5. Once done cooking, do a QPR.
6. Serve and enjoy.

Nutrition information:

Calories per serving: 428; Carbohydrates: 9.2g; Protein: 26.3g; Fat: 24.8g; Sugar: 3.2g; Sodium: 879mg

362. Instant Pot French Onion Soup
(Servings: 2, Cooking time: 23 minutes)

Ingredients:

- 4 tablespoons unsalted butter
- 2 large yellow onions, sliced thinly
- 3 cloves of garlic, minced
- Salt and pepper to taste
- 1 ½ cup chicken broth
- 1 ½ cup beef broth
- 2 tablespoons worcestershire sauce
- 3 slices of French bread, toasted and cubed
- 1 cup mozzarella cheese

Directions for Cooking:

1. Press the Sauté button on the Instant Pot and melt the butter. Sauté the onion and garlic. Keep stirring for 6 minutes until the onions have caramelized. Season with salt and pepper to taste.
2. Add in the chicken broth, beef broth, and Worcestershire sauce.
3. Close Instant Pot, press the button, choose high settings, and set time to 20 minutes.
4. Once done cooking, do a QPR.
5. Serve with slices of French bread on top and mozzarella cheese.
6. Serve and enjoy.

Nutrition information:

Calories per serving: 740; Carbohydrates: 54.8g; Protein: 63.8g; Fat: 29.8g; Sugar: 11g; Sodium: 1733mg

363. Instant Pot Easy Pork Ramen
(Servings: 5, Cooking time: 45 minutes)

Ingredients:

- 2 tablespoons cooking oil
- 1 onion, chopped
- 3 cloves of garlic, minced
- 2 ½ pounds pork spareribs, cut into chunks
- thumb-size ginger, sliced
- ¼ cup soy sauce
- 6 cups water
- Salt to taste
- 5 cups ramen noodles, boiled
- 1 sheet of nori (seaweed wrap)
- Green onions
- Toasted sesame seeds

Directions for Cooking:

1. Press the Sauté button on the Instant Pot and heat the oil. Sauté the onion and garlic until fragrant.
2. Stir in the pork for a minute. Add in the ginger, soy sauce, and water. Season with salt and pepper to taste.
3. Close Instant Pot, press the Manual button, choose high settings, and set time to 40 minutes.
4. Once done cooking, do a QPR.
5. Open the lid and assemble the ramen noodles.
6. First, take out the meat then shred using forks. Set aside.
7. For each serving, place a cup of ramen noodles in a bowl then top with shredded meat. Ladle in the soup and garnish with nori strips, green onions, and sesame seeds.
8. Serve and enjoy.

Nutrition information:

Calories per serving: 856; Carbohydrates:32.4 g; Protein: 66.4g; Fat: 49.8g; Sugar: 4.9g; Sodium: 1129mg

INSTANT POT SOUP RECIPES

364.   Weight Loss Soup
(Servings: 8, Cooking time: 15 minutes)

Ingredients:

- 2 tablespoons olive oil
- 1 onion, chopped
- 8 cloves of garlic, minced
- 2 tablespoons tomato paste
- 1 cup diced zucchini
- 1 cup celery, chopped
- 1 medium carrot, peeled and sliced
- 4 russet potatoes, peeled and quartered
- ¼ cabbage, quartered
- 1 teaspoon each of dried basil, oregano, onion powder, and garlic powder
- Salt and pepper to taste
- 8 cups vegetable broth
- 3 bay leaves

Nutrition information:

Calories per serving:214; Carbohydrates:42.5 g;
Protein: 5.1g; Fat: 3.6g; Sugar: 3g; Sodium: 581mg

Directions for Cooking:

1. Press the Sauté button on the Instant Pot and heat the oil. Sauté the onion and garlic until fragrant.
2. Stir in the tomato paste, zucchini, celery, carrots, potatoes, and cabbages. Season with herbs seasoning, salt and pepper. Keep stirring for at least 3 minutes until the vegetables sweat.
3. Stir in the rest of the ingredients. Adjust the salt if necessary.
4. Close Instant Pot, press the Manual button, choose high settings, and set time to 10 minutes.
5. Once done cooking, do a QPR.
6. Serve and enjoy.

365.   Vegan Red Lentil Soup
(Servings: 3, Cooking time: 60 minutes)

Ingredients:

- 1 tablespoon peanut oil
- 1 onion, chopped
- 1 tablespoon fresh ginger root, grated
- 1 clove of garlic, minced
- 1 pinch fenugreek seeds
- 1 cup dry red lentils, soaked overnight
- 2 cups water,2 tablespoons tomato paste
- 1 teaspoon curry powder
- Salt and pepper to taste
- 2 cups coconut milk

Directions for Cooking:

1. Press the Sauté button on the Instant Pot and heat oil. Stir in the onions, ginger, garlic, and fenugreek seeds until fragrant.
2. Stir in the lentils and pour in water and tomato paste. Season with curry powder, salt and pepper.
3. Close Instant Pot, press the Manual button, choose high settings, and set time to 40 minutes.
4. Once done cooking, do a QPR.
5. Open the lid and stir in the coconut milk.
6. Close the lid again and press the Manual button and set the time to 10 minutes.
7. Do QPR.
8. Serve and enjoy.

Nutrition information:

Calories per serving: 672; Carbohydrates: 57.1g;
Protein: 20.2g; Fat: 44.5g; Sugar: 9.3g; Sodium: 481mg

366. Italian Chicken Soup
(Servings: 12, Cooking time: 20 minutes)

Ingredients:

- 3 pounds whole chicken, cut into parts
- 4 large tomatoes, chopped
- 3 celery stalks, chopped
- 2 large carrots, peeled and halved
- 1 onion, wedged
- 4 cloves of garlic, minced
- 6 black peppercorns
- 1 bay leaf
- 8 cups water
- ¾ cup orzo pasta
- Salt to taste
- Small bunch of basil
- Lemon juice to taste
- Parmesan cheese, grated

Directions for Cooking:

1. Place the chicken, tomatoes, celery, carrots, onion, garlic, peppercorns, bay leaf, water, and pasta in the Instant Pot. Season with salt to taste.
2. Close Instant Pot, press the Manual button, choose high settings, and set time to 20 minutes.
3. Once done cooking, do a QPR.
4. Open the lid and add in the basil leaves last.
5. Before serving, add lemon juice and parmesan cheese on top.
6. Serve and enjoy.

Nutrition information:
Calories per serving: 300; Carbohydrates: 30.7g; Protein: 21.8g; Fat: 10.4g; Sugar: 6.7g; Sodium: 580mg

---

367. Cream of Celery Soup
(Servings: 4, Cooking time: 20 minutes)

Ingredients:

- 6 cups chopped celery
- 1 onion, chopped
- 1 cup coconut milk
- 2 cups water
- ½ teaspoon dill
- Salt to taste

Directions for Cooking:

1. Place all ingredients in the Instant Pot.
2. Once done cooking, do a QPR.
3. Open the lid and transfer into a blender. Pulse until smooth.
4. Serve and enjoy.

Nutrition information:
Calories per serving:174 ; Carbohydrates: 10.5g; Protein: 2.8g; Fat: 14.6g; Sugar:5.2 g; Sodium: 672mg

368.   Instant Pot Pork Shank Carrots Soup
(Servings: 4, Cooking time: 40 minutes)

Ingredients:

- 2 large carrots, chopped
- 1 green radish, peeled and chopped
- 2 pounds pork shank, cut into chunks
- 4 quarts water
- 1 thin slice of ginger
- 2 dried dates, pitted
- 1 small piece of chenpi (dried Mandarin peel)
- Salt to taste

Directions for Cooking:

1. Place all ingredients in the Instant Pot.
2. Close Instant Pot, press the Manual button, choose high settings, and set time to 40 minutes.
3. Once done cooking, do a QPR.
4. Serve and enjoy.

Nutrition information:

Calories per serving: 320; Carbohydrates: 12.1g; Protein: 50.2g; Fat: 6.9g; Sugar: 2.1g; Sodium: 128mg

---

369.   Instant Pot Beef and Vegetable Soup
(Servings: 5, Cooking time: 30 minutes)

Ingredients:

- 2 pounds lean ground beef
- 1 onion, diced
- 2 teaspoons garlic, minced
- 1 can tomatoes
- 4 cups beef broth
- 4 carrots, peeled and chopped
- 3 stalks of celery, diced
- 4 large potatoes, peeled and cut into chunks
- 2 tablespoons tomato paste
- Salt and pepper to taste
- ½ teaspoon ground oregano

Directions for Cooking:

1. Press the Sauté button on the Instant Pot and stir in the beef, onion, and garlic. Stir until the beef slightly turns golden.
2. Add in the rest of the ingredients.
3. Close Instant Pot, press the Manual button, choose high settings, and set time to 25 minutes.
4. Once done cooking, do a QPR.
5. Serve and enjoy.

Nutrition information:

Calories per serving:735; Carbohydrates: 79.2g; Protein: 56.2g; Fat: 20.9g; Sugar: 7.3g; Sodium: 918mg

INSTANT POT SOUP RECIPES

370.   Unstuffed Cabbage Roll Soup
(Servings: 3, Cooking time: 25 minutes)

Ingredients:

- 1 ½ pounds ground beef
- ½ onion, diced
- 2 cloves of garlic, minced
- 1 14-ounce can diced tomatoes
- 1 cup tomato sauce
- ¼ cup liquid aminos
- 3 cups beef broth
- 1 cabbage, chopped
- 3 teaspoons Worcestershire sauce
- Salt and pepper to taste

Directions for Cooking:

1. Press the Sauté button on the Instant Pot and stir in the beef, onions, and garlic until fragrant.
2. Stir in the rest of the ingredients
3. Close Instant Pot, press the button, choose high settings, and set time to 20 minutes.
4. Once done cooking, do a QPR.
5. Serve and enjoy.

Nutrition information:

Calories per serving: 217; Carbohydrates: 6.4g; Protein: 15.6g; Fat: 14.8g; Sugar: 3.1g; Sodium: 731mg

---

371.   Instant Pot Beef Borscht
(Servings: 9, Cooking time: 25 minutes)

Ingredients:

- 1 tablespoon oil
- 1-pound beef steak, cut into strips
- 2 cloves of garlic, minced
- 1 onion, diced
- 3 large beets, peeled and diced
- 3 stalks of celery, diced
- 2 carrots, diced
- 3 cups cabbage, shredded
- 6 cups beef stock
- 1 bay leaf
- Salt and pepper to taste
- ¼ cup fresh dill, chopped
- ½ cup sour cream

Directions for Cooking:

1. Press the Sauté button on the Instant Pot and heat the oil.
2. Stir in the beef steak, garlic, and onion until lightly golden.
3. Stir in the rest of the ingredients.
4. Close Instant Pot, press the Manual button, choose high settings, and set time to 20 minutes.
5. Once done cooking, do a QPR.
6. Serve and enjoy.

Nutrition information:

Calories per serving: 157; Carbohydrates: 10.9g; Protein: 15.5g; Fat: 5.9g; Sugar: 5g; Sodium: 401mg

INSTANT POT SOUP RECIPES

372.   Lemon Chicken Orzo
(Servings: 4, Cooking time: 30 minutes)

Ingredients:

- 1 tablespoon olive oil
- ¾ cup onion, diced
- 1 tablespoon garlic, minced
- ½ pound chicken, cut into small pieces
- ¾ cup celery, chopped
- Salt and pepper to taste
- ½ teaspoon thyme
- 1/3 cup orzo
- 2 cups chicken broth
- 1 tablespoon lemon juice
- ¼ cup heavy cream

Directions for Cooking:

1. Press the Sauté button on the Instant Pot and heat the oil. Stir in the onions and garlic until fragrant.

2. Stir in the chicken and celery. Season with salt and pepper to taste. Keep stirring for three minutes until the chicken becomes lightly golden.
3. Add in thyme, orzo, chicken broth and lemon juice.
4. Close Instant Pot, press the Manual button, choose high settings, and set time to 25 minutes.
5. Once done cooking, do a QPR.
6. Open the lid and press the Sauté button. Add in the heavy cream and allow to simmer.
7. Serve and enjoy.

Nutrition information:

Calories per serving: 282; Carbohydrates: 10g; Protein:15.8g; Fat: 8.7g; Sugar: 3.1g; Sodium: 768mg

---

373.   Winter Melon and Tofu Soup
(Servings: 3, Cooking time: 1 hour and 5 minutes)

Ingredients:

- 1-pound pork bones,
- 5 cups water
- Salt and pepper to taste
- 3 slices of ginger
- 1 cup tofu, cubed
- 1 cup winter melon
- Green onions for garnish

Directions for Cooking:

1. Place the pork bones and water in the Instant Pot. Season with salt and pepper to taste.
2. Close Instant Pot, press the Manual button, choose high settings, and set time to 60 minutes.

3. Once done cooking, do a QPR.
4. Open the lid and take out the bones. Set aside for future use.
5. Press the Sauté button.
6. Stir in the ginger, tofu, and winter melon. Allow to simmer for 5 minutes.
7. Garnish with green onions on top.
8. Serve and enjoy.

Nutrition information:

Calories per serving: 404; Carbohydrates: 27.8g; Protein: 28.8g; Fat: 20.6g; Sugar: 2.9g; Sodium: 1743mg

INSTANT POT SOUP RECIPES

374.   Mexican Albondigas Soup
(Servings: 4, Cooking time: 25 minutes)

Ingredients:

- 1-pound packaged meatballs
- 2 cloves of garlic, minced
- 1 onion, chopped
- ½ green bell pepper, chopped
- 4 carrots, chopped
- 1 can diced tomatoes
- 3 cups chicken broth
- Salt and pepper to taste
- Chopped cilantro for garnish

Directions for Cooking:

1. Place the meatballs, garlic, and onions in the Instant Pot. Press the Sauté button and allow to sear on all sides for three minutes.

2. Stir in the rest of the ingredients except for the cilantro.
3. Close Instant Pot, press the Manual button, choose high settings, and set time to 20 minutes.
4. Once done cooking, do a QPR.
5. Open the lid and stir in the cilantro.
6. Serve and enjoy.

Nutrition information:
Calories per serving: 642; Carbohydrates: 22.6g; Protein: 74.4g; Fat: 27.2g; Sugar: 7.5g; Sodium: 1485mg

375.   Butternut Squash and Cauliflower Soup
(Servings: 4, Cooking time: 12 minutes)

Ingredients:

- 2 tablespoons oil
- 1 onion, diced
- 3 cloves of garlic, minced
- 1-pound frozen cauliflower
- 1-pound frozen butternut squash
- 2 cups of vegetable broth
- 1 teaspoon paprika
- 1 teaspoon dried thyme
- Salt and pepper to taste
- ½ cup half-and-half

Directions for Cooking:

1. Press the Sauté button on the Instant Pot and heat oil.

2. Stir in the onions and garlic. Sauté until fragrant.
3. Add in the rest of the ingredients.
4. Close Instant Pot, press the button, choose high settings, and set time to 10 minutes.
5. Once done cooking, do a QPR.
6. Open the lid and transfer the contents into a blender. Pulse until smooth. Serve with cheese on top if desired.
7. Serve and enjoy.

Nutrition information:
Calories per serving: 98; Carbohydrates:15.2 g; Protein:1.9 g; Fat: 3.8g; Sugar: 3.8g; Sodium:168mg

INSTANT POT SOUP RECIPES

376.   Instant Pot Taco Soup
(Servings: 8, Cooking time: 30 minutes)

Ingredients:

- 2 pounds ground beef
- 1 onion, chopped
- 4 cloves of garlic, minced
- 2 tablespoons chili powder
- 2 teaspoons cumin
- 1 cup diced tomatoes
- 3 cups beef broth
- Salt and pepper to taste
- ½ cup cream cheese
- ½ cup heavy cream

Directions for Cooking:

1. Press the Sauté button on the Instant Pot and stir in the beef, onion, garlic, chili powder, and cumin.
2. Stir in the tomatoes and beef broth. Season with salt and pepper to taste.
3. Close Instant Pot, press the button, choose high settings, and set time to 20 minutes.
4. Once done cooking, do a QPR.
5. Open the lid and press the Sauté button. Stir in the cream cheese and heavy cream.
6. Serve and enjoy.

Nutrition information:
Calories per serving: 386; Carbohydrates: 8g; Protein: 27g; Fat: 28g; Sugar: 4g; Sodium: 831mg

---

377.   En Caldo De Res Soup
(Servings: 6, Cooking time: 20 minutes)

Ingredients:

- 1 tablespoon oil
- 2 pounds beef shank, sliced thinly
- 1 onion, chopped
- 1 chayote, peeled and sliced
- 2 zucchinis, sliced
- 2 carrots, sliced
- 2 corn cut into 3 big pieces
- ½ head of cabbage, cut into wedges
- 1 bay leaf
- Salt and pepper to taste
- 6 cups water
- Lime wedges
- Cilantro for garnish

Directions for Cooking:

1. Press the Sauté button on the Instant Pot and heat oil.
2. Place the beef and onions in the Instant Pot and allow to brown on all sides.
3. Stir in the chayote, zucchini, carrots, corn, cabbage, and bay leaf. Season with salt and pepper to taste. Allow the vegetables to sweat before pouring in water.
4. Close Instant Pot, press the Manual button, choose high settings, and set time to 15 minutes.
5. Once done cooking, do a QPR.
6. Once the lid is open, garnish with lime wedges and cilantro on top.
7. Serve and enjoy.

Nutrition information:
Calories per serving: 171; Carbohydrates: 18g; Protein: 18g; Fat: 3g; Sugar: 4g; Sodium: 76mg

378. Cream of Asparagus Soup
(Servings: 4, Cooking time: 13 minutes)

Ingredients:

- 1 teaspoon coconut oil
- ½ stick butter
- 2 cloves of garlic, minced
- 1 onion, diced
- ½ cup chopped celery
- 1-pound asparagus, chopped
- 2 cups vegetable stock
- 1 cup heavy cream
- Salt to taste

Directions for Cooking:

1. Press the Sauté button on the Instant Pot and heat the oil and butter. Sauté the garlic, onion, and celery until fragrant.
2. Stir in the rest of the ingredients.
3. Close Instant Pot, press the Manual button, choose high settings, and set time to 10 minutes.
4. Once done cooking, do a QPR.
5. Open the lid and transfer into a blender. Pulse until smooth.
6. Serve and enjoy.

Nutrition information:

Calories per serving: 353; Carbohydrates: 20.6g; Protein: 7.1g; Fat: 27.9g; Sugar: 4.8g; Sodium: 183mg

379. Sweet Potato, Black Bean, And Quinoa Chili Soup
(Servings: 6, Cooking time: 30 minutes)

Ingredients:

- 1 bell pepper, diced
- 3 medium-sized sweet potatoes, peeled and diced
- 1 onion, diced
- 3 cloves of garlic, minced
- 3 stalks of celery, chopped
- 4 cups vegetable broth
- 2 tablespoons tomato paste
- 1 cup diced tomatoes
- 1 can black beans, rinsed and drained
- 2 teaspoons each of paprika and cumin
- Salt to taste
- ½ cup quinoa
- 6 cups vegetable broth

Directions for Cooking:

1. Place all ingredients in the Instant Pot. Give a good stir.
2. Close Instant Pot, press the Manual button, choose high settings, and set time to 30 minutes.
3. Once done cooking, do a QPR.
4. Serve and enjoy.

Nutrition information:

Calories per serving:375 ; Carbohydrates: 73.7g; Protein: 18.1g; Fat: g; Sugar: 4.8g; Sodium: 954mg

380. Vietnamese Beef Stew Noodle Soup
(Servings: 5, Cooking time: 30 minutes)

Ingredients:

- 1 cinnamon stick
- 4 star anise
- 5 whole cloves
- 2 ½ pounds beef chuck, cut into chunks
- 1 tablespoon oil
- 2 tablespoons chopped garlic
- ¼ cup yellow onion, chopped
- 3 tomatoes, chopped
- ½ cup red wine
- 1 ginger, sliced
- 6 cups water
- 3 tablespoons fish sauce
- 1 package rice noodles
- Chopped cilantro for garnish

Directions for Cooking:

1. Place the cinnamon stick, star anise, and cloves in a cloth or tea bag. Set aside.
2. Press the Sauté button on the Instant Pot and stir in the beef and oil until lightly golden. Add in garlic and onions.
3. Stir in the tomatoes, red wine, ginger, and water. Season with fish sauce and the spices placed in the tea bag.
4. Close Instant Pot, press the Manual button, choose high settings, and set time to 25 minutes.
5. Once done cooking, do a QPR.
6. Open the lid and press the Sauté button. Stir in the rice noodles and cilantro.
7. Serve and enjoy.

Nutrition information:

Calories per serving: 424; Carbohydrates: 4.9g; Protein: 56g; Fat: 19.8g; Sugar: 2.5g; Sodium: 1037mg

381. Ham and White Bean Soup
(Servings: 5, Cooking time: 45 minutes)

Ingredients:

- 1 tablespoon olive oil
- 3 cloves of garlic, minced
- 1 onion, chopped
- 1-pound ham, sliced
- 1 tomato, chopped
- 1-pound great northern beans, soaked overnight
- 4 cups vegetable stock
- 2 cups water
- Salt and pepper to taste
- 1 teaspoon dried mint
- 1 teaspoon dried paprika
- 1 teaspoon dried thyme

Directions for Cooking:

1. Press the Sauté button on the Instant Pot and heat the oil.
2. Sauté the garlic and onion until fragrant. Stir in the ham and allow to render its fat. Add in the rest of the ingredients.
3. Close Instant Pot, press the Manual button, choose high settings, and set time to 40 minutes.
4. Once done cooking, do a QPR.
5. Serve and enjoy.

Nutrition information:

Calories per serving: 240; Carbohydrates: 16g; Protein: 17g; Fat: 11g; Sugar: 2g; Sodium: 745mg

382. Instant Pot Pasta Fagioli
(Servings: 5, Cooking time: 50 minutes)

Ingredients

- 1 tablespoon olive oil
- 1 onion, chopped
- 5 cloves of garlic, minced
- 1-pound Italian sausage, ground
- 2 stalks of celery, diced
- 1 large carrot, diced
- 1 can diced tomatoes
- 1 can cannellini beans
- 1 can tomato sauce
- 2 bay leaves
- 3 cups chicken broth
- Salt and pepper to taste
- 1 cup pasta, cooked according to package instruction
- ¼ cup parmesan cheese, grated

Directions for Cooking:

1. Press the Sauté button on the Instant Pot and heat the oil. Sauté the onion and garlic until fragrant. Stir in the Italian sausages and celery. Allow to sweat before adding the carrots, tomatoes, beans, tomato, sauce and bay leaves.
2. Pour in the chicken broth and season with salt and pepper to taste.
3. Close Instant Pot, press the Manual button, choose high settings, and set time to 40 minutes.
4. Once done cooking, do a QPR.
5. Open the lid and press the Saute button. Stir in the pasta and parmesan cheese.
6. Serve and enjoy.

Nutrition information:
Calories per serving:709 ; Carbohydrates: 27.8g; Protein: 48.6g; Fat: 43.1g; Sugar: 8.9g; Sodium: 949mg

---

383. Easy Kimchi Soup
(Servings: 5, Cooking time: 35 minutes)

Ingredients:

- 2 tablespoons olive oil
- 2 cloves of garlic, minced
- 1-inch ginger
- 1 onion, chopped
- 2 pounds beef stew, cut into chunks
- Salt and pepper to taste
- 1 cup commercial kimchi
- 5 cups chicken broth
- 1 package firm tofu

Directions for cooking:

1. Press the Sauté button on the Instant Pot and heat the oil. Sauté the garlic, ginger, and onion. Stir in the beef and allow to brown on all sides.
2. Stir in salt and pepper to taste.
3. Add the kimchi and chicken broth.
4. Close Instant Pot, press the Manual button, choose high settings, and set time to 25 minutes.
5. Once done cooking, do a QPR.
6. Open the lid and stir in the tofu. Allow to simmer for at least 5 minutes.
7. Serve and enjoy.

Nutrition information:
Calories per serving:808 ; Carbohydrates: 10.5g; Protein:102.9g; Fat: 39.4g; Sugar: 1.6g; Sodium: 1148mg

---

INSTANT POT SOUP RECIPES

384. Instant Pot Tortellini Soup
(Servings: 6, Cooking time: 25 minutes)

Ingredients:

- 1-pound Italian sausage
- 1 onion, diced
- 2 stalks of celery, diced
- 4 cloves of garlic, minced
- Salt and pepper to taste
- 1/3 cup sherry wine
- 2 carrots, diced
- 1 can diced tomatoes
- 1-pound fresh cheese tortellini
- 8 cups chicken stock
- 3 cups kale, chopped
- Grated parmesan cheese

Directions for Cooking:

1. Press the Sauté button on the Instant Pot and stir in the Italian sausage, onion, celery, and garlic. Season with salt and pepper to taste.

2. Add in the wine, carrots, tomatoes, tortellini, and chicken stock.
3. Close Instant Pot, press the Manual button, choose high settings, and set time to 20 minutes.
4. Once done cooking, do a QPR.
5. Open the lid and press the Sauté button and stir in the kale. Allow to simmer until the kale is cooked through.
6. Serve and enjoy.

Nutrition information:
Calories per serving: 711; Carbohydrates: 56.8g; Protein: 35.7g; Fat: 37.8g; Sugar: 9g; Sodium: 1124mg

385. Beef Stroganoff Soup
(Servings: 6, Cooking time: 25 minutes)

Ingredients:

- 1 ½ pounds stew meat
- 6 cups beef broth
- 4 tablespoons Worcestershire sauce
- ½ teaspoon Italian seasoning
- 1 ½ teaspoon onion powder
- 2 teaspoons garlic powder
- ½ cup sour cream
- 8 ounces mushrooms, sliced
- Salt and pepper to taste
- 8 ounces short noodles, blanched

Directions for Cooking:

1. Place the meat, broth, Worcestershire sauce, Italian seasoning, onion powder, garlic powder, sour cream, and mushrooms. Season with salt and pepper to taste.

2. Close Instant Pot, press the Manual button, choose high settings, and set time to 20 minutes.
3. Once done cooking, do a QPR.
4. Open the lid and press the Sauté button. Stir in the noodles and allow to simmer for 5 minutes.
5. Serve and enjoy.

Nutrition information:
Calories per serving:588 ; Carbohydrates: 65g; Protein: 39.6g; Fat: 20.1g; Sugar: 12.8g; Sodium: 639mg

Instant Pot Rice & Pasta Recipes

386. Shrimp, Mushrooms & Asparagus Risotto
(Servings: 4, Cooking Time: 20 minutes)

Ingredients:

- 2 tsp olive oil
- 1 small red or yellow onion, diced
- 1-1/2 cups Arborio rice
- 1 cup sliced cremini or white button mushrooms
- 1/2 cup dry white wine
- 3-1/2 cups chicken broth
- 1 Tbsp butter
- 1 cup chopped asparagus
- 3/4 lb large shrimp, defrosted if frozen, peeled and deveined
- Heaping 1/4 cup grated Parmigiano-Reggiano cheese
- 1/2 tsp fresh black pepper

Nutrition information:

Calories per serving: 454; Carbohydrates: 28.0g; Protein: 43.1g; Fat: 24.3g; Sugar: 2.1g; Sodium: 1055mg

Directions for Cooking:

1. Press browning button and heat oil. Sauté onions for 3 minutes.
2. Stir in mushrooms and rice. Cook for 5 minutes.
3. Add wine and deglaze pot for a minute.
4. Add chicken broth. Press cancel.
5. Close Instant Pot, press pressure cook button, choose high settings, and set time to 6 minutes.
6. Once done cooking, do a QPR.
7. Press cancel, press brown button, stir in asparagus and butter. Cook for a minute.
8. Add shrimps and stirring frequently, cook for 3 minutes.
9. Serve and enjoy.

---

387. Wild Rice Pilaf
(Servings: 8, Cooking Time: 50 minutes)

Ingredients:

- 2 tablespoons olive oil
- 2 brown onions chopped
- 2 cloves garlic minced
- 12 oz mushrooms sliced
- 1/4 cup white wine
- 1/2 teaspoon salt
- 6 sprigs fresh thyme (or 1/2 tsp dried thyme leaves)
- 2 cups wild rice brown basmati blend
- 2 cups stock
- 1/2 cup parsley chopped
- 1/2 cup pine nuts (or almond slices)

Directions for Cooking:

1. Press sauté and heat oil. Sauté onions for 5 minutes.
2. Add garlic and sauté for another minute.
3. Stir in white wine and deglaze pot for a minute. Press cancel.
4. Stir in salt, thyme, rice, and stock. Mix well.
5. Close Instant Pot, press pressure cook button, choose high settings, and set time to 28 minutes.
6. Once done cooking, do a QPR.
7. Stir in pine nuts and parsley. Serve and enjoy

Nutrition information:

Calories per serving: 263; Carbohydrates: 36.0g; Protein: 8.0g; Fat: 9.0g; Sugar: 3.0g; Sodium: 389mg

388.   Fried Rice with Shrimps
(Servings: 3, Cooking Time: 40 minutes)

Ingredients:

- 2tablespoons of oil, divided
- 1 onion, peeled and diced
- 2 tablespoons of garlic
- 2 eggs, whisked
- 1 cup of uncooked basmati rice
- 2 teaspoons of soy sauce
- 1¼ cup of chicken broth
- ½ cup of mixed frozen vegetables
- 1 pound of frozen shrimp
- 1 cup of water

Directions for Cooking:

1. Add rice, water, and stock in Instant Pot.
2. Close Instant Pot, press rice button.
3. Once done cooking, do a QPR and transfer rice to a bowl.
4. Press cancel, press sauté button and add 1 tbsp oil.
5. Once hot, scramble eggs for 4 minutes. Transfer to a bowl and cut into small pieces.
6. Add remaining oil and once hot sauté garlic for a minute. Stir in onions and cook for another 3 minutes.
7. Add shrimps and cook until opaque, around 5 minutes.
8. Stir in frozen vegetables and cook until heated through around 3 minutes.
9. Stir in rice. Add soy sauce. Mix well and cook for 2 minutes.
10. Serve and enjoy.

Nutrition information:
Calories per serving: 483; Carbohydrates: 32.5g; Protein: 45.5g; Fat: 23.6g; Sugar: 4.0g; Sodium: 1946mg

389.   Risotto Italian Style
(Servings: 4, Cooking Time: 40 minutes)

Ingredients:
- 1 bunch asparagus, sliced thin
- 1 cup broccoli florets
- 1 cup fresh peas or snap peas
- 2 tablespoons and 1 teaspoon extra-virgin olive oil
- 1 onion, diced
- 1 cup leek, diced
- 2 garlic cloves, minced
- 1 teaspoon fresh thyme
- 1 1/2 cups arborio rice
- 4 cups vegetable broth
- 4 tablespoons butter
- 1 cup spinach
- 1/2 bunch chives, sliced thin
- 1/2 teaspoon garlic powder

Directions for Cooking:

1. Pre-heat oven to 400°F. Line a baking sheet with parchment paper. Add asparagus, broccoli, and peas to the baking sheet. Coat with 1 teaspoon extra-virgin olive oil, salt and pepper, toss well. Place in the oven for 15-20 minutes or until broccoli is fork tender. Once done, remove from oven and set aside.
2. Press sauté button on Instant Pot ad heat remaining oil. Cook garlic and onions for 3 minutes.
3. Stir in rice and cook for 2 minutes.
4. Add thyme, butter, and vegetable stock. Mix well. Press cancel.

- 1/4 teaspoon red pepper flakes, more to taste
- 1 teaspoon lemon zest
- 2 tablespoons lemon juice, more to taste

Nutrition information:

Calories per serving: 361; Carbohydrates: 35.1g; Protein: 8.5g; Fat: 27.9g; Sugar: 6.0g; Sodium: 662mg

5. Close Instant Pot, press pressure cook button, choose high settings, and set time to 7 minutes.
6. Once done cooking, do a QPR. Press cancel.
7. Stir in spices, roasted vegetables, chives, and spinach. Toss well to mix. Cover and let it sit for 5 minutes.
8. Serve and enjoy
9.

---

390. Fish Congee Vietnam Style
(Servings: 4, Cooking Time: 25 minutes)

Ingredients:

- 3/4 cup rice (see recipe notes for more details)
- 2 tablespoons mung bean (optional)
- 1 - 1.5 lbs fish bones
- a thumb-sized piece of ginger, peeled and sliced
- 1 shallot, peeled and cut in half
- 6 cups water (boiling water for faster cooking)
- 1 teaspoon salt (plus more to taste)
- 1 tablespoon fish sauce (plus more to taste)
- 1-lb fish fillet (grouper works best)

For Topping Ingredients:

- 1 tbsp fried shallot
- 2 tbsp scallion, thinly sliced
- 1 tbsp Cilantro, roughly chopped
- black pepper to taste

Directions for Cooking:

1. Wash rice and mung bean (if using) and drain, add to Instant Pot.
2. Scrub fish bones with salt and rinse under cold water. Add to pot.
3. Add water, 1 teaspoon salt, 1 tablespoon fish sauce in pot.
4. Close Instant Pot, press porridge button.
5. Meanwhile, slice fish diagonally in ½-inch thick slices. Season with pepper and salt. Set aside.
6. Once done cooking, do a QPR.
7. Fish out the bones and discard. Press cancel, press sauté and stir in fish. Cook for 5 minutes or until cooked.
8. Serve and enjoy with topping ingredients.

Nutrition information:

Calories per serving: 201; Carbohydrates: 12.3g; Protein: 29.7g; Fat: 5.9g; Sugar: 0.9g; Sodium: 1090mg

391. Pasta Puttanesca
(Servings: 4, Cooking Time: 5 minutes)

Ingredients:

- 3 cloves garlic minced
- 4 cups pasta sauce
- 3 cups water
- 4 cups pasta such as penne or fusilli
- 1/4 teaspoon crushed red pepper flakes
- 1 Tablespoon capers
- 1/2 cup Kalamata olives sliced
- salt to taste
- pepper to taste

Directions for Cooking:

1. Press sauté and add a splash of water. Add garlic and sauté for 30 seconds. Press cancel.

2. Stir in olives, capers, crushed red pepper flakes, pasta, water, and pasta sauce. Mix well.
3. Close Instant Pot, press pressure cook button, choose high settings, and set time to 5 minutes.
4. Once done cooking, do a QPR.
5. Mix well and adjust seasoning to taste
6. Serve and enjoy

Nutrition information:
Calories per serving: 504; Carbohydrates: 98.0g; Protein: 18.0g; Fat: 4.0g; Sugar: 13.0g; Sodium: 1620mg

---

392. Barley and Beef Stew
(Servings: 8, Cooking Time: 30 minutes)

Ingredients:

- 2-lbs stew beef
- 2 tbsp olive oil
- 1/2 tsp salt
- 1/2 tsp ground pepper
- 3/4 cup red wine
- 3 cups beef broth
- 2 cloves garlic, finely diced
- 1/2 cup onion, diced
- 2 tbsp tomato paste
- 1/2 tsp dried thyme
- 1 bay leaf
- 1/2 tsp Italian Seasoning
- 14 oz can petite diced tomatoes
- 1 cup carrots, 1/2" pieces
- 2 cups potatoes, diced 1/2" pieces
- 1/2 cup barley

Directions for Cooking:

1. Press brown and heat oil. Once hot, add beef and season with pepper and salt. Cook until browned, around 10 minutes.
2. Add wine and deglaze pot.
3. Stir in broth, garlic, onion, tomato paste, thyme, bay leaf, Italian seasoning, diced tomatoes, carrots, potatoes and barley. Mix well.
4. Close Instant Pot, press stew button, and set time to 30 minutes.
5. Once done cooking, do a QPR.
6. Mix well and discard bay leaf.
7. Serve and enjoy.

Nutrition information:
Calories per serving: 273; Carbohydrates: 21.7g; Protein: 28.1g; Fat: 8.3g; Sugar: 2.2g; Sodium: 522mg

393. Chicken, Chorizo & Seafood Paella
(Servings: 8, Cooking Time: 40 minutes)

Ingredients:

- 1-lb Chicken, diced
- 8 oz. Spicy Chorizo
- 1 tbsp Olive oil
- 1 Onion, diced
- 1/4 tsp Marjoram
- 1/4 tsp Cumin
- 1/8 tsp Whole Saffron
- 15 oz Long-grain rice, uncooked
- 2 cups Chicken Stock
- 1 cup Water
- 2 Cloves garlic, minced
- ½-lb Whole Shrimp
- ½-lb Clams, in the shell, Drained
- 1/2 cup Green Peas; Frozen
- Salt
- 1 Lemon, wedged

Nutrition information:

Calories per serving: 482; Carbohydrates: 50.0g;
Protein: 30.7g; Fat: 16.9g; Sugar: 3.5g; Sodium:
1133mg

Directions for Cooking:

1. Press sauté and heat oil.
2. Sauté saffron, cumin, marjoram, and onions for a minute.
3. Stir in chorizo and chopped chicken for 8 minutes.
4. Stir in rice and cook for a minute.
5. Add water and chicken stock. Deglaze pot.
6. Close Instant Pot, press pressure cook button, choose high settings, and set time to 20 minutes.
7. Once done cooking, do a QPR.
8. Press cancel, press sauté button. Stir in salt, garlic, clams, green peas and shrimp. Cook for 3 minutes.
9. Press cancel and let it sit for 5 more minutes to continue cooking.
10. Serve and enjoy with lemon wedges.

394. Cheesy & Easy Beef Bowties
(Servings: 8, Cooking Time: 20 minutes)

Ingredients:

- 1-lb Farfalle pasta
- 1-lb ground beef
- 1 jar vodka sauce (24 ounce)
- 3 cups beef stock (unsalted)
- 1 tbsp Italian seasoning
- 1 tbsp dry minced onion
- 1 ½ tsp garlic powder
- 1 tsp salt
- ½ tsp pepper
- 1 ½ cups mozzarella (shredded)
- ½ cup parmesan (grated)

Nutrition information:

Directions for Cooking:

1. Press sauté button and once hot cook beef until browned, around 10 minutes.
2. Stir in pepper, salt, garlic powder, Italian seasoning, and minced onion. Cook for 2 minutes.
3. Add beef stock and deglaze pot. Press cancel.
4. Add pasta, pushing it down but not mixing it in.
5. Layer the vodka sauce on top.
6. Close Instant Pot, press pressure cook button, choose high settings, and set time to 5 minutes.

Calories per serving: 297; Carbohydrates: 24.3g; Protein: 27.2g; Fat: 10.1g; Sugar: 3.3g; Sodium: 1098mg

7. Once done cooking, do a 2-minute natural release and then a QPR.
8. Stir in mozzarella and parmesan. Mix well.
9. Serve and enjoy

395.   Fettucine Alfredo
(Servings: 5, Cooking Time: 10 minutes)

Ingredients:

- 3 Tbsp Butter, cut in a few small pieces
- 4 cloves Garlic, pressed/minced
- 2 cups Chicken Broth
- 8 oz Fettuccine Noodles, broken in half
- 1-lb small Chicken Breasts, uncooked cut larger breasts in half
- 1 1/2 cups Heavy Cream
- 1 tsp Salt (or more to taste)
- 1/2 tsp Pepper
- 1 cup Parmesan Cheese, grated

Directions for Cooking:

1. Place the butter and garlic in the pot.
2. Pour in the chicken broth.
3. Sprinkle in the fettuccine noodles, in a random pattern, and gently press them down.

4. If Adding Chicken: Add the chicken breasts, and space evenly over the noodles. Pour the cream over them, then sprinkle with the salt and pepper..
5. Close Instant Pot, press pressure cook button, choose high settings, and set time to 5 minutes.
6. Once done cooking, do a QPR.
7. Stir in Parmesan and mix well. Let it rest for 5 minutes.
8. Serve and enjoy

Nutrition information:
Calories per serving: 469; Carbohydrates: 17.8g; Protein: 37.2g; Fat: 27.1g; Sugar: 1.5g; Sodium: 1405mg

396.   Macaroni Salad
(Servings: 8, Cooking Time: 10minutes)

Ingredients:

- 1 lb elbow pasta
- 4 cups water
- 1 tsp salt
- 1 ½ cups mayonnaise
- ½ cup sour cream
- 2 tsp pickle juice from bread & butter pickle jar
- 2 tsp mustard
- 1 cup shredded lettuce (chopped)
- 1 cup green peas (or one small 8.5 oz can)

2. Close Instant Pot, press pressure cook button, choose high settings, and set time to 0 minutes.
3. Once done cooking, do a QPR. Let pasta sit for 5 minutes.
4. In a small bowl, mix well pickle juice, sour cream, mustard, and mayonnaise. Stir in pot of macaroni and mix well.
5. Stir in olives, peas, lettuce, pickled, and spam. Mix well.

- 1 can Spam (diced)
- ½ cup bread & butter pickles (chopped)
- 1 cup olives

Directions for Cooking:

1. Add water and macaroni in Instant Pot.

6. Transfer to a bowl and refrigerate for at least 4 hours or until cool.
7. Serve and enjoy

Nutrition information:

Calories per serving: 410; Carbohydrates: 31.5g; Protein: 10.9g; Fat: 27.6g; Sugar: 4.6g; Sodium: 1381mg

---

397. Goulash
(Servings: 8, Cooking Time: 25minutes)

Ingredients:

- 1 lb ground turkey
- 1 tablespoon minced garlic
- 2 ½ tablespoons Italian seasoning
- 1 tablespoon minced onion
- 1 teaspoon salt
- 2 bay leaves
- 1 chopped zucchini
- 1 cup chopped red and green bell peppers
- 8 ounces whole wheat pasta
- 1 14-ounce can crushed tomatoes
- 1 can of water

Directions for Cooking:

1. Press sauté button and sauté ground turkey until browned, around 10 minutes.

2. Stir in bay leaves, salt, Italian seasoning, minced onions, and garlic. Mix well.
3. Stir in tomatoes, fill empty can of tomatoes with water and add to pot. Mix well. Stir in pasta.
4. Close Instant Pot, press pressure cook button, choose high settings, and set time to 10 minutes.
5. Once done cooking, do a QPR.
6. Stir in zucchini and bell peppers. Cover and let it sit for 5 minutes.
7. Serve and enjoy

Nutrition information:

Calories per serving: 204; Carbohydrates: 25.7g; Protein: 16.0g; Fat: 4.9g; Sugar: 1.9g; Sodium: 576mg

---

398. Shrimp-Clam Cocktail Risotto
(Servings: 4, Cooking Time: 30 minutes)

Ingredients:

- 4 cups of PC Bacon Flavour Tomato Clam Cocktail (half the bottle)
- 2 tbsp butter
- 1 chopped onion
- 1 tbsp smoked paprika
- 1 tsp dried oregano
- 1/2 tsp salt

Directions for Cooking:

1. Press sauté button and melt butter. Stir in onions and cook for 5 minutes.
2. Add paprika, oregano, salt, and pepper. Sauté for a minute.
3. Add rice and sauté for a minute.

- 1/2 tsp freshly ground black pepper
- 1 1/2 cup arborio rice
- 1 cup of raw deveined shrimp
- ¼ cup freshly grated Parmesan

Nutrition information:

Calories per serving: 398; Carbohydrates: 56.8g; Protein: 16.7g; Fat: 17.9g; Sugar: 12.7g; Sodium: 1612mg

4. Add clam cocktail and deglaze pot. Press cancel.
5. Close Instant Pot, press pressure cook button, choose high settings, and set time to 10 minutes.
6. Once done cooking, do a QPR.
7. Stir in shrimp, mix well, and let it rest for 5 minutes.
8. Add Parmesan and let it rest for 5 minutes more.
9. Serve and enjoy

---

399. Chicken Biryani
(Servings:6, Cooking Time: 45 minutes)

Chicken Ingredients:

- 1 ½-lbs. boneless skinless chicken thighs
- 3/4 cup plain yogurt
- 2 tablespoons olive oil
- 2 tablespoons ginger-garlic paste 1-inch ginger + 6 cloves garlic
- 2 tablespoons chopped cilantro & mint
- 1 tablespoon garam masala
- 1 tablespoon coriander powder
- 2 teaspoons cumin powder
- 1 teaspoon turmeric
- 1/2 teaspoon red chili powder adjust to your spice level
- 2 teaspoons Smoked Paprika
- 1.5 teaspoon salt adjust to taste
- 2 teaspoons lime juice

Rice Ingredients:

- 2 cups Basmati Rice or long grain rice
- 4 cups water
- 2 teaspoons salt
- 1/2 teaspoon garam masala
- 1 teaspoon ghee or oil

Biryani Ingredients:

- 1 tablespoon butter melted : put before shutting lid

Cucumber-Mint Raita Ingredients:

- 1 English cucumber chopped fine
- 2 cups plain yogurt
- 1/2 teaspoon salt
- 1/4 teaspoon pepper
- 1/4 teaspoon sugar optional, but highly recommended
- 1 tablespoon chopped mint

Directions for Cooking:

1. In a large shallow dish, make the chicken marinade by mixing yogurt, olive oil, ginger garlic paste, cilantro & mint, garam masala, coriander, cumin, turmeric, red chili powder, smoked paprika, salt and lime juice. Add chicken and marinate for at least 30 minutes.
2. Partially cook the rice by mixing all rice ingredients in a heatproof bowl. Microwave for 10 minutes and then drain thoroughly.
3. Meanwhile, in a separate bowl whisk well all raita ingredients and then set aside.
4. Press sauté button and add ¼ cup water in pot.
5. Layer chicken on pot bottom and pour in marinade. Evenly spread partially cooked rice over chicken.

- 10 whole cashews
- 1/2 teaspoon saffron soaked in 2 tablespoons warm milk
- 1 teaspoon garam masala : put before shutting lid
- 1/2 cup chopped cilantro & mint
- 1/4 cup fried onion store bought

6. Close Instant Pot, press pressure cook button, choose high settings, and set time to 6 minutes.
7. Once done cooking, do a 5-minute natural release and then do a QPR.
8. Serve and enjoy with the raita dip.

Nutrition information:
Calories per serving: 628; Carbohydrates: 63.0g; Protein: 31.0g; Fat: 26.0g; Sugar: 8.0g; Sodium: 1761mg

---

400.   Broccoli-Beef Rice
(Servings: 4, Cooking Time: 25 minutes)

Ingredients:

- 1 ½-lbs ground beef
- 3 ½ cups water
- 1 ½ cups rice
- 12-oz frozen chopped broccoli
- 1 jar double cheddar pasta sauce
- 1 tsp onion powder
- 1 tsp garlic powder

Directions for Cooking:

1. Press sauté button and brown beef for 10 minutes.

2. Stir in water and rice. Evenly spread rice. Press cancel.
3. Close Instant Pot, press pressure cook button, choose high settings, and set time to 7 minutes.
4. Once done cooking, do a QPR.
5. Stir in garlic powder, onion powder, and broccoli. Let it rest for 5 minutes while covered.
6. Serve and enjoy.

Nutrition information:
Calories per serving: 549; Carbohydrates: 34.1g; Protein: 53.0g; Fat: 28.1g; Sugar: 6.1g; Sodium: 730mg

---

401.   Easy-Creamy Ziti
(Servings: 4, Cooking Time: 20 minutes)

Ingredients:

- 1 1/2 cup chicken broth
- 1 cup heavy cream
- 1 tsp minced garlic dried
- salt and pepper to taste
- 8 oz dry ziti pasta
- 1 cup red pasta sauce

Directions for Cooking:

1. In pot, add broth, cream, garlic, salt, pepper, and noodles. Do not mix but ensure that noodles are covered. You can push pasta down.

- 1 cup parmesan cheese shredded
- 1/2 cup mozzarella cheese shredded

Nutrition information:
Calories per serving: 457; Carbohydrates: 54.6g; Protein: 17.4g; Fat: 19.8g; Sugar: 4.2g; Sodium: 1022mg

2. Close Instant Pot, press pressure cook button, choose high settings, and set time to 6 minutes.
3. Once done cooking, do a 6-minute natural release and then do a QPR.
4. Stir in red pasta sauce. Slowly add the cheese while stirring. Let it rest for 5 minutes.
5. Serve and enjoy.

---

402.   Chicken Noodle Casserole
(Servings: 4, Cooking Time: 20 minutes)

Ingredients:
- 1 ½-lbs of chicken, cut into 2" squares
- 3/4 of a bag of egg noodles
- 1 can of cream of chicken or mushroom
- 1/2 bag of peas and carrots frozen
- 1/2 cup of diced onion
- 2 cloves of garlic
- 1 stalk celery, diced
- Salt and pepper

Directions for Cooking:

1. Add noodles in pot and cover with water. Add another cup of water.
2. Place chicken on top of pasta.
3. Sprinkle carrots, peas, minced garlic, celery, and diced onion on top.
4. Season with pepper and salt. Mix well.
5. Close Instant Pot, press pressure cook button, choose high settings, and set time to 5 minutes.
6. Once done cooking, do a 10-minute natural release and then do a QPR.
7. Stir in cream of mushroom and mix well. Let it rest for 5 minutes covered.
8. Serve and enjoy.

Nutrition information:
Calories per serving: 451; Carbohydrates: 41.1g; Protein: 43.8g; Fat: 11.7g; Sugar: 6.2g; Sodium: 745mg

---

403.   Saffron Rice
(Servings: 4, Cooking Time: minutes)

Ingredients:
- 1 cup basmati rice or Jasmine Rice
- 1 cup water
- 1/2 teaspoon salt
- 1 teaspoon ghee or oil
- 1/2 teaspoon saffron: soaked in 1 tablespoon hot water
- 2 tablespoon slivered almonds : optional
- Other optional ingredients

Directions for Cooking:

1. Rinse and drain rice in Instant Pot insert.
2. Add remaining ingredients.
3. Close Instant Pot, press pressure cook button, choose high settings, and set time to 6 minutes.
4. Once done cooking, do a 10-minute natural release and then do a QPR.
5. Serve and enjoy.

- 1 tablespoon cashews
- 1 tablespoons raisin

Nutrition information:
Calories per serving: 233; Carbohydrates: 41.0g;
Protein: 4.0g; Fat: 5.0g; Sugar: 8.0g; Sodium: 297mg

404. Mac and Cheese
(Servings: 8, Cooking Time: 4 minutes)

Ingredients:

- 1 tbsp olive oil
- 12-oz bacon 1" pieces, diced
- 16-oz rigatoni pasta
- 4 cups water
- 2 cups cheddar cheese sharp or extra sharp and shredded
- 1 cup heavy cream
- 1 tbsp kosher salt
- 1 tbsp dry mustard
- 1 tbsp flour

Directions for Cooking:

1. Press sauté and heat oil. Add bacon and cook for 3 minutes per side until crisped.
2. Press cancel. Drain fat.
3. Place bacon on bottom of pot. Add pasta on top and pour in water.
4. Close Instant Pot, press pressure cook button, choose high settings, and set time to 4 minutes.
5. Once done cooking, do a QPR.
6. Press cancel, press sauté and stir in mustard, salt, cream, and cheese. Mix well.
7. Sprinkle flour, mix well, and cook for 5 minutes.
8. Serve and enjoy.

Nutrition information:
Calories per serving: 356; Carbohydrates: 21.2g;
Protein: 14.1g; Fat: 25.3g; Sugar: 1.5g; Sodium: 1715mg

405. Sausage Rigatoni
(Servings: 6, Cooking Time: 17 minutes)

Ingredients:

- 2 tbsp olive oil
- 5-6 cloves of garlic chopped
- 1-2 red peppers chopped
- 1 onion chopped
- 1 tbsp tomato paste
- 2 tsp dried basil
- 2 tsp dried oregano
- sea salt and black pepper
- 4-5 Italian sausage (remove meat from casing)

Directions for Cooking:

1. Press sauté and heat oil. Stir in pepper, salt, garlic, and onions. Sauté for 5 minutes.
2. Stir in tomato paste, basil, and oregano. Cook for a minute.
3. Add sausage and cook for 8 minutes or until no longer pink.
4. Add water and deglaze pot.
5. Stir in pasta sauce and san Marzano tomatoes. Squish tomatoes and mix well.
6. Press cancel.

- 1 28-oz can san Marzano tomatoes
- 1 3/4 cup tomato puree/pasta sauce
- 3 1/2 cups water
- 1-lb rigatoni

Nutrition information:
Calories per serving: 255; Carbohydrates: 22.2g;
Protein: 10.7g; Fat: 14.5g; Sugar: 8.7g; Sodium: 573mg

7. Close Instant Pot, press pressure cook button, choose high settings, and set time to 10 minutes.
8. Once done cooking, do a QPR.
9. Stir in red peppers and rigatoni. Mix well.
10. Close Instant Pot, press pressure cook button, choose high settings, and set time to 8 minutes.
11. Once done cooking, do a QPR.
12. Serve and enjoy.

406.   Creamy Cajun Pasta
(Servings: 6, Cooking Time: 20minutes)

Ingredients:

- 1 Tbsp Olive Oil
- 1 Tbsp Butter
- 1-lb Andouille Sausage sliced in 1/2" rounds
- 1 Chicken Breast, skinless/boneless
- 1 small Sweet Onion, chopped
- 1/2 cup Celery, diced
- 4 cloves Garlic, pressed or minced
- 1 1/2 Tbsp Cajun Seasoning Blend
- 1 Tbsp Smoked Paprika
- 8 med Mushrooms, sliced
- 1 Red Bell Pepper, chopped
- 4 cups Chicken Broth, low sodium
- 12 to 16 oz Penne Pasta
- 1 cup Parmesan Cheese, grated
- 1 cup Heavy Cream
- 1/4 cup Fresh Flat Leaf Parsley, chopped

Directions for Cooking:

1. Press sauté and then add oil and melt butter.
2. Stir in chicken breast and sausage. Cook for 4 minutes.

3. Add celery and onion, cook for 5 minutes.
4. Add mushrooms, smoked paprika, Cajun spice blend, and garlic. Mix well and sauté for a minute.
5. Add chicken broth and bell pepper. Mix well.
6. Add pasta and push down to submerge. Press cancel.
7. Close Instant Pot, press pressure cook button, choose high settings, and set time to 5 minutes.
8. Once done cooking, do a QPR.
9. Stir in parmesan cheese and let it rest covered for 5 minutes.
10. Mix in parsley and heavy cream. Mix well.
11. Serve and enjoy

Nutrition information:
Calories per serving: 501; Carbohydrates: 34.1g;
Protein: 30.2g; Fat: 27.7g; Sugar: 7.2g; Sodium: 2066mg

INSTANT POT RICE AND PASTA RECIPES

407. Creamy Chicken Pasta the Italian Way
(Servings: 4, Cooking Time: 15 minutes)

Ingredients:

- 1 chicken breast, cubed
- 16-ounces penne pasta
- 1 can diced tomatoes w/green chilies
- 1½ cans water
- ½ teaspoon sea salt
- 1 tablespoon basil
- ¼ teaspoon pepper
- 1 clove garlic, chopped
- ¼ teaspoon paprika
- 1 teaspoon oregano
- 4 ounces cream cheese
- 1 small onion
- ¼ cup Parmesan cheese

Directions for Cooking:

1. Add all ingredients except for cream cheese in Instant Pot. Mix well.
2. Close Instant Pot, press pressure cook button, choose high settings, and set time to 10 minutes.
3. Once done cooking, do a QPR.
4. Stir in cream cheese and let it rest for 5 minutes. Mix well.
5. Serve and enjoy

Nutrition information:

Calories per serving: 392; Carbohydrates: 37.0g; Protein: 22.4g; Fat: 17.5g; Sugar: 1.9g; Sodium: 688mg

---

408. Chili Mac n Cheese
(Servings: 6, Cooking Time: 11 minutes)

Ingredients:

- 1 ½-pounds lean ground beef
- 1 onion, diced
- ½ teaspoon salt
- ¼ teaspoon pepper
- ½ teaspoon dried thyme
- ¼ cup ketchup
- 3 cups elbow macaroni
- 3 cups beef broth
- 1 cup shredded cheddar cheese

Directions for Cooking:

1. Press sauté and cook ground beef and onions for 10 minutes.
2. Season with pepper and salt.
3. Add macaroni, ketchup, beef broth and dried thyme. Mix well. Press cancel.
4. Close Instant Pot, press pressure cook button, choose high settings, and set time to 6 minutes.
5. Once done cooking, do a QPR.
6. Stir in cheese and let it rest for 5 minutes. Mix well.
7. Serve and enjoy

Nutrition information:

Calories per serving: 519; Carbohydrates: 54.2g; Protein: 40.2g; Fat: 14.6g; Sugar: 4.4g; Sodium: 547mg

INSTANT POT RICE AND PASTA RECIPES

409. Cheesy-Tuna Pasta
(Servings: 6, Cooking Time: 10minutes)

Ingredients:

- 1 can tuna drained
- 16-oz egg noodles
- 1 cup frozen peas
- 28-oz can cream mushroom soup
- 4-oz cheddar cheese
- 3 cups water

Directions for Cooking:

1. Add pasta and water in pot.
2. Sprinkle peas, mushroom soup and tuna.
3. Close Instant Pot, press pressure cook button, choose high settings, and set time to 4 minutes.
4. Once done cooking, do a QPR.
5. Stir in cheese and mix well. Let it rest for 5 minutes.
6. Serve and enjoy

Nutrition information:
Calories per serving: 540; Carbohydrates: 67.0g; Protein: 31.0g; Fat: 15.0g; Sugar: 3.0g; Sodium: 1211mg

---

410. Beef n Mac Casserole
(Servings: 8, Cooking Time: 25 minutes)

Ingredients:

- 1 tbsp olive oil
- 1 cup medium onion, chopped
- 4 garlic cloves, minced
- 2-lbs ground beef
- 2 tsp salt
- ½ tsp pepper
- 1 tbsp Worcestershire sauce
- 1 cup frozen corn
- 4 cups beef stock (unsalted)
- 2 cans cream of mushroom soup
- 1-lb elbow pasta
- 1 cup sour cream

Directions for Cooking:

1. Press sauté and heat oil.
2. Add garlic and onions, sauté for 5 minutes.
3. Stir in ground beef and cook for 10 minutes or until browned. Press cancel.
4. Season beef with Worcestershire sauce, pepper, and salt. Stir in corn and mix well.
5. Add beef stock and mushroom soup. Mix well.
6. Add pasta and cover well in mixture.
7. Close Instant Pot, press pressure cook button, choose high settings, and set time to 3 minutes.
8. Once done cooking, do a 2-minute natural release and then a QPR.
9. Stir in sour cream and mix well.
10. Serve and enjoy.

Nutrition information:
Calories per serving: 476; Carbohydrates: 29.8g; Protein: 38.8g; Fat: 22.0g; Sugar: 3.6g; Sodium: 979mg

411.   Chicken Parmesan Casserole
(Servings: 5, Cooking Time: 25 minutes)

Ingredients:

- 2 chicken breasts cut into chunks
- 1/2 onion diced
- 2 tbsp olive oil
- 1 tsp salt to taste
- 1 tsp basil
- 1 jar spaghetti sauce 24 oz.
- 2 cup water
- 2 cup noodles uncooked, small shapes of your choice
- 1 tsp garlic minced
- 2 tbsp butter
- 1/3 cup bread crumbs
- 1 cup parmesan cheese, divided

Directions for Cooking:

1. Press sauté and heat oil.
2. Add chicken and cook for 3 minutes.
3. Stir in garlic and onions and cook for 3 minutes.
4. Mix in water, spaghetti sauce, basil, and salt.
5. Add pasta and push down to drown in sauce.
6. Close Instant Pot, press pressure cook button, choose high settings, and set time to 10 minutes.
7. Once done cooking, do a QPR.
8. Mix in 2/3 cup parmesan cheese. Let it rest for 5 minutes.
9. Meanwhile, in a bowl melt butter and mix in bread crumbs and remaining parmesan.
10. Serve and enjoy with a sprinkle of breadcrumb mixture.

Nutrition information:
Calories per serving: 392; Carbohydrates: 32.0g; Protein: 21.0g; Fat: 20.0g; Sugar: 7.0g; Sodium: 1707mg

412.   Beef Enchilada Pasta
(Servings: 4, Cooking Time: 25 minutes)

Ingredients:

- 8 oz elbow noodles
- 1-lb ground beef
- 1 cup shredded cheese
- 12-oz can enchilada sauce
- 2 cups beef broth (or 15 oz can)
- 2 Tbsp chili powder
- salt & pepper (to taste)

Directions for Cooking:

1. Press sauté and cook beef until browned, around 10 minutes. Drain fat.
2. Stir in chili powder and cook for a minute.
3. Add enchilada sauce, pasta, and broth. Press cancel.
4. Close Instant Pot, press pressure cook button, choose high settings, and set time to 4 minutes.
5. Once done cooking, do a 3-minute natural release and then do a QPR.
6. Stir in pepper, salt, and cheese. Let it rest for 5 minutes.
7. Serve and enjoy.

Nutrition information:
Calories per serving: 516; Carbohydrates: 22.5g; Protein: 39.5g; Fat: 29.4g; Sugar: 3.4g; Sodium: 1248mg

INSTANT POT RICE AND PASTA RECIPES

413. Easy Spaghetti
(Servings: 4, Cooking Time: 30 minutes)

Ingredients:

- 1-lb ground beef
- 1 Tbsp minced onion
- 1 tsp garlic powder
- 26 oz. jar marinara sauce
- 16 oz. spaghetti pasta
- 2 1/2 cups beef stock, chicken stock or water
- ¼ cup Parmesan cheese, as garnish

Directions for Cooking:

1. Press sauté and cook ground beef, onions, and garlic powder for 10 minutes or until beef us browned.
2. Break noodles in half and add to pot.
3. Stir in stock, marinara and spaghetti sauce. Mix well.
4. Close Instant Pot, press pressure cook button, choose high settings, and set time to 6 minutes.
5. Once done cooking, do a QPR.
6. Serve and enjoy with cheese.

Nutrition information:
Calories per serving: 446; Carbohydrates: 24.4g; Protein: 38.0g; Fat: 22.2g; Sugar: 14.4g; Sodium: 2261mg

---

414. Chicken Rice Bowl Thai Style
(Servings: 4, Cooking Time: 10 minutes)

Ingredients:

- 2 Tablespoons olive oil
- 4 chicken breasts (about 2 lbs)
- 1 cup uncooked long-grain white rice
2 cups broth
- 1 Tablespoon peanut butter optional
- 1/2 cup sweet chili Thai sauce
- 3 Tablespoons soy sauce – to taste
- 1/2 Tablespoon fish sauce
- 1/2 Tablespoon ginger minced
- 1/2 Tablespoon garlic minced
- 1 teaspoon lime juice
- 1 teaspoon Sriracha or hot sauce
- Cilantro optional garnish
- Shredded zucchini optional garnish
- Shredded carrots optional garnish
- Bean sprouts optional garnish
- Peanuts optional garnish

Directions for Cooking:

1. Press sauté and heat oil.
2. Sear chicken for 3 minutes per side.
3. Meanwhile, in a baking dish that fits inside your Pot, mix well sriracha, lime juice, garlic, ginger, fish sauce, soy sauce, and chili Thai sauce.
4. Once chicken is done, place in dish of sauce and cover well in sauce. Cover securely with foil. Press cancel.
5. In pot, add rice and broth. Place chicken dish on top.
6. Close Instant Pot, press pressure cook button, choose high settings, and set time to 5 minutes.
7. Once done cooking, do a QPR.
8. Serve and enjoy with optional garnish.

Nutrition information:
Calories per serving: 343; Carbohydrates: 29.0g; Protein: 27.0g; Fat: 12.0g; Sugar: 15.0g; Sodium: 1873mg

415. Beef Plov
(Servings: 8, Cooking Time: 45minutes)

Ingredients:

- 2 1/2 cups short grain brown rice (500 grams), rinsed and drained*
- 1-lb beef chuck or beef stew meat, cut into 3/4" pieces
- 4 Tbsp olive oil
- 4 Tbsp butter
- 1 large onion, diced
- 3 large carrots, thickly julienned
- 3 cups (720 ml) very warm water
- 1 Tbsp salt (we used fine sea salt)
- 1/2 tsp black pepper
- 1/2 tsp ground cumin
- 1/2 tsp ground paprika
- 1/2 tsp ground coriander
- 1 whole head garlic, unpeeled, cut in half crosswise.
- 1 Tbsp freshly chopped parsley to garnish – optional

Directions for Cooking:

1. Rinse rice and drain well. Set aside in strainer.
2. Press sauté and heat oil. Cook beef for 8 minutes until browned.
3. Add butter and onions. Sauté for 3 minutes.
4. Stir in coriander, paprika, cumin, pepper, salt, and carrots. Sauté for 5 minutes.
5. Evenly spread rice on top. Add garlic. Pour in warm water. Create 3-4 holes in the rice to disburse flavor.
6. Close Instant Pot, press pressure cook button, choose high settings, and set time to 30 minutes.
7. Once done cooking, do a QPR.
8. Mix plov and garnish with parsley.
9. Serve and enjoy

Nutrition information:

Calories per serving: 502; Carbohydrates: 60.0g; Protein: 21.0g; Fat: 19.0g; Sugar: 1.0g; Sodium: 917mg

416. Cajun Chicken and Rice
(Servings: 4, Cooking Time: 15 minutes)

Ingredients:

- 1 9 oz package VeeTee Brown Rice
- 1 lb. chicken breast cut thin
- 1 cup chicken broth
- 1 teaspoon Cajun seasoning
- 1 small onion diced
- 1 red bell pepper diced
- 3 cloves garlic minced
- 2 tablespoons tomato pasta
- salt and pepper to taste

Directions for Cooking:

1. Season chicken with Cajun spice.
2. Add all ingredients in pot except for rice.
3. Close Instant Pot, press pressure cook button, choose high settings, and set time to 10 minutes.
4. Once done cooking, do a QPR.
5. Remove chicken and stir in rice. Shred chicken and return to pot.
6. Press brown button and cook for 5 minutes.
7. Serve and enjoy.

Nutrition information:

Calories per serving: 212; Carbohydrates: 24.5g; Protein: 22.4g; Fat: 2.9g; Sugar: 3.5g; Sodium: 1488mg

417.   Buffalo Chicken Pasta
(Servings: 6, Cooking Time: 22 minutes)

Ingredients:

- 1/2 tsp cayenne
- 1/2 tsp salt
- 1/4 tsp black pepper
- 1/4 tsp garlic powder
- 1 ½-lbs boneless skinless chicken breast (about 3 large breasts)
- 1 Tbsp olive oil
- 1 cup diced onion
- 3 garlic cloves, minced
- 1 1/2 cups half and half
- 2 cups unsalted chicken broth, divided
- 1 lb spaghetti
- 3/4 cup buffalo sauce
- 1/4 cup crumbled blue cheese
- 2 Tbsp chopped parsley

Directions for Cooking:

1. Mix well garlic powder, black pepper, salt, and cayenne in a small bowl. Season chicken well with this mixture.
2. Press sauté and heat oil. Cook chicken for 2 minutes per side. Transfer to plate.
3. Stir in garlic and onion. Cook for 2 minutes.
4. Pour in ½ chicken broth and deglaze pot. Stir in half and half, mix well and cook for 2 minutes.
5. Break spaghetti in half and mix in pot. Add chicken on top. Pour in remaining broth. Top with buffalo sauce.
6. Close Instant Pot, press pressure cook button, choose high settings, and set time to 7 minutes.
7. Once done cooking, do an 8-minute natural release and then do a QPR.
8. Remove chicken and mix pot. Slice chicken to bit sized pieces.
9. Transfer pasta to serving plates, top with chicken and sprinkle cheese and chopped parsley.
10. Serve and enjoy

Nutrition information:

Calories per serving: 382; Carbohydrates: 43.0g; Protein: 33.5g; Fat: 8.5g; Sugar: 16.6g; Sodium: 1047mg

---

418.   Creamy Beef and Shells
(Servings: 6, Cooking Time: 15 minutes)

Ingredients:

- 1 tablespoon olive oil
- 1 medium yellow or sweet onion, diced
- 1-pound lean ground beef
- 1 tablespoon Italian seasoning
- 1 teaspoon salt
- 1/2 teaspoon pepper
- 1 teaspoon garlic powder
- 1/4 teaspoon crushed red pepper flakes
- 1 tablespoon tomato paste

Directions for Cooking:

1. Press sauté and heat oil.
2. Add onion and cook for 5 minutes.
3. Stir in beef and cook for 8 minutes.
4. Stir in tomato paste, pepper flakes, garlic powder, pepper, salt, and Italian seasoning. Mix well.
5. Add shells on top of beef evenly.

- 1 (16-ounce) box medium pasta shells, uncooked
- 1 (24-ounce) jar pasta sauce
- 3 cups water
- 1 cup freshly grated Parmesan cheese
- 1 cup heavy cream
- 2 ounces cream cheese, cut into chunks and softened

6. Pour pasta sauce on top of shells. Press cancel.
7. Close Instant Pot, press pressure cook button, choose high settings, and set time to 5 minutes.
8. Once done cooking, do a QPR.
9. Stir in cream cheese, heavy cream, and Parmesan cheese. Let it rest for 5 minutes while covered.
10. Serve and enjoy.

Nutrition information:
Calories per serving: 474; Carbohydrates: 38.9g; Protein: 30.8g; Fat: 22.2g; Sugar: 7.1g; Sodium: 1544mg

---

419. Rice Pudding
(Servings: 6, Cooking Time: 30 minutes)

Ingredients:

- 2 cups raw whole milk or dairy-free milk of choice
- 1 1/4 cups water
- 1 cup basmati rice
- 3/4 cup heavy cream OR coconut cream
- 1/4 cup maple syrup
- 1/8 teaspoon sea salt
- inside scrapings from 1 vanilla bean OR 1 teaspoon vanilla extract

Directions for Cooking:

1. Place rice in fine mesh colander. Rinse well in several changes of water.
2. Then, place rice in Instant Pot. Add water, milk, maple syrup, and sea salt. Stir briefly.
3. Close Instant Pot, press porridge button.
4. Once done cooking, do a 10-minute natural release and then do a QPR.
5. Serve and enjoy.

Nutrition information:
Calories per serving: 198; Carbohydrates: 22.8g; Protein: 5.8g; Fat: 12.3g; Sugar: 12.3g; Sodium: 99mg

---

420. Beef Burgundy Pasta
(Servings:8, Cooking Time: 45minutes)

Ingredients:

- 2 1/2 pounds top sirloin cubed
- 1 teaspoon salt plus additional, to taste
- 3/4 teaspoon fresh ground black pepper plus additional, to taste
- 4 tablespoons vegetable oil divided
- 3 slices uncooked bacon chopped
- 1 cup diced white or yellow onion

Directions for Cooking:

1. Press sauté and heat oil.Cook beef in two batches. Season each batch with pepper and salt. Cook for 5 minutes. Transfer to a plate. Repeat process to next batch.
2. Close Instant Pot, press pressure cook button, choose high settings, and set time to 5 minutes.

- 1 tablespoon minced garlic
- 2 tablespoons tomato paste
- 1 1/2 cups full-bodied red wine
- 2 cups low-sodium beef broth
- 1 tablespoon fresh or 1 teaspoon dried thyme leaves
- 2 bay leaves
- 4 to 5 carrots peeled and chopped diagonally into 1" chunks
- 3 tablespoons softened butter
- 3 tablespoons all-purpose flour
- 9 ounces cremini mushrooms quartered or halved
- 2 tablespoons minced fresh Italian parsley optional
- 1-lb cooked pasta

Nutrition information:

Calories per serving: 528; Carbohydrates: 25.2g; Protein: 34.0g; Fat: 31.5g; Sugar: 3.0g; Sodium: 666mg

3. Add bacon and cook until crisped.
4. Stir in carrots and onions. Cook for 4 minutes. Season with ¾ tsp pepper and 1 tsp salt.
5. Add tomato paste and garlic. Cook for a minute.
6. Add wine and deglaze pot. Cook for 4 minutes.
7. Stir in beef, bay leaves, thyme, and beef broth. Mix well. Press cancel.
8. Close Instant Pot, press pressure cook button, choose high settings, and set time to 15 minutes.
9. Meanwhile, in a small bowl whisk well flour and butter. Set aside.
10. Once done cooking, do a QPR. Press cancel, press sauté.
11. Stir in butter mixture and mushroom mix well. Let it rest for 5 minutes. Mix well.
12. Evenly divide cooked pasta on plates. Top with beef dish.
13. Serve and enjoy

---

421. Cinnamon-Raisin Rice Pudding
(Servings: 4, Cooking Time: 35 minutes)

Ingredients:

- 1 Cup Short Grain Brown Rice
- 1 1/2 Cups Water 1 tbsp Vanilla Extract
- 1 tbsp Vanilla Extract
- 1 Cinnamon Stick
- 1 tbsp butter
- 1 Cup Raisins
- 3 tbsp Honey
- 1/2 Cup Heavy Cream

Directions for Cooking:

1. Add rice, water, vanilla, cinnamon stick, and butter into Instant Pot.

2. Close Instant Pot, press pressure cook button, choose high settings, and set time to 20 minutes.
3. Once done cooking, do a 15-minute natural release and then do a QPR.
4. Discard cinnamon stick.
5. Stir in cream, honey and raisins. Let it rest for 5 minutes.
6. Serve and enjoy.

Nutrition information:

Calories per serving: 414; Carbohydrates: 35.0g; Protein: 1.7g; Fat: 8.9g; Sugar: 23.9g; Sodium: 39mg

422.   Peas &Sausage Rigatoni
(Servings: 6, Cooking Time: 30 minutes)

Ingredients:

- 1-pound Johnsonville® Ground Mild Italian sausage
- 4 garlic cloves, minced
- 1/4 cup tomato paste
- 12 ounces uncooked rigatoni or large tube pasta
- 1-1/2 cups frozen peas
- 1 can (28 ounces) crushed tomatoes
- 1/2 teaspoon dried basil
- 1/4 to 1/2 teaspoon crushed red pepper flakes
- 4 cups water
- 1/2 cup heavy whipping cream
- 1/2 cup crumbled goat or feta cheese
- Thinly sliced fresh basil, optional

Directions for Cooking:

1. Press sauté and cook for 6 minutes the sausage until crumbled.
2. Stir in garlic cook for a minute.
3. Add tomato paste and cook for 2 minutes.
4. Mix in rigatoni, peas, tomatoes, dried basil, red pepper flakes, and water. Mix well. Press cancel.
5. Close Instant Pot, press pressure cook button, choose low settings, and set time to 6 minutes.
6. Once done cooking, do a QPR.
7. Stir in cream. Let it rest for 3 minutes.
8. Serve and enjoy with basil and feta cheese.

Nutrition information:

Calories per serving: 563; Carbohydrates: 60.0g; Protein: 23.0g; Fat: 28.0g; Sugar: 11.0g; Sodium: 802mg

423.   Red Beans and Rice
(Servings: 10, Cooking Time: 30 minutes)

Ingredients:

- 1 package (16 ounces) dried kidney beans (about 2-1/2 cups)
- 2 cups cubed ham (about 1 pound)
- 1 package (12 ounces) andouille chicken sausage, sliced
- 1 medium green pepper, chopped
- 1 medium onion, chopped
- 2 celery ribs, chopped
- 1 tablespoon hot pepper sauce
- 2 garlic cloves, minced
- 1 teaspoon salt
- Hot cooked rice

Directions for Cooking:

1. Rinse beans and soak overnight in water. Discard water the next day.
2. Press sauté button and cook chicken sausage links for 5 minutes.
3. Stir in ham and cook for 2 minutes.
4. Stir in salt, garlic, pepper sauce, vegetables, beans, and about 4 cups of water. Mix well. Press cancel.
5. Close Instant Pot, press pressure cook button, choose high settings, and set time to 30 minutes.
6. Once done cooking, do a QPR.
7. Serve and enjoy with hot cooked rice.

Nutrition information:

Calories per serving: 249; Carbohydrates: 31.0g; Protein: 23.0g; Fat: 5.0g; Sugar: 2.0g; Sodium: 788mg

424.　　　Beef Stroganoff
(Servings: 8, Cooking Time: 30 minutes)

Ingredients:

- 2 tbsp canola oil
- ½ onion diced
- 2 tsp salt, divided
- 2-lbs beef stew meat, cut into 1-inch cubes
- 1 tsp freshly ground black pepper
- 3 cloves garlic, minced
- ½ tsp dried thyme
- 2 tbsp soy sauce
- 3 cups chopped mushrooms
- 2 tbsp all-purpose flour
- 3 cups chicken broth
- 1 16-oz package wide egg noodles
- ¾ cup sour cream

Directions for Cooking:

1. Press sauté and heat oil. Add onion and ½ tsp salt. Cook for 4 minutes.
2. Add beef and season with 1 tsp pepper and 1 tsp salt. Cook for 4 minutes.
3. Stir in thyme and garlic. Cook for a minute.
4. Add soy sauce, and mushrooms. Mix in flour and sauté well until fully mixed in.
5. Pour in broth and remaining salt. Press cancel.
6. Close Instant Pot, press pressure cook button, choose high settings, and set time to 15 minutes.
7. Once done cooking, do a QPR.
8. Stir in noodles. Press cancel, press pressure cook button, choose high, and time for 5 minutes.
9. Do a 5-minute natural release and then do a QPR.
10. Stir in sour cream.
11. Serve and enjoy.

Nutrition information:
Calories per serving: 536; Carbohydrates: 45.2g; Protein: 29.0g; Fat: 26.2g; Sugar: 2.0g; Sodium: 1312mg

---

425.　　　Spicy Mushroom Fried Rice
(Servings: 6, Cooking Time: 25minutes)

Ingredients:

- 2 cups jasmine rice
- 1 tbsp oil
- 1 12-oz jar of sliced mushrooms
- 1/2 cup of diced onion
- 1 jalapeno sliced
- 2 cups chicken broth
- 2 tablespoons soy sauce
- salt and pepper to taste

Directions for Cooking:

1. Press sauté and heat oil.
2. Stir in onion, jalapeno, and mushrooms. Cook for 3 minutes.
3. Stir in rice and sauté for 2 minutes.
4. Add soy sauce, chicken broth, salt and pepper to taste. Mix well. Press cancel.
5. Close Instant Pot, press rice button.
6. Once done cooking, do a QPR.
7. Fluff rice, serve and enjoy

Nutrition information:
Calories per serving: 187; Carbohydrates: 25.5g; Protein: 8.0g; Fat: 11.9g; Sugar: 4.1g; Sodium: 409mg

426.   Spicy Mexican Chicken and Rice
(Servings: 6, Cooking Time: 15 minutes)

Ingredients:

- 1 10 oz package VeeTee Spanish Style Rice
- 2 boneless skinless chicken breasts
- 2 tablespoons olive oil
- 1 cup onion chopped
- 1 green bell pepper chopped
- 1 1 oz packet Chicken Taco Seasoning
- 1 10 oz can red enchilada sauce
- 1 10 oz can diced tomatoes and chilies
- 1 cup shredded Mexican blended cheese
- 1 15 oz can black beans, drained and rinsed
- 1 cup frozen corn
- salt and pepper to taste

Directions for Cooking:

1. Press sauté and heat oil.
2. Stir in chicken. Season with pepper and salt. Cook for 6 minutes.
3. Stir in bell peppers and onions. Cook for 3 minutes.
4. Add enchilada sauce, corn, black beans, chilies, diced tomatoes, taco seasoning, and rice. Mix well. Press cancel.
5. Close Instant Pot, press pressure cook button, choose high settings, and set time to 5 minutes.
6. Once done cooking, do a QPR.
7. Stir in cheese, mix well and let it rest for 5 minutes.
8. Serve and enjoy.

Nutrition information:
Calories per serving: 438; Carbohydrates: 38.4g; Protein: 37.1g; Fat: 16.2g; Sugar: 3.8g; Sodium: 675mg

427.   Cooking a Simple Rice in Instant Pot
(Servings: 4, Cooking Time: 22 minutes)

Ingredients:

- 1 cup Long Grain White Rice,
- 1 1/2 cups Water
- 1 teaspoon Olive Oil
- Pinch of Salt
- Pinch Ground Pepper

Directions for Cooking:

1. Place rice in a strainer and rinse well. Set aside in strainer and drain well.
2. In Instant pot, add oil and coat well sides and bottom of pot.
3. Add rice water, salt and pepper in pot.
4. Close Instant Pot, press rice button.
5. Once done cooking, do a QPR.
6. Serve and enjoy.

Nutrition information:
Calories per serving: 63; Carbohydrates: 11.6g; Protein: 1.1g; Fat: 1.3g; Sugar: 6.1g; Sodium: 585mg

INSTANT POT RICE AND PASTA RECIPES

428. Teriyaki Rice
(Servings: 4, Cooking Time: 22 minutes)

Ingredients:

- 1 tablespoon sesame oil
- 1 medium onion , finely chopped
- 4 cloves garlic , chopped finely
- 2 medium carrots , cubed or sliced
- 2 ribs celery , chopped into small pieces
- 2 large bell peppers, 2 different colors are nice, chopped into bite sized pieces
- 2 cups brown rice
- 1¾ cups water
- ⅓ cup coconut aminos
- ¼ cup rice vinegar
- ¼ cup maple syrup
- ½ teaspoon red chili flakes
- 1 cup frozen peas

Directions for Cooking:

1. Press sauté and heat oil.
2. Stir in celery, carrots, garlic, and onions. Cook for 4 minutes. Press cancel.
3. Mix in all ingredients except for peas. Mix well.
4. Close Instant Pot, press pressure cook button, choose high settings, and set time to 22 minutes.
5. Once done cooking, do a QPR.
6. Stir in peas and let it rest for 3 minutes while covered.
7. Serve and enjoy

Nutrition information:
Calories per serving: 525; Carbohydrates: 104g;
Protein: 10.5g; Fat: 6.9g; Sugar: 21.0g; Sodium: 449mg

---

429. Shrimp Scampi Paella
(Servings: 4, Cooking Time: 5 minutes)

Ingredients:

- 1pound frozen wild caught shrimp, 16-20 count shell & tail on
- 1 cup Jasmine Rice
- 1/4cup butter
- 1/4cup chopped fresh Parsley
- 1teaspoon sea salt
- 1/4teaspoon black pepper
- 1pinch crushed red pepper or to taste
- 1medium lemon, juiced
- 1pinch saffron
- 1 1/2cups filtered water or chicken broth
- 4 cloves garlic minced or pressed

Directions for Cooking:

1. Add all ingredients in pot and mix well.
2. Close Instant Pot, press pressure cook button, choose high settings, and set time to 5 minutes.
3. Once done cooking, do a QPR.
4. Serve and enjoy.

Nutrition information:
Calories per serving: 299; Carbohydrates: 16.1g;
Protein: 27.3g; Fat: 18.5g; Sugar: 0.9g; Sodium: 1174mg

---

430. Osso Buco Rice
(Servings: 4, Cooking Time: 70 minutes)

Ingredients:

- 4 veal osso buco shanks or lamb shanks (about 1.4 lb / 650-700 g with the bone in)
- 1 tablespoon coconut oil or olive oil
- Salt and pepper
- 1 large carrot, diced
- 1 medium onion, diced
- 1 large celery stick, diced1 teaspoon coconut oil or olive oil
- Generous pinch of salt and pepper
- 2 large cloves of garlic, diced or sliced
- ⅓ cup red wine or white wine
- 2 bay leaves
- 2 tablespoons chopped parsley
- 2 cups chicken stock (I used water and 1 cube stock)
- 1 cup tinned chopped tomatoes1 tablespoon Tamari or soy sauce (optional)
- 1 cup uncooked Basmati organic rice

Garnish Ingredients:

- 3-4 tablespoons finely chopped parsley
- 1 small clove of garlic, grated
- Zest of 1 lemon

Directions for Cooking:

1. Pt dry with paper towel the meat and season with pepper and salt.
2. Press sauté and heat oil. Add veal and cook for a minute per side. Transfer to a plate.
3. Stir in celery, carrot, and onion. Season with pepper, salt, and extra oil. Cook for 5 minutes.
4. Add wine and deglaze pot.
5. Stir in the rest of the ingredients except for rice. Add back veal.
6. Close Instant Pot, press pressure cook button, choose high settings, and set time to 45 minutes.
7. Meanwhile, rinse rice and then drain thoroughly in a fine mesh strainer.
8. Once done cooking, do a QPR.
9. Remove meat and bones. Stir in rice. Return meat and bones on top of rice.
10. Press cancel, cover, press rice button and cook.
11. Do a 5-minute natural release and then do a QPR.
12. Serve and enjoy with garnish ingredients.

Nutrition information:

Calories per serving: 506; Carbohydrates: 27.9g; Protein: 67.6g; Fat: 18.5g; Sugar: 5.2g; Sodium: 4656mg

431. Coconut Rice
(Servings: 4, Cooking Time: 10 minutes)

Ingredients:

- 1 1/2 cups Jasmine Rice
- 1 can (14 ounces) Coconut Milk
- 1/2 cup water
- 1 teaspoon sugar
- 1/4 teaspoon salt
- 2 tbsp Toasted coconut, optional

Directions for Cooking:

1. Rinse rice and drain well. Transfer to pot.
2. Stir in all ingredients in pot except for toasted coconut.
3. Close Instant Pot, press pressure cook button, choose high settings, and set time to 3 minutes.
4. Once done cooking, do a 7-minute natural release and then do a QPR.
5. Fluff rice, serve and enjoy with toasted coconut garnish.

Nutrition information:

Calories per serving: 372; Carbohydrates: 28.4g; Protein: 8.2g; Fat: 32.9g; Sugar: 4.5g; Sodium: 171mg

---

432. Sonoma Paella
(Servings: 6, Cooking Time: 20 minutes)

Ingredients:

- 2 Tbs. olive oil
- 1 lb. Spanish chorizo or kielbasa, cut into slices 1/2 inch (12 mm) thick
- 1 yellow onion, chopped
- 3 garlic cloves, minced
- Kosher salt and freshly ground pepper
- 1/2 cup dry white wine
- 2 cups long-grain white rice, such as basmati
- 1 tsp. smoked paprika
- 1/2 tsp. saffron threads, crumbled
- 4 cups chicken broth
- 1 lb. large shrimp, shell and tail intact, or 1 lb.crawfish tails in their shell, or a combination
- 1 lb. small clams, such as littleneck or Manila, scrubbed
- 1/2 cup pitted green olives
- 1 cup sliced roasted red bell peppers

Directions for Cooking:

1. Press sauté and heat oil. Cook chorizo for 3 minutes. Transfer to a plate.
2. Stir in garlic and onions cook for 4 minutes. Season with pepper and salt.
3. Add wine and deglaze pot. Cook for 2 minutes.
4. Add saffron, paprika, and rice. Sauté for a minute.
5. Add a pinch of salt and broth. Mix well. Press cancel.
6. Close Instant Pot, press pressure cook button, choose high settings, and set time to 5 minutes.
7. Once done cooking, do a QPR.
8. Stir in clams and shrimp. Cover and let it rest for 7 minutes or until shrimps are pink and clams have opened.
9. Add bell peppers, olive, and sausage. Toss to mix.
10. Serve and enjoy.

Nutrition information:

Calories per serving: 429; Carbohydrates: 23.4g; Protein: 34.0g; Fat: 21.4g; Sugar: 1.3g; Sodium: 2327mg

433.   Mexican Rice
(Servings: 6, Cooking Time: 30 minutes)

Ingredients:

- 2 cups long-grain rice (such as Lundberg Farms Brown Basmati)
- 1/2 white onion (chopped)
- 1/2 cup tomato paste
- 3 cloves garlic (minced)
- 1 small jalapeño (optional)
- 2 teaspoons salt
- 2 cups water

Directions for Cooking:

1. Press sauté and heat oil.
2. Stir in salt, garlic, onion, and rice. Sauté for 4 minutes.
3. Add tomato paste and water. Mix well. Add jalapeno. Press cancel.
4. Close Instant Pot, press pressure cook button, choose high settings, and set time to 3 minutes.
5. Once done cooking, do a 15-minute natural release and then do a QPR.
6. Serve and enjoy.

Nutrition information:

Calories per serving: 253; Carbohydrates: 53.1g; Protein: 5.9g; Fat: 2.1g; Sugar: 3.8g; Sodium: 759.2mg

---

434.   Mexican Beefy Rice
(Servings: 4, Cooking Time: 16 minutes)

Ingredients:

- 1 tablespoon olive oil
- 1-pound lean ground beef
- 1 cup diced red onion
- 1 teaspoon chili powder Hatch chile powder
- 1/2 teaspoon ground cumin
- 1/2 teaspoon salt
- 1 cup long grain white rice rinsed well and drained
- 2 cups water
- 2 cups chunky salsa
- 15 ounces black beans rinsed and drained
- 1 cup cooked corn kernels
- 2 tablespoons chopped fresh cilantro
- 1 cup shredded cheese 4 Cheese Mexican blend

Directions for Cooking:

1. Press sauté and sauté salt, cumin, chili powder, onion, and beef for 8 minutes until beef is browned and cooked.
2. Stir in salsa, water, and rice. Deglaze pot. Press cancel.
3. Close Instant Pot, press pressure cook button, choose high settings, and set time to 8 minutes.
4. Once done cooking, do a QPR.
5. Press cancel and press brown button.
6. Stir in cilantro, corn, and black beans. Cook for 3 minutes while stirring frequently.
7. Stir in cheese.
8. Serve and enjoy.

Nutrition information:

Calories per serving: 622; Carbohydrates: 48.7g; Protein: 48.2g; Fat: 26.0g; Sugar: 9.9g; Sodium: 1999mg

435. Chicken & Boiled Egg Congee
(Servings: 6, Cooking Time: 20 minutes)

Ingredients:

- 1 cup uncooked jasmine rice
- 2 cloves garlic, smashed and peeled
- 1-2 inches fresh ginger, peeled and sliced
- 3 shitake mushrooms, sliced
- 2 lb. bone-in chicken pieces
- 7 cups water
- 1/2 Tbsp salt (or to taste)

Topping Ingredients:

- 3 green onions, sliced
- 3 hardboiled eggs, peeled and sliced
- 1/3 cup peanuts, chopped
- 1 Tbsp soy sauce
- 1 Tbsp toasted sesame oil

Directions for Cooking:

1. In pot, place rice in an even layer. Add garlic, ginger, and sliced mushrooms.
2. Place chicken pieces on top. Season with salt.
3. Add water.
4. Close Instant Pot, press porridge button.
5. Once done cooking, do a QPR.
6. Remove chicken, chop and discard bones.
7. Ladle into bowls, evenly divide chicken meat on top followed by equal servings of garnish.
8. Serve and enjoy.

Nutrition information:
Calories per serving: 342; Carbohydrates: 13.7g; Protein: 38.6g; Fat: 17.0g; Sugar: 1.2g; Sodium: 775mg

---

436. Cajun Red Beans & Rice
(Servings: 10, Cooking Time: minutes)

Ingredients:

- 1 medium onion diced
- 1 bell pepper diced
- 3 celery stalks diced
- 3 cloves garlic minced
- 1-pound dry red kidney beans
- 1 tsp salt or more to taste
- 1/2 tsp black pepper
- 1/4 tsp white pepper (optional)
- 1 tsp hot sauce
- 1 tsp fresh thyme or ½ tsp dried thyme
- 2 leaves bay
- 7 cups water
- 1-pound chicken andouille sausage cut into thin slices
- 10 cups cooked rice

Directions for Cooking:

1. Except for rice and sausage, mix all ingredients in Instant Pot.
2. Close Instant Pot, press pressure cook button, choose high settings, and set time to 28 minutes.
3. Once done cooking, do a QPR.
4. Add sausage. Press cancel, close pot, press manual, choose high pressure, cook for 15 minutes.
5. Do a full natural release.
6. Serve and enjoy on top of rice.

Nutrition information:
Calories per serving: 461; Carbohydrates: 77.0g; Protein: 21.0g; Fat: 7.0g; Sugar: 2.0g; Sodium: 735mg

437.   Ground Lamb & Fig Rice Pilaf
(Servings: 4, Cooking Time: 25minutes)

Ingredients:

- 1 medium brown onion, finely diced
- 1 tablespoon olive oil
- 1 + ½ teaspoons salt
- About 1 lb. or 400-450 g of ground lamb (lamb mince)
- 2 teaspoons ground cumin
- 1 teaspoon ground cinnamon
- ½ teaspoon Allspice
- 1 teaspoon coriander seed powder
- ½ teaspoon pepper
- ½ teaspoon turmeric powder
- 3 large cloves of garlic, finely diced
- Zest of ½ lemon
- 1 stick celery, diced
- 1 medium to large carrot, diced
- 5 dried figs, diced
- 2 tablespoons almond flakes
- 1½ cups rice
- 1 + ⅓ cup vegetable stock
- ½ cup tinned tomatoes

Garnish Ingredients:

- Zest of the remaining ½ lemon
- Juice of ½ lemon
- 1 tablespoon almond flakes
- 7-8 mint leaves, finely sliced
- Greek yoghurt or sour cream, to serve

Directions for Cooking:

1. Soak the rice in a bowl or pot with cold water for 5-10 minutes, then rinse 4-5 times.
2. Press sauté and heat oil.
3. Sauté onion and a tsp of salt for 3 minutes.
4. Stir in ground lamb and cook for 8 minutes.
5. Add lemon zest, garlic, ½ tsp salt, ground cumin, ground cinnamon, Allspice, coriander seed powder, pepper, and turmeric powder. Cook for 3 minutes.
6. Stir in rice, almonds, figs, carrots, and celery. Mix well.
7. Pour in tomatoes and stock. Deglaze pot. Press cancel.
8. Close Instant Pot, press pressure cook button, choose high settings, and set time to 4 minutes.
9. Once done cooking, do a 2-minute natural release and then do a QPR.
10. Serve and enjoy with equal servings of garnish ingredients.

Nutrition information:

Calories per serving: 298; Carbohydrates: 39.1g;
Protein: 11.7g; Fat: 17.7g; Sugar: 8.8g; Sodium: 738mg

438. Chai Spiced Rice Pudding
(Servings: 4, Cooking Time: 15 minutes)

Ingredients:

- 1 cup short grain rice (also sold as pudding rice)
- 1 cup almond milk (unsweetened)
- 1 cup coconut milk
- 1 + ½ cups water
- 2 tablespoons brown sugar
- 6 Medjool dates, sliced (peeps out)
- 1 teaspoon cinnamon powder
- 1 teaspoon ground ginger powder
- ¼ teaspoon ground nutmeg
- 5 cardamom pods
- 2 cloves or ¼ teaspoon Allspice powder
- 1 teaspoon vanilla extract
- Pinch of salt
- garnish: berries, nuts, chopped dates or other dried fruit

Directions for Cooking:

1. Combine all ingredients in Instant Pot except for garnish ingredients.
2. Close Instant Pot, press pressure cook button, choose high settings, and set time to 10 minutes.
3. Once done cooking, do a 5-minute natural release and then do a QPR.
4. Serve and enjoy with desired garnish.

Nutrition information:

Calories per serving: 535; Carbohydrates: 81.5g; Protein: 8.4g; Fat: 21.7g; Sugar: 32.2g; Sodium: 56mg

439. Chinese Sausage on Brown Rice
(Servings: 4, Cooking Time: 30 minutes)

Ingredients:

- 1/2 cup dried shrimp
- 4 Chinese dried mushrooms
- 3 Chinese sausage (lap cheung), diced
- 2 tablespoons cooking oil
- 1 shallot, minced
- 2 1/4 cups brown rice, rinsed and drained
- 3 cups chicken or vegetable broth
- 1/4 cup chopped cilantro

Directions for Cooking:

1. Soak the dried ingredients: In a small bowl, add the dried shrimp and cover with just-boiled hot water. Let soak up for 10 minutes and drain, discarding water.
2. In a separate small bowl, add the dried mushrooms and cover with just-boiled hot water. Let soak up for 30 minutes, and drain, discarding water. Chop/dice the shrimp and the mushrooms.
3. Press sauté and heat oil. Sauté shallot for 30 seconds.
4. Add shrimp and cook for 2 minutes.
5. Add Chinese sausage and mushrooms cook for a minute.
6. Add rice and chicken broth. Deglaze pot. Press cancel.
7. Close Instant Pot, press pressure cook button, choose high settings, and set time to 5 minutes.
8. Once done cooking, do a 15-minute natural release and then do a QPR.
9. Serve and enjoy with cilantro as garnish.

Nutrition information:

Calories per serving: 473; Carbohydrates: 58.9g; Protein: 18.6g; Fat: 17.9g; Sugar: 2.9g; Sodium: 1056mg

440. Garlic Noodles
(Servings: 3 , Cooking Time: minutes)

Ingredients:

- 6 oz chow mein noodles
- 3 to 4 tablespoons peanut oil
- 4 green onions , chopped, white and green parts separated
- 4 cloves garlic , minced
- 2 teaspoon ginger , minced
- 1 bell pepper, thinly sliced

Sauce Ingredients:

- 1/4 cup chicken broth
- 2 tablespoons Shaoxing wine , or dry sherry
- 2 tablespoons oyster sauce
- 1 tablespoon soy sauce
- 1/2 teaspoon sesame oil

Directions for Cooking:

1. In a small bowl, whisk well all sauce ingredients.
2. Boil noodles according to package instructions. Pour into colander and run under tap water to stop the cooking process. Drain well.
3. In Instant Pot, press sauté button and heat 3 tbsps oil. Heat for 4 minutes. Once hot add noodles and cook for a minute.
4. Stir in ginger and garlic. Cook for a minute until fragrant.
5. Stir in bell pepper and cook for 2 minutes.
6. Add sauce and toss noodles to coat well.
7. Serve and enjoy

Nutrition information:

Calories per serving: 426; Carbohydrates: 45.9g; Protein: 8.0g; Fat: 24.7g; Sugar: 2.7g; Sodium: 908mg

Instant Pot Dessert Recipes

INSTANT POT DESSERT RECIPES

441.   Curried Tahini Carrots
(Servings: 6, Cooking Time: 10 minutes)

Ingredients:

- 2 carrots, peeled and julienned
- 1 cup organic raisins
- ¼ cup pumpkin seeds, roasted
- 1/3 cup tahini
- 2 tablespoons curry powder
- ¼ cup lemon juice
- 2 tablespoons maple syrup
- ¼ teaspoon ground black pepper

Directions for Cooking:

1. Mix all ingredients in pot.
2. Close Instant Pot, press pressure cook button, choose high settings, and set time to 10 minutes.
3. Once done cooking, do a full natural release.
4. Serve and enjoy.

Nutrition information:

Calories per serving: 142; Carbohydrates: 12.1g; Protein: 4.3g; Fat: 9.8g; Sugar: 0g; Sodium: 44mg

---

442.   Zucchini & Walnut Bread
(Servings: 6, Cooking Time: 6 hours)

Ingredients:

- 1 ¾ cups brown rice flour
- ½ teaspoon baking soda
- ¼ teaspoon baking powder
- 2 eggs
- 2 cups grated zucchini
- ¾ cup dates, pitted and chopped
- ¾ cup walnuts, chopped

1.

Directions for Cooking:

1. Grease the inner pot with olive oil.
2. In a mixing bowl, combine all ingredients to create a dough.
3. Place the dough in the greased inner pot.
4. Close Instant Pot, press slow cook button, choose low settings, set vent to venting, and set time to 6 hours.
5. Serve and enjoy

Nutrition information:

Calories per serving: 329; Carbohydrates: 50.9g; Protein: 8.3g; Fat: 11.1g; Sugar: 5.8g; Sodium: 144mg

INSTANT POT DESSERT RECIPES

443.   Cranberry Nut Bread
(Servings: 12, Cooking Time: 6 hours)

Ingredients:

- 2 cups brown rice flour
- ¼ cup chopped dates
- ¼ cup chopped figs
- ¾ teaspoon salt
- 1 ½ teaspoon baking powder
- ½ teaspoon baking soda
- 1 cup chopped cranberries
- ½ cup chopped almonds
- 1 tablespoon orange zest
- 1 egg, beaten
- 1 cup orange juice, freshly squeezed
- ½ cup coconut milk

Directions for Cooking:

1. In a mixing bowl, combine all ingredients until you form a batter.
2. Grease the inner pot of the Instant Pot or place a parchment paper at the bottom.
3. Pour the batter into the pot.
4. Close Instant Pot, press slow cook button, choose low settings, set vent to venting and set time to 6 hours.
5. Once done cooking, serve and enjoy

Nutrition information:

Calories per serving: 169; Carbohydrates: 30.7g; Protein: 3.2g; Fat: 4.1g; Sugar: 1.3g; Sodium: 212mg

---

444.   Nuts & Dates Bar
(Servings: 12, Cooking Time: 6 hours)

Ingredients:

- 2 cups dates, chopped
- 1 cup maple syrup
- 1/8 teaspoon ground cinnamon
- ¾ teaspoon salt
- 1/8 teaspoon ground nutmeg
- 1 cup brown rice flour
- 1 cup coconut milk
- ½ cup walnuts, chopped
- ½ cup cashews, chopped

Directions for Cooking:

1. Combine all ingredients in Instant Pot.
2. Close Instant Pot, press slow cook button, choose low settings, set vent to venting and set time to 6 hours.
3. Once done cooking, do a let it cool.
4. Serve and enjoy

Nutrition information:

Calories per serving: 318; Carbohydrates: 50.8g; Protein: 3.8g; Fat: 13.1g; Sugar: 0g; Sodium: 185mg

---

445. Nuts & Cherry Delight
(Servings: 4, Cooking Time: 4 hours)

Ingredients:

- ¼ cup walnuts
- ½ cup chopped dates
- ¼ cup chopped figs
- ½ cup coconut flakes
- 1 organic egg
- 1 teaspoon vanilla extract
- 2 cups chopped cherries

Directions for Cooking:

1. Add all ingredients in Instant Pot.
2. Close Instant Pot, press slow cook button, choose low settings, set vent to venting and set time to 4 hours.
3. Once done cooking, serve and enjoy

Nutrition information:

Calories per serving: 236; Carbohydrates: 37.2g; Protein: 5.1g; Fat: 8.9g; Sugar: 2.1g; Sodium: 66mg

---

446. Cherry-Chocolate Pudding
(Servings: 8, Cooking Time: 6 hours)

Ingredients:

- 1 ½ cup coconut milk
- ¼ cup chia seeds
- 3 tablespoons raw cacao powder
- 3 tablespoons maple syrup
- ½ cup brown rice flour
- ½ cup cherries, pitted and chopped

Directions for Cooking:

1. Grease Instant Pot.
2. In a bowl, whisk well ingredients. Pour into pot.
3. Close Instant Pot, press slow cook button, choose low settings, set vent to venting and set time to 6 hours.
4. Once done cooking, refrigerate until cool.
5. Serve and enjoy

Nutrition information:

Calories per serving: 195; Carbohydrates: 19.1g; Protein: 2.9g; Fat: 12.9g; Sugar: 0g; Sodium: 11mg

---

255

447. Choco-Dipped Frozen Bananas
(Servings: 6, Cooking Time: 10 minutes)

Ingredients:

- 3 large bananas, cut into thirds
- 12 ounces dark chocolate
- 1 cup salted pistachios
- ½ cup cocoa nibs

Directions for Cooking:

1. Insert popsicles on the banana slices.
2. Place the bananas in the fridge for 4 hours to freeze them.
3. Mix together the pistachios and cocoa nibs in a glass and mix until well combined. Set aside.
4. Meanwhile, put the chocolate in the instant Pot and press the Sauté button.
5. Heat to melt the chocolate. Place in a deep glass.
6. Dip the frozen bananas in the melted chocolate before dredging into the pistachio mixture.
7. Place in the fridge to harden.

Nutrition information:

Calories per serving:531; Carbohydrates: 51.6g; Protein: 10.1g; Fat: 34.5g; Sugar: 2.7g; Sodium: 101mg

448. Dark Chocolate Glaze
(Servings: 4, Cooking Time: 10minutes)

Ingredients:

- 3 tablespoons coconut oil
- 8 ounces dark chocolate
- ¼ cup coconut sugar
- 1/3 cup coconut milk

Directions for Cooking:

1. Place in the Instant Pot and press the Sauté button.
2. Allow to simmer until all ingredients are well incorporated.
3. Drizzle glaze over your favorite dessert or store in an airtight container in the fridge.

Nutrition information:

Calories per serving: 177; Carbohydrates: 18.1g; Protein:1.6g; Fat:18.1g; Sugar: 3.4g; Sodium: 8mg

INSTANT POT DESSERT RECIPES

449.   Dark Chocolate Hot Cocoa
(Servings: 1, Cooking Time: 15 minutes)

Ingredients:

- 1 cup coconut milk
- 1 ½ teaspoon coconut sugar
- 2 ounces dark chocolate
- A dash of cinnamon

Directions for Cooking:

1. Place the coconut milk, coconut sugar, and dark chocolate in the Instant Pot.
2. Close the lid and make sure that the steam release valve is set to "Sealing."
3. Press the Manual button and adjust the cooking time to 15 minutes.
4. Do quick pressure release.
5. Garnish with a dash of cinnamon before serving.

Nutrition information:

Calories per serving: 906; Carbohydrates: 43.1g; Protein: 9.9g; Fat: 81.3g; Sugar: -5.7g; Sodium: 47mg

---

450.   Lemon Blueberry Cake
(Servings: 5, Cooking Time: 10 minutes)

Ingredients:

- ½ cups coconut flour
- 4 large eggs
- 1 teaspoon baking soda
- ½ cup coconut milk
- ½ teaspoon lemon zest

Directions for Cooking:

1. Combine all ingredients in a mixing bowl.
2. Pour into a mug.
3. Place a steam rack in the Instant Pot and pour a cup of water.
4. Place the mug on the steam rack.
5. Close the lid and make sure that the vent points to "Sealing."
6. Press the "Steam" button and adjust the time to 10 minutes.
7. Do natural pressure release.

Nutrition information:

Calories per serving: 259; Carbohydrates: 10.3g; Protein: 7.2g; Fat: 20.9g; Sugar: 0g; Sodium: 34mg

---

451.   Choco-Coco Macaroons
(Servings: 15, Cooking Time: 10 minutes)

Ingredients:

- 3 cups coconut flakes
- ¼ cup coconut oil
- 3 eggs, beaten
- 1/3 cup cocoa powder
- 1 tablespoon liquid stevia

Directions for Cooking:

1. Press the "Sauté" button on the Instant Pot.
2. Add all ingredients and pour ¼ cup water.
3. Stir constantly for 10 minutes.
4. Turn off the Instant Pot and scoop small balls from the mixture.
5. Allow to set in the fridge for 1 hour.

Nutrition information:

Calories per serving:141; Carbohydrates:8.1 g;
Protein: 2.6g; Fat: 15.2g; Sugar: 0g; Sodium: 69mg

---

452.   Brownie Fudge
(Servings: 10, Cooking Time: 6 hours)

Ingredients:

- ¾ cup coconut milk
- 2 tablespoons butter, melted
- 4 egg yolks, beaten
- 5 tablespoons cacao powder
- 1 teaspoon erythritol

Directions for Cooking:

1. Place all ingredients in the Instant Pot and mix until well combined.
2. Pour the batter into the greased inner pot.
3. Close the lid and make sure that the vent points to "Venting."
4. Press the "Slow Cook" button and adjust the time to 6 hours.

Nutrition information:

Calories per serving: 84; Carbohydrates: 1.2g; Protein: 1.5g; Fat: 8.4g; Sugar: 0g; Sodium: 25mg

---

INSTANT POT DESSERT RECIPES

453. Berry Compote
(Servings: 10, Cooking Time: 6 hours)

Ingredients:

- 1 cup raspberries
- 1 cup full fat coconut milk

Directions for Cooking:

1. Place the raspberries in the Instant Pot.
2. Add 1/8 cup of water.
3. Close the lid and make sure that the vent points to "Venting."
4. Press the "Slow Cook" button and adjust the time to 6 hours.
5. While the berry compote is cooking, make the coconut cream.
6. In a bowl, place the coconut milk.
7. Use a hand mixer and whisk until it becomes thick and foamy.
8. Place on a bowl and top with the berry compote.

Nutrition information:

Calories per serving: 78; Carbohydrates: 7.3g; Protein:0.8 g; Fat: 8.1g; Sugar: 2.4g; Sodium: 4mg

---

454. Creamy Choco Mousse
(Servings: 4, Cooking Time: 10 minutes)

Ingredients:

- 2 cups coconut milk, freshly squeezed
- 2 teaspoons vanilla extract
- 2 tablespoons erythritol
- 2 tablespoons cocoa powder, sifted
- Cocoa nibs for garnish

Directions for Cooking:

1. Place the coconut milk, vanilla extract, sweetener, and cocoa powder in the Instant Pot.
2. Press the "Sauté" button and allow to simmer for 10 minutes.
3. Pour into the ramekins and allow to set in the fridge for an hour.
4. Garnish with cacao nibs before serving.

Nutrition information:

Calories per serving:291; Carbohydrates: 9.2g; Protein: 3.5g; Fat: 29.5g; Sugar: 0g; Sodium: 19mg

INSTANT POT DESSERT RECIPES

455.   Vanilla Jello
(Servings: 6, Cooking Time: 6 minutes)

Ingredients:

- 1 cup boiling water
- 2 tablespoons gelatin powder, unsweetened
- 3 tablespoons erythritol
- 1 cup heavy cream
- 1 teaspoon vanilla extract

Directions for Cooking:

1. Place the boiling water in the Instant Pot.

2. Press the "Sauté" button on the Instant Pot and allow the water to simmer.
3. Add the gelatin powder and allow to dissolve.
4. Stir in the rest of the ingredients.
5. Pour the mixture into jello molds.
6. Place in the fridge to set for 2 hours.

Nutrition information:

Calories per serving: 105; Carbohydrates: 5.2g; Protein: 3.3; Fat: 7.9g; Sugar: 0g; Sodium: 31mg

---

456.   Salted Caramel Icing on Apple Bread
(Servings: 12, Cooking Time: 35 minutes)

Ingredients:

- 2 eggs
- 2 sticks butter
- 3 cup sugar
- 1 tablespoon apple pie spice
- 3 cups apples, peeled and cubed
- 2 cups flour
- 1 tablespoon baking powder
- 1 tablespoon vanilla
- 1 cup heavy cream
- 2 cups powdered sugar

Directions for Cooking:

1. In a mixing bowl, combine the eggs, 1 stick butter, 1 cup sugar, and apple pie spice. Mix until creamy and smooth. Add in the apples and mix well.

2. In another bowl, mix together flour and baking powder. Add this mixture to the apple mixture. Stir and pour the batter into a greased spring form pan.
3. Place a steamer rack in the Instant Pot and pour 1 ½ cup water. Place the pan on the trivet.
4. Close the lid and press the manual button. Cook on high for 35 minutes.
5. Do a natural pressure release.
6. Meanwhile, make the icing by mixing 1 stick butter, 2 cups sugar, heavy cream and powdered sugar. Heat over medium low flame.
7. Pour the icing on top of the apple bread.

Nutrition information:

Calories per serving: 494; Carbohydrates: 87.7g; Protein: 4.0g; Fat: 15.0g; Sugar: 69.6g; Sodium: 101mg

457.   Pumpkin, Banana, Choo-Chip Bundt Cake
(Servings: 12, Cooking Time: 35 minutes)

Ingredients:

- ¾ cup whole wheat flour
- ¾ cup all-purpose flour
- 1 teaspoon baking soda
- ½ teaspoon salt
- ½ teaspoon baking powder
- ¾ teaspoon pumpkin pie spice
- 1 medium banana, mashed
- ¾ cup sugar
- ½ cup Greek yogurt
- 2 tablespoon canola oil
- 1 egg
- ½ can pureed pumpkin
- ½ teaspoon vanilla extract
- 2/3 cup semi-sweet chocolate chips

Directions for Cooking:

1. In a mixing bowl, mix together the two types of flour, baking soda, salt, baking powder, and pumpkin pie spice.

2. Using an electric mixer, combine the banana, sugar, yogurt, oil, egg, pureed pumpkin, and vanilla in a separate bowl.
3. Mix the dry ingredients and wet ingredients. Fold until well combined. Stir in the chocolate chips.
4. Transfer the batter in a greased Bundt pan.
5. Cover the pan with foil and make sure that it is sealed.
6. Add 1 ½ cups of water into the Instant Pot and place the steamer rack.
7. Place the Bundt pan on top of the rack.
8. Close the lid and press the manual button. Cook on high for 35 minutes.
9. Do natural pressure release.
10. Serve chilled.

Nutrition information:

Calories per serving: 127; Carbohydrates: 21.2g; Protein: 3.5g; Fat: 3.5g; Sugar: 8.0g; Sodium: 214mg

458.   Mini Lava Cake
(Servings: 3, Cooking Time: 6 minutes)

Ingredients:

- 1 egg
- 4 tablespoon sugar
- 2 tablespoon olive oil
- 4 tablespoon milk
- 4 tablespoon all-purpose flour
- 1 tablespoon cacao powder
- ½ teaspoon baking powder
- Pinch of salt
- Powdered sugar for dusting

Nutrition information:

Calories per serving: 193; Carbohydrates: 20.0g; Protein: 3.5g; Fat: 11.1g; Sugar: 11.5g; Sodium: 31.0mg

Directions for Cooking:

1. Grease the ramekins with butter or oil. Set aside
2. Pour 1 cup of water in the Instant Pot and place the steamer rack.
3. In a medium bowl, mix all the ingredients except the powdered sugar. Blend until well combined.
4. Pour in the ramekins.
5. Place the ramekins in the Instant Pot and close the lid.
6. Press the manual button and cook on high for 6 minutes.
7. Once the Instant Pot beeps, remove the ramekin and sprinkle powdered sugar.
8. Serve and enjoy.

459.   Berry-Choco Cheesecake
(Servings: 8, Cooking Time: 10 minutes)

Ingredients:

- 4 tablespoon butter, melted
- 1 ½ cup chocolate cookie, crumbed
- 3 packages low-fat cream cheese
- 2 tablespoon cornstarch
- 1 cup sugar
- 3 large eggs
- ½ cup plain Greek yogurt
- 1 tablespoon vanilla extract
- 4-ounce milk chocolate
- 4-ounce white chocolate
- 4-ounce bittersweet chocolate
- 1 cup sugared cranberries

Directions for Cooking:

1. Brush ramekins or a spring form pan with oil. Set aside.
2. Make the crust by combining butter with cookie crumbs. Press the dough at the bottom of the pan. Place in the freezer to set.
3. Beat the cream cheese with a mixer on low speed until smooth. Add cornstarch and sugar and continue mixing until well combined. Mix in eggs one at a time while continuing to beat. Scrape the sides of the bowl as needed. Add the yogurt and vanilla and mix until well combined.
4. Divide the batter in three bowls. Set aside
5. Melt the milk chocolate in the microwave oven for 30 seconds twice until completely melted. Whisk the chocolate into one of the bowl of the cheesecake batter. Do the same thing with the white and bittersweet chocolates.
6. Take the spring form pan out from the fridge. Pour the dark chocolate batter as the first layer, followed by the white chocolate and milk chocolate. Put aluminum foil on top of the spring form pan.
7. Pour water on the Instant Pot and place the steamer rack. Place the spring form pan and close the lid.
8. Cook on high for 10 minutes.
9. Do natural pressure release to open the lid.
10. Take the cheesecake out and refrigerate for 1 hour.
11. Serve with sugared cranberries.

Nutrition information:

Calories per serving: 554; Carbohydrates: 50.1g; Protein: 15.2g; Fat: 32.6g; Sugar: 41.7g; Sodium: 569mg

INSTANT POT DESSERT RECIPES

460.   Apple Crisp
(Servings: 4, Cooking Time: 25 minutes)

Ingredients:

- 5 medium apples, peeled and chopped
- ½ teaspoon nutmeg
- 2 teaspoon cinnamon
- 1 tablespoon maple syrup
- ½ cup water
- 4 tablespoon butter
- ¾ cup old fashioned rolled oats
- ¼ cup brown sugar
- ¼ cup flour
- ½ teaspoon salt

Directions for Cooking:

1. Place the apples in the Instant Pot and sprinkle with nutmeg and cinnamon. Pour in maple syrup and water.

2. In a small bowl, melt the butter in the microwave oven. Add to the melted butter oats, brown sugar, flour and salt.

3. Drop a spoonful of mixture on the apples.

4. Close the lid on the Instant Pot. Press the manual setting and cook on high for 8 minutes.

5. Use natural pressure release.

6. Serve warm and topped with vanilla ice cream.

Nutrition information:

Calories per serving: 362; Carbohydrates: 67.1g; Protein: 4.7g; Fat: 13.3g; Sugar: 40.3g; Sodium: 390mg

---

461.   Toffee Pudding
(Servings: 12, Cooking Time: 20 minutes)

Ingredients:

- ¼ cup blackstrap molasses
- ¾ cup boiling water
- 1 ¼ cup dates, chopped
- 1 ¼ cup all-purpose flour
- ¼ teaspoon salt
- 1 teaspoon baking powder
- 1/3 cup unsalted butter + ¼ cup unsalted butter
- 1 ¾ cup brown sugar
- 1 egg
- 2 teaspoon vanilla extract
- 1/3 cup whipping cream

Nutrition information:

Calories per serving: 263; Carbohydrates: 49.7g; Protein: 2.9g; Fat: 6.6g; Sugar: 35.8g; Sodium: 74mg

Directions for Cooking:

1. Brush butter on ramekins and set aside.

2. In a bowl, mix together molasses, boiling water and dates. Mix in the flour, salt and baking soda. Place in a blender and pulse until fine.

3. In a separate bowl, cream the 1/3 cup butter and ¾ cup brown sugar using a hand mixer Do this until the butter becomes fluffy. Add the eggs and 1 teaspoon vanilla. Pour in the date mixture.

4. Divide the batter and distribute to the ramekins.

5. Cover the ramekins with foil and make sure that it is sealed well.

6. Place a steamer rack in the instant pot. Pour 2 cups of water.

7. Close the lid and press the manual button. Cook on high for 20 minutes.

8. Meanwhile, make the caramel sauce by mixing together the remaining vanilla, butter, and brown sugar. Add the whipping cream. Bring to a boil in a saucepan heated over medium low flame. Set aside.

9. Once the pudding is done, do quick natural release.

10. Remove the ramekins and pour the caramel sauce.

---

462.   Thai Coconut Rice
(Servings: 4,Cooking Time: 20 minutes)

Ingredients:

- 1 cup Thai sweet rice
- 1 ½ cups water
- 1 can full fat coconut milk
- A pinch of salt
- 4 tablespoon pure sugar
- ½ teaspoon cornstarch + 2 tablespoon water
- 1 large mango, sliced
- Sesame seeds for garnish

Directions for Cooking:

1. Place rice and water in the Instant Pot.
2. Close the lid and press the manual button. Cook on high for 5 minutes.
3. Turn off the Instant Pot and do natural pressure release for 10 minutes.
4. While the rice is cooking, place the coconut milk, salt, and sugar in a saucepan. Heat over medium heat for 10 minutes while stirring constantly.
5. Once the Instant Pot lid can be open, add the coconut milk mixture. Stir well. Place a clean kitchen towel over the opening of the lid and let it rest for 10 minutes.
6. Meanwhile, mix cornstarch with water and add to the rice. Press the sauté button and mix until the rice becomes creamy and thick.
7. Serve with mango slices and sesame seeds.

Nutrition information:
Calories per serving: 301; Carbohydrates: 36.5g; Protein: 3.5g; Fat: 17.5g; Sugar: 21.6g; Sodium: 163mg

INSTANT POT DESSERT RECIPES

463.   Applesauce
(Servings: 8, Cooking Time: 8 minutes)

Ingredients:

- 8 medium apples, peeled and cored
- 1 cup water
- 2 teaspoon cinnamon, ground

Directions for Cooking:

1. Place the apples in the Instant Pot. Pour in the water.
2. Close the lid and press the manual button. Cook on high for 8 minutes.
3. Do natural pressure release and open the lid.
4. Remove the excess water.
5. Place the apples in a blender and process until smooth.
6. Add the rest of the ingredients.
7. Serve chilled.

Nutrition information:

Calories per serving: 96; Carbohydrates: 25.7g; Protein: 0.5g; Fat: 0.3g; Sugar: 18.9g; Sodium: 2mg

---

464.   Custard Cheesecake
(Servings: 6, Cooking Time: 25 minutes)

Ingredients:

- 1 ½ cup custard cream biscuits
- ¼ cup melted butter
- 2 cup full fat cream cheese
- ½ cup caster sugar
- 2 large eggs
- 1 teaspoon vanilla
- 2 drops of almond extract
- ¾ cup double cream

Directions for Cooking:

1. Place the custard cream biscuits and butter in the food processor and pulse until a fine crumb is formed. This will be the dough
2. Press the dough in ramekins or small spring form pans.
3. Clean the food processor and pour in the cream cheese, caster sugar, eggs, vanilla extract, almond extract, and double cream. Process until well combined.
4. Pour the mixture to the ramekins or cake pan. Place a kitchen towel on top of the ramekin to absorb the excess liquid from forming on the cheesecake
5. Pour 1 ½ cup of water to the Instant Pot and place a trivet. Place the ramekins or cake pan on the trivet.
6. Close the lid and select the manual button. Cook on high for 25 minutes.
7. Do natural pressure release then remove the lid. Remove the kitchen towel.
8. Refrigerate.

Nutrition information:

Calories per serving: 459; Carbohydrates: 18.5g; Protein: 9.8g; Fat: 39.0g; Sugar: 16.2g; Sodium: 387mg

465. Deliciously Good Peach Dessert
(Servings: 8, Cooking Time: 15 minutes)

Ingredients:

- 8 cups peaches, thinly sliced
- ¼ cup brown sugar
- 1 teaspoon cinnamon
- 1/8 teaspoon salt
- ¼ cup butter

Directions for Cooking:

1. Place the peaches in a mixing bowl and add brown sugar, cinnamon and salt. Toss to combine everything. Add butter and mix again.
2. Place the peaches inside ramekins.
3. Place a steamer rack in the Instant Pot.
4. Arrange the ramekins on the steamer rack.
5. Close the lid and press the manual button. Cook on high for 15 minutes.
6. Do natural pressure release.
7. Serve and enjoy warm or cold.

Nutrition information:

Calories per serving: 272; Carbohydrates: 59.2g; Protein: 1.3g; Fat: 6.0g; Sugar: 55.5g; Sodium: 102mg

466. Berry Cobbler
(Servings: 4, Cooking Time: 10 minutes)

Ingredients:

- 30 ounces frozen mixed berries
- ½ cup granulated white sugar, divided
- 2 ½ cup commercial baking mix
- ½ cup light vanilla soy milk
- 3 tablespoon whipped butter
- 2 teaspoon cinnamon

Directions for Cooking:

1. Prepare the filling by mixing berries with ¼ cup white sugar and ½ cup commercial baking mix.
2. In another bowl, prepare the topping by combining 2 cups commercial baking mix, soy milk, ¼ cup white sugar, butter and cinnamon.
3. Place the filling in ramekins. Add the topping mixture.
4. Place a trivet or steam rack at the bottom of the Instant Pot and pour 1 cup water.
5. Place the ramekins on the rack.
6. Close the lid and press the manual button. Cook on high for 10 minutes.
7. Do natural pressure release for 10-minutes.
8. Serve and enjoy.

Nutrition information:

Calories per serving: 243; Carbohydrates: 30.1g; Protein: 1.8g; Fat: 14.8g; Sugar: 20.5g; Sodium: 72mg

INSTANT POT DESSERT RECIPES

467. Mini Peanut Butter Choco Cakes
(Servings: 4, Cooking Time: 15 minutes)

Ingredients:

- 1 can black beans, drained and rinsed
- ½ cup cocoa powder, unsweetened
- ½ cup egg whites
- 1/3 cup canned pumpkin
- 1/3 cup unsweetened applesauce
- ¼ cup brown sugar
- 1 teaspoon vanilla extract
- 1 ½ teaspoon baking powder
- ¼ teaspoon salt
- 3 tablespoon peanut butter baking chips

Directions for Cooking:

1. Place all the ingredients except the peanut butter chips inside a food processor. Process until smooth.
2. Add the peanut butter chips and fold until evenly distributed within the batter.
3. Place the batter in a ramekin sprayed with cooking oil.
4. Place a steam rack in the Instant Pot and add 1 ½ cup water.
5. Place the ramekins with the batter onto the steamer rack.
6. Close the lid and press the manual button. Cook on high for 10 minutes.
7. Do natural pressure release.
8. Insert a toothpick in the middle of the cakes and check if it comes out clean.
9. Serve chilled.

Nutrition information:
Calories per serving: 218; Carbohydrates: 34.9g; Protein: 12.0g; Fat: 6.5g; Sugar: 15.9g; Sodium: 229mg

---

468. Mocha Pudding Cake
(Servings: 6, Cooking Time: 25 minutes)

Ingredients:

- 2/3 cup granulated sweetener
- 5 large eggs
- 1/8 teaspoon salt
- 1/3 cup almond flour
- 4 tablespoons unsweetened cocoa powder
- 1 teaspoon vanilla extract
- 2 tablespoons instant coffee crystals
- ½ cup heavy cream
- 2-ounces unsweetened chocolate
- ¾ cup butter
- Coconut oil spray

Nutrition information:
Calories per serving: 397; Carbohydrates: 27.9g; Protein: 3.6g; Fat: 31.2g; Sugar: 21.9g; Sodium: 253mg

Directions for Cooking:

1. Grease sides and bottom of Instant Pot with cooking spray.
2. Press sauté button.
3. Add butter and chocolate. Mix well. Make sure to mix constantly so as the bottom doesn't burn. Once fully incorporated, press cancel to keep warm.
4. Meanwhile, in a small bowl whisk well vanilla, coffee crystals, and heavy cream.
5. In another bowl, mix well salt, almond flour, and cocoa powder.
6. In a mixing bowl, beat eggs until thick and pale, around 5 minutes while slowly stirring in sweetener.
7. While beating, slowly drizzle and mix in melted butter mixture.

8. Mix in the almond flour mixture and mix well.
9. Add the coffee mixture and beat until fully incorporated.
10. Pour batter into Instant Pot.
11. Place a paper towel on top of pot this will absorb condensation.
12. Cover pot, press slow cooker button, and adjust to 2-hour cooking time.

---

469. Brownies & Macadamia Nuts
(Servings: 9, Cooking Time: 10 minutes)

Ingredients:

- 1 teaspoon instant coffee
- 1 teaspoon vanilla extract
- 1 ½ teaspoon baking powder
- 2 large eggs
- 3 tablespoon cocoa powder
- 5 tablespoon salted butter
- ¼ cup coconut oil
- ¾ cup macadamia nuts
- ¾ cup erythritol
- ¾ cup Honeyville almond flour

Directions for Cooking:

1. In a mixing bowl, cream butter.
2. Add erythritol and coconut oil and mix well.
3. Add vanilla and eggs, mix for around a minute or until fully incorporated.
4. Add coffee and cocoa powder and mix well.
5. Add almond flour and baking powder and mix thoroughly.
6. With a spatula, fold in macadamia nuts.
7. Transfer batter to a heat proof dish that fits inside your Instant Pot.
8. Spread evenly and cover top with foil.
9. On Instant Pot, add a cup of water and steamer basket.
10. Place dish of batter in side steamer basket.
11. Cover, press steam button.
12. Allow for natural release, slice into 9 equal servings, and enjoy.

Nutrition information:
Calories per serving: 189; Carbohydrates: 3.3g;
Protein: 1.9g; Fat: 20.0g; Sugar: 0.6g; Sodium: 38mg

INSTANT POT DESSERT RECIPES

470.   Choco Fudge
(Servings: 24, Cooking Time: 25 minutes)

Ingredients:

- 3 ¼-ounces dark chocolate with a minimum of 70% cocoa, chopped
- 3 ¼-ounces butter
- 1 teaspoon vanilla extract
- 2 cups heavy whipping cream

Directions for Cooking:

1. Press sauté button on Instant Pot.
2. Add vanilla and heavy cream and bring to a simmer.
3. Continue simmering for 20 minutes or until mixture is reduced to 50% its original amount. Stir frequently to prevent burning.
4. Press cancel button and stir in butter.
5. Mix well until butter is melted and thoroughly incorporated.
6. Add chocolate and mix until thoroughly melted and combined.
7. In a square baking dish, grease bottom and sides with cooking spray, pour in chocolate mixture.
8. Stick into the fridge for at least 4 hours.
9. Slice into 24 equal pieces and enjoy.
10. Refrigerate at all times.

Nutrition information:

Calories per serving: 83; Carbohydrates: 2.3g; Protein: 0.6g; Fat: 8.1g; Sugar: 2.0g; Sodium: 31.0mg

471.   Salted Choco Treat
(Servings: 10, Cooking Time: 15 minutes)

Ingredients:

- Sea salt
- 1 tablespoon pumpkin seeds
- 2 tablespoons roasted unsweetened coconut chips
- 10 hazelnuts or pecan/walnuts
- 3 ½-ounces dark chocolate (minimum of 70% cocoa solids)

Directions for Cooking:

1. On Instant Pot, add 1/2 cup of water and press sauté button.
2. On a heat proof bowl, place chocolate and slowly lower into Instant Pot.
3. Continue heating bowl until chocolate is melted. If needed you can add more water into Instant Pot.
4. Once chocolate is melted, stir in salt, pumpkin seeds, coconut chips, and walnuts.
5. Refrigerate for at least two hours, cut into strips and enjoy.

Nutrition information:

Calories per serving: 83; Carbohydrates: 8.1g; Protein: 1.3g; Fat: 5.1g; Sugar: 5.1g; Sodium: 13.0mg

472.   Whipped Brown Sugar on Creamy-Berry cake
(Servings: 1, Cooking Time: 10 minutes)

Ingredients:

- ¼ cup mixed berries
- ¼ cup almond flour
- 2 tablespoons organic cream cheese
- 2 tablespoons ghee
- ¼ cup sugar-free vanilla bean sweetener syrup,2 large eggs
- ¼ cup heavy whipping cream
- ½ tablespoon sugar-free brown sugar syrup

Directions for Cooking:

1. In a blender, mix cream cheese, ghee, vanilla bean sweetener, and eggs until smooth.
2. Transfer into a heat proof bowl and cover top with foil.
3. Add a cup of water in Instant Pot.
4. Add steamer basket and place bowl on top.
5. Cover and press steam button.
6. Meanwhile, whip your cream until stiff and slowly add the brown sugar syrup. Store in fridge.
7. Once done steaming, do a quick release and allow cake to cool.
8. Refrigerate for at least 2 hours, top with whipped cream, and enjoy.

Nutrition information:

Calories per serving: 495; Carbohydrates: 67.7g; Protein: 9.1g; Fat: 21.1g; Sugar: 51.5g; Sodium: 258mg

---

473.   Tapioca Pudding
(Servings: 4, Cooking Time: 20 minutes)

Ingredients:

- ½ lemon, zested
- ½ cup sugar
- ½ cup water
- 1 ¼ cups whole milk
- 1/3 cup seed tapioca pearls

Directions for Cooking:

1. Prepare the Instant Pot by placing the inner pot inside.
2. Add steamer basket and a cup of water.
3. In fine mesh strainer, rinse tapioca pearls and pour into heat proof bowl. Mix in sugar, zest, water, and milk.
4. Place bowl in steamer basket.
5. Cover and lock lid. Close the pressure release valve and press soup/stew button. Set the timer to 20 minutes.
6. Once done cooking, press cancel, and do the natural release method.
7. Serve while warm or place in the fridge to cool and enjoy.

Nutrition information:

Calories per serving: 164; Carbohydrates: 33.9g; Protein: 2.3g; Fat: 2.4g; Sugar: 22.6g; Sodium: 35.0mg

474. Blueberry & Strawberry Cheesecake
(Servings: 8, Cooking Time: 45 minutes)

Ingredients:

- 1 cup strawberry, sliced in half
- ½ cup blueberry
- 2 eggs
- 1 teaspoon vanilla extract
- 1 tablespoon all-purpose flour
- ¼ cup sour cream
- ½ cup sugar
- 16-ounces cream cheese
- 2 tablespoons melted butter
- 1 cup crushed cookie crumbs
- 1 tablespoon sugar, optional

Directions for Cooking:

1. Line a spring form pan with foil.
2. Mix melted butter and cookie crumbs in a small bowl. Then press on the bottom of a spring form pan.
3. In mixing bowl, whisk well eggs, vanilla extract, flour, sour cream, sugar, and cream cheese. Pour on top of crust.
4. Prepare the Instant Pot by placing the inner pot inside.
5. Place a wire rack and 1 cup of water. Place pan on wire rack.
6. Cover and lock lid. Close the pressure release valve and press chicken/meat button. Set the timer to 25 minutes.
7. Meanwhile, in a small pot cook blueberry and strawberries for 5 minutes. You can mix in a tablespoon of sugar if desired.
8. Once done cooking, press cancel, open the pressure release valve, and wait until steam is released completely before you remove the lid.
9. Remove pan from pot or let it cool completely there. Refrigerate for at least 4 hours.
10. Serve and enjoy.

Nutrition information:

Calories per serving: 243; Carbohydrates: 19.4g; Protein: 7.4g; Fat: 15.2g; Sugar: 15.3g; Sodium: 264mg

475. Leche Flan
(Servings: 4, Cooking Time: 30 minutes)

Ingredients:

- 1 teaspoon almond extract
- ¾ cup sugar
- 3 egg whites
- 6 eggs
- 2 cups milk

Caramel Syrup Ingredients:

- ½ teaspoon lemon juice
- 2-ounce water
- 2 cups sugar

Directions for Cooking:

1. In heavy bottomed skillet, add lemon juice, water, and sugar. Heat until sugar is melted. Pour into a baking dish that fits inside your Instant Pot. Let it harden.
2. In a mixing bowl, mix well almond extract, sugar, egg whites, eggs, and milk. Then pour on top of hardened caramel sugar.
3. Cover dish with foil.
4. Prepare the Instant Pot by placing the inner pot inside.
5. Place wire rack and 2 cups of water. Place dish on wire rack.

6. Cover and lock lid. Close the pressure release valve and press chicken/meat button. Set the timer to 15 minutes.
7. Once done cooking, press cancel, open the pressure release valve, and wait until steam is released completely before you remove the lid.
8. Remove dish from pot, let it cool completely, and refrigerate for at least 4 hours.
9. Remove foil cover, place a plate on top of dish and invert dish.
10. Serve and enjoy.

Nutrition information:

Calories per serving: 256; Carbohydrates: 25.3g; Protein: 14.9g; Fat: 10.5g; Sugar: 24.9g; Sodium: 188mg

---

476.   Cranberry-Orange Bread Pudding
(Servings: 4, Cooking Time: 20 minutes)

Ingredients:

- ¾ cup cranberries
- 2 tablespoons butter, softened
- ¾ cup sugar
- ½ tablespoon vanilla
- 1 orange juice and zest
- 2 cups half and half
- 3 cups brioche, cube
- 4 egg yolks

Directions for Cooking:

1. In a 6-inch square baking dish, mix well vanilla extract, half & half, orange juice, zest, juice, cranberries, and eggs. Mix thoroughly.
2. Add cubed brioche and toss well to coat in egg mixture. Let it soak for ten minutes. Cover the top with foil.
3. Prepare the Instant Pot by placing the inner pot inside.
4. Place wire rack inside and add 2 cups of water.
5. Place baking dish on wire rack.
6. Cover and lock lid. Close the pressure release valve and press chicken/meat button. Set the timer to 15 minutes.
7. Once done cooking, press cancel, open the pressure release valve, and wait until steam is released completely before you remove the lid.
8. Let it cool completely before serving.

Nutrition information:

Calories per serving: 287; Carbohydrates: 48.6g; Protein: 5.9g; Fat: 12.0g; Sugar: 31.9g; Sodium: 171mg

INSTANT POT DESSERT RECIPES

477.   Cherry Compote
(Servings: 8, Cooking Time: 10 minutes)

Ingredients:

- 1 package frozen cherries
- 2 tablespoon lemon juice
- ¾ cup sugar
- 2 tablespoon cornstarch
- 2 tablespoon water
- ¼ teaspoon almond extract

Directions for Cooking:

1. Place the cherries, lemon juice and sugar in the Instant Pot. Stir to mix everything.
2. Close the lid and press the Fish/Veg/Steam button. Adjust the cooking time to 5 minutes.

3. Do natural pressure release.
4. Meanwhile, mix the cornstarch, water and almond extract.
5. Once the lid is open, pour the slurry over the cherries. Press the same button and cook until the sauce thickens.
6. Once done cooking, refrigerate until cool.
7. Serve and enjoy.

Nutrition information:

Calories per serving: 46; Carbohydrates: 11.6g; Protein: 0g; Fat: 0g; Sugar: 9.4g; Sodium: 0mg

478.   Hazelnut Flan
(Servings: 4, Cooking Time: 50 minutes)

Ingredients:

- ¾ + 1/3 cup granulated sugar
- ¼ cup water
- 3 eggs
- 2 egg yolks
- A pinch of salt
- 2 cups milk
- ½ cup whipping cream
- 1 teaspoon vanilla extract
- 2 tablespoon hazelnut syrup

Directions for Cooking:

1. Prepare the caramel base by heating the ¾ cup sugar and ¼ cup water. Bring to a boil and place on ramekins before it hardens. Set aside.
2. Place a trivet or steamer basket in the Instant Pot and add 1 ½ cups of water.

3. In a mixing bowl, beat the eggs, yolks and 1/3 cup of sugar. Add a pinch of salt.
4. Heat milk in a saucepan over medium heat until it bubbles. Add milk to eggs to temper the eggs.
5. Stir in the cream, vanilla and Hazelnut syrup.
6. Pour mixture on ramekins and cover with tin foil.
7. Place inside on the steamer basket and close the lid.
8. Press the Fish/Veg/ Steam button and adjust the cooking time to 50 minutes.
9. Do natural pressure release.

Nutrition information:

Calories per serving: 325; Carbohydrates:35.12g; Protein: 12.16g; Fat: 15.16g; Sugar:34.21g; Sodium: 141mg

### 479.	Carrot Pudding Cake
(Servings: 8, Cooking Time: 50 minutes)

Ingredients:

- ½ + ½ cup brown sugar
- ¼ cup molasses
- 2 eggs
- ½ cup flour
- ½ teaspoon cinnamon
- ½ teaspoon allspice
- ½ teaspoon nutmeg
- ½ teaspoon baking soda
- ¼ teaspoon salt
- 2/3 cup shortening, frozen and grated
- ½ cup carrots, grated
- ½ cup raisins
- 1 cup bread crumbs
- ½ cup pecans, chopped
- 4 tablespoon butter
- ¼ cup cream
- 2 tablespoon rum
- ¼ teaspoon cinnamon, ground

Directions for Cooking:

1. Place a steamer rack in the Instant Pot and add 1 ½ cups of water.

2. In a mixing bowl, whisk ½ cup of brown sugar, molasses and eggs.
3. Pour in the flour and the spices, baking soda and salt. Mix until well combined.
4. Add the shortening, carrots, bread crumbs and pecans.
5. Pour the batter in a baking pan that will fit the Instant Pot. Cover with aluminum foil and place on the trivet.
6. Close the lid and press the Fish/Veg/Steam button. Adjust the cooking time to 50 minutes.
7. Meanwhile, prepare the rum sauce by mixing in a saucepan the remaining brown sugar, butter, cream, rum and cinnamon. Heat over low flame until reduced.
8. Once the Instant Pot beeps, do natural pressure release.
9. Pour over the rum sauce on top.

Nutrition information:
Calories per serving:428; Carbohydrates:31.92g; Protein: 4.27g; Fat: 31.55g; Sugar:22.53g; Sodium: 260mg

### 480.	Key Lime Pie
(Servings: 8 , Cooking Time: 15 minutes)

Ingredients:

- ¾ cup graham cracker crumbs
- 3 tablespoon butter, melted
- 1 tablespoon sugar
- 1 can condensed milk
- 4 large egg yolks
- ½ cup key lime juice
- 1/3 cup sour cream
- 2 tablespoon key lime zest

Directions for Cooking:

1. Place a trivet or steamer rack in the Instant Pot and pour 1 ½ cups of water.
2. Coat a spring form pan that will fit in the Instant Pot with cooking spray.
3. In a bowl, mix together the graham crackers, butter and sugar. Press evenly on the bottom of the pan to form the crust.

Place inside the fridge to set.
4. In another bowl, beat the egg yolks until light yellow. Add the condensed milk gradually. Beat in the lime juice and beat until smooth. Stir the sour cream and lime zest.
5. Pour the batter in the spring form pan and cover the top with aluminum foil.
6. Place inside the Instant Pot and close the lid.
7. Press the Fish/Veg/Steam button and adjust the cooking time to 15 minutes.
8. Do natural pressure release once you hear the beep sound.
9. Place in the fridge to cool.

Nutrition information:
Calories per serving: 93; Carbohydrates: 4.67g; Protein: 1.9g; Fat: 7.74g; Sugar:1.72g; Sodium: 53mg

INSTANT POT DESSERT RECIPES

481.   Keto Ranch Dip
(Serves: 8, Cooking Time: 2 minutes)

Directions for Cooking:

Ingredients:

- 1 cup egg white, beaten
- 1 lemon juice, freshly squeezed
- Salt and pepper to taste
- 1 teaspoon mustard paste
- 1 cup olive oil

1. Place all ingredients in the Instant Pot and whisk vigorously.
2. Press the "Sauté" button and allow to heat up for 2 minutes while stirring.
3. Do not allow to simmer.
4. Pour into container and store in the fridge for 2 weeks.

Nutrition information:

Calories per serving: 258; Carbohydrates: 1.2g;
Protein: 3.4g; Fat: 27.1g; Sugar: 0g; Sodium: 58mg

---

482.   All-Around Gravy
(Serves: 6, Preparation Time: 5 minutes, Cooking Time: 10 minutes)

Ingredients:

- 2 tablespoons butter
- 1 white onion, chopped
- ¼ cup coconut milk
- 2 cups bone broth
- 1 tablespoon balsamic vinegar

Directions for Cooking:

1. Press the "Sauté" button on the Instant Pot.Melt the butter and sauté the onions for 2 minutes.
2. Add the rest of the ingredients.
3. Stir constantly for 5 minutes or until slightly thickened.

Nutrition information:

Calories per serving: 59; Carbohydrates: 1.1g;
Protein: 0.2g; Fat: 6.3g; Sugar: 0g; Sodium: 33mg

---

483.   Béarnaise Sauce
(Serves: 4, Cooking Time: 3 minutes)

Ingredients

- 2/3 pounds butter
- 4 egg yolks, beaten
- 2 teaspoons lemon juice, freshly squeezed
- ¼ teaspoon onion powder
- 2 tablespoon fresh tarragon

Directions for Cooking:

1. Press the "Sauté" button on the Instant Pot.
2. Melt the butter for 3 minutes.
3. Transfer into a mixing bowl.
4. While whisking the melted hot butter, slowly add the egg yolks.
5. Continue stirring so that no lumps form.
6. Add the lemon juice, onion powder, and fresh tarragon.
7. Store in the fridge for up to 2 weeks.

Nutrition information:

Calories per serving: 603; Carbohydrates: 1.4g;
Protein: 3.5g; Fat: 66.2g; Sugar: 0g; Sodium:497 mg

INSTANT POT DESSERT RECIPES

484.   Caesar Salad Dressing
(Serves: 6, Cooking Time: 3 hours)

Ingredients:

- ½ cup olive oil
- 1 tablespoon Dijon mustard
- ½ cup parmesan cheese, grated
- 2/3-ounce anchovies, chopped
- ½ lemon juice, freshly squeezed

Directions for Cooking:

1. Place all ingredients in the Instant Pot.
2. Add ¼ cup of water and season with salt and pepper to taste.
3. Close the lid and make sure that the vent points to "Venting."
4. Press the "Slow Cook" button and adjust the time to 3 hours.

Nutrition information:

Calories per serving:203; Carbohydrates: 1.5g; Protein: 3.4g; Fat: 20.7g; Sugar: 0g; Sodium: 296mg

---

485.   Cranberry Sauce
(Servings: 8, Cooking Time: 6 hours)

Ingredients:

- 1-pound cranberries
- ½ cup water
- 1 stick butter
- 1 lemon, juice and zest

Directions for Cooking:

1. Place all ingredients in the Instant Pot.
2. Close the lid and make sure that the vent points to "Venting."
3. Press the "Slow Cook" button and adjust the time to 6 hours.
4. Open the lid and strain the cranberry sauce.
5. Discard the strained solid.

Nutrition information:

Calories per serving:174; Carbohydrates: 8.1g; Protein: 0.9g; Fat: 15.5g; Sugar: 1.2g; Sodium: 127mg

---

486.   Chia-Blackberry Jam
(Servings: 6, Cooking Time: 6 hours)

Ingredients:

- 3 cups blackberries, fresh
- 4 tablespoons lemon juice, freshly squeezed
- ¼ cup erythritol
- 4 tablespoons chia seeds
- 5 tablespoons butter

Directions for Cooking:

1. Place all ingredients in the Instant Pot.
2. Close the lid and make sure that the vent points to "Venting."
3. Press the "Slow Cook" button and adjust the time to 6 hours.

Nutrition information:

Calories per serving:236; Carbohydrates: 33g; Protein: 2.9g; Fat: 11.8g; Sugar: 0g; Sodium: 81mg

---

INSTANT POT DESSERT RECIPES

487.   Caramel Sauce
(Servings: 9, Cooking Time: 6 hours)

Ingredients:

- ¼ cup butter
- ½ cup coconut milk
- ¼ teaspoon xanthan gum
- 2 tablespoons water
- ½ cup erythritol

Directions for Cooking:

1. Place all ingredients in the Instant Pot.

2. Close the lid and make sure that the vent points to "Venting."
3. Press the "Slow Cook" button and adjust the time to 6 hours.

Nutrition information:
Calories per serving: 76; Carbohydrates: 0.7g; Protein: 0.4g; Fat: 8.3g; Sugar: 0g; Sodium: 43mg;

---

488.   Hot Fudge Sauce
(Servings: 9, Cooking Time: 5 hours)

Ingredients:

- 1 cup whipping cream
- 1/3 cup powdered Swerve sweetener
- 2 ½ ounces chocolate, unsweetened
- ½ teaspoon vanilla extract

Directions for Cooking:

1. Place all ingredients in the Instant Pot.

2. Close the lid and make sure that the vent points to "Venting."
3. Press the "Slow Cook" button and adjust the time to 5 hours.
4. Mix before serving.

Nutrition information:
Calories per serving: 126; Carbohydrates: 3.7g; Protein: 1.7g; Fat: 14.8g; Sugar: 0g; Sodium: 19mg

---

489.   Dulce De Leche
(Servings: 4, Cooking Time: 30 minutes)

Ingredients:

- 1 can sweetened condensed milk
- 16 ounces of canning jar
- 8 cups of water

Directions for Cooking:

1. Pour the condensed milk into a 16 ounce of canning jar.
2. Place the lid on.
3. Place the steamer rack in the Instant Pot and add 8 cups of water.

4. Place the jar with condensed milk on the steamer rack.
5. Close the lid and press the Fish/Veg/Steam button. Adjust the cooking time to 30 minutes.
6. Let the pressure release naturally.

Nutrition information:
Calories per serving: 525; Carbohydrates: 84.26g; Protein: 8.16g; Fat: 17.8g; Sugar: 25.29g; Sodium: 510mg

---

INSTANT POT DESSERT RECIPES

490.   Creamy Artichoke Dip
(Servings: 8, Cooking Time: 15 minutes)

Ingredients:

- ½ cup dry cannellini beans, soaked overnight
- 8 medium-sized artichokes, cleaned and trimmed
- 1 cup water
- ½ lemon, juiced
- 2 cloves of garlic, minced
- ¾ cup plain non-fat yogurt
- 1 teaspoon salt
- ¼ teaspoon pepper
- ¾ cup grated parmigiana cheese

Directions for Cooking:

1. Place the beans, artichokes and water in the Instant Pot.
2. Close the lid and press the Fish/Veg/Steam button. Set the cooking time to 15 minutes.
3. Do quick pressure release and drain the water.
4. In a food processor, place the beans and artichokes.
5. Season with lemon juice, garlic, yogurt, salt and pepper.
6. Pulse until fine.
7. Add the grated parmigiana cheese.

Nutrition information:
Calories per serving: 134; Carbohydrates: 20.95g; Protein: 9.36g; Fat:3.27g; Sugar: 3.46g; Sodium: 629mg

---

491.   Colorful Peperonata Sauce
(Servings: 6, Cooking Time: 6 minutes)

Ingredients:

- 1 tablespoon olive oil
- 1 red onion, sliced into strips
- 2 cloves of garlic
- 2 red peppers, sliced into thick strips
- 2 yellow peppers, sliced into thick strips
- 1 green pepper, thinly sliced
- 2 medium tomatoes, sliced
- 1 bunch of basil
- Salt and pepper

Directions for Cooking:

1. Without the lid on, press the sauté button and heat the oil.
2. Sauté the onion and garlic for 3 minutes.
3. Add the peppers and tomatoes.
4. Stir in basil and season with salt and pepper to taste.
5. Close the lid, press cancel, press manual, and adjust the cooking time to 3 minutes.
6. Do a QPR.
7. Adjust seasoning to taste and enjoy.

Nutrition information:
Calories per serving: 36; Carbohydrates: 3.55g; Protein: 0.68g; Fat: 2.38g; Sugar:1.92g; Sodium: 31mg

---

INSTANT POT DESSERT RECIPES

492.   Creamy Chicken Liver Pate
(Servings: 8, Cooking Time: 15 minutes)

Ingredients:

- 1 tablespoon butter
- ¾ pounds chicken liver
- 1 onion, chopped
- 1 bay leaf
- ¼ cup red wine
- 2 anchovies in oil
- 1 tablespoon capers
- 1 teaspoon rum
- Salt and pepper to taste

Directions for Cooking:

1. Without the lid on, place butter in the Instant Pot and press the Meat button.
2. Add the chicken livers, onions and bay leaves. Stir to combine everything.
3. Close the lid and adjust the cooking time to 15 minutes.
4. Once the Instant Pot is done, do natural pressure release.
5. Remove the bay leaves and transfer the contents in a food processor or blender.
6. Add the red wine, anchovies, capers, and rum.
7. Season with salt and pepper.
8. Pulse until smooth.

Nutrition information:
Calories per serving: 111; Carbohydrates:4.68g; Protein: 6.32g; Fat: 7.1g; Sugar: 0.88g; Sodium:239mg

---

493.   Olive Oil & Eggplant Dip
(Servings: 6, Cooking Time: 5 minutes)

Ingredients:

- 4 tablespoon olive oil
- 2-pounds eggplant, sliced
- 4 garlic cloves
- 1 teaspoon salt
- 1 lemon, juiced
- 1 tablespoon tahini
- ¼ cup black olives, pitted and sliced
- A few sprigs of thyme
- A dash of extra virgin oil

Directions for Cooking:

1. Press the Fish/Veg/Steam button on the Instant Pot.
2. Heat the oil and add the eggplants. Fry the eggplants for 3 minutes on each side. Stir in the garlic.
3. Add 1 cup of water and close the lid. Press the Fish/Veg/Steam and cook for 5 minutes.
4. Do natural pressure release and take the eggplants out and transfer to a food processor.
5. Add in salt, lemon juice and tahini.
6. Pulse until smooth.
7. Place in a bowl and garnish with olives, thyme and a dash of extra virgin olive oil.

Nutrition information:
Calories per serving: 155; Carbohydrates: 16.8g; Protein: 2g; Fat:11.7g; Sugar: 5.6g; Sodium: 820.9mg

INSTANT POT DESSERT RECIPES

494.   Chickpea Hummus
(Servings: 8, Cooking Time: 18 minutes)

Ingredients:

- 1 cup chickpeas
- 4 cloves of garlic
- 1 bay leaf
- 2 tablespoon tahini
- 1juice of lemon
- ¼ teaspoon cumin
- ½ teaspoon salt
- A dash of paprika
- ½ teaspoon parsley
- A dash of extra virgin olive oil

Directions for Cooking:

1. Place the chickpeas in the Instant Pot and add 6 cups of water. Add two cloves of garlic and bay leaf in the pot.

2. Close the lid of the Instant Pot and press the Beans/Lentils button and adjust the cooking time for 18 minutes.
3. Do natural pressure release.
4. Transfer the chickpeas in a food processor and add the remaining garlic, tahini, lemon, cumin, and salt.
5. Pulse until smooth.
6. Transfer to a bowl and garnish with paprika, parsley and olive oil.

Nutrition information:
Calories per serving: 109.1; Carbohydrates: 0.2g; Protein: 4.1g; Fat: 3.8g; Sugar:0.2g; Sodium: 332.9mg

---

495.   Cheesy Bacon n Corn Southwest Dip
(Servings: 8, Cooking Time: 15 minutes)

Directions for Cooking:

Ingredients:

- 2 tbsp olive oil
- 4 strips of bacon (cut into small pieces)
- 1/2 medium sized white onion, diced
- 1.5 cups frozen corn
- 1 jalapeno pepper, seeds removed and chopped
- 1 clove garlic, minced
- 1 14 oz can diced tomatoes
- 1 4 oz can diced green chilis
- 2 tsp chili powder
- 1 tsp cumin
- 1/2 tsp salt
- 8 oz cream cheese, softened to room temperature
- 1 cup shredded cheddar cheese or pepper jack cheese
- 3 tbsp fresh cilantro (for garnish)

1. Press sauté and heat oil.
2. Cook bacon for 7 minutes or until crispy. Transfer bacon to a plate.
3. Stir in jalapeno, corn, and onion in pot and sauté for 5 minutes.
4. Stir in garlic and cook for a minute.
5. Stir in chili powder, cumin, and salt. Mix well. Add cream cheese, green chili, add tomatoes. Mix well. Press cancel.
6. Close Instant Pot, press the Manual button, choose high settings, and set time to 5 minutes.
7. Once done cooking, do a QPR.
8. Serve and enjoy with chips and cilantro.

Nutrition information:
Calories per serving: 222.2; Carbohydrates: 13.0g; Protein: 11.2g; Fat: 14.2g; Sugar: 4.3g; Sodium: 631.2mg

INSTANT POT DESSERT RECIPES

496.   Buffalo Chicken Dip
(Servings: 15, Cooking Time: 20 minutes)

Ingredients:

- 2 chicken breasts
- 2 (8-ounce) packages of cream cheese (I used low-fat)
- 1 cup ranch dressing or you can use blue cheese dressing if you want
- 3/4 cup Louisiana hot sauce
- 2 cups shredded cheddar cheese
- 3 Tbs. butter
- 2 green onions, chopped
- 2-3 packages of Crunch master Crackers

Directions for Cooking:

1. Mix in ranch, hot sauce, butter, cream cheese, and chicken in instant Pot.
2. Close Instant Pot, press the Manual button, choose high settings, and set time to 20 minutes.
3. Once done cooking, do a QPR.
4. Remove chicken and mix in cheese.
5. Shred chicken and return to pot. Mix well.
6. Sprinkle with green onions.
7. Serve and enjoy with crackers.

Nutrition information:
Calories per serving: 270; Carbohydrates: 6.1g; Protein: 20.6g; Fat: 18.0g; Sugar:1.9g; Sodium: 607mg

---

497.   Huge Vat of Tomato Sauce
(Servings: 8, Cooking Time: 25 minutes)

Ingredients:

- 4 tablespoons olive oil
- 2-3 medium yellow onions, sliced into rings
- 2 large carrots, roughly chopped
- 1 celery stalk, roughly chopped
- 6 pounds (3k) plum tomatoes, quartered
- 6-8 fresh basil leaves

Directions for Cooking:

1. Press sauté and heat oil.
2. Sauté onions for 5 minutes.
3. Add celery and carrots, sauté for 5 minutes.
4. Add tomatoes and mix well. Mash tomatoes with a potato masher. Cook until it begins to boil.
5. Close Instant Pot, press the Manual button, choose high settings, and set time to 5 minutes.
6. Once done cooking, do a QPR.
7. Mix contents well. With an immersion blender, puree tomatoes.
8. Transfer to jars for storage and use when ready.

Nutrition information:
Calories per serving: 171.6; Carbohydrates: 0.4g; Protein: 4.0g; Fat: 8.4g; Sugar:0.4g; Sodium: 48mg

---

498.   Blood Orange Marmalade
(Servings: 8, Cooking Time: 18 minutes)

Ingredients:

- 4 whole blood oranges
- 1 lemon juice
- 1.5 x weight of fruit in caster sugar

Directions for Cooking:

1. Weighing blood oranges and note the weight (about 600-650g usually).
2. Wash them under hot wash. Scrubbing to get any waxy coat off.
3. Cut the blood oranges in quarters and slice them as thinly as you can possibly manage - use a mandolin. Discard pips.
4. Scoop the sliced fruit into the Inner Pot with all their juice plus that of the lemon. Add 250-ml water and close the lid, setting to 12 minutes Manual (High). Allow a NPR. Cancel the Keep Warm function
5. Weigh out 1.5 x the weight of the oranges in caster sugar (you can go as low as 1.2 if you prefer it less sweet) and add to the cooked fruit, stirring to help it dissolve.
6. Press Sauté and stirring constantly to avoid catching and burning on the bottom of the pot, heat until an instant read thermometer shows 104.5°C. Take off the heat and allow to cool briefly.
7. If wishing to make shredless marmalade, simply pass it through a fine meshed sieve, pressing firmly to ensure as much pulp goes through just leaving the peel behind. Scrape the jelly off the underside of the sieve. Ladle into the hot sterile jars, sealing the lids immediately. If leaving the peel in, then simply ladle into jars, trying to distribute the peel evenly between them.

Nutrition information:
Calories per serving: 8; Carbohydrates: 2.0g; Protein: 0g; Fat: 0.1g; Sugar:1.0g; Sodium: 54mg

---

499.   Artichoke-Spinach Dip
(Servings: 10, Cooking Time: 4 minutes)

Ingredients:

- 8-oz cream cheese
- 10-oz box Frozen spinach
- 16-oz Shredded Parmesan cheese
- 8-oz Shredded mozzarella
- 1/2 cup chicken broth
- 14-oz can artichoke hearts
- 1/2 cup sour cream
- 1/2 cup mayo
- 3 cloves garlic
- 1 tsp onion powder

Directions for Cooking:

1. Squeeze out excess water from spinach.
2. Add all ingredients in Instant pot except for cheese. Mix well.
3. Close Instant Pot, press the Manual button, choose high settings, and set time to 4 minutes.
4. Once done cooking, do a QPR.
5. Stir in cheese.
6. Serve and enjoy.

Nutrition information:
Calories per serving: 330; Carbohydrates: 6.0g; Protein: 15.0g; Fat: 26.0g; Sugar:1.0g; Sodium: 844mg

500. Strawberry Jam

(Servings: 20, Cooking Time: 26 minutes)

Ingredients:

- 2 pounds fresh strawberries , hulled and halved
- 1 cup granulated sugar
- 2 Tablespoons lemon juice
- 3 Tablespoons cornstarch
- 1 1/2 Tablespoons water

Directions for Cooking:

1. Mix in lemon juice, sugar, and strawberries in Instant Pot. Let it stand for 10 minutes.

2. Close Instant Pot, press the Manual button, choose high settings, and set time to 1 minutes.

3. Once done cooking, do a 15-minute natural release and then a QPR.

4. Mix water and cornstarch in a small bowl. Stir in pot and stir until thickened.

5. Let jam cool completely and transfer to a lidded jar.

Nutrition information:

Calories per serving: 58; Carbohydrates: 14.7g; Protein: 0.3g; Fat: 0.1g; Sugar:12.2g; Sodium: 1.0mg

Measurement Conversion Charts

Volume Equivalents(Liquid)

US Standard	US Standard(Ounces)	Metric(Approximate)
2 tablespoons	1 fl.oz.	30 mL
1/4 cup	2 fl.oz.	60 mL
1/2 cup	4 fl.oz.	120 mL
1 cup	8 fl.oz.	240 mL
1 1/2 cup	12 fl.oz.	355 mL
2 cups or 1 pint	16 fl.oz.	475 mL
4 cups or 1 quart	32 fl.oz.	1 L
1 gallon	128 fl.oz.	4 L

Volume Equivalents (DRY)

US standard	Metric (Approximate)
1/8 teaspoon	0.5 mL
1/4 teaspoon	1 mL
1/2 teaspoon	2 mL
3/4 teaspoon	4 mL
1 teaspoon	5 mL
1 tablespoon	15 mL
1/4 cup	59 mL
1/2 cup	118 mL
3/4 cup	177 mL
1 cup	235 mL
2 cups	475 mL
3 cups	700 mL
4 cups	1 L

MEASUREMENT CONVERSION CHARTS

Weight Equivalents

US Standard	Metric (Approximate)
1/2 ounce	15g
1 ounce	30g
2 ounce	60g
4 ounce	115g
8 ounce	225g
12 ounce	340g
16 ounces or 1 pound	455g

Oven Temperatures

Fahrenheit (F)	Celsius(C) (Approximate)
250	121
300	149
325	163
350	177
375	190
400	205
425	218
450	232

Made in the USA
Columbia, SC
06 December 2018